Lecture Notes in Computer Science 11190

Commenced Publication in 1973
Founding and Former Series Editors:
Gerhard Goos, Juris Hartmanis, and Jan van Leeuwen

More information about this series at http://www.springer.com/series/7409

Kim Marriott · Falk Schreiber
Tim Dwyer · Karsten Klein
Nathalie Henry Riche · Takayuki Itoh
Wolfgang Stuerzlinger · Bruce H. Thomas (Eds.)

Immersive Analytics

Editors
Kim Marriott
Monash University
Melbourne, VIC, Australia

Falk Schreiber
University of Konstanz
Konstanz, Germany

Tim Dwyer
Monash University
Melbourne, VIC, Australia

Karsten Klein
University of Konstanz
Konstanz, Germany

Nathalie Henry Riche
Microsoft
Redmond, WA, USA

Takayuki Itoh
Ochanomizu University
Tokyo, Japan

Wolfgang Stuerzlinger
Simon Fraser University
Surrey, BC, Canada

Bruce H. Thomas
University of South Australia
Adelaide, SA, Australia

ISSN 0302-9743 ISSN 1611-3349 (electronic)
Lecture Notes in Computer Science
ISBN 978-3-030-01387-5 ISBN 978-3-030-01388-2 (eBook)
https://doi.org/10.1007/978-3-030-01388-2

Library of Congress Control Number: Applied For

LNCS Sublibrary: SL3 – Information Systems and Applications, incl. Internet/Web, and HCI

Cover illustration: The illustration on the cover appears in this volume on p. 2, used with permission.

This Springer imprint is published by the registered company Springer Nature Switzerland AG
The registered company address is: Gewerbestrasse 11, 6330 Cham, Switzerland

Foreword

We live in an age where the amount and complexity of data available to us far surpass our ability to understand or to utilise them in decision-making. Analysis of such data is not only common in the physical, social, and life sciences, but is becoming an integral part of effective planning in business, government, e-health, and many other aspects of modern society. Furthermore data analytics is no longer solely the preserve of scientists and professional analysts as personalised data analytics becomes increasingly common.

Visual analytics has become a key technology for human-in-the-loop data analysis. While the standard definition for visual analytics is agnostic of the actual interface devices employed by visual analytics systems, the affordances of the display and input devices used for analysing data strongly affect the experience of the users of such systems and, thereby, their degree of engagement and productivity. For practical visual analytics tools, the platform for interaction is almost always a standard desktop computer. A systematic approach to developing analysis and decision support tools that move beyond the desktop is lacking.

Immersive analytics is a new interdisciplinary field that brings together researchers and practitioners from data visualisation, visual analytics, virtual and mixed reality, human–computer interaction, and human-in-the-loop algorithmics to explore these new forms of analytics tools. The goal is to remove barriers between people, their data, and the tools they use for analysis by developing more engaging, embodied analysis tools that support data understanding and decision-making everywhere and by everyone, either working individually or collaboratively.

This book is the outcome of two coordinated workshops on immersive analytics held in 2016. The first in Shonan, Japan, took place in February and organised by Takayuki Itoh, Kim Marriott, Falk Schreiber, and Uwe Wössner with the help of Karsten Klein, the second was held in June at Dagstuhl, Germany, and was organised by Tim Dwyer, Nathalie Henry Riche, Wolfgang Stuerzlinger, and Bruce H. Thomas, again with the help of Karsten Klein. In all, 25 leading international experts in data visualisation, visual analytics, human–computer interaction, virtual reality and augmented reality attended the first workshop, with another 38 experts attending the second. There was a sizeable overlap of experts between the two workshops that provided a sensible continuity of concepts.

The two workshops explored the definition of immersive analytics and identified the structure and focus of this book. A working group for each chapter was formed at the workshops, with the participation of invited experts as needed, and the groups wrote the chapters contained in this book. A critical goal was to develop a vision of the research domain for immersive analytics and a roadmap for future investigations. Authors submitted manuscripts for their chapters in mid-2017. These initial versions were first reviewed "internally" by one of the book editors. After an initial round of revision based on these internal reviews, the updated manuscripts were sent to expert reviewers invited from the community. We are grateful to these people for their detailed and insightful reviews.

September 2018

Kim Marriott
Falk Schreiber
Tim Dwyer
Karsten Klein
Nathalie Henry Riche
Takayuki Itoh
Wolfgang Stuerzlinger
Bruce H. Thomas

Table of Contents

Contributors

Benjamin Bach University of Edinburgh, Edinburgh, UK

Anastasia Bezerianos Inria and Universite Paris-Saclay, Paris, France

Mark Billinghurst University of South Australia, Mawson Lakes, Australia

Wolfgang Büschel Technische Universität Dresden, Dresden, Germany

Tom Chandler Monash University, Melbourne, Australia

Jian Chen The Ohio State University, Columbus, USA

Maxime Cordeil Monash University, Melbourne, Australia

Tobias Czauderna Monash University, Melbourne, Australia

Raimund Dachselt Technische Universität Dresden, Dresden, Germany

Pierre Dragicevic Inria, Rocquencourt, France

Steven Drucker Microsoft Research, Redmond, USA

Tim Dwyer Monash University, Melbourne, Australia

Neven A. M. ElSayed Benha University, Benha, Egypt

Niklas Elmqvist University of Maryland, College Park, USA

Carla Dal Sasso Freitas Federal University of Rio Grande do Sul, Porto Alegre, Brazil

Carsten Görg University of Colorado, Denver, USA

Jason Haga National Institute of Advanced Industrial Science and Technology, Tokyo, Japan

Marcel Hlawatsch University of Stuttgart, Stuttgart, Germany

Christophe Hurter Ecole Nationale de l'Aviation Civile (ENAC), Toulouse, France

Pourang Irani University of Manitoba, Winnipeg, Canada

Petra Isenberg Inria, Paris, France

Tobias Isenberg Inria and University Paris-Saclay, Paris, France

Takayuki Itoh Ochanomizu University, Tokyo, Japan

Yvonne Jansen Sorbonne University, Paris, France

Andreas Kerren Linnaeus University, Växjö, Sweden

Jinman Kim University of Sydney, Sydney, Australia

Matthias Klapperstück Monash University, Melbourne, Australia

Karsten Klein Monash University, Melbourne, Australia; University of Sydney, Sydney, Australia; University of Konstanz, Konstanz, Germany

Torsten Wolfgang Kuhlen RWTH Aachen University, Aachen, Germany

Bongshin Lee Microsoft Research, Redmond, USA

Todd Margolis Qlik, Irvine, CA, USA

Kim Marriott Monash University, Melbourne, Australia

Jon McCormack Monash University, Melbourne, Australia

Thomas Morgan Monash University, Melbourne, Australia

Miguel A. Nacenta University of St Andrews, St Andrews, Scotland

Chris North Virginia Tech, Blacksburg, USA

Steffen Oeltze-Jafra University of Leipzig, Leipzig, Germany

Huamin Qu Hong Kong University of Science and Technology, Kowloon, Hong Kong

Guido Reina University of Stuttgart, Stuttgart, Germany

Nathalie Henry Riche Microsoft, Redmond, USA

Jonathan C. Roberts Bangor University, Bangor, UK

Gerik Scheuermann University of Leipzig, Leipzig, Germany

Dieter Schmalstieg Graz University of Technology, Graz, Austria

Falk Schreiber University of Konstanz, Konstanz, Germany; Monash University, Melbourne, Australia

Ross T. Smith University of South Australia, Adelaide, Australia

Björn Sommer Monash University, Melboume, Australia; University of Konstanz, Konstanz, Germany

Wolfgang Stuerzlinger Simon Fraser University, Burnaby, Canada

Aurélien Tabard University Lyon, Lyon, France

Bruce H. Thomas University of South Australia, Adelaide, Australia

Gregory F. Welch University of Central Florida, Orlando, USA

Wesley Willett University of Calgary, Calgary, Canada

1. Immersive Analytics: An Introduction

Tim Dwyer[1], Kim Marriott[1], Tobias Isenberg[2], Karsten Klein[3], Nathalie Riche[4], Falk Schreiber[1,3], Wolfgang Stuerzlinger[5], and Bruce H. Thomas[6]

[1] Monash University, Australia
[Tim.Dwyer, Kim.Marriott]@monash.edu
[2] Inria and University Paris-Saclay
tobias.isenberg@inria.fr
[3] ? University of Konstanz, Germany
[Karsten.Klein, Falk Schreiber]@uni-konstanz.de
[4] Microsoft, USA
Nathalie.Henry@microsoft.com
[5] Simon Fraser University, Canada
w.s@sfu.ca
[6] University of South Australia
bruce.thomas@unisa.edu.au

Abstract. Immersive Analytics is a new research initiative that aims to remove barriers between people, their data and the tools they use for analysis and decision making. Here we clarify the aims of immersive analytics research, its opportunities and historical context, as well as providing a broad research agenda for the field. In addition, we review how the term immersion has been used to refer to both technological and psychological immersion, both of which are central to immersive analytics research.

Keywords: immersive analytics, multi-sensory, 2D and 3D, data analytics, decision making

1.1. What is Immersive Analytics?

Immersive Analytics is the use of engaging, embodied analysis tools to support data understanding and decision making. Immersive analytics builds upon the fields of data visualisation, visual analytics, virtual reality, computer graphics, and human-computer interaction. Its goal is to remove barriers between people, their data, and the tools they use for analysis. It aims to support data understanding and decision making everywhere and by everyone, both working individually and collaboratively. While this may be achieved through the use of immersive virtual environment technologies, multisensory presentation, data physicalisation, natural interfaces, or responsive analytics, the field of immersive analytics is not tied to the use of specific techniques.

We live in an age where the amount and complexity of data available to us far surpass our ability to understand or to utilise in decision making. This is not only

K. Marriott et al. (Eds.): Immersive Analytics, LNCS 11190, pp. 1–23, 2018.
https://doi.org/10.1007/978-3-030-01388-2_1

Fig. 1: The research field of immersive analytics is exploring techniques that will enable seamless local and remote collaborative work informed by data in immersive environments. While the ideal technologies are not yet quite available (left), researchers can already explore the design space and develop the necessary display and interaction techniques using existing technologies (right). (Figure © 2015 IEEE. Reprinted, with permission, from Chandler *et al.* [16]).

true for business analysts, scientists, and policymakers, but also for members of the general public who have increasing access to, for instance, personalised health data, IoT and other sensor data, as well as social media. In recent years we have seen rapid progress in the development and availability of immersive technologies such as head-mounted Virtual and Augmented Reality (VR and AR), large wall-mounted, hand-held, or wearable displays. Similarly, progress in sensor technology and the application of machine learning technologies to interpret user gestures and utterances have fuelled the development of natural interfaces making use of speech, gesture and touch. The combination of these new kinds of display and interaction technologies is building towards a(nother) revolution in how people use computers and offers a new approach to data analytics and decision making; one that liberates these activities from the office desktop and supports both collocated and remote collaboration (see Figure 1).

Immersive visual analytics has the potential to dramatically improve all areas of our lives. One example application is healthcare, see Chapter 10 (*Immersive Analytics Applications in Life and Health Sciences*). For medical specialists treating a patient with a complex multi-faceted medical condition, a mix of AR headsets and tiled wall displays potentially support collocated and remote collaboration, see Chapter 8 (*Immersive Collaborative Analytics*). This collaboration may be synchronous, such as a group of nurses and doctors conducting surgery, or asynchronous, where the collaborators participate at different times, perhaps throughout the entire course of the medical treatment. Current technologies allow specialists to create and remotely share immersive data visualisations. In the near future they will be able to see, hear, touch and perhaps even smell an anatomically correct model of the patient. They will be able to walk through the model, overlaying it with, for example, 2D and 3D scans, or population-based tumour occurrence models. By using AR to overlay the patient's body with visualisations of their internal organs, they will be able to show the patient what they believe is happening and the impact of possible treatment options.

Another example is urban planning and disaster management, as detailed in Chapter 11 (*Exploring Immersive Analytics for Built Environments*). Urban planners, engineers, and local authorities will soon be able to collaboratively explore different flood, wildfire or other disaster mitigation strategies using a 3D-printed topographical model of the affected area, overlaying it with personal and shared holographic displays and showing the results of computer simulations. These technologies allow the local community to more deeply engage in decision making by using immersive VR or AR to viscerally understand the complex impact that these choices will have on their local neighbourhood.

Even more excitingly, these new technologies potentially democratise the use of sophisticated data analysis and decision support tools, taking them outside the workplace and into everyday life, see Chapter 7 (*Situated Analytics*). Already, GPS-based navigation tools—computing optimal routes to the desired destination using current location and live traffic data—have changed the way in which most people navigate while driving. Ubiquitous AR promises a future in which we live in a mixed-reality environment, where physical objects are overlaid with virtual data and everyday analysis and decisions are computer-mediated. For instance, when walking through a supermarket, products could be overlaid with personalised dietary, ethical and pecuniary information to inform and guide purchase decisions.

However, while many of the display and interaction hardware technologies required for these scenarios already exist, the fundamental knowledge of how to design appropriate human-computer interfaces and data visualisations is missing. This is the subject of Immersive Analytics (IA). As the brief examples above illustrate, IA offers several opportunities beyond more traditional visual analytics:

- The first opportunity is *situated analytics* in which user-controlled data analytics information is linked with objects in the physical world. This might be products in a supermarket, attendees at a conference, machinery in a workshop, instruments in a lab, or objects at a building site. This has many applications in the workplace and even more in other aspects of everyday life through ubiquitous personalised analytics [37] (see Chapter 7).
- The second opportunity is *embodied data exploration*. By moving away from the mouse and keyboard, it is hoped that touch, gesture, voice and tangible interaction allow more intuitive and engaging data exploration in which the computer becomes invisible, but continues to facilitate analytics behind the scene. These topics are covered in Chapter 4 (*Interaction for Immersive Analytics*) and Chapter 5 (*Immersive Human-Centered Computational Analytics*).
- The third opportunity is *collaboration*, where the collaboration might be collocated or remote as well as synchronous or asynchronous. IA potentially supports deeper, more equitable and socially engaging collaboration (see Chapter 8).

- The fourth opportunity is *spatial immersion.* Moving away from the desktop allows users to use the space around them as a three-dimensional workspace in which they place coordinated 2D, $2\frac{1}{2}$D, and 3D visualisations, see Chapter 2 (*Immersive Analytics: Time to Reconsider the Value of 3D for Information Visualisation*).
- The fifth opportunity is *multi-sensory presentation.* Traditional visual analytics has focussed on visualisation but audio and the other senses can also be used to provide additional information or as an alternative to vision where this is unavailable or not useful. This topic is discussed in detail in Chapter 3 (*Multisensory Immersive Analytics*).
- The final opportunity is more informed and increased *engagement* in data-informed decision making by the general public and other stakeholders. Immersive interactive narrative visualisations can be used, for instance, to engage the local community in climate change mitigation or to see the potential impact of their local carbon footprint. Such immersive visual data stories are discussed in Chapter 6 (*Immersive Visual Data Stories*).

Immersive analytics brings together researchers and data practitioners from data visualisation and visual analytics, virtual and mixed reality, human-computer-interaction and human-in-the-loop algorithmics. This book provides the first comprehensive introduction to this emerging interdisciplinary research field. We survey academic research and provide the necessary background material for new PhD students or for more experienced researchers who wish to work in this field. In addition, the book gives a roadmap of open questions to guide further research. It is also designed to be accessible to a broader audience who are interested in how emerging technologies may be used in data analysis applications in science, technology, business, health, or other aspects of modern life.

1.2. Historical Context

Today we interact with computers through phones, laptops and other devices so regularly and ubiquitously that many people forget or are unaware that such activities were once almost unimaginable. Before the 1980s, however, computers were intimidating and expensive tools. Computing pioneer Howard Aiken once reminisced of the early days of computing: "there was no thought in mind that computing machines should be used for anything except out-and-out mathematics" [18]. It took considerable time and research effort [44, 87] for the human imagination to move beyond the notion that computers were centralised resources to be used only by skilled technicians for very "serious" applications.

1.2.1. Human-Computer Interaction

Researchers in computing labs in the 1960s foresaw that this rapidly evolving technology could play a more transformative role. For example, Engelbart and English saw their computing lab at Stanford as "a research center for augmenting human intellect" [28]. Their work led to the first demonstrations of a windowed UI, the mouse, hyperlinked documents, video conferencing, and visual word processing. Around the same time, Ivan Sutherland at Harvard demonstrated direct interaction with a graphical display using a light pen [92] and then the first mixed reality head-mounted display system [93].

An early journal, *Man-Machine Studies*, began to link technologies for computer interaction with more human-focussed studies in 1969 [56]. The increased use of computers in real-time applications such as avionics meant that the initial focus was on making interaction as simple and efficient as possible. Then, as computers became cheaper and smaller, they moved into mainstream use. The focus changed to computer use by non-specialists, and the field of Human-Computer Interaction (HCI) emerged at the intersection of the previously disparate disciplines of computer science, cognitive and perceptual psychology, and ergonomics. The creation of the ACM SIGCHI organisation and its first conference in 1982, established HCI as an important new field of computer science.

The history of HCI is intricately bound to developments in interaction technologies. Sometimes research in HCI drives innovation in hardware and devices, for example the light pen or the mouse. Sometimes hardware innovation drives HCI research by allowing new ways to integrate computers into our work and our lives. For example, motion tracking—conceived as a means to create lifelike animated movie characters—is now supported by consumer devices[1] and has become a viable input for interaction, as processor speeds and algorithms for feature detection have improved allowing real-time gesture recognition. Motion tracking is only one example of an emerging technology that allows more natural, fluid, and *embodied*[2] interaction with computers. Such natural and fluid interaction is a potential key to engaging users in their data, a primary goal of immersive analytics (as further discussed in Section 1.3.).

1.2.2. Graphics and Visualisation

In addition to input devices, the other critical technological advance that has opened up new ways to interact with computers has been display technologies. This advance began in the 1950s with computer-driven oscilloscopes that were able to trace lines to form what we now call *vector graphics*. Once again, research that began in labs made its way into the mainstream over the course of several decades. With the introduction of the ACM SIGGRAPH conference series in 1974, graphics was recognised as a distinct sub-field of computer science. Computer graphics research rapidly evolved, and many sought to achieve photo-realistic renderings of virtual scenes. By the 1980s, the opportunities for visualising

[1] Examples of low-cost motion tracking devices being Microsoft Kinect [60]—launched in 2010—and Leap Motion [49]—launched in 2013.

[2] Embodied interaction refers to the notion that the affordances of a user interface or interaction device somehow naturally embody the purpose or nature of the intended action [24]. See Chapter 4 for more background on this and other aspects of immersive interaction.

data were evident, especially to the scientists already using powerful computers with sophisticated graphics capabilities. A report based on the NSF sponsored workshop on "Visualization in Scientific Computing" in 1987 [58] gave rise to the IEEE Visualization conference series in 1990.

As mentioned earlier, virtual reality (VR) and augmented reality (AR) prototypes were demonstrated by Ivan Sutherland in the late 1960s [93]. However, it was not until the 1990s that advances in dedicated graphics hardware and real-time rendering techniques led to the first practical interactive virtual reality systems. An early example of such a VR system was the CAVE [19]. Research interest in the area in industry and university labs was such that a dedicated conference series, IEEE Virtual Reality (IEEE VR), was established in 1993.

After successful workshops in the two preceding years, the first Symposium on 3D User Interfaces (3DUI) was held in 2006. This symposium series focussed on the interaction aspects of VR and AR systems. Reflecting a growing interest in interaction with virtual content, the ACM Symposium on Spatial interaction (SUI) was established in 2013. Then, as a result of a convergence of research within virtual reality, IEEE VR and 3DUI merged into the IEEE Conference on Virtual Reality and 3D User Interfaces in 2018.

As of early 2018, there are several well-established commercial virtual reality equipment providers. Some notable examples of VR equipment include: HTC Vive,[3] Oculus Rift,[4] Microsoft Mixed Reality,[5] and Google Daydream.[6] What is important about this latest generation of VR equipment is that they are modestly priced, compatible with mid-range graphics PCs, and simple to set up as they are a fully integrated system. In contrast, only a few years ago, head-mounted displays and tracking subsystems were sold separately, and the input devices were, by and large, custom-made by the end user. Furthermore, a major barrier to the widespread use of earlier VR equipment was that integration of the subsystems was left to the end user, and included such fundamental operations as mounting tracking sensors onto the head mounted display.

In the past, while there have been commercial software development environments for VR, these were not widely used. WorldViz[7] is an early example of an easy to use VR development and runtime software environment, but it was not commonly employed. This has changed, and emerging software standards are allowing the rapid growth of VR applications and software ecosystems. Games engines such as Unity 3D[8] and UnReal Engine[9] provide support for the development and deployment of VR applications while software tools such as SteamVR[10] provide cross-platform support.

---

[3] https://www.vive.com/
[4] https://www.oculus.com/
[5] https://www.microsoft.com/en-us/store/collections/vrandmixedrealityheadsets
[6] https://vr.google.com/daydream/
[7] http://www.worldviz.com/
[8] https://unity3d.com/
[9] https://www.unrealengine.com/
[10] http://store.steampowered.com/steamvr

The visualisation field's early emphasis on scientific applications concentrated on data that had a natural spatial embedding in two or three dimensions. This included geographic data such as ocean currents or architectural, physical or biological data such as fluid flows in wind-tunnels or density in medical scans. Such data was naturally visualised using immersive 3D display environments. Early pioneers (e. g., Card *et al.* [15]) enthusiastically explored immersive visualisation of data that was more abstract, i. e., purely numerical or relational and, therefore, with more freedom in how it could be represented and spatially embedded. Exploration of this design space of spatial mappings for abstract data became a key theme of a new sub-field of visualisation called Information Visualisation (InfoVis). Information visualisation built upon the work of graphic designers such as Bertin [3], statisticians such as Tukey [99], Tufte [98], and Cleveland [17], as well as HCI researchers such Card, McKinley, and Shneiderman [14], and many others, to create a new interdisciplinary field that explored how to effectively utilise computer graphics for abstract data visualisation and its interactive exploration. In 1995, the new IEEE Symposium on Information Visualization (IEEE InfoVis) was established to focus on this new theme, becoming a conference in 2007.[11]

Despite an early enthusiasm for the kind of 3D representations of abstract data made possible by first-generation graphics hardware (e. g., Figure 2), in the 2000s information visualisation researchers became more conservative. As information visualisation established itself as a new research discipline, researchers concentrated on techniques suited to standard desktop and WIMP interfaces, rather than to immersive technologies which, at that time, were only available in labs. This conservatism was supported by studies finding that some 3D representations of abstract data on standard 2D monitors were not particularly useful. It remains an open question whether 3D representations of abstract data can be more effective in genuinely immersive environments, for some settings or application scenarios. More generally, the question of how we should be using the space around users for representing data in immersive environments (whether VR or AR) is a much more complicated issue than simple 2D versus 3D effectiveness. Both questions are discussed in detail in Chapter 2.

1.2.3. Visual Analytics

In the early 2000s, national security concerns and exponential growth in data and communication on the internet created an urgent need for more effective techniques to analyse large, complex data. By this time information visualisation research had shown some promise and developed novel techniques along with guidelines for the design of useful visual data representations. However, this new urgency suggested a need for a more holistic but also pragmatic research agenda to tackle the grand challenge of creating tools that genuinely met the requirements of big data analytics. In their agenda for the new National Visualization and Analytics Center, Thomas and Cook called for a new science called

[11] For a brief history of the IEEE VIS conferences see Section 2.2 in [40].

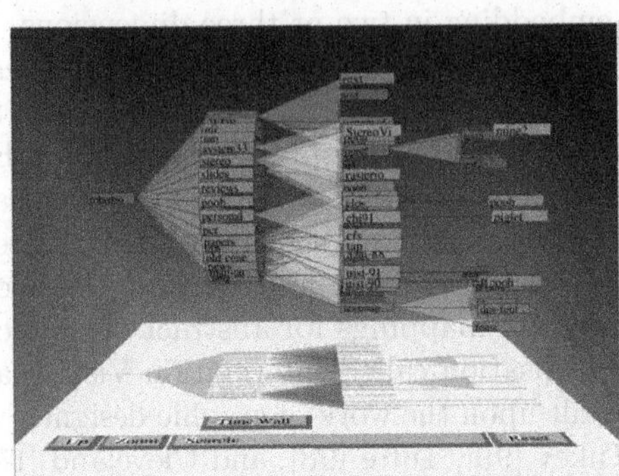
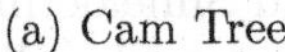

(a) Cam Tree

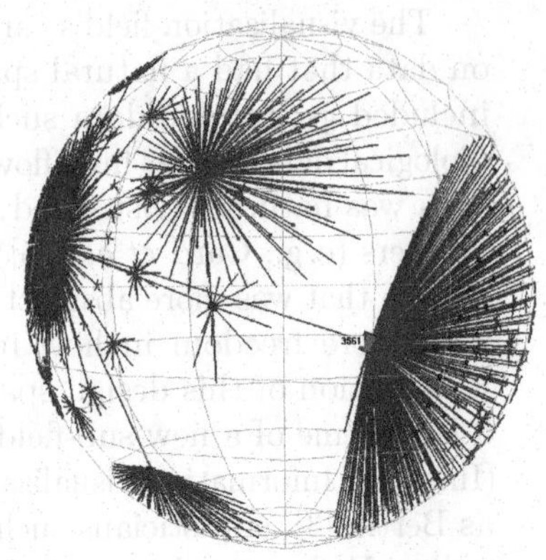

(b) 3D Hyperbolic Network Layout

Fig. 2: Early enthusiastic exploration of immersive visualisation of abstract data. (a) Cone Trees and the horizontal variant Cam Trees were introduced by Robertson *et al.* in 1991 as a way to navigate complex tree structures [80]. The internal nodes of the tree could be rotated to bring a different children to the fore, exploiting perspective distortion as a "focus and context" technique. (b) In 1997 Munzner introduced a 3D hyperbolic network browser that exploited an even more exotic space for focus and context [63]. (Figure (a) courtesy of S. Card, J. Mackinlay and G. Robertson and used with permission from Xerox, Figure (b) © 1998 IEEE. Reprinted, with permission, from [63])

Visual Analytics concerned with "analytical reasoning facilitated by interactive visual interfaces" [96]. They made 19 high-level recommendations for the field of visual analytics and, in particular, in contrast to earlier work on information visualisation, they called for research that would enable visualisation techniques to:

- scale to huge data [96, pg. 7] and
- enable a higher-level discourse between analyst and information [96, pg. 77] rather than what they saw as a focus by information visualisation on straightforward and low-level analysis tasks.

Thomas and Cook's definition of visual analytics was agnostic of the actual interface and display devices employed by visual analysis systems. Nevertheless, most visual analytics researchers inherited a certain scepticism of immersive environments from the InfoVis community and continued to focus on developing techniques for traditional desktop environments. However, as discussed in regard to human-computer interaction, the affordances of the display and input devices strongly affect the experience of users and so their degree of engagement and productivity. While it may be that work in visual analytics has tried to have a high-level focus on human cognition and workflows for "sense making" rather than on the details of devices and computing environments, we feel that the embodiment of data afforded by the new generation of immersive environment technologies fundamentally impacts the analyst's experience and warrants consideration.

1.2.4. The Birth of Immersive Analytics

We contend that emerging display and interaction technologies open up new possibilities for achieving Thomas and Cook's goals for visual analytics described above. But, in addition, as discussed in Section 1.1. these technologies can bring data analytics:

- to a wider audience through tools and technologies that more fully engage the senses,
- to a new generation whose first "language" of computer interaction is not the mouse and keyboard,
- to new situations where desktop computing is impossible, and
- to teams of people where all participants are equally empowered.

This potential has already excited a large community of researchers from the various fields we have discussed above. The idea that information should be immersive is at least as old as the early work of Robertson, Card, and McKinley [15]. However, the belief that visualisation and visual analytics needed to embrace the explosion of new interaction paradigms took off in 2014, with a workshop entitled "Death of the Desktop: Envisioning Visualization without Desktop Computing" at IEEE VIS 2014.[12]

Shortly after this, the name Immersive Analytics was coined by researchers exploring possibilities for data visualisation in virtual and mixed reality [16] and introduced at IEEE BDVA 2015. Two coordinated workshops under the banner of Immersive Analytics were held in 2016. The first at Shonan, Japan, with 25 invited international experts on visualisation, visual analytics, human-computer interaction and virtual and augmented reality [41] and the second was held soon after at Dagstuhl, Germany with an additional 38 experts spanning similar disciplines [27]. It was at these workshops that a broader understanding of immersive analytics and the chapter topics for this book emerged. Most authors of chapters in this book attended one of the two workshops, but some additional experts were invited as required.

Since then there has been a flood of workshops on immersive analytics and the community has grown rapidly. Immersive analytics workshops were held at:

- IEEE BDVA in 2016 and 2017, Australia
- IEEE VR 2016, USA
- Interactive Surfaces and Spaces 2016, Canada
- IEEE VIS 2017, USA

And, in 2018, the first symposium with an explicit call for Immersive Analytics submissions will be held in Germany at *IEEE Big Data Visual and Immersive Analytics*.[13]

---

[12] http://dataphys.org/workshops/vis14/tag/visualization/

[13] http://bdva.net/2018/

1.3. Engagement and Immersion

Engagement and immersion are at the heart of immersive analytics. We broadly distinguish between *technological immersion*—which relates to the technologies used in VR to immerse the user in a virtual world—and *psychological immersion*—which relates to the cognitive state experienced by a user when they are absorbed by some task. The latter could also be called *engagement*. As both technical and psychological immersion are relevant to immersive analytics research, we provide a brief review here. While clearly different they are connected: technological immersion is, for example, widely employed in computer gaming with the belief that it will increase psychological immersion.

1.3.1. Technological Immersion/Presence

A primary focus of VR research has been to develop technologies that immerse the user in a virtual world by providing a sensory experience that is so similar to that offered by the real world that the user feels and behaves like they are indeed present in the virtual world, temporarily unaware that they are inhabiting a computer-mediated environment. This is the intended meaning of "immersive" in the terms "immersive environments" or "immersive technologies". A significant focus of immersive analytics is the use of immersive technologies to support collaboration and embodied data exploration and decision making. Therefore, a common, shared understanding of technological immersion is necessary for immersive analytics researchers.

Following Slater [91], we distinguish between *presence* (the subjective psychological experience of being in a virtual or remote space) and *immersion* (the objective characteristics of the technology used to present the virtual space). Since the term telepresence was introduced to describe the experience of being virtually transported via telecommunication systems to another physical location [62], there has been considerable research into different aspects of technological immersion and presence by IT researchers and psychologists, e. g., [25, 26, 34, 53, 54, 77, 82–85, 88, 90, 91, 101].

Immersive technologies can produce three main kinds of presence:

- *Spatial presence* is the psychological state in which the environment and objects in the virtual world are experienced as actual physical objects [50]. According to Slater [88] it is (a) the sense of "being there" in the world depicted by the virtual environment (VE), (b) the extent to which the VE becomes the dominant one—i. e., the tendency to respond to events in the VE rather than in the "real world", and (c) the extent to which participants remember the VE experience as having visited a "place" rather than just having seen images generated by a computer [88].
- *Social presence* is the "sense of being with another" [6] or, more broadly, the psychological state in which virtual social actors (both human and artificial) are experienced as actual social actors [50]. Many different aspects have been identified [6, 50, 53, 67]. One is *co-presence* which requires the actors to be

in the same virtual space and measures the degree of mutual awareness and psychological involvement between actors [6]. Another aspect (confusingly also called social presence) is the degree to which the actors believe the virtual world supports interpersonal communication. This was originally introduced to measure the effectiveness of telecommunication technologies. Related to social presence is the notion of cultural presence [57].
- *Self presence* is the psychological state in which virtual selves are experienced as the actual self [50] and measures the "effect of the VE on the perception of one's body (i. e., body schema or body image), psychological states, emotional states, perceived traits and identity" [5] or "the extent to which some aspect of a person's proto (body-schema) self, core (emotion-driven) self, and/or extended (identity-relevant) self is relevant during media use" [76].

Researchers have found that different kinds of presence are correlated (e. g., [67]) and that many features of the VE have been identified as affecting the subjective feeling of presence. These include:

- *Inclusiveness:* the degree to which the virtual world blocks out the real world [91].
- *Extensiveness:* the range of sensory channels (visual, audio, haptic, olfactory etc.) provided in the environment [91]. While vision remains the primary channel in VE, studies show that the use of spatialised audio and the provision of other sensory channels increase the sense of spatial presence [23,35,36,75, 82].
- *Vividness:* the degree of visual realism or fidelity of the virtual environment [91]. Studies have found that higher frame rate, stereopsis and large field of view can increase spatial presence [82]. Surprisingly, visual realism does not seem to have a significant impact [82].
- *Proprioceptive matching:* the degree to which the perceptual effects of movement by the user in the virtual world mirror their effects in the real world [91]. For instance, head tracking and the ability to walk through the virtual world increase presence [82].
- *Autonomous action:* the extent to which the participant can act autonomously and interact with objects in the VE and the affordances provided [30,86,102]. As Schultze writes: "The sense of 'being there' is grounded in the ability to 'do there.' " [79,84].
- *Representation of virtual self:* the degree of realism of the representation of the participant in the VE. This affects self-presence and behaviour [43,68].
- *Plausability:* the extent to which objects and actors in the virtual world exhibit real-world behaviour [89].
- *Representation of others:* the degree of realism of the representation of other actors in the VE [48].
- *Communication channels:* the range of ways, e. g.verbal and nonverbal, in which communication is made available to individuals or groups in the environment. Communication greatly benefits from awareness features in VE [66].

1.3.2. Psychological Immersion/Engagement

Even more central to immersive analytics research is understanding how to cognitively immerse the user in the analytics or decision-making task. Such task immersion has been studied by psychologists, computer game, user interface (UI) and other researchers.

Csikszentmihalyi *et al.* [20, 21] extensively studied intrinsically motivated activity in both work and play settings. They introduced the notion of *flow* to describe the enjoyable subjective state that people experience when they are completely involved in something to the point of forgetting time, fatigue and everything but the activity itself. This might come from reading an engrossing novel, playing chess or when engaging in sport. Flow is an example of psychological absorption, the term describing total engagement in the present experience. Unlike some other kinds of psychological absorption [39], flow is always enjoyable.

Flow is characterised by: intense and focussed concentration on what one is doing in the current moment; merging of action and awareness; loss of reflective self-consciousness; a sense of control; temporal disassociation (typically time passes faster than usual); and enjoyment of the activity itself rather than only the outcome [64]. Two necessary preconditions for flow are that the perceived challenges or opportunities stretch existing skills but are not over-demanding, and that there are clear sub-goals with immediate feedback on performance.

Flow has been applied to software use [1, 97, 100]. Building upon the notion of flow, Agawal and Karahanna [1] define cognitive absorption as "a state of deep involvement with software". It is characterised by: focussed immersion and total engagement in using the software; temporal disassociation; enjoyment; a sense of control and curiosity. Like flow, cognitive absorption requires an extreme state of engagement.

It seems unrealistic to expect that immersive analytics systems will regularly engender the degree of immersion required for flow or cognitive absorption. A more general notion of software engagement has been studied by HCI researchers wishing to move beyond usability and to characterise and design more engaging interfaces [2, 69, 70]. They have found that an engaging experience is encouraged by the aesthetic and sensory appeal of the software and that the task should be regarded as interesting or novel, be sufficiently challenging and provide regular feedback. Engaged users are emotionally involved, motivated and perceive themselves to be in control. However, while the user must be focussed on the activity, engagement, unlike flow, does not require them to be so focussed that they lose all awareness of the surrounding world.

Software engagement and immersion has been most extensively studied for computer games [7, 11, 13]. Immersion is commonly used in the games industry to refer to the feeling of "being in the game". Unlike flow, but like software engagement, games immersion is not an all or nothing experience [9]. The first level of immersion is called *engagement*, simply investing enough time and energy to play the game, the next level is *engrossment* at which point the players devote considerable effort and have an emotional attachment. The final level is *total immersion* in which the player is completely involved in the game and nothing else matters. This is similar to flow, though more transient. It is important to note that being "in the game" does not refer to immersion in a virtual world but to a cognitive state and can occur in both digital and non-digital games.

Jennett *et al.* [42] identified five constituent factors to immersion: emotional involvement, cognitive involvement, real-world disassociation, challenge, and control, while Ermi and Mäyrä [29] identified three kinds of immersive experience: sensory, challenge-based, and imaginary. These are related: challenge-based corresponds to cognitive involvement, challenge, and control, while imaginary relates to emotional involvement and sensory to real-world disassociation through the use of immersive technologies to create a sense of presence [11]. More generally, Poels *et al.* [73] identified the following dimensions to descriptions of the gaming experience by digital game players: enjoyment, flow, imaginative immersion, sensory immersion, suspense, competence, control, social presence, as well as negative affect.

It is implicit in many discussions of immersion in computer gaming that the use of immersive technologies will increase player engagement and sense of "being there" in the game. However, study results are somewhat mixed [11, 33]. Social presence is now recognised as an important aspect of many digital games [22] and high social presence, i. e., the sense of being socially connected to others, leads to greater enjoyment [31] and to increased immersion [12]. There is some evidence that flow in immersive environments leads to better performance, though this may be confounded by non-congruent interfaces [4].

Narrative has been identified as another factor contributing to immersion [74] and increased engagement [33], though there is some disagreement as to whether digital games make use of narrative. If we mean the use of storytelling techniques to emotionally engage the player in the characters and setting of the game, then it is clear that some games utilise narrative while others, such as *Tetris*, do not [11].

Narrative as a device for immersion has been previously studied in literature and film-making [32, 65, 81]. Like engagement in games, immersion in a book or film is graduated. Nell [65] writes of *absorption* sometimes deepening to become *entrancement*, while Ryan [81] identifies four successively deeper levels of immersion: *concentration*, in which the reader is focusing on reading or understanding the text itself and is hardly immersed; *imaginative involvement* in which the users engages emotionally and imaginatively with the text but is also aware of the text and in the case of non-fiction will critically analyse the arguments; *entrancement* in which the reader is wholly engaged in the book and cannot easily put it down but is still aware that the textual world is not real; and the pathological state of *addiction* in which the reader cannot distinguish between the fictional and real world or compulsively reads book after book without finding pleasure. Immersion in a text or film relies "on being transported" to the textual world [32]. It may involve spatial or sensorial immersion, social connection with the characters, or game-like engagement in the plot.

The line between literature and film and new digital media is blurring. Increasingly, journalists are utilising computer games, online communities and immersive technologies to present news stories interactively. An extreme form of such immersive journalism uses VR to recreate the news event and allow the user to experience it as one of the actors [71]. Undoubtedly, immersive analytics can learn from the techniques and tricks used by UI and game designers and journalists to engage their audience using immersive technologies, social connection, narrative as well as responsive interfaces that allow the user to feel in control through frequent feedback.

1.4. Overview of this Book

The chapters of this book study different aspects of immersive analytics, focusing on potential opportunities and applications. The chapters are self-contained and are intended to provide background for researchers and interested practitioners outside the field as well as a theoretical framework for future research. All chapters provide a list of research issues and questions.

In Chapter 2, Marriott *et al.* explore spatial immersion and investigate whether immersive analytic applications should continue to use traditional 2D information visualisations or whether there are situations when the use of 3D depth cues may offer benefits. They also discuss the opportunity that spatial immersion provides to arrange multiple views in the 3D space around the user.

In Chapter 3, McCormack *et al.* look at another important aspect of technological immersion. They review how non-visual sensory channels—audio, haptic, smell and taste—can be used to present data, both as an adjunct to vision and as a replacement when vision is unavailable. They summarise the physiological characteristics of each channel, current presentation technologies including data physicalisation, and provide a preliminary investigation of the resulting design space for multisensory data exploration.

As mentioned in Sections 1.2. and 1.3. of this introductory chapter, effective interaction is key to giving people a fluid and, hence, immersive experience while exploring their data. The state of the art in immersive interaction technologies and the ramifications of these is discussed by Büschel *et al.* in Chapter 4.

Chapter 5 discusses the broader question of how to immersively integrate the "human in the loop" of automated machine processes for processing data. In this chapter, Stuerzlinger *et al.* reinterpret the sense-making loop of visual analytics as it applies to user engagement during data exploration in immersive environments.

We have identified the potential of immersive analytics for data-driven storytelling (also known as narrative visualisation). This is explored by Isenberg *et al.* in Chapter 6. They give examples of immersive storytelling and review the theoretical frameworks for understanding data-driven narratives. In particular, they provide a detailed analysis of how immersion has been understood in related fields such as gaming and relates this back to data-driven storytelling.

Thomas *et al.*, in Chapter 7, explore another potential benefit of immersive analytics. They provide a theoretical framework for understanding situated analytics—the use of "data representations organised in relation to relevant objects, places, and persons in the physical world for the purpose of understanding, sense-making, and decision-making". They characterise its properties, give a number of examples, and clarify the relationship to related fields and concepts.

The chapter by Bezerianos *et al.* (Chapter 8) explores the shared use of immersive technologies to support collaborative analytical reasoning and decision making. They provide a taxonomy of collaborative systems based on space and time, give examples of immersive applications, and analyse the different roles people may play in these systems.

In Chapter 9, Marriott *et al.* present an initial design framework for immersive analytics that extends Brehmer and Munzner's "What, Why and How" [8] data visualisation framework by considering display and interaction capabilities, collaboration and all sensory channels.

The two final chapters in the book look in more detail at application domains of immersive analytics. The chapter by Czauderna *et al.* (Chapter 10) investigates typical use-cases of immersive analytics in life and health sciences ranging from structural biology to neurosciences.

Chandler *et al.*, in Chapter 11, present immersive analytics applications to simulations of built environments. They investigate virtual prototyping tools, 3D simulation of urban areas, and the reconstruction and crowd simulation of the medieval Cambodian temple complex of Angkor Wat.

Chapter Review Process The chapter groups were formed across the Shonan and Dagstuhl immersive analytics workshops in 2016. Authors submitted manuscripts for their chapters in mid-2017. These initial versions were reviewed at first "internally" by one of the book editors. After an initial round of revisions based on the recommendations of these internal reviews, updated manuscripts were sent to expert reviewers invited from the community. We are grateful to these people for their detailed and insightful reviews.

1.5. Research Agenda

While the chapters provide a detailed introduction to the field of immersive analytics, they also make it clear that we have only begun to scratch the surface of this new field and that many questions remain. While the individual chapters detail research questions for a particular topic, we can group these under the following seven headings.

1.5.1. Underpinning Theory

We have seen how technological and psychological immersion has been studied for virtual environments [10], telepresence [94], telecommunications, and gaming [95]. A fundamental question for immersive analytics is how to modify these theories to identify and formalise the various kinds of immersion and engagement that might occur during data analytics and decision making. Such a theory would need to extend the current understanding of physical or spatial presence from representation of virtual worlds in virtual reality to representation of abstract data in mixed reality [61] and even data physicalisation [10]. It will need to clarify the links between technological and psychological immersion, the connection between these and the emotional state of the viewer, as well as the relationship with user performance.

Immersive analytics also requires the development of models for the processes and workflows employed by users. Variants of the sense-making loop underpin visual analytics [45,72] and recently the problem-solving loop was introduced for interactive optimisation [52]. Is it possible to develop a more general model of human-in-the-loop decision making? Furthermore, current models do not capture all of the activities of users in immersive analytics. They focus on the analyst, not on the stakeholders trying to understand and evaluate the result of the analysis. They do not adequately consider collaboration and the different roles that people may play in this process (see Chapter 8).

1.5.2. Effectiveness

A necessary question is to identify when immersive analytics techniques are useful. When (if ever) does the use of immersive technologies offer benefits over current desktop visual analytics tools? Traditionally data visualisation researchers have focussed on task performance, typically accuracy and speed. As Chapter 2 identifies, the use of depth cues may improve task effectiveness for some kinds of visualisation tasks. However, task performance is not the only measure of effectiveness. Emotional engagement and recall may also be important, especially when communicating findings to stakeholders. There is some evidence that both presence and emotional engagement improves recall [55]. In general, presence is bi-directionally linked to the emotional state of the viewer: the emotional state is influenced by the degree of presence and the feeling of presence is increased in "emotional" environments [78]. More research is required to understand this in the context of immersive data-driven narratives (see Chapter 6) and other aspects of immersive analytics.

Such an understanding crucially relies on methodologies for measuring the various aspects of user engagement and immersion [47]. These are most commonly evaluated using self-reported measure and a number of surveys have been developed to measure spatial and social presence [6,51,67,101] in virtual worlds and immersion in games [22,42,74]. Less subjective measures include behavioural measures such as the responses to virtual and external stimuli and psychophysiological measures such as skin conductance, heart rate, or brain activity [38,46,59].

1.5.3. Responsive Analytics

Few machine learning, data mining, optimisation, or simulation algorithms are designed to be used in responsive, interactive analytics applications. Human-in-the-loop algorithmics is still an emerging research field (see Chapter 5). More research is required to understand the trade-offs between responsiveness, predictability and the quality of answer, as well as how to design systems that leverage from the real-world knowledge of the human analyst.

1.5.4. Work Flows and Work Spaces

Immersive analytics, in particular situated analytics, allows very different work flows in which analytics can be employed in virtually any process or situation. What are general guidelines for doing this? Collaboration raises many additional questions, e. g., division and allocation of work, group dynamics and consensus. A related question is how to organise both shared and individual workspaces. Some further background on these questions is provided in Chapters 5 and 8.

1.5.5. Design Space

Many of the chapters have identified the need to explore and understand the design space for immersive analytics applications. Chapter 9 presents a preliminary framework but decades of research will be required to refine and validate this framework. Particular areas that require attention are interaction, mixed reality, collaboration and the use of audio and haptic feedback. The difficulty is compounded by rapidly changing technology, which means that previous findings and guidelines may no longer apply.

1.5.6. Applications

In this book, we have presented two possible application domains: life and health sciences, and the built environment, but there are many more. Examples include disaster management (where participants must quickly plan and direct reactions to threats), healthcare, including personalised health, manufacturing applications, and so on.

1.5.7. Societal Impact

The democratisation of data analysis and decision making has potentially far-reaching consequences for our society. There are also potential dangers: Will the use of emotionally engaging immersive data-driven narratives lead to less objective and possibly worse decisions by stakeholders (Chapter 6)? What will be the health effects and impact on social cohesion of increased use of virtual environments at work as well as at home?

Acknowledgements

Early efforts that prompted the conversations and workshops that have eventually led to this book were strongly supported by the Monash University Faculty of Information Technology. Chapters in this book were written by working groups formed at workshops on Immersive Analytics at Shonan, Meeting 2016-2 [41], and Dagstuhl, Seminar 16231 [27]. Continuing work by the authors of this chapter was funded by the Australian Research Council Discovery Scheme, project DP180100755 and the German Research Foundation (DFG), project D4 of SFB/Transregio 161.

References

1. Agarwal, R., Karahanna, E.: Time flies when you're having fun: cognitive absorption and beliefs about information technology usage. MIS Quarterly pp. 665–694 (2000)
2. Attfield, S., Kazai, G., Lalmas, M., Piwowarski, B.: Towards a science of user engagement (position paper). In: WSDM Workshop on User Modelling for Web Applications. pp. 9–12 (2011)
3. Bertin, J.: Semiology of graphics: diagrams, networks, maps. University of Wisconsin press (1983)
4. Bian, Y., Yang, C., Zhou, C., Liu, J., Gai, W., Meng, X., Tian, F., Shen, C.: Exploring the weak association between flow experience and performance in virtual environments. In: Proceedings of the Conference on Human Factors in Computing Systems (CHI). pp. 401:1–401:12. ACM (2018)
5. Biocca, F.: The cyborg's dilemma: progressive embodiment in virtual environments. Journal of Computer-Mediated Communication 3(2), 12–26 (1997)
6. Biocca, F., Harms, C., Burgoon, J.K.: Towards a more robust theory and measure of social presence: Review and suggested criteria. Presence: Teleoperators & Virtual Environments 12(5), 456–480 (2003)
7. Boyle, E.A., Connolly, T.M., Hainey, T., Boyle, J.M.: Engagement in digital entertainment games: a systematic review. Computers in Human Behavior 28(3), 771–780 (2012)
8. Brehmer, M., Munzner, T.: A multi-level typology of abstract visualization tasks. IEEE Transactions on Visualization and Computer Graphics 19(12), 2376–2385 (2013)
9. Brown, E., Cairns, P.: A grounded investigation of game immersion. In: CHI'04 extended abstracts on Human Factors in Computing Systems. pp. 1297–1300. ACM (2004)
10. Burdea, G.C., Coiffet, P.: Virtual Reality Technology. John Wiley & Sons, Inc., New York, NY, USA, 2 edn. (2003)
11. Cairns, P., Cox, A., Nordin, A.I.: Immersion in digital games: review of gaming experience research. Handbook of Digital Games 339, 337–361 (2014)
12. Cairns, P., Cox, A.L., Day, M., Martin, H., Perryman, T.: Who but not where: the effect of social play on immersion in digital games. International Journal of Human-Computer Studies 71(11), 1069–1077 (2013)
13. Calleja, G.: In-game: From immersion to incorporation. MIT Press (2011)
14. Card, S.K., Mackinlay, J.D., Shneiderman, B.: Readings in information visualization: using vision to think. Morgan Kaufmann (1999)
15. Card, S.K., Robertson, G.G., Mackinlay, J.D.: The information visualizer, an information workspace. In: Proceedings of the SIGCHI Conference on Human Factors in Computing Systems. pp. 181–186. ACM (1991)
16. Chandler, T., Cordeil, M., Czauderna, T., Dwyer, T., Glowacki, J., Goncu, C., Klapperstueck, M., Klein, K., Marriott, K., Schreiber, F., Wilson, E.: Immersive analytics. In: IEEE 2015 Big Data Visual Analytics (BDVA). pp. 1–8 (2015)

17. Cleveland, W.S., McGill, R.: Graphical perception: Theory, experimentation, and application to the development of graphical methods. Journal of the American Statistical Association 79(387), 531–554 (1984)
18. Cohen, I.B.: Howard Aiken on the number of computers needed for the nation. IEEE Annals of the History of Computing 20(3), 27–32 (1998)
19. Cruz-Neira, C., Sandin, D.J., DeFanti, T.A., Kenyon, R.V., Hart, J.C.: The CAVE: audio visual experience automatic virtual environment. Commun. ACM 35(6), 64–72 (1992)
20. Csikszentmihalyi, M.: Beyond boredom and anxiety. Jossey-Bass Publishers (1975)
21. Csikszentmihalyi, M., Abuhamdeh, S., Nakamura, J.: Flow. In: Flow and the Foundations of Positive Psychology, pp. 227–238. Springer (2014)
22. De Kort, Y.A., IJsselsteijn, W.A., Poels, K.: Digital games as social presence technology: development of the social presence in gaming questionnaire (SPGQ). Proceedings of PRESENCE 195203 (2007)
23. Dinh, H.Q., Walker, N., Hodges, L.F., Song, C., Kobayashi, A.: Evaluating the importance of multi-sensory input on memory and the sense of presence in virtual environments. In: Proceedings IEEE Virtual Reality. pp. 222–228 (1999)
24. Dourish, P.: Where the action is: the foundations of embodied interaction. MIT Press (2004)
25. Draper, J.V., Kaber, D.B., Usher, J.M.: Telepresence. Human Factors 40(3), 354–375 (1998)
26. Durlach, N., Slater, M.: Presence in shared virtual environments and virtual togetherness. Presence: Teleoperators & Virtual Environments 9(2), 214–217 (2000)
27. Dwyer, T., Riche, N.H., Klein, K., Stuerzlinger, W., Thomas, B.: Immersive analytics (Dagstuhl seminar 16231). Dagstuhl Reports 6(6), 1–9 (2016)
28. Engelbart, D.C., English, W.K.: A research center for augmenting human intellect. In: Proceedings of the December 9-11, 1968, Fall Joint Computer Conference, Part I. pp. 395–410. AFIPS '68 (Fall, part I), ACM (1968)
29. Ermi, L., Mäyrä, F.: Fundamental components of the gameplay experience: analysing immersion. Worlds in Play: International Perspectives on Digital Games Research 37(2), 37–53 (2005)
30. Flach, J.M., Holden, J.G.: The reality of experience: Gibson's way. Presence: Teleoperators & Virtual Environments 7(1), 90–95 (1998)
31. Gajadhar, B.J., De Kort, Y.A., Ijsselsteijn, W.A.: Shared fun is doubled fun: player enjoyment as a function of social setting. In: Fun and Games, pp. 106–117. Springer (2008)
32. Gerrig, R.J.: Experiencing narrative worlds: on the psychological activities of reading. Yale University Press (1993)
33. Gorini, A., Capideville, C.S., De Leo, G., Mantovani, F., Riva, G.: The role of immersion and narrative in mediated presence: the virtual hospital experience. Cyberpsychology, Behavior, and Social Networking 14(3), 99–105 (2011)
34. Hartmann, T., Wirth, W., Vorderer, P., Klimmt, C., Schramm, H., Böcking, S.: Spatial presence theory: state of the art and challenges ahead. In: Immersed in Media, pp. 115–135. Springer (2015)
35. Hoffman, H.G.: Physically touching virtual objects using tactile augmentation enhances the realism of virtual environments. In: Proceedings IEEE 1998 Virtual Reality Annual International Symposium. pp. 59–63 (1998)
36. Hoffman, H.G., Hollander, A., Schroder, K., Rousseau, S., Furness, T.: Physically touching and tasting virtual objects enhances the realism of virtual experiences. Virtual Reality 3(4), 226–234 (1998)

37. Huang, D., Tory, M., Aseniero, B.A., Bartram, L., Bateman, S., Carpendale, S., Tang, A., Woodbury, R.: Personal visualization and personal visual analytics. IEEE Transactions on Visualization and Computer Graphics 21(3), 420–433 (2015)
38. IJsselsteijn, W.A., de Ridder, H., Freeman, J., Avons, S.E.: Presence: Concept, determinants and measurement. In: Human Vision and Electronic Imaging. vol. 3959, pp. 520–529 (2000)
39. Irwin, H.J.: Pathological and nonpathological dissociation: the relevance of childhood trauma. The Journal of Psychology 133(2), 157–164 (1999)
40. Isenberg, P., Heimerl, F., Koch, S., Isenberg, T., Xu, P., Stolper, C.D., Sedlmair, M., Chen, J., Möller, T., Stasko, J.: vispubdata.org: A metadata collection about IEEE visualization (VIS) publications. IEEE Transactions on Visualization and Computer Graphics 23(9), 2199–2206 (Sep 2017)
41. Itoh, T., Marriott, K., Schreiber, F., Wössner, U.: Immersive analytics: a new multidisciplinary initiative to explore future interaction technologies for data analytics. Shonan Reports (2016)
42. Jennett, C., Cox, A.L., Cairns, P., Dhoparee, S., Epps, A., Tijs, T., Walton, A.: Measuring and defining the experience of immersion in games. International Journal of Human-Computer Studies 66(9), 641–661 (2008)
43. Jin, S.A.A.: Avatars mirroring the actual self versus projecting the ideal self: The effects of self-priming on interactivity and immersion in an exergame, wii fit. CyberPsychology & Behavior 12(6), 761–765 (2009)
44. Kay, A., Goldberg, A.: Personal dynamic media. Computer 10(3), 31–41 (1977)
45. Kerren, A., Schreiber, F.: Toward the role of interaction in visual analytics. In: Rose, O., Uhrmacher, A.M. (eds.) Prodeedings Winter Simulation Conference. p. 420 (2012)
46. Kober, S.E., Kurzmann, J., Neuper, C.: Cortical correlate of spatial presence in 2D and 3D interactive virtual reality: an EEG study. International Journal of Psychophysiology 83(3), 365–374 (2012)
47. Laarni, J., Ravaja, N., Saari, T., Böcking, S., Hartmann, T., Schramm, H.: Ways to measure spatial presence: review and future directions. In: Immersed in Media, pp. 139–185. Springer (2015)
48. Latoschik, M.E., Roth, D., Gall, D., Achenbach, J., Waltemate, T., Botsch, M.: The effect of avatar realism in immersive social virtual realities. In: 23rd ACM Symposium on Virtual Reality Software and Technology (VRST). pp. 39:1–39:10 (2017)
49. Leap Motion. http://www.leapmotion.com, accessed: January 2018
50. Lee, K.M.: Presence, explicated. Communication Theory 14(1), 27–50 (2004)
51. Lessiter, J., Freeman, J., Keogh, E., Davidoff, J.: A cross-media presence questionnaire: the itc-sense of presence inventory. Presence: Teleoperators & Virtual Environments 10(3), 282–297 (2001)
52. Liu, J., Dwyer, T., Marriott, K., Millar, J., Haworth, A.: Understanding the relationship between interactive optimisation and visual analytics in the context of prostate brachytherapy. IEEE Transactions on Visualization and Computer Graphics 24(1), 319–329 (2018)
53. Lombard, M., Ditton, T.: At the heart of it all: the concept of presence. Journal of Computer-Mediated Communication 3(2) (1997)
54. Lombard, M., Jones, M.T.: Defining presence. In: Immersed in Media, pp. 13–34. Springer (2015)
55. Makowski, D., Sperduti, M., Nicolas, S., Piolino, P.: Being there and remembering it: presence improves memory encoding. Consciousness and Cognition 53, 194–202 (2017)

56. International journal of man-machine studies (From 1969 to 1993)
57. Mantovani, G., Riva, G.: ?Real? presence: how different ontologies generate different criteria for presence, telepresence, and virtual presence. Presence: Teleoperators & Virtual Environments 8(5), 540–550 (1999)
58. McCormick, B.H.: Visualization in scientific computing. Computer Graphics 21(6), 1–14 (1987)
59. Meehan, M., Insko, B., Whitton, M., Brooks Jr, F.P.: Physiological measures of presence in stressful virtual environments. ACM Transactions on Graphics (TOG) 21(3), 645–652 (2002)
60. Microsoft Kinect. https://en.wikipedia.org/wiki/Kinect, accessed: January 2018
61. Milgram, P., Kishino, F.: A taxonomy of mixed reality visual displays. IEICE Transactions on Information and Systems 77(12), 1321–1329 (1994)
62. Minsky, M.: Telepresence. Omni (1980)
63. Munzner, T.: Exploring large graphs in 3D hyperbolic space. IEEE Computer Graphics and Applications 18(4), 18–23 (1998)
64. Nakamura, J., Csikszentmihalyi, M.: The concept of flow. In: Flow and the Foundations of Positive Psychology, pp. 239–263. Springer (2014)
65. Nell, V.: Lost in a book: the psychology of reading for pleasure. Yale University Press (1988)
66. Nguyen, T.T.H., Duva, T.: A survey of communication and awareness in collaborative virtual environments. In: Proceedings of IEEE International Workshop on Collaborative Virtual Environments (3DCVE) (2014)
67. Nowak, K.: Defining and differentiating copresence, social presence and presence as transportation. In: Presence 2001 Conference, Philadelphia, PA. pp. 1–23 (2001)
68. Nowak, K.L., Biocca, F.: The effect of the agency and anthropomorphism on users' sense of telepresence, copresence, and social presence in virtual environments. Presence: Teleoperators & Virtual Environments 12(5), 481–494 (2003)
69. O'Brien, H.L., Toms, E.G.: What is user engagement? A conceptual framework for defining user engagement with technology. Journal of the Association for Information Science and Technology 59(6), 938–955 (2008)
70. O'Brien, H.L., Toms, E.G.: The development and evaluation of a survey to measure user engagement. Journal of the Association for Information Science and Technology 61(1), 50–69 (2010)
71. De la Peña, N., Weil, P., Llobera, J., Giannopoulos, E., Pomés, A., Spanlang, B., Friedman, D., Sanchez-Vives, M.V., Slater, M.: Immersive journalism: immersive virtual reality for the first-person experience of news. Presence: Teleoperators & Virtual Environments 19(4), 291–301 (2010)
72. Pirolli, P., Card, S.: The sensemaking process and leverage points for analyst technology as identified through cognitive task analysis. In: Proceedings of International Conference on Intelligence Analysis. vol. 5, pp. 2–4 (2005)
73. Poels, K., De Kort, Y., Ijsselsteijn, W.: It is always a lot of fun!: exploring dimensions of digital game experience using focus group methodology. In: Proceedings of the 2007 Conference on Future Play. pp. 83–89. ACM (2007)
74. Qin, H., Patrick Rau, P.L., Salvendy, G.: Measuring player immersion in the computer game narrative. International Journal of Human-Computer Interaction 25(2), 107–133 (2009)
75. Ranasinghe, N., Jain, P., Thi Ngoc Tram, N., Koh, K.C.R., Tolley, D., Karwita, S., Lien-Ya, L., Liangkun, Y., Shamaiah, K., Eason Wai Tung, C., Yen, C.C., Do, E.Y.L.: Season traveller: Multisensory narration for enhancing the virtual reality experience. In: Proceedings of the 2018 CHI Conference on Human Factors in Computing Systems (CHI). pp. 577:1–577:13. ACM (2018)

76. Ratan, R.: Self-presence, explicated: body, emotion, and identity. Handbook of Research on Technoself: Identity in a Technological Society (2012)
77. Riva, G., Davide, F., Ijsselsteijn, W.: Being there: the experience of presence in mediated environments. Being there: Concepts, Effects and Measurement of User Presence in Synthetic Environments 5 (2003)
78. Riva, G., Mantovani, F., Capideville, C.S., Preziosa, A., Morganti, F., Villani, D., Gaggioli, A., Botella, C., Alcañiz, M.: Affective interactions using virtual reality: the link between presence and emotions. CyberPsychology & Behavior 10(1), 45–56 (2007)
79. Riva, G., Waterworth, J.A., Waterworth, E.L., Mantovani, F.: From intention to action: The role of presence. New Ideas in Psychology 29(1), 24–37 (2011)
80. Robertson, G.G., Mackinlay, J.D., Card, S.K.: Cone trees: animated 3D visualizations of hierarchical information. In: Proceedings of the SIGCHI Conference on Human Factors in Computing Systems. pp. 189–194. ACM (1991)
81. Ryan, M.L.: Narrative as virtual reality: immersion and interactivity in literature and electronic media. Johns Hopkins University Press (2001)
82. Sanchez-Vives, M.V., Slater, M.: From presence to consciousness through virtual reality. Nature Reviews Neuroscience 6(4), 332–339 (2005)
83. Schuemie, M.J., Van Der Straaten, P., Krijn, M., Van Der Mast, C.A.: Research on presence in virtual reality: a survey. CyberPsychology & Behavior 4(2), 183–201 (2001)
84. Schultze, U.: Embodiment and presence in virtual worlds: a review. Journal of Information Technology 25(4), 434–449 (2010)
85. Sheridan, T.B.: Musings on telepresence and virtual presence. Presence: Teleoperators & Virtual Environments 1(1), 120–126 (1992)
86. Sheridan, T.B.: Further musings on the psychophysics of presence. Presence: Teleoperators & Virtual Environments 5(2), 241–246 (1996)
87. Shneiderman, B.: Direct manipulation: A step beyond programming languages. In: ACM SIGSOC Bulletin. vol. 13 (2-3), p. 143. ACM (1982)
88. Slater, M.: Measuring presence: A response to the Witmer and Singer presence questionnaire. Presence: Teleoperators & Virtual Environments 8(5), 560–565 (1999)
89. Slater, M.: Place illusion and plausibility can lead to realistic behaviour in immersive virtual environments. Philosophical Transactions of the Royal Society of London B: Biological Sciences 364(1535), 3549–3557 (2009)
90. Slater, M., Lotto, B., Arnold, M.M., Sanchez-Vives, M.V.: How we experience immersive virtual environments: the concept of presence and its measurement. Anuario de psicología/The UB Journal of psychology 40(2), 193–210 (2009)
91. Slater, M., Wilbur, S.: A framework for immersive virtual environments five: speculations on the role of presence in virtual environments. Presence: Teleoperators & Virtual Environments 6(6), 603–616 (1997)
92. Sutherland, I.E.: Sketchpad a man-machine graphical communication system. Transactions of the Society for Computer Simulation 2(5), R–3 (1964)
93. Sutherland, I.E.: A head-mounted three dimensional display. In: Proceedings of the December 9-11, 1968, Fall Joint Computer Conference, Part I. pp. 757–764. AFIPS '68 (Fall, part I), ACM (1968)
94. Tachi, S.: Telexistence. In: Virtual Realities, pp. 229–259. Springer (2015)
95. Thomas, B.H.: A survey of visual, mixed, and augmented reality gaming. Computers in Entertainment (CIE) 10(1), 3 (2012)
96. Thomas, J.J., Cook, K.A.: Illuminating the path: the research and development agenda for visual analytics. National Visualization and Analytics Ctr (2005)

97. Trevino, L.K., Webster, J.: Flow in computer-mediated communication: electronic mail and voice mail evaluation and impacts. Communication Research 19(5), 539–573 (1992)
98. Tufte, E.R.: Envisioning information. Graphics press (1990)
99. Tukey, J.W.: Exploratory data analysis. Reading, Mass. (1977)
100. Webster, J., Trevino, L.K., Ryan, L.: The dimensionality and correlates of flow in human-computer interactions. Computers in Human Behavior 9(4), 411–426 (1993)
101. Witmer, B.G., Singer, M.J.: Measuring presence in virtual environments: a presence questionnaire. Presence: Teleoperators & Virtual Environments 7(3), 225–240 (1998)
102. Zeltzer, D.: Autonomy, interaction, and presence. Presence: Teleoperators & Virtual Environments 1(1), 127–132 (1992)

2. Immersive Analytics: Time to Reconsider the Value of 3D for Information Visualisation

Kim Marriott[1], Jian Chen[2], Marcel Hlawatsch[3], Takayuki Itoh[4], Miguel A. Nacenta[5], Guido Reina[6], and Wolfgang Stuerzlinger[7]

[1] Monash University, Australia
Kim.Marriott@monash.edu
[2] The Ohio State University, USA
chen.8028@osu.edu
[3] University of Stuttgart (VISUS), Germany
Marcel.Hlawatsch@visus.uni-stuttgart.de
[4] Ochanomizu University, Japan
itot@is.ocha.ac.jp
[5] University of St Andrews, Scotland
mans@st-andrews.ac.uk
[6] University of Stuttgart (VISUS), Germany
guido.reina@visus.uni-stuttgart.de
[7] Simon Fraser University, Canada
w.s@sfu.ca

Abstract. Modern virtual reality display technologies engender spatial immersion by using a variety of depth cues such as perspective and head-tracked binocular presentation to create visually realistic 3D worlds. While 3D visualisations are common in scientific visualisation, they are much less common in information visualisation. In this chapter we explore whether immersive analytic applications should continue to use traditional 2D information visualisations or whether there are situations when 3D may offer benefits. We identify a number of potential applications of 3D depth cues for abstract data visualisation: using depth to show an additional data dimension, such as in 2.5D network layouts, views on non-flat surfaces and egocentric views in which the data is placed around the viewer, and visualising abstract data with a spatial embedding. Another important potential benefit is the ability to arrange multiple views in the 3D space around the user and to attach abstract visualisations to objects in the real world.

Keywords: immersive analytics, data visualisation, information visualisation, 3D

2.1. Introduction

In this chapter we are concerned with *spatial immersion*, in which the viewer is immersed within a virtual world that is perceptually convincing. We focus on

K. Marriott et al. (Eds.): Immersive Analytics, LNCS 11190, pp. 25–55, 2018.
https://doi.org/10.1007/978-3-030-01388-2_2

the visual aspects of this immersion and its relevance for data visualisation. An important component of spatial immersion in mixed reality systems[1] is the use of depth cues like occlusion and linear perspective, global lighting effects like shadows, texture rendering, as well as head tracking and binocular display technologies to simulate three-dimensional (3D) vision. Consequently these technologies support perceptually convincing rendering of data visualisations that make use of three dimensional space either in the visualisation itself or by allowing the visualisations to be placed anywhere in the viewer's environment.

Scientific visualisation researchers have been quick to adopt mixed reality display technologies, especially virtual reality systems, since most scientific data already lives in a 3D world. In contrast, information visualisation researchers have been very cautious about the use of 3D representations for abstract data and have therefore seen little benefit in the use of spatially immersive technologies. Most information visualisation researchers have continued to focus on flat 2D data visualisation designed for presentation on desktop computers, with a few forays into touch interfaces [51] and tangible graphics [52].

This conservatism is quite deliberate and is a response to the "unbridled enthusiasm" [71] of information visualisation researchers in the late 1980s and early 1990s for 3D representations. This was the time when the first 3D graphic workstations, such as those made by Silicon Graphics, were hitting the mass market and many information visualisation researchers were convinced that 3D visualisations utilising linear perspective, shading and shadows offered benefits over traditional 2D representations. For example, cone trees were introduced as an interactive way of visualising hierarchical data in 3D [78] (see Figure 1), the perspective wall [65] as a 3D focus+context way of viewing traditional 2D tables, while 3D desktops such as the data mountain [77] were introduced as a way of taking advantage of 3D spatial memory. The infamous 3D Pie or Bar Charts [80] that popular spreadsheet applications and business graphics showcased were also introduced at this time. Subsequent user studies, however, failed to find any benefits for these 3D representations over the traditional 2D representations in abstract data visualisation [16,19] and this early enthusiasm for 3D was replaced by a strong scepticism. Thus, in a recent popular text on data visualisation, Munzner [71] cautions against the "unjustified use" of 3D representations and immersive environments for representation of abstract data.

However, we believe that with the arrival of commodity immersive VR and AR devices such as the HTC Vive or Microsoft HoloLens it is timely to explore how to best visualise abstract data in such immersive environments and whether immersive analytic applications should continue to use traditional 2D information visualisations or whether there are situations in which 3D offers benefits. There are several reasons for doing so:

- **Potential of immersive displays.** Head-mounted mixed reality displays are almost certainly going to become much more common. As discussed

[1] We use the term mixed reality to refer to the continuum from pure virtual reality in which the user is totally immersed in the virtual environment, to augmented reality in which the physical environment is overlaid with virtual information [70].

in Chapter 1 these new platforms will free analytics applications from the desktop and encourage their use in all aspects of life. Furthermore these devices support situated analytics, embodied data exploration, collaboration as well as more engaging narrative visualisations. It is inevitable that mixed reality displays will be used for presentation of abstract data regardless of how well suited they are to this. We therefore need evidence-based guidelines on how to present abstract data on these devices, even if we find that the best way is to simply show abstract data on a flat 2D "billboard".

- **Additional visual channel.** Allowing a third spatial dimension provides another visual channel for data visualisation. While prone to occlusion, depth disparity and foreshortening [71], as we shall discover, a number of studies demonstrate that there are benefits in using this channel for certain kinds of abstract data and tasks: we require a more nuanced understanding of when it is beneficial to do so.
- **Improving technology.** Furthermore, immersive display technologies have advanced considerably in the last decade. Modern displays have much higher resolution and less latency than the devices used in these earlier studies, as well as providing head-tracked binocular presentation[2] and supporting a wider range of interaction technologies. This means that modern immersive displays overcome at least some of the previously identified problems of viewing 3D visualisations on a flat desktop display.
- **Immersive work spaces.** Head-mounted mixed reality devices potentially allow the analyst to use the space around them as their workspace, placing data visualisations where they please, and in the case of augmented reality using the physical environment as the workspace. Such an immersive workspace is dramatically different from the traditional flat and workspace provided by desktop machines. As yet we do not know how to best use this extra freedom and what, if any, benefits it offers.
- **Beyond task effectiveness.** Information visualisation researchers have typically focussed on task effectiveness of data visualisations by measuring accuracy and speed. In immersive analytics we wish to understand effectiveness in a broader sense that includes other aspects of the user experience (Chapter 1). Does spatial immersion support deeper collaboration? Does it provide a more enjoyable, engaging, affective or memorable experience? Answers to these questions are vital if we want analytics applications to be used by the general public, not just professional analysts.

This chapter is intended to be a starting point for research into visual idioms for presenting and arranging abstract data in spatially immersive environments. In particular, it investigates the use of 3D for abstract data visualisation. However, a key problem in any discussion about the value of 3D visualisation is that the term 3D has been used to refer to very different things at different periods in time. In the 1980's, 3D generally referred to graphics that rendered objects with three

[2] We avoid the use of the term stereoscopic, which derives from the greek σπερεως, meaning "solid" (not "dual", a common misconception). For an in-depth discussion see [98].

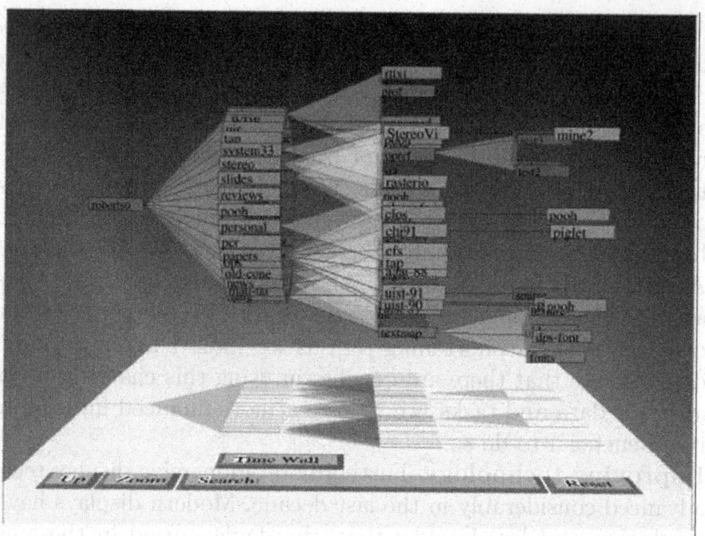

Fig. 1: Cone Trees and the horizontal variant Cam Trees were introduced by Robertson *et al.* in 1991 as a way to navigate large tree structures [80]. (Figure courtesy of S. Card, J. Mackinlay and G. Robertson and used with permission from Xerox.)

spatial dimensions (i. e., objects with volume) on to a flat (hence 2D) electronic screen while more recently 3D has become a synonym for (possibly head-tracked) binocular presentation. Thus it is important to clearly distinguish between the use of a 3D visualisation and the way in which this is presented to the viewer. We need to tease apart the effect of the different kinds of technologies and the depth cues they provide. As Ware argues, the use of 3D in data visualisation is really all about choosing the right depth cues [101]. We believe a major direction for immersive analytics research will be to investigate how to best make use of the depth cues provided in common spatially immersive environments for abstract data analysis. Our chapter provides the basis for this research by providing:

- A discussion of depth cues from a perceptual and technical perspective (*Section 2.2.*).
- A review of user studies evaluating the use of 3D in abstract data visualisation (*Section 2.3.*).
- Identification of applications and tasks for which spatially immersive visualisations may provide advantages over traditional 2D abstract data visualisation (*Section 2.4.*).

We finish the chapter with a number of open research questions.

2.2. Background: Perception and Presentation of 3D

As discussed in the introduction, one of the difficulties in understanding the value of 3D visualisation is that the term 3D has been used to refer to very different things depending upon sub-discipline and the time period. During the advent of the first powerful graphic workstations in the 1980's, 3D generally referred to graphics that rendered objects with three spatial dimensions (i. e., objects with volume) on to a flat (hence 2D) electronic screen.

More recently 3D has become a synonym for binocular presentation. Visualisation using this kind of 3D has been a popular area of research since the 80s (e. g., [76]), as sophisticated presentation technologies (e. g., binocular CAVEs, binocular head-mounted displays) were available to researchers before they were commercially viable for the general public. The assumption in this body of work, which we review in subsequent sections of this chapter, is that modes of presentation that are more faithful to how humans perceive the world will allow visualisations to take better advantage of the additional depth channel by overcoming the problems of the "flattened" 3D representations. For example, we might be able to overcome the inaccuracy in perceiving depth through the extra information contained in the differences between the images perceived by each eye, or the problem of occlusion [31] if we can move our heads (or ourselves) around a representation. This kind of thinking, in its limit, is exemplified by the relatively recent *physical visualisation* sub-area of data visualisation research [52], in which data is represented directly using real solid objects. Physical visualisation provides a representation that is not only faithful to real-world perception; it actually *is* real-world perception.

Obviously there are great differences between a 3D pie chart [80] printed on paper, a cone tree [78] seen through the Oculus Rift, or a bar chart printed with a volumetric 3D printer. For our purpose, a *3D visualisation* is any visualisation that *maps data to three different spatial dimensions*, independently of *how* these dimensions are presented to the viewer[3] and independently of whether these mappings are inherent in the semantics of the data (what is traditionally referred to as Scientific Visualisation) or they are abstract or arbitrary. A 3D visualisation may be good or bad depending on the device it is being viewed on, and devices will be different from each other depending on how they cater to the different ways of the human visual system to perceive depth dimension (depth cues).

We now provide a brief introduction into the perceptual and hardware terms that we will use in the rest of the chapter. First we summarise existing depth cues and attempts to rank them in order of strength, second we describe the most common presentation technologies and systems in connection to the cues that they support.

[3] This definition is related to the process called *spatialisation* [94] and resonates with the presentation-representation distinction made by Spence in his visualisation textbook [83], but we will not use this terminology since the distinction of representation and presentation is sometimes not clear and is intertwined with considerations of interactivity.

Depth perception The types of information that the visual system relies on for perceiving depth are called *depth cues.* Although there are multiple classifications and research is still ongoing (we do not know yet whether some of these cues actually provide information about depth to the visual system), we will use Cutting and Vishton's nomenclature [24], as well as mentioning some additional cues (or subcues) that are of relevance.

Occlusion refers to how objects that are closer in space prevent us seeing objects that are behind. This depth cue is ordinal, in the sense that it does not tell us how much further an object is if it is occluded, just that it is behind.

Relative size refers to the phenomenon that two objects of the same size that are at different distances from the observer will project a differently sized image in the eye. If we have an idea of the approximate size of an object, how big or small it appears in our field of view will give us information about how far it is.

Relative density relates to how spatial patterns of objects or visual features will appear more dense as the distance to the pattern increases. For example, if looking at a barley field, the individual spikes of the barley plants will be more concentrated and closer to each other in the retinal image of those parts of the field that are further away than those that are closer.

Height in visual field. If we assume that the space in front of us is approximately flat and that objects are bound to rest on the ground (due to the action of gravity), the position of their retinal images (or at least, their base) with respect to the horizon provides a proxy for their distance, since objects that are closer will be resting further from the horizon (or closer to our own feet).

The four cues described above, in combination, are often clustered as *linear perspective* [12] and are mostly a consequence of the projective properties of the eye as a sensor. Relative size, density and height in visual field are often also referred as *foreshortening.*

Aerial perspective refers to the change in colour properties (e. g., hue, saturation, lightness) of objects at large distances, caused by the scattering of light of the atmosphere in between the observer and the objects. This cue only works when distances are very large or when the atmosphere is optically dense (e. g., on a misty day).

Motion perspective is based on movement. If an object or the observer moves, the projection of the object in the retina changes, and the form and magnitude of these changes provide additional information about the 3D structure of the object [23] as well as its distance [79]. For example, when looking from a side window in a moving car, and assuming that most objects are static, we can perceive that objects that move faster in our field of view are closer to us, whereas objects in the horizon stay relatively static. Motion perspective is supported by head-tracking.

Binocular disparity and *stereopsis* are the cues most commonly associated with the modern popular understanding of 3D. Small differences in the images received by the left and the right eye (disparity), are processed in the brain to interpret depth and 3D shape of objects.

Accommodation refers to effects of dynamic physiological changes in the shape of each eye and the consequences on the retinal image. Specifically, accommodation is most evident in how objects that are not focused on appear proportionally blurry in relation to the distance to the current focus depth. This blur occurs because the eye lens works like a camera with a limited depth of field which adapts dynamically its focal length according to the object that is the center of attention. The amount of blur of the background and other objects provides information about their relative distances [66], although the amount of blur is also generally dependent on the lightness of the scene (a lighter scene causes the pupil to contract and, in consequence, the depth of field increase because the eye comes closer to a *pin hole camera*, which has almost infinite depth of field, i. e., all objects are in focus).

There are two additional possible sources of information from *accommodation*. The first is that the human nervous system controls the size of the pupil and the shape of the eye's lens, which could provide an additional input about the distance of an object (how much the body needs to stretch the lens for an object for it to be in focus is a function of its distance). The other is that different light frequencies are bent by the lens in slightly different ways. This results in subtle "halos" around objects that can be red or blue depending on which object is in focus and at which distance [46, 97], a manifestation of the chromatic aberration phenomenon.

Cast shadows can be an effective cue for judging the height of an object above the plane and act as an indirect depth cue by linking the depth of an object with that of the location on which its shadow falls [103].

Convergence refers to the change in rotation of the eyes that takes place to align the object or region of interest in the center of both eye's foveas. This is a reflex from the visual system [38]. Since the eye orientations are known by the perceptual system and are related to the distance of the object, the visual perceptual system can use this information to infer distance, although generally only in the short range (less than 3m) due to the fact that angle changes for far objects become increasingly small and therefore difficult to distinguish.

User interaction can provide further depth information by complementing or enhancing the above visual cues.

Controlled point of view refers to the ability of people to manipulate their point of view in a virtual space. This is common in desktop VR reality systems where the location of the point of view used to render a scene can be changed by the user through some input device, typically the mouse. This provides additional 3D information because the user knows what positional change she has triggered through her actions on the input device and therefore can expect different kinds of visual changes depending on the position and depth of the objects in the scene. Therefore this additional cue takes advantage of a closed feedback loop involving perception and motor action, and relies on the senses of touch and proprioception to complement mostly the *motion perspective* visual cue described above, but also triggering changes in most of the other cues (e. g., changes in vergence for binocular displays if an object comes close to the viewer).

Subjective motion is related to controlled point of view in that the viewer can change the perspective of the scene. However, in subjective motion the changes are triggered through the actual physical motion in space of the observer. These changes can be subtle (small changes in head position) or more dramatic if they involve walking. Subjective motion involves proprioception and motor action control as in the controlled point of view but, importantly, it provides additional information through the vestibular system (balance and movement detection). Equivalently to controlled point of view, this information is complementary to a range of visual cues [86].

Object manipulation through touch, using one's (tracked) hands, or input devices can change the position of objects with respect to the observer and therefore trigger motion perspective and changes in other cues. The change in relative position between the observer and the object of interest (virtual or physical) produces alterations of the information projected in the retina equivalent to what controlling the virtual point of view or moving oneself does, but it is generally limited to a single object (rather than the rest of the environment in the previous two), and it does not trigger vestibular system signals [72]. It still relies on touch (somatic), motor, and proprioceptive information.

3D display technologies By replicating all the cues listed above with electronic displays it is conceivable that we could recreate a (dynamic) experience of 3D perception that is very close to regular perception of physical objects in the real world. However, existing display technologies represent an additional bottleneck, since not all cues can be replicated simultaneously in a dynamic form. Therefore it is important to not only qualify what kind of depth perception cues our data representations will be depending on, but also which cues can actually be supported by the display itself.

Table 1 provides a summary of current display technologies and links it to the cues that they support. A technology can: a) clearly support a particular cue, b) might possibly support it, c) might only partially support it (or only in certain circumstances), and d) might intrinsically not support it. For more explanation of the technologies: Fishtank VR [104], Stereo CAVE [22], Accomodation Optics VR Headset [57], Holografika Holovizio see http://www.holografika.com, Optical 3D Displays [55], Volumetric 3D display [95] and Physical Displays [52]. Augmented reality (AR) provides a direct or indirect view of reality, augmented by computer-generated imagery. AR typically provides stereoscopic views, but monoscopic variants exist as well. Most AR systems are based on head-mounted devices, but some hybrid systems use large transparent displays in front of the scene to display the computer-generated content, e. g. [56].

Limitations of depth perception Knowing when and how best to use 3D for data visualisation requires us to understand the limitations of human depth perception and the additional limitations arising from current immersive display technologies. It is important to highlight that, although supported multi-modally by a plethora of cues as we have seen above, the perception of spatial 3D in

Table 1: Mapping between 3D display technologies and depth cues. "Y" (yes–Dark Green) indicates that existing systems do this. "P" (Possible–Light Green) indicates that existing systems could potentially do this. "D" (Depends/To Some Extent–Yellow) indicates that the specific property is achievable to some degree, although not completely, or needs to be simulated. "N" (No–Red) indicates that this is not currently possible.

	Linear Perspective	Aerial Perspective	Occlusion	Motion Perspective	Accommodation	Convergence	Binoc. Disparity and Stereopsis	User-controlled PoV	Subjective Motion	Interactive Content Manipulation	Examples
Regular photography or print	Y	Y	Y	N	N	N	N	N	N	N	
Desktop Computer Virtual Reality	Y	P	Y	Y	N	D	D	Y	N	D	[87]
Fishtank Virtual Reality	Y	P	Y	Y	N	D	D	P	Y	D	[104]
Non-disparity monocular/binocular viewing	Y	P	P	P	N	N	N	P	P	D	[99]
Head-mounted Binocular Displays	Y	P	Y	Y	N	Y	Y	P	Y	D	[90]
Multi-display Environments, Large Displays	Y	P	Y	Y	N	N	N	P	P	D	[43, 72, 73]
Binocular CAVEs	Y	P	Y	Y	N	Y	Y	P	Y	D	[22]
Gazer (Simulation of Accommodation)	Y	P	P	P	D	P	P	P	P	D	[66, 67]
Accommodation Optics VR Headset	Y	P	P	P	Y	Y	Y	P	Y	D	[81]
Multiview Autostereoscopic	Y	P	Y	Y	D	Y	Y	P	Y	D	[25, 49]
Volumetric 3D Displays	Y	N	N	Y	Y	Y	Y	P	Y	D	[36]
Optical Holographic 3D Displays	Y	N	N	Y	Y	Y	Y	P	Y	D	[55]
Augmented Reality (AR)	Y	P	D	Y	D	D	Y	N	Y	D	[5]
AR Hybrids	Y	P	Y	Y	D	D	Y	D	P	D	[56]
Physical Visualisations (reality)	Y	P	Y	Y	Y	Y	Y	N	Y	Y	[52]

humans is, strictly speaking, not *volumetric*, but instead layered and multiplexed in time. This is why the previous section describes the perception of depth (not 3D perception) and why Ware has argued that human visual perception is not 3D, not 2.5D, but instead closer to 2.05D [102].

Studies also indicate that more than 30% of the population may experience some form of binocular deficiency [47], and binocular acuity generally decreases with age [110]. Gracia *et al.* [39] identified several issues arising in 3D visualisation: line-of-sight ambiguity, occlusion and linear perspective distortion. Line-of-sight ambiguity refers to the fact that we can only see a single datapoint along each line of sight, whereas we can see many more across the field of view, text legibility, inappropriate view scale and movement distortion were also identified as potential issues. Text legibility is a particularly important issue as text and numbers are common in abstract data visualisations. Problems with legibility arise because current head-mounted AR and VR displays typically have lower resolution than desktop systems. This is compounded by foreshortening and 3D orientation, i. e., when the text is not directly facing the viewer [41, 62, 73].

An observer that has sufficient cues will be able to determine within a certain range of accuracy the 3D position of one particular object, but as the number of objects increases, or if the datum itself is continuous in the volume (e. g., the temperature of the water in a cube of $1km \times 1km \times 1km$) the dataset typically needs to be filtered and looked at a small number of layers at a time. With increasing numbers of objects, occlusion becomes a major limiting factor. The alternative of using transparency is limited by the fact that even the best 3D volume rendering techniques suffer from errors of 25% or more [33].

Apart from "true 3D" displays - volumetric display devices that show the graphics for a virtual object at the *actual depth* of the object, all other prevalent 3D stereo technologies, including stereo monitors and head-mounted displays, show the image on a different plane relative to where the eyes converge to in depth for objects away from the screen plane. Given that the eyes naturally focus onto the monitor image, this causes vergence-accomodation conflicts, e. g., [48], which affect the perception of 3D scenes. Moreover, if the disparity is too large, it results in double images (diplopia), which can also be effectively used by the perceptual system to infer depth [27].

Other limitations of spatially immersive data visualisation arise with interaction. These are discussed more fully in Chapter 4, but we point out that that navigation in 3D spaces is more challenging than 2D navigation, especially for abstract spaces, and 3D interaction is more difficult than 2D interaction as more degrees of freedom have to be controlled.

Following the review of depth perception and 3D presentation technologies, we now look at previous work that compare 2D and 3D representations.

2.3. Prior Research Comparing 2D with 3D Representations

In this section we review empirical studies comparing 2D with 3D representations and critically evaluate whether these support the orthodoxy that 2D is best for abstract data representations. As discussed earlier, as immersive technologies have improved what is implied when speaking of "3D" has changed so it is important to understand the depth cues as well as the kinds of interaction provided in the studies.

Cone trees and data mountains Cone trees [78] and the data mountain [77] were two very influential 3D visualisations from the 1990s which were claimed to have significant advantages over traditional 2D visualisations. Both visualisations were intended for use on a 3D graphics workstation with mouse interaction. There was no head tracking or binocular presentation, and by today's standards resolution was low. Later empirical studies critically evaluated the claim that cone trees and the data mountain offered benefits over 2D visualisations. As these significantly contributed to the subsequent scepticism of information visualisation researchers of the use of 3D in abstract data visualisation, we discuss these studies in some detail.

Robertson *et. al.* [78] argued that cone trees were more effective than traditional 2D trees because: (i) linear perspective provides a focus+context view of the tree; (ii) 3D cues of perspective, lighting and shadows help shape understanding; (iii) interactive animation reduces cognitive load by exploiting the visual system's object tracking; (iv) users enjoyed the visualisations because they were more "alive"; and (v) 3D allows more effective use of the display space by using depth which means that larger trees can be displayed.[4] Cockburn and McKenzie [16] conducted a user study comparing cone trees with a traditional indented list-like representation for navigating through a hierarchy to find particular nodes. They found that task performance was slower with cone trees and that users rated the cone interface as worse for seeing and for interacting with the hierarchy. They did not evaluate understanding of structure, but participant comments "indicated that cone trees may perform relatively better in [such] tasks". Caveats were that participants were much more familiar with the traditional indented list like representation, the cone tree was rendered with low fidelity because of implementation efficiency, and cone tree rotation was slower than scrolling in 2D.

The data mountain allowed the user to arrange documents on a virtual 3D desktop in front of them. The bottom of the billboard-like representations was always in contact with the desktop so it was really a 2.5D visualisation.[5] The

[4] Though not necessarily perceived because of linear perspective and occlusion.

[5] Unfortunately the term 2.5D visualisation is commonly used in several different ways. Here we are using it in the sense of Ware [101] in which the visualisation is essentially 2D but selected depth cues are used to provide some suggestion of 3D. In GeoVis 2.5D refers to showing a 2D continuous surface in 3D, while in network visualisation 2.5D refers to stacked 2D visualisations.

viewpoint of the user was fixed and occlusion, shadows and linear perspective were used to create the illusion of depth. Audio cues were also used. Motivations for using 3D were to: (i) allow more objects on the desktop (with linear perspective providing a focus+context view), (ii) a natural metaphor for grouping, and (iii) to leverage from 3D spatial memory. Robertson *et al.* [77] compared bookmark retrieval times and error rates with the Data Mountain and Internet Explorer (IE4). They found the data mountain led to increased efficiency and lower error rates. However since the two representations were quite different this did not directly address the question of whether 3D offered benefits over 2D. This was investigated by Cockburn and McKenzie [17] in a user study comparing a low fidelity implementation of the Data Mountain interface with the equivalent 2D interface in which thumbnails of web pages were organised on the screen much like in a standard window manager. There was no foreshortening and the user could bring thumbnails to the front or back. They found that participants were faster with the 2D interface than with 3D (though this was not statistically significant) but that the participants believed the 3D interface was more effective. They suspected that foreshortening (and low resolution) meant that in the 3D condition it was difficult to visually match thumbnails that were in the top half of the screen. In a subsequent study Cockburn [15] compared recall of non-overlapping 'cards' arranged on a desktop in horizontal rows. This compared a 2D presentation with a 3D presentation using foreshortening, shadows and proximity luminance covariance, i. e., cards at the front were lighter than things at the back. He found no difference between the two conditions. Another study compared the effectiveness of spatial memory in 2D, 2.5D (2D + linear perspective), and full 3D in both virtual and physical environments [18]. Flaws in the design and implementation mean it is difficult to draw conclusions from the physical implementation. While 2.5D outperformed 2D, which in turn outperformed 3D, the differences were not statistically significant.

So what can we take home from these evaluations of cone trees and the data mountain? It is fair to conclude that they show that 3D does not offer "magic" benefits over 2D for data visualisation because of its "naturalness". In hindsight, cone trees, because of occlusion and the inherent slowness of tree rotation, are a poor representation for hierarchical data. In the case of document management there is no difference between 2 and 2.5D. Indeed in some sense most window managers are 2.5D since they provide occlusion, the most powerful depth cue (hence the question: which depth cues are useful?). Thus, these studies do not rule out the use 2.5 or 3D in abstract data visualisation but rather suggest that depth cues need to be used carefully. We now look at the findings from other evaluations of 3D. These are organised by the kind of data being visualised.

Aviation Haskell and Wickens [45] compared 2D orthogonal views with 3D perspective for aviation displays showing current position and predicted flight path. The 3D display was better for lateral and altitude flight path tracking but worse for accurate measurement of airspeed. The display was not binocular or interactive. Van Orden and Broyles [95] compared a variety of 2D and 3D displays for judging aircraft altitude or speed, route planning (vectoring) and collision detection. Air traffic controllers were more accurate with 2D views except collision avoidance in which task the laser-based 3D volumetric display led to significantly more accurate performance than the other 2D or 3D displays.

3D shapes and landscapes St John *et al.* [84] compared a 3D orthographic perspective view with side-by-side 2D orthogonal views of complex block shapes. Shadows, motion and binocular cues were not used. 3D views were better for understanding the overall shape while 2D orthogonal views were better for precisely judging relative position.

Tory *et al.* [92] compared 2D, 3D, and combined visualisations for some basic tasks like position estimation and orientation. They suggest the combination of 2D and 3D views to improve precision. In further studies, Tory *et al.* [91] compared 2D orthogonal, 3D rotated orthographic projection, and combinations of 2D and 3D for determining relative position of a ball and complex block shape and for orienting a plane to cut a torus in half (Figure 2). They also compared two ways to orient and couple 2D planes with 3D. They concluded that 3D was effective for approximate navigation and relative positioning but combination 2D/3D displays were better for precise orientation and positioning.

In another study St John *et al.* [85] compared: (i) a 3D perspective view of a landscape; (ii) a topographic map with contours and (iii) a side-by-side combination of these two views. One task involved computing the best routing for antennas so that they were in line of sight. Participants were fastest with the side-by-side view, then the 2D view and slowest with the 3D perspective view. In a second study participants were asked to choose the best route from three given routes with either the 3D or the plan view. In this case the 3D view led to faster performance. These suggest that the 3D view is best for overall orientation and understanding, the 2D view is better for precise manipulation, and that it is beneficial to combine them using 3D for orientation and 2D for manipulation ("Orient and Operate").

Network visualisation Ware and Franck [100] report the results of a user study in which graph visualisation with 2D and different 3D displays were compared. According to their results, the 3D displays allowed participants to decide if there is a path between highlighted nodes with the same accuracy for graphs up to three times larger than in the 2D case. They found that both motion and binocular depth cues were beneficial. A binocular display was found to be 1.6 times more accurate than a 2D display when detecting paths of length two through the complex structure, and binocular presentation combined with head-coupled motion produced the best results.

The Ware and Frank study was replicated in [105] while Greffard *et al.* found benefits for binocular 3D over 2D for community detection in social networks [40]. Van Schooten [96] evaluated the impact of motion cues and binocular presentation on path following in 3D maze-like solid shaded structures (based on vascular structures). They found that the motion cue was more important than binocular

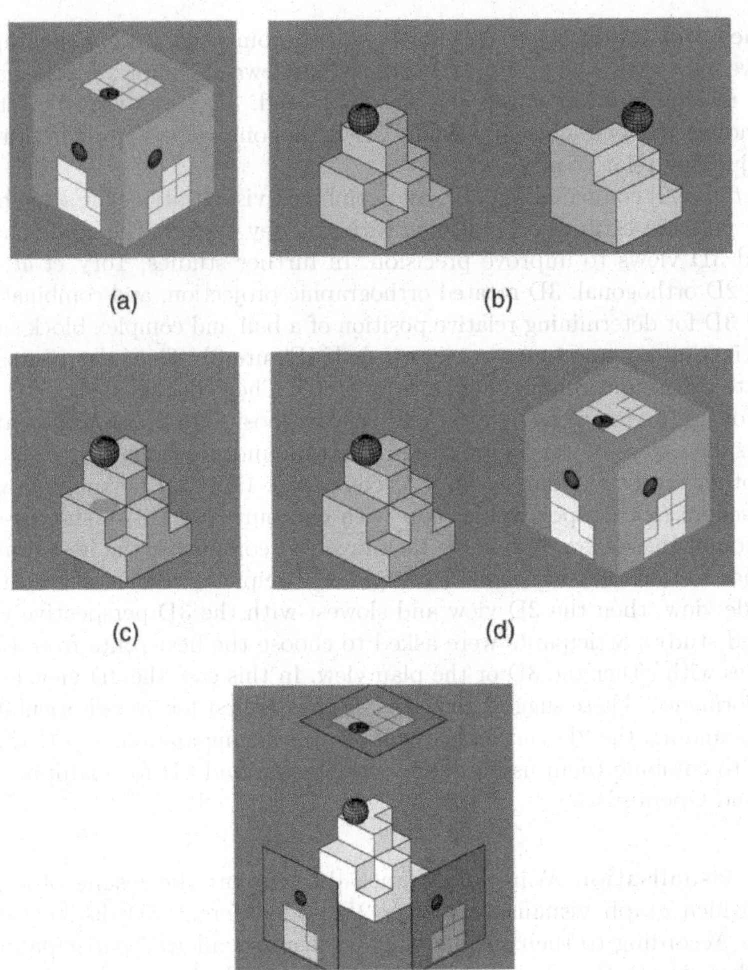

Fig. 2: Example stimuli from Tory *et al.* [91]. Position estimation of the ball relative to the block shape using the following visualisation techniques: (a) 2D, (b) 3D rotated, (c) 3D shadow, (e) Integrated 2D and 3D display. (Figure © 2006 IEEE. Reprinted, with permission, from [91])

presentation and that binocular presentation had little added benefit if motion cue was provided. Belcher *et al.* [5] found similar benefits to 3D and motion cues but not binocular views when viewing graphs using augmented reality.

Irani and Ware [50] found that 3D glyphs rendered using shading, surface texture and lighting as 3D cues where more easily recognised and remembered than flat 2D silhouettes of the glyphs. They studied this in the context of UML-like network diagrams. The diagrams themselves were laid out in a flat plane, only the glyphs utilised depth.

Kwon *et al.* recently proposed an immersive graph visualisation system [60,61]. Previous studies into 3D graph layout used exocentric layouts in which the user was outside the layout. They introduced an egocentric layout in which the graph is laid out in a sphere around the user's head and viewed using a binocular HMD VR environment. Their user study [60] found that their spherical layout outperformed a traditional 2D layout.

Alper *et al.* designed depth highlighting of 2D graph visualisation on binocular displays [1] (Figure 3). The technique makes use of depth cues to enable focus+context visualisation by overlaying a detailed image of a region of interest on the overall graph, which is visualized at a further depth with correspondingly less details. Their empirical study results show that binocular highlighting had about the same performance as the static visual highlighting and that performance was improved when binocular and static visual highlights were combined.

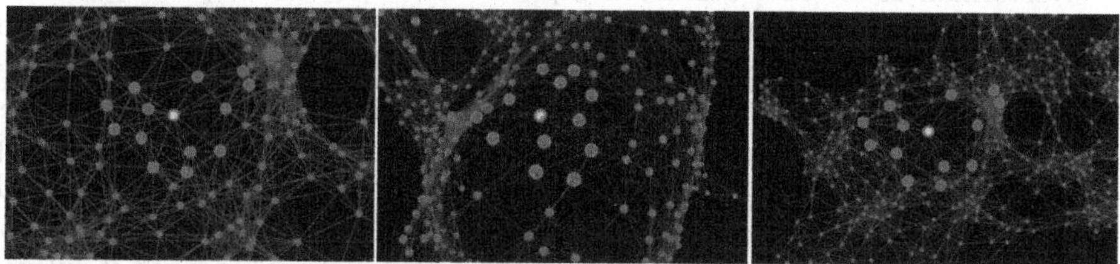

Fig. 3: Focus+context views from [1] for different visualisations illustrating how an increasingly large portion of graph nodes is kept in view from left to right, 2D, 3D, and 2.5D views. (Figure © 2011 IEEE. Reprinted, with permission, from [1])

Multivariate data visualisation An early paper by Lee *et al.* [63] ran two small user studies comparing 2D graphics with 3D graphics shown using a polarising binocular view on a standard monitor. They found that performance was more accurate with a 3D scatter plot of a three-dimensional data set than with three 2D scatter plots of the data, but that for another data set accuracy was the same with a 3D histogram as a multidimensional table. In a related study Wickens *et al.* [108] evaluated the use of 3D and a split-view orthogonal 2D representation of three-dimensional economic data. They found that participants using 3D were faster than those using 2D when answering integrative questions involving all three dimensions, while performance was similar for more focused questions involving fewer dimensions. In the 3D condition they found a positive effect for binocular depth cues while allowing user-controlled rotation or providing a mesh had no effect.

Wegman and Symanzik [106] reviewed the use of immersive technologies for visual exploration of multidimensional data (visual data mining). There are several empirical studies and the results are mixed. An early study by Nelson *et al.* [74] compared exploration of multidimensional data sets using brushing and a grand tour in 2D on a computer monitor and in 3D using binocular VR with head tracking. They found that 3D provided a large advantage in cluster identification and some advantage in identifying the shape of the cluster and similar performance when identifying the dimensionality of the data. More recently, Gracia *et al.* [39] evaluated the effectiveness of dimensionality reduction of a multidimensional dataset to a 3D scatterplot and to a 2D scatterplot. Both were shown in monocular 3D on a standard monitor. The extra dimension in the 3D condition meant that distances in the visualisation more closely matched the actual distances between points in the higher dimensional space. They found that with the 3D scatter plot users could more accurately compare distances between points (with respect to actual distance in multidimensional space) and more accurately detect outliers but had similar accuracy when classifying points. They were slower with 3D on the last two tasks. However, in both studies the number of participants was small and statistical significance was not reported. Westerman *et al.* [107] evaluated exploration of document spaces presented in two and three dimensions. They found that interaction and navigation was slower in 3D space. They used monocular 3D on a standard computer monitor.

Sedlmair *et al.* [82] evaluated two users ranking of cluster separation using a number of dimension reduction techniques for 2D scatterplots, scatterplot matrices (SPLOMs) and 3D scatterplots shown in monocular 3D on a standard monitor. They found that cluster separation was generally ranked to be the same or less with 3D scatterplots than with 2D scatterplots. This result is surprising given that that an extra dimension should allow the underlying structure to be revealed more clearly.

Tory *et al.* [93, 94] evaluated the usefulness of both 2D and 3D landscapes for enhancing understanding of clustering in 2D scatterplots. The first task was to identify the spatial region with the most values in a particular interval. Both 2D and 3D spatial encoding redundantly encoded the data value intervals. They found that the spatial landscape was detrimental and that the 3D landscape was worse than the equivalent 2D landscape. This may be the result of using the landscape color and/or height to encode attribute value range rather than density of data points which would have been more salient. They also evaluated the effect of 2D and 3D landscapes on recall. Recall without landscapes was more accurate, and 3D was generally better than 2D landscapes.

Spatial and spatio-temporal data visualisation Yalong *et al.* [109] compared task performance for three standard geographic tasks using different 2D and 3D representations for the Earth. It is one of the few studies to compare 2D and 3D representations in VR and used a head-tracked binocular HMD. They compared a 3D exocentric globe placed in front of the viewer, an egocentric 3D globe placed around the viewer, a flat map (rendered to a plane in VR) and a curved map, created by projecting the map onto a section of a sphere curved around the user. They found that (a) the exocentric globe was more accurate than the egocentric globe and the flat map for distances comparison, (b) for comparison of areas, more time is required with exocentric and egocentric globes than with flat and curved maps, and (c) that for direction estimation, the exocentric globe is more accurate and faster than the other visual presentations. There was a weak preference for the exocentric globe. Generally, the curved map had benefits over the flat map. In almost all cases the egocentric globe was found to be the least effective visualisation.

Kjellin *et al.* [59] compared 3D space-time cubes with 2D map + animation and a pure 2D representation in which tracks are drawn on a map and time is shown by annotating the tracks with orthogonal cross-lines spaced at regular time intervals. A Head-tracked binocular display was used for the 3D visualisation. It does not appear that the participants could interactively control their point of view or speed of the animation. They found that performance with the pure 2D representation was better than with the other two representations for predicting the point where 3 vehicles would meet in the future. In a final experiment they compared the pure 2D representation with the space-time cube and asked participants to determine the relative order 4 vehicles had passed through a particular point. For this task performance was better with the space-time cube. Kjellin *et al.* explained this in terms of Todd *et al.*'s theory [88,89] that tasks that can be solved by estimating properties of a viewed scene that are invariant under affine transformations are perceptually easier than those that are invariant only under Euclidean transformations. In another study Kjellin *et al.* [58] compared performance with monocular and head-tracked binocular presentation of a 3D space-time cube showing discrete spatiotemporal data. The task was to find the data set which had a cone like shape and the largest geographic spread. They found no difference between the conditions and believe this was because the task was essentially affine preserving and that there was little clutter, so little need for additional depth cues.

Summary It is clear from the studies that 3D representations are not generally better than 2D representations, but nor are 2D representations always better than 3D: which is better depends upon the kind of task. Previous studies suggest that 3D representations may show overall structure in multidimensional spaces more clearly: 3D shapes and terrain [84, 85], multidimensional data [39, 63, 74, 108], and networks [40, 100, 105]. On the other hand some of these studies also found that 2D representations were preferable for precise manipulation or accurate data value measurement or comparison and advocated the use of linked 2D and 3D representations [85, 91].

It also seems that the choice of technology and depth cues makes a significant difference to the effectiveness of 3D visualisations. Ragan *et al.* [75] found that combining binocular presentation and head-tracking contributed to improved spatial judgment accuracy when participants need to distinguish between structural gaps and intersections between components of 3D models in a simulated underground systems. Two papers review user studies comparing binocular 3D with non-binocular 3D in wide variety of applications including scientific, medical and military [36, 69]. The most recent, McIntire *et al.* [69], summarised 180 experiments and found performance benefits for binocular 3D in 60% of the studies but little or no benefit in the others. They conclude that binocular 3D is beneficial for depth-related tasks including spatial understanding of complex scenes and spatial manipulation, especially when the objects were close and the tasks were difficult. This may help to explain the previously discussed mixed results on the effectiveness of 3D scatter plots when compared to 2D scatter plots. Studies providing binocular depth cues found benefits [63,74,108], while those using only monocular clues were mixed with one finding benefits [39] but others finding 2D was more effective [82,107,107]. It would be interesting to replicate these experiments using modern head-tracked binocular displays.

Finally, details of representation are important. For instance, Kjellin *et al.* [59] found that hanging the trajectory representation from a line to a stepped staircase of rectangles in the 3D space-time cube improved performance with the space-time cube considerably (though it was still worse than with the pure 2D representation).

2.4. Potential Benefits of Immersive Visualisation

In the preceding section we have reviewed user studies comparing 2D and 3D representations, In this section we present five reasons why immersive 3D display environments may offer advantages over traditional 2D visualisations on a desk display. Further information visualisation applications and concepts that might benefit from 3D representations or binocular displays are discussed by Brath [9] and McIntire and Liggett [68].

Using depth to show an additional abstract dimension In the last section we saw that two studies [39, 74] found benefits in using 3D scatter plots to understand structure in multi-dimensional data while three studies did not [82, 107]. Notably the three studies which did not find benefits did not use head-tracked binocular 3D while it was used in one of the studies finding benefits. If the data has more dimensions then projecting onto an additional dimension means that there will be less *stress* (error) in the multidimensional projection: the distance between data points in the projected 3D space will be closer to the distance between them in the original multi-dimensional space than when they are projected to a 2D space. Thus it seems plausible that clusters and other structure are likely to be more clearly shown in the 3D scatter plot. However for this benefit to be realised there need to be sufficient depth cues for the viewer to see the structure without the need for interaction beyond head movement.

Even if the primary visualisation is a 2D scatter plot, 3D may be used to show the relationship between different plots, for instance Elmqvist *et al.* [30] use an animated 3D cube to transition between different plots.

We have seen that there is empirical evidence that laying out node-link diagrams in 3D can benefit path following [100,105]. This may be because depth cues help to clarify edge crossings and resolve node-edge overlap. 3D network diagrams may also more clearly show structure [40] since (as discussed above) the extra dimension means that layouts can have less stress in the sense that the distance between nodes more closely reflects the graph theoretic distance between them and the edges have more uniform length.

Judicious use of depth cues may be beneficial even with essentially 2D representations of networks. For instance Alper *et al.* [1] found that using binocular "pop out" was beneficial for highlighting elements. In 2D node-link diagrams it is common to use occlusion to indicate that one edge crosses over another, so as to enforce the perception of the edges as separate objects. Other depth cues might also be beneficial. We also note that Irani and Ware [50] found benefits in using depth cues with glyphs in UML diagrams.

Several researchers have investigated different kinds of 2.5D layouts of network diagrams in which nodes in the network are laid out on 2D planes stacked on top of each other. For instance Brandes *et al.* [8] use stacked 2D layouts of metabolic pathways to compare pathways in different organisms while Eades and Feng used stacked layouts to show the hierarchical structure [29]. Another use of stacked 2D network representations is to show network changes over time. Each plane is a snapshot of the network at a particular point in time. Dwyer and Eades [28] used these to visualise trading data.

The use of the third dimension to show time is a successful idiom that has been employed with many kinds of data [4]. We have seen it used for showing trajectories and for dynamic network diagrams. It has also been used to show time series data from oscilloscopes organised in a layered eye diagram [64]. This uses an orthogonal projection to show time series wrapped in time with different slices clustered together behind one another.

Views on non-flat surfaces Another possible advantage of 3D is that 2D data with cyclic dimensions or without natural boundaries can be laid out on the surface of a sphere [10] or a cylinder so as to remove the visual illusion of a break in the dimension when the data is laid out in 2D. While it is not clear that this outweighs the problem of occlusion when viewed from outside the sphere or cylinder, Yalong *et al.* [109] found that an exocentric globe or curved map outperformed a standard flat map for some common geographic tasks. Non-flat viewing canvases also allow an egocentric view of the data from inside. Results comparing egocentric and exocentric views of abstract data are mixed. The study reported in Kwon *et al.* [60, 61] suggests that such an egocentric view is useful for network visualisation but Yalong *et al.* [109] found that for geographic tasks an exocentric globe outperformed an egocentric globe.

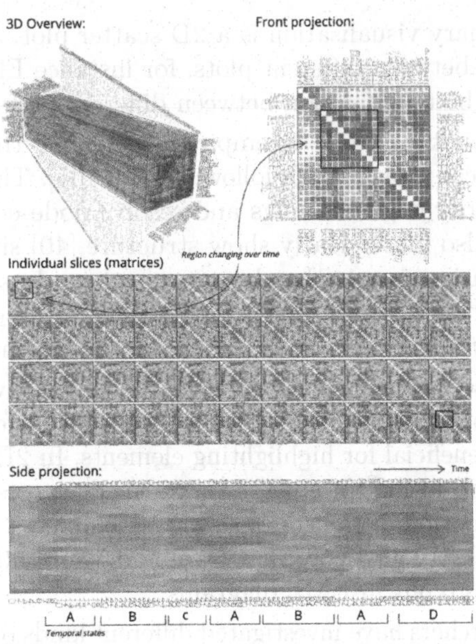

Fig. 4: Matrix cubes for visualising dynamic networks are an example of the use of the third dimension to show time [3]. (Figure courtesy Benjamin Bach.)

Visualising abstract data with a spatial embedding 3D has also been used quite successfully for visualising abstract data with a geographic embedding. Here it is natural to use two dimensions to show a map and use the third dimension to show a data attribute or to overlay data attributes in either 2D or 3D visualisations on a 3D landscape. Dübel *et al.* [26] classifies such visualisations based on whether the reference space (i. e., the map or surface) is shown in 2D or 3D and/or whether the abstract attribute is shown in 2D or 3D. Prism maps are widely used as an alternative to choropleth maps and allow more accurate comparison of data values so long as occlusion is not a problem. Vertical pins can be used to show magnitude of a data attribute at a particular location on a map rather than using proportional symbols such as a circle [9]. Another widely used example is the space-time cube. Introduced by Hägerstrand [42] in 1970 this shows trajectories across a map using time as a third (vertical) dimension. As we saw in the section it is well-suited to some tasks but for others a pure 2D representation may be more effective.

More generally 3D is potentially useful for showing abstract data with a 3D spatial embedding [54]. Bowman *et al.* defined the integration of spatial and non-spatial data as information-rich virtual environment [7]. The goal is to enhance spatial data with abstract information, which is the type of data that is not directly *perceptible* in the physical world but *added* to the 3D world (e. g., text labels to show velocity at every point in a complex vector field, trees, networks, and other multiple-dimensional information). The information-rich virtual environment defines the forms of the display, e. g., temperature in a room can be recorded spatially but cannot be directly perceived visually thus will need to be encoded (either with colour or texts). The follow-up lab-based experiment by Chen et al. [13] found that 2D-billboard style text display is better than 3D texts attached directly on spatial objects.

This might be by overlaying 2D or 3D abstract data representations on to 3D visualisations of say buildings or organisms, or by having separate 2D and 3D views linked in some way. For example, multi-dimensional scaling (MDS) techniques have been developed to to embed a 3D diffusion magnetic resonance imaging (DMRI) into a low-dimensional 2D representation [14]. Distance measurements (e. g., similarity) are also adopted to further cluster the 2D embedding [53]. Recently, Zhang *et al.* uses a topological approach to represent DTI using a contour tree to show brain water diffusion rate measured by fractional anisotropy in a brain [111].

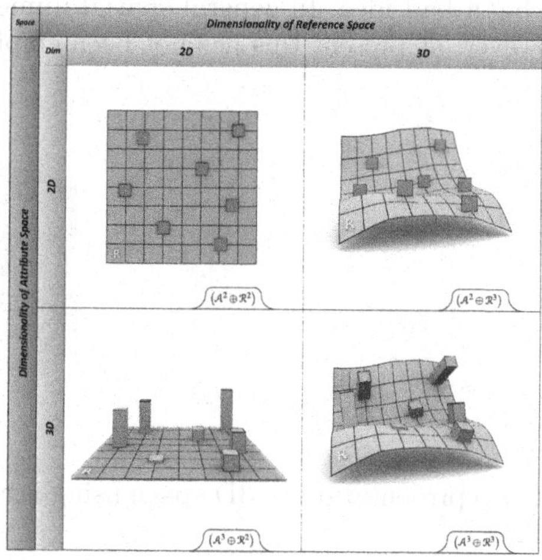

Fig. 5: Dübel *et al.* [26] categorise geo-visualisation techniques based on the dimensionality of the attribute space and reference space presentation. (Figure courtesy Steve Dübel).

Arranging multiple views in 3D space Another possible benefit of immersive 3D is that it allows the analyst to arrange their views in 3D space. Mixed mode displays, for instance, allow the use of virtual Powerwalls which provide unlimited display space and use linear perspective to provide an easily understood focus+context view [9].[6] Such a virtual Powerwall potentially provides the same benefits as actual physical Powerwalls for visual analytics [2].

[6] In a sense they are a modern equivalent of the perspective wall.

At present there is no agreed windowing metaphor in mixed mode applications and this is a research topic that warrants attention. Some researchers have suggested the use of flat 2D views whose position may be fixed with respect to the world or with respect to some part of the user's body, e.g., [34, 35, 37], while others have suggested more embodied three-dimensional data views, e.g., [11, 21], or blended views in which physical objects provide the view frame, e.g., [32].

Closely related to 2.5D layouts of networks are Collins and Carpendale's technique [20] of linking 2D representation laid out as views in 3D space by using arcs between elements in the different views to show connectivity with selected elements.

Engagement The final benefit of depth cues is that they may help to engage the reader. In many previous studies users indicated they preferred 3D representations even if they did not improve task performance. Of course this has to be done judiciously, adding gratuitous 3D depth cues to pie charts or bar charts is, and always will be, a bad idea. In general spatial immersiveness may aid user engagement. However, at present this has not been empirically investigated.

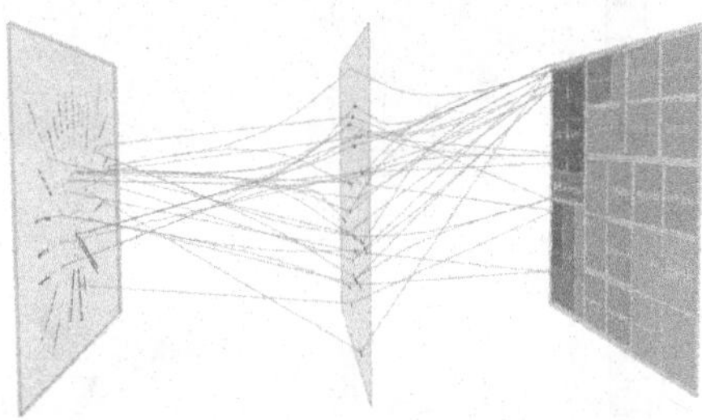

Fig. 6: Linking 2D representation in 3D space using arcs [20]. (Figure courtesy Christopher Collins.)

2.5. Research Questions and Issues

This chapter suggests a large number of different research directions and questions. One of the most obvious is to develop general, evidence based design rules and a portfolio of effective visual and interaction idioms for data visualisation in mixed reality environments. Some interesting questions are

- What should the data analyst's workspace look like in mixed reality applications? We have seen a variety of different suggestions, ranging from 2D windows similar to those found on a desktop to embodied scatter plots or parallel coordinates [11, 21, 34, 37]. At present there is no agreed approach and little empirical data. Closely related is the question of how to link different viewing canvases. Is brushing enough or should explicit links be drawn [20]? How do we guide/direct the analyst's attention in their immersive workspace, in particular how to communicate that there are important things behind them in the virtual space? (The same issues arise in video games and 360° immersive movies.)

- Some studies have advocated the use of tightly linked 2D and 3D representations [85, 91], with the 3D view providing overall orientation and understanding while the 2D view is better for precise manipulation and data comparison. Is this a general idiom that we should support in spatially immersive analytics applications?
- Egocentric data views potentially offer a more engaging user experience. However, studies comparing exocentric and egocentric views are mixed [60, 109]. When if ever, are egocentric views of data preferable to exocentric? Should the user be able to move between egocentric and exocentric views of the data analogously to the way the Magic Book allows the viewer to view actors in the story from outside or to transport themselves into the scene [6]? Is rapid motion in immersive egocentric data views unpleasant to the user and lead to motion sickness? If so, how best to change the position of the user in such views? One solution, used in video games, is teleportation of the user – is this also appropriate for immersive analytics?
- What are the differences between VR and AR environments and how do these affect the choice of immersive visualisation idiom?
- Parallel perspective–oblique, isometric, etc–is widely used in technical drawing as such projections have a uniform scale in each dimension and parallel lines remain parallel. An interesting question is when, if ever, is parallel perspective more appropriate than linear perspective for showing abstract data? It may for example have benefits when multiple users are looking at the same representation from slightly different viewpoints [44, 72].
- What is the influence of different aspects of spatial immersion—depth cues, realism of the rendering, integration of the environment in an AR setting (e. g., things are placed on the real table), consistency of multi-sensory output, egocentric vs. exocentric views, etc.—on all aspects of user experience and performance. In particular, how does spatial immersiveness affect longer-term engagement with the data/content (beyond the first "cool" impression)?
- To answer these questions we will need to devise and verify measures and ways of evaluating the effectiveness and usefulness of spatially immersive environments for data visualisation

One strong recommendation echoing that of McIntire [69], is that in all papers describing user studies involving some kind of 3D the technology and supported depth cues as well as available interactions and interaction devices are carefully described: In many existing papers this is unclear, yet it is now apparent that these significantly impact user performance and must be taken into account.

2.6. Conclusion

Mixed-reality display technologies utilise a variety of techniques such as depth cues (like occlusion, linear perspective or head-tracked binocular presentation) to enhance spatial immersion. In this chapter we have explored the potential use of these techniques to visualise abstract data in immersive analytics applications. Almost certainly more and more people will be using immersive environments as the technology matures and on occasions they will want to visualise data in these environments, not just on a desktop. We need to know the best way of supporting this.

While 3D visualisations are common in scientific visualisation, they are much less common in information visualisation. Indeed the accepted wisdom is that 3D effects are rarely useful for showing abstract data. In Section 2.3. we investigated the empirical evidence for this viewpoint in order to understand whether immersive analytics applications should continue to use traditional 2D information visualisations or whether there are situations when use of 3D depth cues may offer benefits. We found that previous user studies suggest that 3D representations more clearly show overall structure in higher dimensional datasets such as 3D terrain, networks or multidimensional data and are useful for providing orientation while 2D representations are preferable for precise manipulation or accurate data value measurement or comparison. Thus, it may be useful to provide linked 2D and 3D representations in immersive analytics applications.

In Section 2.4. we further explored the potential applications of depth cues for abstract data visualisation. These include: using depth to show an additional abstract dimension, such as in 2.5D network layouts, views on non-flat surfaces and egocentric views in which the data is placed around the viewer, visualising abstract data with a spatial embedding as well as arranging multiple views in 3D space.

Based on the discussions above, we feel that the current scepticism by information visualisation researchers for 3D visualisation of abstract data is too negative and that there are situations in which judicious use of depth cues to provide 2.5 or 3D views is warranted. We also believe that allowing the user to arrange views in the 3D space around them in mixed-reality settings offers benefits over traditional desktop windows management. We believe that further exploration of these topics should be a major focus of immersive analytics research.

Acknowledgements

We are thankful for the helpful suggestions of Benjamin Bach, Tim Dwyer and Mark Billinghurst. Marriott acknowledges the support of the Australian Research Council Discovery Scheme for this research through project DP180100755.

References

1. Alper, B., Hollerer, T., Kuchera-Morin, J., Forbes, A.: Stereoscopic highlighting: 2D graph visualization on stereo displays. IEEE Transactions on Visualization and Computer Graphics 17(12), 2325–2333 (2011)
2. Andrews, C., Endert, A., North, C.: Space to think: large high-resolution displays for sensemaking. In: Proceedings of the SIGCHI Conference on Human Factors in Computing Systems. pp. 55–64. ACM (2010)
3. Bach, B., Pietriga, E., Fekete, J.D.: Visualizing dynamic networks with matrix cubes. In: the SIGCHI Conference on Human Factors in Computing Systems. pp. 877–886 (2014)
4. Bach, B., Dragicevic, P., Archambault, D., Hurter, C., Carpendale, S.: A review of temporal data visualizations based on space-time cube operations. In: Eurographics Conference on Visualization (EuroVis) (2014)
5. Belcher, D., Billinghurst, M., Hayes, S., Stiles, R.: Using augmented reality for visualizing complex graphs in three dimensions. In: Proceedings of the 2nd IEEE/ACM International Symposium on Mixed and Augmented Reality. p. 84. IEEE Computer Society (2003)
6. Billinghurst, M., Kato, H., Poupyrev, I.: The magicbook: a transitional ar interface. Computers & Graphics 25(5), 745–753 (2001)
7. Bowman, D.A., North, C., Chen, J., Polys, N.F., Pyla, P.S., Yilmaz, U.: Information-rich virtual environments: theory, tools, and research agenda. In: Proceedings of the ACM Symposium on Virtual Reality Software and Technology. pp. 81–90. ACM (2003)
8. Brandes, U., Dwyer, T., Schreiber, F.: Visual understanding of metabolic pathways across organisms using layout in two and a half dimensions. Journal of Integrative Bioinformatics 1(1) (2004)
9. Brath, R.: 3D infovis is here to stay: deal with it. In: 2014 IEEE VIS International Workshop on 3DVis. pp. 25–31 (2014)
10. Brath, R., MacMurchy, P.: Sphere-based information visualization: challenges and benefits. In: IV. pp. 1–6 (2012)
11. Butscher, S., Hubenschmid, S., Müller, J., Fuchs, J., Reiterer, H.: Clusters, trends, and outliers: How immersive technologies can facilitate the collaborative analysis of multidimensional data. In: Proceedings SIGCHI Conference on Human Factors in Computing Systems. pp. 90:1–90:12 (2018)
12. Carlbom, I., Paciorek, J.: Planar geometric projections and viewing transformations. ACM Computing Surveys (CSUR) 10(4), 465–502 (1978)
13. Chen, J., Pyla, P.S., Bowman, D.A.: Testbed evaluation of navigation and text display techniques in an information-rich virtual environment. In: IEEE Proceedings of Virtual Reality. pp. 181–289. IEEE (2004)
14. Chen, W., Ding, Z., Zhang, S., MacKay-Brandt, A., Correia, S., Qu, H., Crow, J.A., Tate, D.F., Yan, Z., Peng, Q.: A novel interface for interactive exploration of DTI fibers. IEEE Transactions on Visualization and Computer Graphics 15(6), 1433–1440 (2009)
15. Cockburn, A.: Revisiting 2D vs 3D implications on spatial memory. In: Proceedings of the fifth conference on Australasian user interface-Volume 28. pp. 25–31. Australian Computer Society, Inc. (2004)
16. Cockburn, A., McKenzie, B.: An evaluation of cone trees. In: People and Computers XIV Usability or Else!, pp. 425–436. Springer (2000)

17. Cockburn, A., McKenzie, B.: 3D or not 3D?: evaluating the effect of the third dimension in a document management system. In: Proceedings of the SIGCHI conference on Human Factors in Computing Systems. pp. 434–441. ACM (2001)
18. Cockburn, A., McKenzie, B.: Evaluating the effectiveness of spatial memory in 2D and 3D physical and virtual environments. In: Proceedings of the SIGCHI conference on Human Factors in Computing Systems. pp. 203–210. ACM (2002)
19. Cockburn, A., McKenzie, B.: Evaluating spatial memory in two and three dimensions. International Journal of Human-Computer Studies 61(3), 359–373 (2004)
20. Collins, C., Carpendale, S.: VisLink: revealing relationships amongst visualizations. IEEE Transactions on Visualization and Computer Graphics 13(6), 1192–1199 (2007)
21. Cordeil, M., Cunningham, A., Dwyer, T., Thomas, B.H., Marriott, K.: ImAxes: Immersive axes as embodied affordances for interactive multivariate data visualisation. In: Proceedings of the 30th Annual ACM Symposium on User Interface Software and Technology. pp. 71–83. ACM (2017)
22. Cruz-Neira, C., Sandin, D.J., DeFanti, T.A., Kenyon, R.V., Hart, J.C.: The CAVE: audio visual experience automatic virtual environment. Commun. ACM 35(6), 64–72 (1992)
23. Cutting, J.E.: Rigidity in cinema seen from the front row, side aisle. Journal of Experimental Psychology: Human Perception and Performance 13(3), 323–334 (1987)
24. Cutting, J.E., Vishton, P.M.: Perceiving layout and knowing distances: The integration, relative potency, and contextual use of different information about depth. In: Perception of space and motion, pp. 69–117. Elsevier (1995)
25. Dodgson, N.A.: Autostereoscopic 3D Displays. Computer 38(8), 31–36 (2005)
26. Dübel, S., Röhlig, M., Schumann, H., Trapp, M.: 2D and 3D presentation of spatial data: a systematic review. In: IEEE VIS International Workshop on 3DVis. pp. 11–18. IEEE (2014)
27. Duwaer, A., Van Den Brink, G.: What is the diplopia threshold? Attention, Perception, & Psychophysics 29(4), 295–309 (1981)
28. Dwyer, T., Eades, P.: Visualising a fund manager flow graph with columns and worms. In: Proceedings Sixth International Conference on Information Visualisation. pp. 147–152. IEEE (2002)
29. Eades, P., Feng, Q.W.: Multilevel visualization of clustered graphs. In: International Symposium on Graph Drawing. pp. 101–112. Springer (1996)
30. Elmqvist, N., Dragicevic, P., Fekete, J.D.: Rolling the dice: multidimensional visual exploration using scatterplot matrix navigation. IEEE Transactions on Visualization and Computer Graphics 14(6), 1539–1148 (2008)
31. Elmqvist, N., Tsigas, P.: A taxonomy of 3D occlusion management for visualization. IEEE Transactions on Visualization and Computer Graphics 14(5), 1095–1109 (2008)
32. ElSayed, N.A., Smith, R.T., Marriott, K., Thomas, B.H.: Context-aware design pattern for situated analytics: Blended model view controller. Journal of Visual Languages & Computing 44 (2018)
33. Englund, R., Ropinski, T.: Evaluating the perception of semi-transparent structures in direct volume rendering techniques. In: SIGGRAPH ASIA 2016 Symposium on Visualization. pp. 9:1–9:8. ACM (2016)
34. Ens, B., Hincapié-Ramos, J.D., Irani, P.: Ethereal planes: a design framework for 2D information space in 3D mixed reality environments. In: Proceedings of the 2nd ACM Symposium on Spatial User Interaction. pp. 2–12. ACM (2014)

35. Ens, B.M., Finnegan, R., Irani, P.P.: The personal cockpit: a spatial interface for effective task switching on head-worn displays. In: Proceedings of the SIGCHI Conference on Human Factors in Computing Systems. pp. 3171–3180. ACM (2014)
36. Favalora, G.E.: Volumetric 3D displays and application infrastructure. Computer 38(8), 37–44 (2005)
37. Feiner, S., MacIntyre, B., Haupt, M., Solomon, E.: Windows on the world: 2D windows for 3D augmented reality. In: Proceedings of the 6th Annual ACM Symposium on User Interface Software and Technology. pp. 145–155. ACM (1993)
38. Fincham, E., Walton, J.: The reciprocal actions of accommodation and convergence. The Journal of Physiology 137(3), 488–508 (1957)
39. Gracia, A., González, S., Robles, V., Menasalvas, E., von Landesberger, T.: New insights into the suitability of the third dimension for visualizing multivariate/multidimensional data: a study based on loss of quality quantification. Information Visualization 15(1), 3–30 (2014)
40. Greffard, N., Picarougne, F., Kuntz, P.: Visual community detection: An evaluation of 2D, 3D perspective and 3D stereoscopic displays. In: Graph Drawing. pp. 215–225. Springer (2011)
41. Grossman, T., Wigdor, D., Balakrishnan, R.: Exploring and reducing the effects of orientation on text readability in volumetric displays. In: Proceedings of the SIGCHI Conference on Human Factors in Computing Systems. pp. 483–492. ACM (2007)
42. Hägerstrand, T.: What about people in regional science? Regional Science Association 24(1), 7–24 (1970)
43. Hancock, M., ten Cate, T., Carpendale, S., Isenberg, T.: Supporting sandtray therapy on an interactive tabletop. In: Proceedings of the SIGCHI Conference on Human Factors in Computing Systems. pp. 2133–2142. CHI '10, ACM (2010)
44. Hancock, M., Nacenta, M., Gutwin, C., Carpendale, S.: The effects of changing projection geometry on the interpretation of 3D orientation on tabletops. In: Proceedings of the ACM International Conference on Interactive Tabletops and Surfaces. pp. 157–164. ACM (2009)
45. Haskell, I.D., Wickens, C.D.: Two-and three-dimensional displays for aviation: A theoretical and empirical comparison. The International Journal of Aviation Psychology 3(2), 87–109 (1993)
46. Held, R., Cooper, E., Banks, M.: Blur and disparity are complementary cues to depth. Current Biology 22(5), 426–431 (2012)
47. Hess, R.F., To, L., Zhou, J., Wang, G., Cooperstock, J.R.: Stereo vision: the haves and have-nots. i-Perception 6(3), 2041669515593028 (2015)
48. Hoffman, D.M., Girshick, A.R., Akeley, K., Banks, M.S.: Vergence–accommodation conflicts hinder visual performance and cause visual fatigue. Journal of Vision 8(3), 33–33 (2008)
49. Inc., H.: Holografika website. http://www.holografika.com, accessed: 2017-10-17
50. Irani, P., Ware, C.: Diagramming information structures using 3D perceptual primitives. ACM Transactions on Computer-Human Interaction (TOCHI) 10(1), 1–19 (2003)
51. Isenberg, P., Isenberg, T., Hesselmann, T., Lee, B., von Zadow, U., Tang, A.: Data visualization on interactive surfaces: a research agenda. IEEE Computer Graphics and Applications 33(2), 16–24 (2013)
52. Jansen, Y., Dragicevic, P., Isenberg, P., Alexander, J., Karnik, A., Kildal, J., Subramanian, S., Hornbæk, K.: Opportunities and challenges for data physicalization. In: Proceedings of the 33rd Annual ACM Conference on Human Factors in Computing Systems. pp. 3227–3236. CHI 15, ACM (2015)

53. Jianu, R., Demiralp, C., Laidlaw, D.: Exploring 3D DTI fiber tracts with linked 2D representations. IEEE Transactions on Visualization and Computer Graphics 15(6), 1449–1456 (2009)
54. Kerren, A., Schreiber, F.: Why integrate InfoVis and SciVis?: an example from systems biology. IEEE ComputerGraphics & Application 34, 69–73 (2014)
55. Khan, J., Can, C., Greenaway, A., Underwood, I.: A real-space interactive holographic display based on a large-aperture hoe. In: Proc. SPIE. vol. 8644, p. 86440M (2013)
56. Kim, M., Lee, J., Stuerzlinger, W., Wohn, K.: Holostation: augmented visualization and presentation. In: SIGGRAPH Asia 2016 Symposium on Visualization. pp. 12:1–12:9. ACM (2016)
57. Kiyokawa, K., Kurata, Y., Ohno, H.: An optical see-through display for mutual occlusion with a real-time stereovision system. Computers & Graphics 25(5), 765–779 (2001)
58. Kjellin, A., Pettersson, L.W., Seipel, S., Lind, M.: Different levels of 3D: an evaluation of visualized discrete spatiotemporal data in space-time cubes. Information Visualization 9(2), 152–164 (2010)
59. Kjellin, A., Pettersson, L.W., Seipel, S., Lind, M.: Evaluating 2D and 3D visualizations of spatiotemporal information. ACM Transactions on Applied Perception (TAP) 7(3), 19:1–19:23 (2010)
60. Kwon, O.H., Muelder, C., Lee, K., Ma, K.L.: A study of layout, rendering, and interaction methods for immersive graph visualization. IEEE Transactions on Visualization and Computer Graphics 22(7), 1802–1815 (2016)
61. Kwon, O.H., Muelder, C., Lee, K., Ma, K.L.: Spherical layout and rendering methods for immersive graph visualization. In: 2015 IEEE Pacific Visualization Symposium (PacificVis). pp. 63–67 (2015)
62. Larson, K., van Dantzich, M., Czerwinski, M., Robertson, G.: Text in 3D: some legibility results. In: CHI'00 extended abstracts on Human Factors in Computing Systems. pp. 145–146. ACM (2000)
63. Lee, J.M., MacLachlan, J., Wallace, W.A.: The effects of 3D imagery on managerial data interpretation. MIS Quarterly pp. 257–269 (1986)
64. Lopez-Hernandez, R., Guilmaine, D., McGuffin, M.J., Barford, L.: A layer-oriented interface for visualizing time-series data from oscilloscopes. In: IEEE Pacific Visualization Symposium (PacificVis). pp. 41-48. IEEE (2010)
65. Mackinlay, J.D., Robertson, G.G., Card, S.K.: The perspective wall: detail and context smoothly integrated. In: Proceedings of the SIGCHI Conference on Human Factors in Computing Systems. pp. 173–176. ACM (1991)
66. Mauderer, M., Conte, S., Nacenta, M.A., Vishwanath, D.: Depth perception with gaze-contingent depth of field. In: Proceedings of the SIGCHI Conference on Human Factors in Computing Systems. pp. 217–226. ACM (2014)
67. Mauderer, M., Nacenta, M.A., Morrison, D.: Gazer: Application for gaze-contingent viewing of images(Apr 2018), https://github.com/MichaelMauderer/Gazer, original-date: 2015-06-16T12:05:34Z
68. McIntire, J.P., Liggett, K.K.: The (possible) utility of stereoscopic 3D displays for information visualization: The good, the bad, and the ugly. In: IEEE VIS International Workshop on 3DVis. pp. 1–9 (2014)
69. McIntire, J.P., Havig, P.R., Geiselman, E.E.: Stereoscopic 3D displays and human performance: A comprehensive review. Displays 35(1), 18–26 (2014)
70. Milgram, P., Takemura, H., Utsumi, A., Kishino, F.: Augmented reality: a class of displays on the reality-virtuality continuum. Proc. SPIE 2351, 282–292 (1995)

71. Munzner, T.: Visualization analysis and design. CRC Press (2014)
72. Nacenta, M.A., Hancock, M., Gutwin, C., Carpendale, S.: The effects of changing projection geometry on perception of 3D objects on and around tabletops. ACM Transactions on Computer-Human Interaction (TOCHI) 23(2), 11:1–11:54 (2016)
73. Nacenta, M.A., Sakurai, S., Yamaguchi, T., Miki, Y., Itoh, Y., Kitamura, Y., Subramanian, S., Gutwin, C.: E-conic: a perspective-aware interface for multi-display environments. In: Proceedings of the 20th Annual ACM Symposium on User Interface Software and Technology. pp. 279–288. ACM (2007)
74. Nelson, L., Cook, D., Cruz-Neira, C.: Xgobi vs the c2: results of an experiment comparing data visualization in a 3-D immersive virtual reality environment with a 2-D workstation display. Computational Statistics 14(1), 39–52 (1999)
75. Ragan, E.D., Kopper, R., Schuchardt, P., Bowman, D.A.: Studying the effects of stereo, head tracking, and field of regard on a small-scale spatial judgment task. IEEE Transactions on Visualization and Computer Graphics 19(5), 886–896 (2013)
76. Rekimoto, J., Green, M.: The information cube: Using transparency in 3D information visualization. In: Proceedings of the Third Annual Workshop on Information Technologies & Systems (WITS'93). pp. 125–132 (1993)
77. Robertson, G., Czerwinski, M., Larson, K., Robbins, D.C., Thiel, D., Van Dantzich, M.: Data mountain: using spatial memory for document management. In: Proceedings of the 11th Annual ACM Symposium on User Interface Software and Technology. pp. 153–162. ACM (1998)
78. Robertson, G.G., Mackinlay, J.D., Card, S.K.: Cone trees: animated 3D visualizations of hierarchical information. In: Proceedings of the SIGCHI Conference on Human Factors in Computing Systems. pp. 189–194. ACM (1991)
79. Rogers, B., Graham, M.: Motion parallax as an independent cue for depth perception. Perception 8(2), 125–134 (1979)
80. Schonlau, M., Peters, E.: Graph comprehension: An experiment in displaying data as bar charts, pie charts and tables with and without the gratuitous 3rd dimension. Social Science Research Network Working Paper Series pp. 1–16 (2008)
81. Schowengerdt, B.T., Seibel, E.J.: True three-dimensional displays that allow viewers to dynamically shift accommodation, bringing objects displayed at different viewing distances into and out of focus. CyberPsychology & Behavior 7(6), 610–620 (2004)
82. Sedlmair, M., Munzner, T., Tory, M.: Empirical guidance on scatterplot and dimension reduction technique choices. IEEE Transactions on Visualization and Computer Graphics 19(12), 2634–2643 (2013)
83. Spence, R.: Information visualization. Springer (2001)
84. St. John, M., Cowen, M.B., Smallman, H.S., Oonk, H.M.: The use of 2D and 3D displays for shape-understanding versus relative-position tasks. Human Factors: The Journal of the Human Factors and Ergonomics Society 43(1), 79–98 (2001)
85. St. John, M., Smallman, H.S., Bank, T.E., Cowen, M.B.: Tactical routing using two-dimensional and three-dimensional views of terrain. In: Proceedings of the Human Factors and Ergonomics Society Annual Meeting. vol. 45, pp. 1409–1413. SAGE Publications (2001)
86. Sun, H.J., Chan, G.S.W., Campos, J.L.: Active navigation and orientation-free spatial representations. Memory & Cognition 32(1), 51–71 (2004)
87. Tait, A.: Desktop virtual reality. In: IEE Colloquium on Using Virtual Worlds. pp. 5/1–5/5 (1992)

88. Todd, J.T., Norman, J.F.: The visual perception of 3-D shape from multiple cues: are observers capable of perceiving metric structure? Perception & Psychophysics 65(1), 31–47 (2003)
89. Todd, J.T., Oomes, A.H., Koenderink, J.J., Kappers, A.M.: On the affine structure of perceptual space. Psychological Science 12(3), 191–196 (2001)
90. Tomilin, M.G.: Head-mounted displays. Journal of Optical Technology 66, 528–533 (1999)
91. Tory, M., Kirkpatrick, A.E., Atkins, M.S., Möller, T.: Visualization task performance with 2D, 3D, and combination displays. IEEE Transactions on Visualization and Computer Graphics 12(1), 2–13 (2006)
92. Tory, M., Moller, T., Atkins, M.S., Kirkpatrick, A.E.: Combining 2D and 3D views for orientation and relative position tasks. In: Proceedings of the SIGCHI conference on Human Factors in Computing Systems. pp. 73–80. ACM (2004)
93. Tory, M., Sprague, D.W., Wu, F., So, W.Y., Munzner, T.: Spatialization design: comparing points and landscapes. IEEE Transactions on Visualization and Computer Graphics 13(6), 1262–1269 (2007)
94. Tory, M., Swindells, C., Dreezer, R.: Comparing dot and landscape spatializations for visual memory differences. IEEE Transactions on Visualization and Computer Graphics 15(6), 1033–1040 (2009)
95. Van Orden, K., Broyles, J.: Visuospatial task performance as a function of two-and three-dimensional display presentation techniques. Displays 21(1), 17–24 (2000)
96. Van Schooten, B.W., Van Dijk, E.M., Zudilova-Seinstra, E., Suinesiaputra, A., Reiber, J.H.: The effect of stereoscopy and motion cues on 3D interpretation task performance. In: Proceedings of the International Conference on Advanced Visual Interfaces. pp. 167–170. ACM (2010)
97. Vishwanath, D., Blaser, E.: Retinal blur and the perception of egocentric distance. Journal of Vision 10(10) (2010)
98. Vishwanath, D.: Toward a new theory of stereopsis. Psychological Review 121(2), 151–178 (2014)
99. Vishwanath, D., Hibbard, P.B.: Seeing in 3D with just one eye: stereopsis without binocular vision. Psychological Science 24(9), 1673–1685 (2013)
100. Ware, C., Franck, G.: Viewing a graph in a virtual reality display is three times as good as a 2D diagram. In: Proceedings of the IEEE Symposium on Visual Languages. pp. 182–183 (1994)
101. Ware, C.: Designing with a 2 1/2-D attitude. Information Design Journal 10(3), 258–258 (2001)
102. Ware, C.: Visual thinking: for design. Morgan Kaufmann (2010)
103. Ware, C.: Information Visualization: Perception for Design (3rd Ed.). Elsevier (2013)
104. Ware, C., Arthur, K., Booth, K.S.: Fish tank virtual reality. In: Proceedings of the INTERACT and CHI Conference on Human Factors in Computing Systems. pp. 37–42. CHI '93, ACM (1993)
105. Ware, C., Mitchell, P.: Reevaluating stereo and motion cues for visualizing graphs in three dimensions. In: Proceedings of the 2nd Symposium on Applied Perception in Graphics and Visualization. pp. 51–58. ACM (2005)
106. Wegman, E.J., Symanzik, J.: Immersive projection technology for visual data mining. Journal of Computational and Graphical Statistics 11(1), 163–188 (2002)
107. Westerman, S.J., Cribbin, T.: Mapping semantic information in virtual space: dimensions, variance and individual differences. International Journal of Human-Computer Studies 53(5), 765–787 (2000)

108. Wickens, C.D., Merwin, D.H., Lin, E.L.: Implications of graphics enhancements for the visualization of scientific data: Dimensional integrality, stereopsis, motion, and mesh. Human Factors: The Journal of the Human Factors and Ergonomics Society 36(1), 44–61 (1994)
109. Yang, Y., Jenny, B., Dwyer, T., Marriott, K., Chen, H., Cordeil, M.: Maps and globes in virtual reality. Computer Graphics Forum (2018)
110. Zaroff, C.M., Knutelska, M., Frumkes, T.E.: Variation in stereoacuity: normative description, fixation disparity, and the roles of aging and gender. Investigative ophthalmology & visual science 44(2), 891–900 (2003)
111. Zhang, G., Kochunov, P., Hong, E., Carr, H., Chen, J.: Towards visual mega-analysis of voxel-based measurement in brain cohorts. In: Proceedings of the Eurographics/IEEE VGTC Conference on Visualization: Short Papers. pp. 55–59. Eurographics Association (2016)

3. Multisensory Immersive Analytics

Jon McCormack[1], Jonathan C. Roberts[2], Benjamin Bach[3], Carla Dal Sasso Freitas[4], Takayuki Itoh[5], Christophe Hurter[6], and Kim Marriott[7]

[1] Monash University, Australia
Jon.McCormack@monash.edu
[2] Bangor University, UK
j.c.roberts@bangor.ac.uk
[3] University of Edinburgh
benj.bach@gmail.com,
[4] Federal University of Rio Grande do Sul
carla@inf.ufrgs.br
[5] Ochanomizu University, Japan
itot@is.ocha.ac.jp
[6] Ecole Nationale de l'Aviation Civile (ENAC), France
christophe.hurter@enac.fr
[7] Monash University
Kim.Marriott@monash.edu

Abstract. While visual cues are traditionally used for visual analytics, multimodal interaction technologies offer many new possibilities. This chapter explores the opportunities and challenges for developers and users to utilize and represent data through non-visual sensory channels to help them understand and interact with data. Users are able to experience data in new ways: variables from complex datasets can be conveyed through different senses; presentations are more accessible to people with vision impairment and can be personalized to specific user needs; interactions can involve multiple senses to provide natural and transparent methods. All these techniques enable users to obtain a better understanding of the underlying information. While the emphasis of this chapter is towards non-visual immersive analytics, we include a discussion on how visual presentations are integrated with different modalities, and the opportunities of mixing several sensory signals, including the visual domain.

Keywords: immersive visual analytics, multisensory visualization, haptic data visualization

3.1. Introduction

We live in a world that excites all our senses. When walking down the corridor the clatter of our footsteps changes as the corridor ends and the stairwell starts. As a person in this workplace, we understand that we have moved from one location to another. The feeling of the roughness of our feet on the stairs, as we

K. Marriott et al. (Eds.): Immersive Analytics, LNCS 11190, pp. 57–94, 2018.
https://doi.org/10.1007/978-3-030-01388-2_3

walk down each step, gives us feedback that we are walking downstairs and helps us to stand upright rather than falling down at each step. We feel the change in pressure on our muscles as we walk, and the smoothness of the wooden hand-rail as we balance our steps. We can hear the sounds of our colleagues talking at the bottom of the stairs, long before we can see them. Furthermore, we readily realize that a colleague has previously walked along the same way because we can smell their perfume in the air. We become immersed in these surroundings. We see, hear, touch and even smell aspects of the building. All these different sensory cues help us to understand where we are, that we are going in the right direction (down the stairs towards our colleagues talking) and that we are able to understand data from the environment (such as guessing how many colleagues are downstairs, just by hearing them). We are certainly immersed in this world.

In immersive analytics we wish to achieve the same result. We want to be immersed in data in such a way that we can perceive all the nuances of the underlying information. Not only should it therefore be possible to visually see our data but to hear, touch and smell the data as well. Furthermore, we would be able to interact through forces, select through gestures or zoom by just by moving our body.

Using all our senses to perceive and interact with the information affords new possibilities. Interfaces can be built that are more natural, which match well to the day-to-day movements of our bodies. We have opportunities to display substantial quantities of data, and use human metaphors such as front and back (where interesting aspects are in front of us, with those items of less interest pushed behind us). We can also include more users, and perform collaborative tasks with them. For example, tangible objects can be used with virtual displays with the implicit notion that whoever holds the object can speak and express their views on the data that is being displayed.

As authors of this chapter, we're excited about the potential and possibilities of this new frontier in immersive analytics. Navigating the research across multiple senses and modalities is complex and difficult. So we organise the material in this chapter by the five main senses: Vision, Sound, Haptics (touch), Smell and Taste.

Using vision (Section 3.4.) to understand data has been extensively studied (e. g., [18, 84, 117]), and consequently it would be possible to create (another) whole book about visualization. This is obviously not our goal. Issues of spatially immersive visualization are covered in great detail in Chapter 2. Here, we review the most important concepts relevant to multisensory immersion.

Sound (Section 3.5.) includes abstract sounds and audible signals, as well as spoken words (auralization) and forms of spatialised sound.

Haptics (Section 3.6.), especially tactile interactions enable the user to feel different textures on their hands and body. Kinesthetic interaction deals with issues of muscle movement and position. We are able to feel and exert forces with our arms and feet.In fact, haptic devices can also simultaneously be actuators, providing both input and output.

Smell and Taste (Section 3.7.) are covered in the same section, not only because the semiochemistry is linked, but also there are fewer designs of data visualization and interaction in this category.

There are many ways to design these systems, and definitely many issues when combining multiple senses together. In Section 3.8. we explore how the user may benefit when the same data is displayed through different senses as complementary presentations. We explore issues of technology and capability of humans to comprehend large quantities of data. We conclude in Section 3.9. with a discussion of future work and directions for multisensory immersive analytics.

3.2. Multisensory Presentation and Analysis

Looking at prior research it can be observed that developers have created numerous multisensory interactive devices. For instance, fun-rides at a fair or resort, excite all our senses, and furthermore there are often rides that use three-dimensional screens, haptic feedback and high-quality sound.

Indeed, it is clear that multisensory storytelling and multisensory visual presentation has been explored in the past. An excellent early example is Morton Heilig's Sensorama system (see [100]). Sensorama placed the user in a multisensory environment allowing them to smell, hear stereo sound, feel vibrations of the seat, and feel the wind in their hair: in combination creating the illusion of presence within another world. Even since 1962 (when Sensorama was patented) researchers have investigated different technologies to display data through multiple senses. However, recently we have seen a step-change in the engineering capability of virtual and augmented reality technologies. Sensors and actuators are smaller, lighter, cheaper, more readily available and easily to connect with each other. Generic, low-power micro-controllers and micro-computers (such as Arduino, Raspberry Pi or BeagleBone) have become small and light, which enable developers to quickly build demonstration interfaces that investigate a variety of multisensory techniques and novel ideas, and companies have produced many excellent commercial devices (such as Oculas Rift, Microsoft HoloLens, HTC Vive, Nintendo Wii).

Any modern computer or digital device employs multisensory interaction: visual displays, touch screens, stereo or multichannel sound and haptic feedback are commonly found on many everyday devices.

The information visualization field has also matured. Researchers have discovered ways to display large abstract datasets, either by using large displays (e. g., [10, 60, 102] or employing some dimensionality reduction method [28, 31] that allows for large data sets to be displayed in regular-sized or even small screens. Visual analytics interfaces have been developed that adapt parameters for the underlying algorithms. Machine learning, data mining, filtering, statistical and other analytic algorithms can all be run interactively. The visual mappings and the underpinning analytics functions are being integrated, such to provide the user with powerful exploratory and intelligent analytic tools. While these systems are extremely useful, they are not spatially immersive in the sense that the user feels like they are located in a virtual "data world" and for the most part they do not utilize or excite all the human senses, only vision.

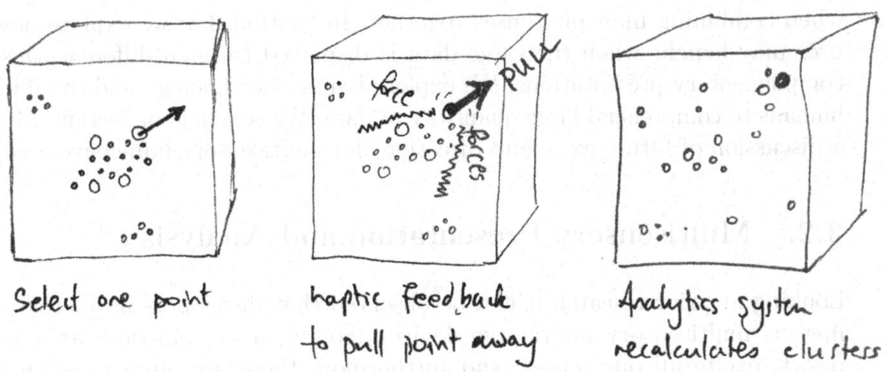

Fig. 1: In this conceptual example, the user is immersed in a large scatterplot. They can select one or more points, move them away (feeling forces related to their closeness to the rest of the points) and place them in a new position, where upon the analytic grouping re-calculates and displays the new clusters.

This chapter explores possibilities and potential design challenges for multisensory immersive analytics, where the user is placed in the heart of their data, they can interact with the information using touch, their body, or arms (for instance), and the data is presented through multisensory stimuli. To motivate this research, let us consider three illustrative examples.

The first is an imaginary example where the user is placed inside a three-dimensional scatterplot of their data, see Figure 1. We could imagine that the scatterplot represents an international company's credit card transactions over one year. The user wishes to investigate how fraudulent transactions spread over the globe. The scatterplot itself would be a multi-dimensional scaling of many variables, with color presenting the cost of a transaction. An immersed user would be able to stand inside the plot, surrounded by billions of data points. They could move their hands through the data, like moving their hands through water, to push some of the points around. Spatialised sound could be used to highlight potential fraud occurrences and draw the user's attention to particular locations, even those outside the current field of view. They could select a group of points with their hand, and start to move them away, with the idea of moving them closer to another group. Forces could be mapped onto clusters to keep them together in one unit, but the user could temporarily pull clusters away to explore them, which snaps them back to their original position when they have completed their operation. In another interaction style, the user could group points together, gesture to move them to a new position, at which point an analytic algorithm re-evaluates the statistics and a new dimension-reduction result is displayed back to the user. This dynamic interaction enables the user to be immersed in a multisensory environment: to see, hear and feel the data in a spatial datasphere.

The second example relates to air traffic controllers and the emerging usage of remote towers. Thanks to technological improvements, live video stream of an air field can be broadcast to remote site where air traffic controller can monitor and regulate aircraft movements. In this specific example, it is important to provide sufficient information so that the immersed user can have a suitable situational awareness. Remote towers encompass a multisensory virtual environment with the visualization of the air field, haptic feedback, audio and multimodal interaction systems [26].

Our third example of multisensory analytics are situations when data analytics is required but vision cannot be employed for this purpose. The most obvious reason for this is that the analyst is blind or has severe vision-impairment but other reasons might be that the environment is dark such as when soldiers are patrolling at night[1] or that vision is required for another purpose. There has been considerable research into how sound and touch can be used by people with severe vision impairment to understand data. For example, sonification of line charts and bar charts (see Section 3.5.) or haptic presentation of spatial and network data (see Sections 3.6. and 3.6.4.). In the near future one can imagine using interactive data physicalisation augmented with audio feedback to provide an immersive interactive data exploration tool for data scientists with severe vision impairment.

As our three examples illustrate, multisensory approaches can enrich the fidelity of our experiences with data analytics, making data more accessible, our experience of it potentially more memorable, and less cognitively challenging in critical situations.

3.3. A Framework for Multisensorial Immersive Analytics

Figure 2 provides a schematic drawing of a design framework for multisensory immersive analytics. The framework aims to help users understand their data better by providing a multisensory environment that utilises traditional visualization (data visualization), sound (sonification), touch (haptification) and even smell (olfaction) or taste (gustation) to immerse the user in their data. As the visual sense is certainly the most explored and used in current analytics systems, through data visualizations, we start by recapitulating the most important concepts from visualization.

In traditional data visualization data elements and their attributes are mapped to geometric elements and their visual and spatial attributes [84]. The rules dictating how the data is mapped to the *visual variables* is called the *visual*

[1] Braille is based on a tactile writing system invented by Charles Barbier for the French army so as to allow soldiers to safely communicate during the night.

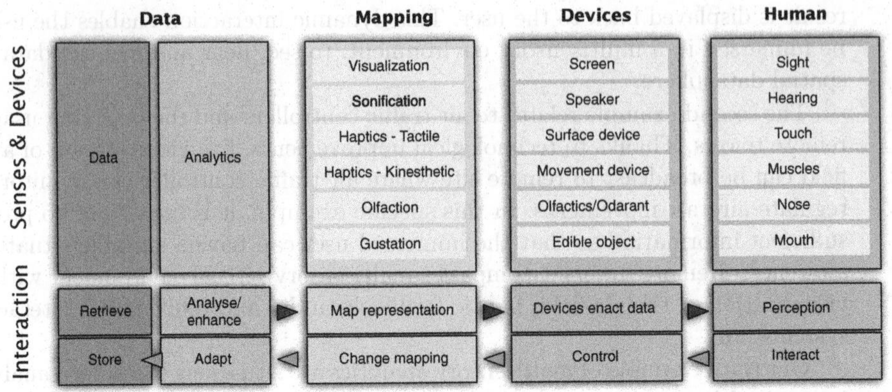

Fig. 2: The design framework for multisensory immersive analytics. Data is mapped onto sensorial channels in the different sensory channels and presented using a variety of devices to the corresponding human sensory system.

mapping (or *visual encoding*). For example, a visual mapping might map each car in a data set to a filled circle and the car's gas consumption to the area of the circle. The resulting picture is the visual representation (or visualization) of the data.

Multisensorial immersive analytics generalises this to other senses. We define a **sensorial mapping** as *a mapping from data elements and data attributes to sensory channels (sight, hearing, touch, proprioception, smell and taste) and their respective sensorial variables (color, pitch, roughness, etc.).* This sensorial mapping is then rendered perceivable through different kinds of *devices* that then stimulate the human senses (Figure 2). In principle, any value can be mapped onto any sensory channel and sensorial variable. For example, a larger value can be mapped onto a darker color, a louder sound, or faster vibration on a vibro-tactile device.

However, because of the characteristics of the human sensory system or limitations of the display device some mappings will be more effective than others, as shown for visualization in the work by Mackinlay [74]. By this we mean that the chosen sensorial variables are more effective in their mission to allow the user to discriminate and compare data values. For example, an effective sensorial mapping would map four categories of elements to four clearly distinctive colors such as red, blue, bright-orange, and green. An ineffective mapping would map the four categories to four very similar colors. Similarly, an ineffective mapping would be to map, for example, dozen values to dozen very different colors, as the human visual system may be incapable of memorizing and clearly decoding a large number of different colors [92,117].

The data is not simply presented to the user passively: the user can actively interact and explore it. Not only does the user wish to see, feel and hear the data, but they also wish to interact with it. Interaction is two-way. It is clear, that some modalities are readily input/output. The movement of our arms (kinaesthetic forces) act both as input devices and output devices. We can hear data through our ears (sonification), but we use our mouth (or maybe our body) to create sounds. Different senses therefore afford different types of representation and interaction.

We represent this two-way interaction in Figure 2 by arrows. In particular, this is one of the areas where immersive analytics needs much research. For instance, it is not clear (for a given task) how the data should be mapped into (say) the visual channel, or how a user could interact with the data haptically (for instance), or then what type of interaction method (menu, gesture, etc.) is used to control the functions to alter the data analytics. Within this system the user is immersed as a human-in-the loop. We encourage the reader to refer to Chapters 4 and 5 for more information about interactive systems and human-in-the-loop analytics.

In the remainder of this chapter we will look at the different sensory channels and variables and how they might be used to understand data. In order to do this it is useful to consider the kinds of dataset that the user might be interested in exploring [84]. These include: *tabular* data, which is conceptually organised into a table with each row corresponding to a different data point or item, and each column corresponding to a different data attribute; *network* data consisting of nodes (or items) and links between these nodes representing different kinds of abstract relationships; *spatial* data in which items are associated with a geographic location or region, and this geographic key is a natural way for organising and understanding the data; *field* datasets that are sampled from a continuous, conceptually infinite domain and *textual* datasets.

Attributes in data items are values that can be measured or logged. They can be [9] *categorical* or *ordered.* Categorical data does not have an inherent ordering. The nationality of people is categorical. Moreover, categorical data is often organised into a hierarchy. An example would be the rank of a specimen in the taxonomy tree of living species. Ordered data has a natural ranking of elements. It has two subtypes: *ordinal* and *quantitative.* Ordinal data can be ranked but the difference between items does not make arithmetic sense, for instance in degrees of preference. An example would be names. For quantitative data differences in value can be compared, e. g., height or weight. The respective data type of attributes can have implications on the sensorial mapping [9].

Furthermore, the analyst may not only interested in visualising the raw data. They may also wish to transform and generate new measures from it. For instance they may wish to simplify, aggregate, arrange, re-arrange, average, calculate and display a range of the data, and so on.

3.4. Visual Presentation

Human vision is the most investigated channel for data presentation, e. g., [18, 84, 117] to name but a few. This section summarizes the most important findings for data visualization in order to provide a benchmark for the design and discussion of data presentation using other sensorial channels in sections that follow.

3.4.1. Physiological Characteristics of Vision

Vision is the main sense for perceiving our environment. It has evolved to allow us to quickly build a 3D model of the objects in our environment from the essentially 2D projection of the environment on our eyes. The visual system has sensors that respond to light. It has a wide area of perception–approximately 100° vertical and 200° horizontal–that provides parallel information acquisition in a continuous flow as well as a narrow focus of attention frame (the *fovea*) which can provide detailed information [117]. It does not need to have physical contact with objects to acquire this information.

The visual system has three main levels or stages [117]: (1) Parallel processing to extract low level properties: color, texture, lines and movement; (2) Rapid serial processing divides the visual field into regions of similar color or texture and achieves *proto-object* recognition of surfaces, boundaries and relative depth. This is driven both top-down by visual attention and bottom-up by low level properties and (3) visual working memory: object recognition and attention, this is under conscious control.

Pre-attentiveness: Low-level visual processing occurs *pre-attentively* and in parallel. This means that visual encodings of data do not have to be consciously recognised by the user. Instead a user can perceive a piece of information before any conscious cognitive activity has happened. Thus red objects "pop out" from blue objects.

Gestalt Theory: Much work on perception of graphic representations is based on Gestalt Theory [118]. This investigated the basic perceptual laws that the human brain uses to pre-attentively group graphic elements as part of proto-object recognition. Elements are grouped by proximity, similarity (e. g., same color or shape), closure and common region, explicit connection (e. g., lines connecting points), continuity and common fate [117].

Depth cues: The visual system uses a wide variety of depth cues to infer the shape of 3D objects from the essentially 2D images falling on the eye. Depth cues include occlusion, linear perspective, changes due to motion of the viewer or object, blurriness due to accommodation, convergence and binocular disparity. See Chapter 2 for more details.

3.4.2. Visual Elements, Variables and Idioms

The visual system allows a rich variety of visual elements and visual variables to be employed for representing different aspects of data. Jaques Bertin [9] identified three kinds of visual elements: points, lines, and areas. More recent literature includes *surfaces* and *volumes* in graphical 3D space [78]. Attributes of data elements can be conveyed by **visual variables** applied to these visual elements. Bertin [9] identified seven visual variables *location, size, color, opacity, orientation, texture,* and *shape.* More recently the use of digital and dynamic computer displays has allowed Bertin's initial set of visual variables to be extended by *containment*, *volume*, *slope* etc. [74] and variables of motion (flicker *frequence*, *direction of movement*, *rythm*, *onset*, etc.) [19, 63].

A large number of studies [24, 32] have investigated the comparative effectiveness of these visual variables for different kinds of data representation. The results are summarised in [78, 84]. For instance, in order of decreasing effectiveness, size, color, motion and shape can be used to show categorical attributes while linear position, length, angle, area, depth, color and curvature and volume can be used to show ordinal attributes. Due to several studies, it is already well known which visual variables can be distinguished pre-attentively and their separability, i. e., how much different variables interfere with each other in pre-attentive processing [117].

Over the last five hundred years a wide variety of ingenious visual idioms have been invented to show different kinds of data with these visual elements and variables. For instance, bar charts, scatter plots and line charts all use position but with different visual elements to show different kinds of tabular data, choropleth and other kinds of data maps show spatial data, while node-link diagrams and adjacency matrices show network data. These components: visual elements, visual variables and visual idioms a provide a basic structure for understanding, describing, and creating visualizations. It also allows – to some extent – evaluation of the perceptual effectiveness of a visualization. However, assessing the *real value* of any visualization is still complex.

3.4.3. Presentation Technology

Emerging presentation technologies for VR and AR are discussed more fully in Chapter 2. For our purposes what is interesting about this technology is that as well as providing immersive visualization it routinely provides stereo or even surround audio and haptic feedback is becoming increasingly common. For instance, the controllers for the HTC Vive or Oculus Rift incorporate haptic feedback and the Nintendo Switch Joy-Con controllers have multiple haptic motors that considerably enhance the sense of immersion when used in games.

3.4.4. Vision in Immersive Analytics

Vision is the basis for visual analytics and will undoubtedly remain the primary sensory channel in most immersive analytics applications apart from those in which for some reason vision cannot be employed. The reasons for this are that vision provides multiple sensorial variables, high bandwidth and parallel pre-attentive processing. There are well established frameworks and tools for creating effective visualizations as well as commodity technologies for presentation.

3.5. Sonification and Auralization

Like vision, hearing is a highly immersive and important sense, often considered the second most important after vision. Humans can become highly sensitive to different nuances in sound through training, prominent examples being visually impaired persons and musicians. With specialised training it is even possible to use sound and hearing as a form of echolocation: to understand oneself spatially in an environment and successfully navigate it without vision [64].

3.5.1. Perceptual Characteristics of Sound

Sound is the movement of vibrational energy through a physical medium (typically air, but sound can also be heard underwater, for example). By *sound*, we are actually referring to a collection of psychophysical aspects. The three most prominent being *loudness*, *pitch* and *timbre*. A young, healthy human adult can detect pitches with frequencies ranging from 20Hz to 20kHz. As frequencies drop below 20Hz the sound perception transitions to rhythmic sensation, as each sound pressure peak can be individually resolved. Sounds can be sensed as quietly as -20dB and are perceived as pain above 140dB. The ear is more sensitive at certain frequencies than others. Sound is perceived best between 1 and 4 kHz (the characteristic frequencies of human speech). The smallest noticeable difference (or *just noticeable distance*, JND) between two tones (pitches) is typically 5-6 cents, 1 cent being 1/100 of the distance between two semitones with 12 semitones in one octave. Timbre (sometimes referred to as tone color) is our identification of the frequency characteristics of a specific sound. For example, a violin and trumpet can play the same pitch, but sound different due to the different levels of harmonics from the fundamental frequency of the note. Moreover, perceived sound can consist of multiple individual sources (such as a symphony orchestra), as well as varying overtones. Together, all these characteristics can produce a unique and distinguishable "sound image", similar to a picture, visual object, or visual glyph.

In addition to recognising loudness, pitch and timbre, humans are also able to recognise rhythmic patterns and to spatially locate the source of a sound in space, including sounds that come from behind or above (although not with the same accuracy uniformly around the body). Spatial location comes predominantly from the sound source arriving at different times in each ear and from cues due to reflections off surfaces in the listening environment. Analogous to stereo vision, good sensing of a sound's location is dependent on having two functioning ears.

3.5.2. Comparison to Vision

In fact, sound has many analogous perceptual characteristics to vision. It can be processed in parallel (multiple sounds at the same time) and position cues with gestalt rules including similarity common fate and proximity are used to build up a 3D model of the objects in the environment [34]. Like vision there is no need to have contact with objects to sense them. Often, the same terms are used to describe characteristics of visual stimuli and aural stimuli; loud, salient, warm, contrast, blur etc. (A fact which holds for other senses as well, e. g., the tactile senses.) Finally, sound is omnipresent meaning that the user does not have to focus his/her attention on it (similar to vision, for example) but also that he/she cannot easily escape a perception. Constant, low-level sounds rapidly fade from conscious awareness (e. g., background sounds like office air conditioning or background traffic noise), so one needs to be careful when using them in an immersive analytics application. Similarly, loud fluctuating sounds immediately attract attention, but cause fatigue or even distress if people are exposed to them for too long.

3.5.3. Perceiving Data with Sound

Communicating information with sound is very common, even though often we don't think of it as "information" in a traditional sense: medical monitoring instruments, sonar, Geiger counters, bell tower clocks with different bells for hours and quarter hours. Similar to visual mappings, those "instruments" map (encode) characteristics of the data or information to characteristics of the sound (*frequency/pitch*, *volume*, *timbre*, *localization*, etc). Such a mapping can be called *sonification* [46, 47, 69]. For example, low pitched values can be mapped to low quantitative values in the data and higher pitches to higher values.

Examples of Data Sonification Many existing data sonifications are inspired by those in the visual domain, such as Franklin and Roberts' pie chart sonification [36], Dingler and Brewster's AudioFeeds [30] which spatialises social network data in a soundscape that surrounds the user, or Saue's [104] work to present a general model for sonification of large spatial datasets. Further examples of existing sonifications include an interactive sonification of multidimensional data where users can change parameters of the data-to-sound mapping while listening [4]; the "Iraq body count" explores the relationship between deaths in Iraq and the oil price through sound [110]. Finally, Xi *et al.* present a tool for the sonification of general time series data [121]. Further examples can be found in [73]. Conferences such as the *International Conference on Auditory Display* specifically focus on research regarding the sonification of data from technical, aesthetic and psychological perspectives.

Scanetti *et al.* [105] discussed the merits of using sound to represent meaning in data, introducing their own sonification system. Madhyastha *et al.* [76] summarized sound attributes for data sonification and then introduced an example sonification toolkit. A study by Flowers *et al.* [33] showed equivalent performance for users interpreting scatterplots visually, and through a mapping to sound. More topics and issues on sonification are introduced in a book [46] and a survey paper [68].

As already mentioned, sound can be used in situations where no visual display is present or a visual display is ineffective or distracting (e. g., Geiger counter). Sound is indirect, i. e., a user is free to look and move where they want. Sound can be present in the background for monitoring purposes (although as discussed above, continuous sounds with little variation quickly fade from conscious perception), and come into attention in critical moments via changes in perceptible characteristics. Sound can further be used to enhance another modality; for example, Baum *et al.* [7] discuss how immersive sound can be used within a CAVE environment, and Hoggan and Brewster [49] studied the mix of audio and tactile feedback in information visualization on a mobile touch screen.

Sound is also effective as a cue to notify variation of data. Madhyastha *et al.* [76] categorizes acoustic attributes effectively applied to sonification as follows:

Pitch: One of the most intuitive ways to express relative magnitude. Mapping to musical notes is more likely to form human-recognizable patterns rather than mapping to arbitrary frequencies (note that frequency and pitch are related logarithmically).

Loudness: Useful to attract attention. Needs to be used carefully as different pitch or timbre may cause differently perceived loudness.

Timbre: Useful to draw distinctions among multiple data categories and many tools allow the choice of voices or tones from predefined sets.

Location: Effectively used only to categorize several discrete values, because precise perception of the elevation of sound source location is relatively poor.

Musical components: Effective to represent particular patterns. For example, change of rhythm patterns can notify temporal separation of information. Melody is a good associative element that allows users to remember associations.

3.5.4. Designing with Sound

One of the important applications of sonification has been for users who are blind or partially sighted. For example, Brewster and his colleagues have explored the use of speech and non-speech audio for presenting tabular data to people with vision impairment [15, 94] while Zhao *et al.* [124] investigated the presentation of maps and tabular data.

However, despite initial research on the perception of auditory variables (e. g., [33, 40]), design guidelines and practices about how to build "auditory displays" for data analysis, are still lacking [69]. Ludovico's sonification space [73] and their differentiation into *sonic plots* (parametric auditory mapping of data to sonic characteristics), system-state description (no precise parameter mapping), auditory support of interactive exploration tasks such as navigation, or in augmented reality setups, are a first step towards a more general framework similar to the one in visualization. Indeed, several concepts [73] are already similar to visualization: orthogonality of auditory variables [67], perceptibility and the number of distinct values (of pitch, volume, etc.) that humans are able to perceive [88], and redundant encoding [66]. Furthermore, as Ludovico *et al.* further point out, *"many symbolic aspects of sound are culture-dependent, so it is difficult to create a sonification having a universally accepted meaning"*.

Sound, music and voice are also an important narrative devices, as becomes immediately apparent when trying to watch a cinematic film with the sound turned off. In cinema for example, musical scores serve many purposes beyond just aural aesthetics. These purposes include: the anticipation of future events, the arrival or return of a character, reinforcement of visual movement or action, reflection on past events, even action or events that occur off screen.

3.6. Haptic Displays

The sense of touch is important to human beings. As we move our muscles we gain an understanding (proprioception) of our body orientation. As we grab a cup we can ascertain (through touch) what type of material the cup is made from, how hot the drink is inside, and how much force we need to hold it. As we pick up a shirt we feel the properties of the fabric, its texture and silkiness, and might be able to understand its composition. We can also feel its weight. All this sensory input helps us to build up a mental model of the object and make deductions about the quality of the garment we are holding. We understand the world, not only through sight, but actively through our sense of touch.

The word haptics comes from the Greek word haptikós, which literally explains our ability to touch or grasp something. We not only can feel the forces exerting on us, but we can engage with the scene and push or pick up the object that we are observing. Therefore, when we perceive characteristics of the object through the sense of touch, haptics is being used as output to us; when we use our forces to interact with objects in the scene, haptics is being used as input to the objects we are interacting with.

3.6.1. Physiological Characteristics of Haptics

We sense touch and movement through many interrelated receptors that are located all over our body. Through our experience of touching and manipulating many different objects we build a deep understanding of how various materials react and feel. That is used to decide what type of object we are holding. For example, we know that metals are generally cold and wood is warm to touch. We can also use this sense to perceive changes in the temperature of bodies, for example, to help us figure out whether someone is probably becoming ill, because temperature is increasing along time.

Our body is full of receptor cells that when stimulated send signals along nerve cells to the brain. These network of nerve endings and receptors is known as the somatosensory system (see [93], Chapter 8). Humans can distinguish between brief tactile sensations and continuous touch, and can understand what part of the body a force has been applied and when an stimulus triggers a pain sensation. There are four main types of receptors: mechanoreceptors, thermoreceptors, proprioceptors and nociceptors.

Mechanoreceptors detect indentations and vibrations on the skin. These types of receptors give rise to sensations including pressure, vibrations and texture. The two most sensitive mechanoreceptors are found in the top layers of the skin and on non-hairy parts of the body such as the lips, tongue, palms, or the soles of our feet. Merkel's disks enable the sensation of slowly adapting change, whereas Meissner's corpuscles react to rapid change. Together these allow humans to understand how long something has been touched. Along tendons, joints and muscles we find Ruffini and Pacinian corpuscles, which detect vibrations in our bones, stretching of skin and movement of limbs [39].

Thermoreceptors enables humans to perceive the temperature of objects on the skin and are found all over the body [45]. Cold receptors work at lower temperatures, and hot receptors work to sense hotter skin temperatures until the pain receptors take over. Early works on this kind of receptors identified that response to warm and cold temperatures are localized, i. e., separate spots in the skin respond to selectively to temperature. Moreover, there is a continuum between these two sensations: from *indifferent - lukewarm - warm - hot - heat pain* on the warm side to *indifferent - cool - cold - cold pain* on the cold side [45].

Proprioceptors help humans understand their own body, by providing continuous and detailed information about the position of limbs and other body parts. These receptors are found in muscles, tendons and joints, and in fact are low-threshold mechanoreceptors specialized for conveying information from the musculoskeletal system. In the case of the head position and movement, proprioceptors are integrated with the vestibular system [93], Chapter 8.

Nociceptors enable humans to perceive pain and help to protect the body from harm. There are different nociceptors that enable to sense excess of mechanical stimuli and temperatures, and chemical substances (such as from an insect sting or various spices). Thus, the other receptors respond from stimuli within certain range; when the stimuli go beyond a certain threshold the nociceptors trigger a signal which is eventually translated as a pain sensation. There are three major classes of nociceptors in the skin: mechanosensitive nociceptors, mechanothermal nociceptors, and polymodal nociceptors. The first two classes are faster-conducting nociceptors that are organized as clusters of sensitive spots and respond selectively to noxiously intense mechanical or thermal stimuli. The polymodal nociceptors tend to respond to thermal, mechanical, and chemical stimuli [93]-Chapter 9.

3.6.2. Comparison to Vision

It is well known that vision provides more information from the external world than all the other senses combined [117]. But this also ignores the complexity of understanding our surroundings. Although it is true that our eyes can detect very detailed and complex light changes, each sense should be considered important, complementary yet different. Humans build a picture of the world using all possible sensory input. Our brain will acquire signals from different sensors (including hands and eyes) [113]. In fact, depending on the task, one type of haptic receptor can be more important than the other [13]. For instance, if an object is too hot, we will instantly drop it, and only after fully perceive that the object is hot.

Our eyes are set at the front of our face, separated so that the brain can build a stereo picture, with vision forward-facing. Thus to see something that is located behind us we need to physically turn our whole body. As we rotate our body, the proprioceptors in our muscles send signals to our brain to say how much we have moved. In immersive analytics we need to be mindful of the relationships between different senses. For example, imagine you have a large display. There are two options to make the picture bigger: you can either increase the size of the displayed object or get the user to physically move closer [3]. As the person walks they are judging distances and can use this information to understand how large the observed object really is.

We can also consider other advantages in using haptic sensors. First, because the receptors are located over the whole body (rather than just at the front of our head), they could potentially be used to create a better sense of immersion. With an actuated body-suit, for instance, the user would instantly know something in front of them or behind them. Second, it is possible to physically move someone, perhaps on a treadmill or robotic arm. The computer can literally be used to effect or refocus the users' attention to something else. This is similar to leading someone by the hand through a space. Third, we use our arms, hands and fingers to input commands to a computer, and also receive feedback from the computer itself. Our bodies may occasionally perceive lights with our vision passively, but haptics is more bidirectional, because we sense the position of our muscles as well as moving them. It is possible therefore that the computer changes haptically at the same time as the user pushes the device, thus creating a dynamic feedback loop.

Much published research supports the notion that the haptic system is less accurate than the visual system at object identification, or that sight dominates touch. However, many of these supporting papers get the user to manipulate abstract (non familiar) objects, or static raised maps [72] that are meant to be read by a finger. While people may struggle to accurately recognise arbitrary objects, haptics can be very effective to identify familiar objects [61]. For example, in a game to select a specific toy from a bag of general toys, the player will easily (and quickly) put their hand in the bag and pick the right toy. When locating the toy, we use fine motor controls, understand the texture, temperature and roughness of the objects through our fingertips. Current technology is problematic, because most haptic devices only activate one type of receptor. This technological limitation has implications for immersive analytics. Ideally we need to have display technologies that can mimic the intricate and nuanced properties of real objects. Indeed, an important aspect to be considered in artificially generating a sensation that can be used for recognizing some object (or data) is the fact that haptic modalities interact. An interesting study by Rincon-Gonzalez *et al.* [97] examined the relationships between tactile and proprioceptive modalities. They showed that signals, which would normally be attributed to tactile senses and self-movement, interact both perceptually and physiologically in ways that complicate the understanding of haptic processing. Another finding was that tactile sensation induced on the fingertips can vanish by the changing the posture of the fingers. Although their primary aim was to improve neuroprosthetic systems by investigating the neural processes underlying haptics, they also provided an interesting discussion about the difficulties in designing effective information representation through haptics.

3.6.3. Data Perception and Understanding Through Haptics

The purpose of immersive analytics is to support the process of obtaining insights from data, i. e., to gain *value* from the data whatever the form in which it is represented. In other words, the sense that we use (be it vision, touch, or something else) should represent the information and allow us – in the case of haptics – to perceive a force, weight, or temperature, for example, and associate the perceived stimulus with a value. We may be accurate in our sensing and say "the first bar in my bar chart represents a value of 90%", or we may be able to ascertain relative values: "the first bar is bigger than the second, so there are clearly more women than men in my class".

A question we should ask ourselves as researchers in immersive analytics is: "how can we effectively display data through the sense of touch?'. In other words, "What haptic variables do we have available?" As previously discussed, in visualization the visual variables [9] include size, position, color (hue, saturation, value) and texture. The haptic variables include force, position, vibration, texture and temperature. To represent value, these cues are adapted. For instance, a larger value in a dataset could be mapped to a higher frequency vibration, greater force, or a hotter temperature. Complex structures can also be communicated as one unit. For instance, in Braille, letters are organised as a unit of raised dots, or a set of vibration, movement and forces could present a haptic glyph [99].

Another question relates to suitable technologies: "What technologies do we have to excite these senses and to allow us (the user) to understand the value of the underlying data?" To answer this question we need to think how we haptically manipulate an object. When we pick up an object in our hands we will move it around, use two or more fingers to judge distances, feel how the object pokes into our skin (to understand how textured the object feels). In our manipulation, we may even pass it from one hand to another. We are not merely picking the object up and holding it still, we are instead actively investigating it with our hands. It is through this motion that we explore the object, exciting a range of receptors, from the slow to the fast response, sensing small textures and the principal corners and edges of an object. Therefore, we can either create static objects and allow the user to explore them through manipulation, or use a computer controlled device to mimic different forces and textures, to excite the receptors on the body. This gives rise to two distinct approaches: data physicalization and haptic data visualization (HDV) or haptification, using haptic devices.

Data Physicalization. In this modality the developer creates a haptic object that presents the data. Static tangible objects are very effective. This is especially relevant for immersive analytics. It is easy and cheap to 3D print objects from CAD models. These can become digital surrogates, or miniature representations of objects. For example, archaeologists in the field can survey buildings or monuments, create 3D models and print 3D digital representations. The heritage project Together.org [82] has used such tangible models of prehistoric standing stones as *interface devices.* The models can be positioned on a table-top display to load specific data relevant to the object that is placed on the table. However, when these tangible objects encode data, they are often called *physical visualizations.*

Physical visualizations have been used for many years. In the late 1950's researchers started to use physical representations of molecules [59] that developed into the so-called "ball and spoke" models, which are widely used in chemistry and biology education. Some data physicalizations have become works of art in their own right. They are beautiful, but explain and encode underlying data. Jansen and colleagues explain many opportunities for physical data visualizations [54].

Currently there is considerable interest in the use of 3D printed models for presenting graphical information to people who are blind or severely vision impaired. Brown and Hurst [14] describe a tool for automatically generating 3D printed line graphs from equations or tabular data sets, while Hu [52] investigated 3D printed bar charts.

An interesting area of current research is to use static tangible models and to project dynamic content. For instance, public art events project dynamically moving video onto the side of buildings, architects have started to project moving imagery onto models and miniatures of buildings, while scientists have projected fluid flow simulation and visualization data onto sand [96]. These tangible visualizations are both static (because they have a fixed tangible content) and dynamic (because moving simulation data, and dynamic data visualizations are augmented on top).

More recently, there has also been promising research into dynamic, tangible visualizations. These works blur the lines between haptic physicalisations and haptic data-visualization devices. Actuators, solenoids or stepper-motors are used to move bars or paddles such to dynamically encode information. For example, McGookin *et al.* [79] developed a tangible user interface (TUI) that could display line and bar graphs in a form that could be touched, whereas Crider *et al.* [27] used a tangible mixing-board to control filtered values in a visualization application [27]. The inForm system [35] or the Haptic Edge Display [53] (both from MIT) enable different physicalisations to become dynamic. They allow the computer to represent data in a tactile way, and enable the user to feel the data as the input data values change.

Haptic Devices. Different devices have been created to recreate forces, vibrations, textures, temperature changes or even induce pain. Much like with the display of graphical cues, whereby the user understands that an object is three dimensional because it has a shadow and has light and dark side, haptic cues enable the user perceive shape. A force applied to a finger could represent an edge of an object, a vibration could present an event has happened, etc. Haptic interaction then may occur directly, such when the user directly touches the device with their finger, or indirectly through the use of a tool (such as using a pencil or scissors).

Haptic research has a long history. Early researchers created remote teleoperation devices, often used in dangerous or remote locations (such as the 1950s Argonne National Laboratory device to remotely handle radioactive material); researchers in the late 1990s invented many new haptic devices that were small and used by researchers in academic institutions (such as the popular Phantom force feedback device [77]). The 2000s saw widespread commercialisation and use of these small devices (such as vibrotactile devices in mobile phones and game controllers).

Due to the interest and widespread potential use of haptics, a number or survey papers have been published. These cover devices, techniques and applications (see, for example, [42,75,89]). Hayward and MacLean [42] recognise four methods for creating haptic sensations: vibrotactile devices, force-feedback systems, surface displays, and distributed tactile displays. In their review, they describe the means to construct experimental devices and the software components needed to drive them. In their companion paper [75] they address the problem of designing interaction with such devices, but also discuss the role of haptics in "offering an additional communication conduit, providing we recognize the importance of attentional design and the overall user environment and its loading". Finally, Panëels and Roberts [89] comprehensively survey the use of haptics in data visualization.

3.6.4. Tactile and Kinaesthetic Technologies

To simplify the haptic sensory field many researchers divide the domain of haptics into two categories: tactile (or cutaneous) and kinaesthetic cues. This is a convenient simplification and can be used to classify much of the research within the haptics domain. Moreover, many of the developed technologies either elicit small movements and excite the receptors in our skin, or provide large forces that change human muscle and limb positions. Consequently we focus on cutaneous and kinaesthetic display technology here.

Cutaneous devices. Imagine holding a glass of hot water. Through our fingertips we notice the temperature of the glass (and therefore conclude the temperature of the water), along with the texture and smoothness of the glass. We might also understand the frictional force of the glass (by understanding how much we need to grip the glass with our fingers, such that it will not fall out of our hands). We can also feel the force applied by gravity, and maybe understand how the water moves or vibrates. These are therefore some of our haptic variables that we have the potential to use, and display data therein. Others include: *temperature* [56], *contact geometry* [22], *slippage* [16], and *vibration* [103].

The popularity of vibrotactile devices has certainly been helped by the growth of mobile and smart technologies. Every mobile phone has a vibrotactile device that vibrates when the phone rings, or vibrates when the user touches the display to press a button. Vibration devices can also be used to assist navigation (such as mimicking bumps and collisions in games) and providing cues that allow the user to infer about an object location or direction to be followed. Vibrotactile devices have also been woven into clothing, from a tactile array sleeve [11] to gloves [85].

A well-known application area for cutaneous haptic technologies is to present data for blind or severely vision-impaired users. A common technique is to use tactile graphics, which are raised line drawings shown on some kind of tactile display. Vidal-Verdu and Hafez [116] present a survey of different kinds tactile displays categorising them as either *refreshable* or *non-refreshable*. Refreshable displays use actuators that dynamically change the object, while non-refreshable displays are static, such as produced by embossing with raised dots using a Braille embosser, printing onto swell paper and thermoforming.

Researchers are starting to explore and develop technology that presents other forms of cutaneous response. Devices such as T-pad [120] or TeslaTouch [6] enable friction to be created through electrovibration. These devices create electrostatic friction that allow different frictional values to be represented to the user. Several surveys on tactile devices and techniques [8, 111] present different examples and allow understanding the evolution of this technology.

A recent technology that shows huge promise for dynamic visualizations, is airborne haptics. Projects such as the noncontact tactile display [50] and UltraHaptics [20] provide a way for mid-air forces to be felt on (say) the hand of the user. While the forces that have been created by airborne haptics are currently very low, they have huge potential to change the way we feel and interact with three-dimensional environments.

Kinaesthetic devices. Recalling our previous example of holding a glass of water, we can perceive its weight and the hardness of the material it is made from through our sense of touch. Instinctively, we apply a force that is capable of holding the glass without deforming it. If someone slides an object on a table and we have to grab it, the force we have to apply must be enough to stop it: we would somehow feel the inertia that is moving that object in our direction.

Kinaesthetic devices have been used for many years usually to provide force feedback for users while they are interacting with virtual representations of physical objects. These devices allow sensing the object's *weight*, *hardness* and *inertia* [16]. This *resistance* to users' action can be used to encode data, and as such weight, stiffness and inertia are our haptic variables in this modality.

Force feedback devices have been largely used in simulators to convey intrinsic information regarding the object or phenomena the user is manipulating or studying. For example, in medical simulators, force-feedback devices have been employed for training students in different tasks from simple palpation with a virtual finger [21] and needle insertion [44] to minimally invasive surgeries [5, 43]. Coles *et al.* [25] present a thorough survey of the use of haptic devices in medical training applications, giving many examples of commercial and experimental systems, many of them employing immersive technologies. The use of haptics in medical training applications is in continuous development and mostly task-specific, such as the force-feedback devices developed by Dargar *et al.* [29]. Among other application domains that benefit from such techniques we can cite driver assistance systems [90] and haptic exploration of computational fluids [23].

Since these applications are intended to provide kinaesthetic sensations about objects or phenomena, they map the properties of objects to those on the device. The accuracy of such mappings is essential for a correct analysis. Recent work on data-driven haptic rendering [122] aims at modelling and rendering both stiffness and friction of a deformable object, by providing frictional slip interaction within sliding exploration on a large surface area on an inhomogeneous deformable object, with a perceptually acceptable accuracy level. The authors claim their system is among the first to support fully unconstrained exploration of deformable objects including rubbing, poking, and stroking, with reasonable accuracy.

3.6.5. Haptics in Immersive Analytics

There are many opportunities to more effectively use haptics in immersive analytics. The first obvious way is to physically move the human in the world. In the large, solutions such as cable robots can place the human on a chair in the centre of a room, and as the chair is physically moved in the room, the user moves in the data space. Through this technology users can feel immersed in the centre of their data. Other solutions, such as treadmills or walking platforms, help to sense walking motions, but keep the user in a static location. In fact, one challenge for immersive visualization is that the user is often physically located in a relatively small space, making it difficult for the VR system to track the user over the long distances that would be useful to mimic very large virtual spaces. Redirected walking [95] is one solution where the visual simulation tricks the users into believing that they are walking in a straight line when in fact they are walking (for instance) in a circle.

Haptic wearables or even a full-body haptic interaction suit would also be useful in immersive analytics. Many of these suits and wearables use vibrotactile devices to present a haptic response. Forces are possible, through using exoskeleton devices. Shull and Damian [109] provide a review of haptic wearables and Bogue [12] reviews exoskeleton and robotic prosthetics.

Another possibility of providing a sense of immersion in a data space coupled with analytics features could be achieved by combining vibrotactile, head-mounted displays with dynamic tangible objects. Vibrotactile head-mounted displays allow a more accurate, precise, and faster target localization in an active head pointing task [55], and could be used to locate points of interest in the data space. Dynamic tangible devices such as the Haptic Edge Display [53] and the Emergeables [101] allow investigation of interesting interactive techniques that could be used to analyze data subsets. As mentioned before, the Haptic Edge Display [53] represents data through actuated pins placed on the side of a mobile display, which can be sensed and manipulated. Emergeables [101] is based on the concept of creating a physical (deformable) surface that displays data and presents physical controls like buttons and sliders. More interesting, these controls emerge from the display when needed and disappear back into the surface when they are no longer needed. The inForm system [35] could also be used to allow sensing and interacting with a specific subset of data points located in a (virtual) surrounding space.

3.7. Smell/Olfaction, Taste/Gustation

The sense of smell and taste are connected. Smell is a chemical reaction where odorant molecules bind to the olfactory receptors in the nose. Our tongue can distinguish five distinct qualities, whereas the nose can discern hundreds of different substances. Smell and taste receptors combine together to give us the sense of flavour. Smell is a perceptual phenomenon which depends not only on the odorant molecules but the environment and the person [1]. Smells are linked closely to memories, and through perceiving a smell we can recall specific situations or events. Smell also conjures a vast range of emotions. Smells also act subconsciously, and may effect the way we choose our partners. Smells are also used by the body to detect dangers, such as smoke or the smell of rotten food.

3.7.1. Suitability of Olfaction and Gustation Senses for Immersive Analytics

Smells are everywhere in the real world: for example, we notice smells of coffee from a room next to ours, or we smell the perfume of someone who had long since walked down the corridor. Thus, using smells in immersive analytics may help the user to believe that a virtual world is more natural or realistic. But how can smell be used to display data? It is easy to imagine that stronger smells could be used to represent larger values in our dataset, or that sweet or pungent smells be used to present categorical data. However, the dimensions of smell perception are not well understood. Zarzo and Stanton [123] provide a review of different odour maps, and Koulakov [65] provide a (MDS) scaling of the dimensions as a picture, with four main segments, as follows:

- sickening, putrid, sharp, pungent, acid, heavy, fatty sour, etc.
- burnt, smoky, nutty, woody, peanut butter, warm, dry, etc.
- fragrant, sweet, floral, light, rose, etc.
- chemical, medical, disinfectant, gasoline, solvent, cool, paint, etc.

Smell and taste vocabulary is an interesting area because often, when faced with some data, a user may need to express what they have discovered. For visualization, a user would be able to express that a value is larger, or smaller, based on the difference in length of a bar on a barchart, for example. The user readily understands the vocabulary of visualization because they are used to plots and pictures, and the (visual) words are more common in every-day language. However, with smell and taste, users are less likely to understand the vocabulary, which is less familiar. Wilson and Stevenson write "*the vocabulary of olfaction almost invariably ties the odour to its physical source, e. g., orange or coffee or cheese odours. This is distinctly different than, for example, the vocabulary for color, in which blue, yellow, and red can be distinct percepts in themselves, separate from whatever object produces those reflected wavelengths*" [119].

3.7.2. Smell and Taste Technologies

One of the main problems is to understand the make-up of the molecules that create particular smells. The same is true for a given chemical mixing: it is difficult to predict how the created molecule will smell. It is well understood that small volatile molecules diffuse fast over a small distance, while other larger molecules linger longer, but understanding what smell is perceived from a specific chemical is more complex. Sometimes similar molecules produce similar smells, whereas molecules that are mirror-symetric to each other could produce different odour sensations [1].

Therefore, current smell systems use arrays of pre-mixed chemicals and when a specific scent is required the lid of a pot is opened such to allow it to disperse. An example of this type of technology is the Olfactory Display [87] from the Tokyo Institute of Technology that can create a range of different smells using a solenoid valves to control which canister is open. Some commercial tools have been created to deliver scent, including DigiScents iSmell, ScentWave, and other devices that have scents on a USB stick to deliver perfumes where you are working. However, each of these technologies have limited use for immersive visualization because they only deliver a few different smells.

One of the challenges with smell is that it disperses in the room, and that the odour can stay for a long time. This means that it is difficult to represent rapidly changing values through the sense of smell. One of the possible solutions is to deliver smell as close to the user's nose. A tube could be run close (or even up) the user's nose. Subsequently, a smaller dose of scent would be needed to be distinguished by the user. And a fan could be used to readily disperse the smell away from the user, to enable more data to be represented. It could be easy to imagine that someone wearing a Head Mounted Display could also receive odours. The sense of smell has been used as a diagnostic tool for physicians for centuries. Recently research has begun to explore how technology can be used to identify and classify odours [86,114]. Many olfactory stimulants carry a strong associative memory with a particular place or event, so in addition to their potential for analytic mapping, they can be used to make a particular multisensory immersion more memorable.

3.8. Designing Multisensorial Immersive Systems

As humans evolved in a multi-sensorial environment, our perception has learned to adapt, to optimize, and to work with multiple simultaneous stimuli. A common example is perceiving food taste and recognizing food. As the tongue has only a very limited number of different sensors for different tastes, most of our perceived taste requires olfactory information. Our senses work *together*, delivering information and a more rich picture about the environment we are currently in.

Immersive environments can employ multiple sensorial channels to communicate information. Such *information* in multisensorial systems can be information about the data, about the state of the system, or about external issues that the immersed user is deprived to perceive (e. g., visual perception of the real world in VR). Multisensorial systems may be able to increase the degree of immersion and help users stay focused and maintain a state of flow.

Building multisensorial systems comes with a number of challenges regarding the components involved in such a system—human, computer machinery, display and input technology—and their respective relationships and combinations. In this section, we discuss questions and challenges related to the design of such multi-sensorial immersive systems with a focus on the *combination* of multiple sensorial channels for communicating information. We first describe how stimuli from multiple sensory sources can be combined to represent data values. Then, we describe capabilities and limitations of the the human perceptual and cognitive system with respect to multiple sensorial stimuli. Finally, we discuss further implications and conditions such as context and training.

3.8.1. Multi-Sensorial Representations

In visualization, there are established visual *representations* for specific purposes and data sets such as node-link diagrams, scatterplots, parallel coordinates, tree maps, Euler diagrams, and many others [84].

Such representations employ lower level components (e. g., visual marks [9]), their sensorial attributes (e. g., visual variables [9]), as well as rules for placing elements on a 2D space (e. g., force-directed layout, axis values on a scatterplot). Representations can be learned and applied to different problems (data), or serve as blueprints and being modified and extended. Some representations support specific tasks; a node-link diagram supports path following tasks in networks, while adjacency matrices support cluster detection; scatterplots allow guessing about the correlation between two variables (dimensions), but parallel coordinate plots show more dimensions simultaneously.

In multi-sensorial systems the concept of the visual representation must be re-conceptualised into a *sensorial representation* and the combination of multiple sensorial representations: a *multi-sensorial representation.* As defined previously, a sensorial representation results from a sensorial mapping and as such, it can involve a variety of sensorial channels.

Some questions arise from this definition: *What is a {sensorial, auditory, olfactorial, haptic, etc.} representation?* Are there specific recurring design patterns for auditory or haptic communication suitable for data representations? What are the correspondents to *visual element* and *layout* in the non-visual channels? What is the equivalent of a node-link diagram or barchart in haptics or audition?

At first, existing representations (in some sensorial channel) can serve as basis to build multi-sensorial systems by augmenting this base representation through other channels.

This leads to two questions in combining multi-sensorial representations:

1. *Which individual sensorial representations does my system (need to) support?*, and

2. *How to combine these sensorial representations into a consistent user interface experience?*

Answering the first question refers to the variety of external and empirical factors: which technology is available to the interface designer and end user, how effective are individual sensorial channels, how real should the sensorial mappings be, e. g., representing olfactorial data through olfactorial stimuli, or affective issues such as the wish to represent specific values through silent and others through loud sounds in order to provoke a feeling of contrast or even physical discomfort.

The second question about *how* to combine multiple sensorial representations into a consistent user interface experience is certainly much less constrained by external factors, but tied to individual and technological factors. There may be several modes in which combinations can happen, such as

- *redundant* or *complementary*
- *synchronous* or *asynchronous*
- *permanent* or *on-demand*
- and certainly others.

For example, visualization designers can decide to redundantly encode the same data value by two complementary visual variables. Redundant encoding aims to increase the precision with which users can decode the visualization, as two stimuli encode the same value. Redundant encoding in multisensorial systems means to combine stimuli across sensorial channels, for example, colour and sound pitch can both be used to encode the same data value. There could even be three or more redundant mappings for the same value, eventually including all senses. Moreover, the sound can be played on-demand only when the user hovers a data point in visual representation or when he/she touches an element in a physical visualization. Here, the sound can even encode additional information about the touched/hovered data object. Eventually, sound or olfaction can be permanent ambient stimuli giving some background information about the data.

For example, haptic representation is often augmented with audio. The TTT (Talking Tactile Tablet) [71] uses a printed tactile graphic on top of a pressure-sensitive touchpad, and an appropriate audio file is played when an object is touched. In MultiVis [80] the authors used a force-feedback device and non-speech audio to provide quick overviews of bar charts while Petrie *et al.* [91] used a mixture of sound and haptic guidance with a force-feedback joystick to present UML diagrams to blind software engineers. More recently, GraVVITAS [38] uses a combination of audio and vibratory feedback to present a variety of information graphics on a touch screen without the need for printed tactile overlays.

3.8.2. Leveraging Human Perceptual Abilities

Differentiation. When mapping data to sensorial channels and stimuli, some senses may perform better depending on the data attribute to be represented as well as the task at hand. Visual perception is definitely one of the most important factors of human perception concerning to immersive visualization/analytics; mappings from data elements to visual elements, such as colour, shape, position, texture, and transparency have been well discussed [78,115] to achieve effective visualization. Similarly, data sonification can be studies by considering relationships between acoustic features [37], such as loudness, frequency, tone, and human perception. Impression and emotion are well associated with visual/acoustic expressions. For example, Hervner [48] proposed eight groups of words to express the impressions and emotions evoked by music. In other words, it is important to appropriately select the diverse, sensorial representations to realize impressive and emotional immersive analytics.

Haptic devices will be often useful to operate and control immersive analytics systems. However, effectiveness, safety and comfort of immersive analytics will depend on how we consider ability of perceiving and tolerating haptic features such as temperature, texture, vibration, weight, hardness, inertia, and even pain. Sense of smell and taste are also important to realize impressive and realistic immersive analytics. Technologies for these sense are expected to be applied to immersive analytics systems.

Focus and Training. Humans can focus on specific sensorial stimuli (*focused attention*) as well as train their sensitivity for a specific visual channel. For example, we can focus on shapes or colours in visual search while ignoring shapes or positions of objects. There are cases where a stimulus in one channel can break this attention and force the brain to pay attention to this stimulus. Common examples include a loud sound, a sharp smell, or a moving visual object.

The brain can also be trained to detect dissonances, position, and distance in sound through shorter or livelong learning processes, like what happen with musicians, artists, dancers, and parfumiers. Besides training for profession, disabled persons often develop specific skills in certain senses. Examples include fine haptic differences and the learning of complex haptic patterns such as in Braille as well as determining the location where a sound comes from.

In the contrary case, we try to avoid any stimuli, when, for example, we try to sleep or concentrate on a demanding task. In a way, our brain is constantly processing input to deliver information and create a reality around us.

However, there are cases where such multimodal perception can be tricked and misleading, especially in virtual environments where almost each stimulus has an artificial origin.

3.8.3. Perceptual and Cognitive Challenges

Human perception is impressive but far from perfect—in an absolute sense. Besides natural limitations such as visible and auditory spectra, we may have limitations on our perception due to some impairment from birth, ageing, or accident. It is important to discuss how to consider any perceptual limitation so that we can develop immersive analytics systems able to be used by wide range of users.

Individual sensorial channels. In terms of visual representation, object arrangements and their relative positions is very important. This is especially true in 3D environment with stereoscopic visualization. *Visual occlusion*, the way that objects are tangled or shaded, gives a powerful visual clue with the visual perception of the depth ordering. This information is not the same than the depth perception that can be retrieved from stereoscopic visualization. The occlusion can work by itself on 2D screen to perceive the depth ordering, but in 3D environment it is crucial that both occlusion and depth represent the same information. If this is not the case, the user will be confused and disoriented. This triggers potential complex problem when dealing with transparency and colour blending [117]. The *Stroop effect* [112] demonstrates an interference effect between the text we read and its visual colour. In terms of cognitive workload, it is hard to read the name of a written colour than to say its colour. This effects shows how colour perception overtake the reading process, and such phenomena is widely used to create psychological test (e. g., double tasks). Further limitations for vision result from diseases and defects: myopia, astigmatism, presbyopia, and colour-blindness.

Sound that reaches our ear has naturally been distorted by the environment and its perceptual capability, such as through distance (sounds getting quieter), masking (loud sounds mask quite sounds), or echo. The making effect has been successfully turned into an asset to store and compress sound in the MP3 audio *compression*. Roger Shepard *blends between two different sounds* to create a musical scale, which can seem to increase in pitch forever [107]. In the same way, Jean-Claude Risset extended this to rhythm perception where the tempo never stops to decrease [98]. Eventually, people suffer from natural hearing loss due to age or over-exposure.

Contradicting stimuli. In the simplest case, stimuli from two different senses contradict each other; we smell a certain food but consistency or even taste are not as expected; we see but do not hear the electric car on the street; we hear but do not see the airplane in the cloudy sky; etc. Another example which considerable consequences in virtual environments are visual stimuli contradicting our sense of balance and orientation; an environment that visually is moving but not physically can cause motion sickess. The inverse, an environment that physically is moving but not visually, causes problems for some people on ships and on curvy car tracks.

Moreover, it is not only the actual senses that make up reality, but also knowledge about the world and about what to expect and what not. For example, seeing an object with a realistic stone texture lets us assume it is heavy and we are surprised if lifting it is easy (in fact, our brain unconsciously prepares our muscles to lift an object of that perceived size and weight).

Sensory crosstalk. Multisensory stimuli can lead to the perception of *false* and non-existent stimuli, as the brain is constantly interchanging signals between brain regions responsible for processing stimuli from different senses [17, 51].

Sensory-crosstalk, a term used by Howes [51] can range from two stimuli being truly equivalent in their information, over an enhancement, to eventually the emergence of information.

For example, in the McGurk effect [81] the visual sense interferes with the auditorial sense creating wrong auditory information; the same sound (e. g., *ba*) while watching lip movement for another sounds (e. g., *ga*) becomes a third sound in the brain (in this case *da*). The other way is possible, too, as shown by Shams *et al.* [106]; the frequency of a visual signal can be tricked by the frequency of a "synchronized" audio signal.[2] Shams *et al.* synchronized the single flashing of a dot with two and more auditory beep-signals, leading study participants to perceive two and more visual flashes.

In multisensorial systems, such effects can eventually lead to the falsification of signals. However, which respective cases do enhance or falsify has been little investigated so far.

We have to be careful not only about the way in which stimuli from different sources are being combined, but even simpler, about their number. Again, more stimuli (more information) can improve our brain in perceiving and deciding for the "the right" information but too much information can result in the contrary: perceptual and cognitive overload leading to ignoring stimuli or problems in deciding with stimuli to trust in cases where stimuli are contradicting each other.

Perceptual overload. Perceptual or sensorial overload occurs when the brain is confronted with too many stimuli from the same or different channels and possibly over a longer time. Perceptual overload requires the brain to filter and concentrate on a subset of stimuli. While this can lead to selective attention, in other cases perceptual overload can lead to missing information and in the worst case to stress-like symptoms and a temporary decrease in cognitive abilities. The case is well known from visualization where too many visual elements with different visual encodings reduce an observers ability to correctly decode information; cluttered node-link diagrams and parallel coordinates plots, maps and scatterplots with too many visual variables; inappropriate use of colour, animation, and animated visual variables such as flickering, in general. The same principles hold for the other channels; too many tones, too many combination of aural variables, and so forth.

In any case, the purpose of any system with the goal of communicating information through multiple senses is to carefully select the channels best suited for some information and to carefully combine them. One goal could be to reduce a possible sensorial overload in one sense by distributing information over several senses.

Cognitive overload. Similar to sensorial overload, and a possible consequence of sensorial overload is cognitive overload. While sensorial overload is specific to one or multiple senses simultaneously, and describes an overload for what and

[2] https://www.youtube.com/watch?v=D3Z1cxA2Tp0

how things are perceived, cognitive (or information) overload usually refers to processing an abundance of perceived information [62]. Cognitive overload can be caused by switching tasks rapidly (though not taking breaks), multi-tasking, distraction and interruption [41]. As Miller writes, the human brain is able to keep between 5-9 "items" in memory simultaneously [83]. Interruptions and sudden changes in sensorial input can influence the current state of the brain in a way that makes us forget what we have been just thinking [62, 83]. In multi-sensorial information systems this can result from signals interrupting the user in the task s/he is currently focusing on (e. g., an aural notification that some data has been updated).

The challenge in multi-sensorial information systems is to support a users mental state of flow, to minimize distraction and to adapt all, or at least the majority of sensorial stimuli to the task the user is currently performing. For example, stimuli signalling system states should be muted according to non-relevance to the current task; stimuli from different sources should focus on the current user tasks and deliver a holistic picture of information; stimuli should complement each other or encode information redundantly.

Pre-knowledge and Training. As occurs with many computational systems, users of immersive analytic applications may have a wide range of knowledge and experience levels. Besides knowledge on the application domain, users also may have a wide range of skills and experiences of the underlying technologies used in visual analytics, virtual/augmented reality, and human-computer interaction. One may need to consider these differences for developing useful immersive analytics systems. For example, users may need to train 3D recognition skills such as spatial awareness or shape understanding for using spatially immersive environments. Also, 3D operations skills using walkthrough interfaces and haptic devices may be required. If the application demands creative or artistic activities during analytics processes, users may need to train immersive-specific skills. For example, 3D modeling and music playing are typical activities which users may need to train for using immersive environments.

3.8.4. Context and Environment

We may need to consider the context of applications and runtime environments while designing immersive analytics systems. Typical factors that we may need to consider are task models, including collaborative tasks, and the physical environment where they are to be used.

Task models and collaborative tasks. Visualization research communities have a history of defining task models. We can start from the information visualization mantra by Shneiderman [108] and the visual analytics mantra by Keim *et al.* [58], both simply defining repetitive tasks. The sense-making loop is well defined for visual analytics [57], being a good reference for system design of immersive analytics tools.

As occurs with many virtual reality applications, immersive analytics may also be useful for collaborative tasks, which assume that multiple users are immersed into the same (virtual) analytics space and collaboratively work there. Typical applications where collaborative tasks in immersive environments can be borrowed from many virtual reality application domains:

- Physical space simulation and analysis for various academic and industrial fields such as fluid dynamics and bioinformatics.
- Industrial design, where designers, engineers, salesmen and employers may work collaboratively in immersive environments.
- Transportation/disaster/security analysis, where experts from different fields of domain may use immersive analytics.

User Environment: Immersive analytics systems are often built on top of existing virtual/augmented reality environments. There are several surveys discussing what kinds of technologies have evolved from virtual/augmented reality systems [2,70]. A number of typical environments and technologies exist, which we may need to be appropriately select for developing immersive analytics systems.

- Diverse computing environments: large-scale, personal, or mobile computers can be used for immersive analytics.
- Display systems: stereoscopic or head-mounted displays are often mandatory for immersive system development. The size of displays is also an important factor for system design.
- Speakers systems: surround audio systems or head-phones are often mandatory for immersive acoustic systems.
- Input devices for navigation, pointing, and gesture.
- Haptic technologies for sensing forces, temperature, vibration, and other stimuli.

In some cases, no visual output may be available while doing other tasks. For example, it is difficult to carefully look at the display of car navigation systems during driving a car. We also need to consider that no- or one-hand operation may be only allowed while doing other tasks. Again, alternative sensory is desirable for such situations. In other cases, we are often not allowed to use input/output sounds or perform large gestures during immersive analytics, for example in public spaces. Alternative sensory is desirable to make the system suitable for use under such situations.

3.9. Discussion and Research Challenges

Auditory interfaces: To date, sound has been largely underutilized in multisensory immersive analytic applications. Just as visual representations require good visual design skills, auditory interfaces require good sonic design skills (a topic not as widely taught as visual design). Moreover, many environments are not ideal for critical listening, due to ambient noise, room coloration or reverberation, for example. Recent HMD devices have included stereo headphones which can help minimise some of these problems. What remains an important research challenge is in the successful mapping of data variables to sonic variables. Unlike visualization, few conventions exist, so the user must necessarily learn mappings anew. Spatialization and immersion are two important features that sound can effectively exploit; the challenge is how to integrate sound into multisensory systems so that the auditory components work in harmony with the other sensory stimuli effectively.

Haptic interfaces: Haptic technologies have huge potential for integration in immersive analytics. We can readily consider three sizes of devices. First, there is huge potential for large-scale physical dynamic devices that control the whole body of a user. For example, treadmills, chairs or even small rooms can be vibrated, moved and rotated. These provide physical sensations that enable the users to move and position themselves directly inside large scale data space. But these devices are typically expensive and require careful health and safety controls. Second, wearable technologies are developing fast and have many uses for immersive analytics. This has been aided by the pervasiveness of cheap and robust vibrotactile devices and the acceptability of wearable devices and clothes. There are many research challenges, and opportunities. While several companies have tried to build haptic suits they have not been currently successful. There is a need to develop modular systems that are robust and cost effective. Third, there are important opportunities for high-fidelity dynamic tactile devices. Currently there are several device types that are being explored in research laboratories, from friction-based displays and vibro-tactile head mounted displays to airborne haptics. However, each of these technologies need to mature further and become cheaper. Finally, there are huge opportunities to integrate tangible objects into virtual worlds and use them for immersive analytics. While three dimensional printing is cheap, and is becoming widely used, there are few middleware libraries or applications that utilise them effectively.

Olfactorial interfaces: Technologies to integrate smell and taste in an immersive analytics system are probably the least mature of all the senses. Certainly, because of the complexity of how humans perceive smell, it is impossible to create and mix smells dynamically. Therefore current technological solutions issue pre-canned odours on demand. Another challenge for immersive analytics is how to deliver the appropriate smells to the user. Odours linger in the room, and need to be flushed out by neutral odours, it would be better to deliver smaller quantities of odour directly to participants, through a personal delivery system. However this can be intrusive and would need the user to wear some kind of nose-mounted display.

Multisensorial representations: Combining sensorial data representation is still an open field where there are many opportunities worth to be explored to leverage user data perception. For instance, sensorial prioritisation triggers numerous questions. While visualization has the largest bandwidth in terms of data communication power, little is known regarding how interruption is prioritized by the human perception system within multi-modal senses. More open questions are concerned with how to create effective combinations. The purpose of a combination may be exploratory, analytical, aiming at presentation and "telling stories about data" or creating a sense of immersion, presence, and experience. Further chapters discuss other issues in combining different sensorial data representations.

Interaction: Interaction in multisensorial systems will most likely happen through haptics, e. g., pressing buttons, touching surfaces, grabbing and reaching to objects, etc. However, there are already cases that involve speech (e. g. Microsoft Hololens). More futuristic scenarios envision human-brain interaction (BCI). BCI is a communication pathway between human brain and an external device. Such techniques are usually envisaged for impaired users but they open promising opportunities to enhance user cognitive perception with a direct and more controlled communication channel.

3.10. Conclusion

Multisensory immersive analytics is an exciting frontier and natural extension of research in visualization and visual analytics. As we have outlined in this chapter, the potential applications are widespread across many different disciplines and tasks. While we have shown a number of examples that demonstrate existing achievements in this field, there remains many important challenges in order for the multisensory experience to reach its full potential (see [69] for examples in sonification).

Other issues include how to map data to multisensory channels and how interaction is interwoven with those sensory channels. We also need to more effectively create data representations tailored to emerging multisensory display technologies. As the capability of technology to realise more immersive multisensorial experiences becomes more prevalent, the impact and application for more fully understanding data will be achieved.

References

1. Auffarth, B.: Understanding smell – the olfactory stimulus problem. Neuroscience & Biobehavioral Reviews 37(8), 1667–1679 (2013)
2. Azuma, R.T.: A survey of augmented reality. Presence: Teleoperators and Virtual Environments 6(4), 355–385 (1997)
3. Ball, R., North, C., Bowman, D.A.: Move to improve: Promoting physical navigation to increase user performance with large displays. In: Proceedings of the SIGCHI Conference on Human Factors in Computing Systems. pp. 191–200. CHI '07, ACM (2007)
4. Barrett, N.: Interactive spatial sonification of multidimensional data for composition and auditory display. Computer Music Journal (2016)
5. Basdogan, C., De, S., Kim, J., Muniyandi, M., Kim, H., Srinivasan, M.A.: Haptics in minimally invasive surgical simulation and training. IEEE Computer Graphics and Applications 24(2), 56–64 (2004)

6. Bau, O., Poupyrev, I., Israr, A., Harrison, C.: Teslatouch: electrovibration for touch surfaces. In: Proceedings of the 23nd Annual ACM Symposium on User Interface Software and Technology. pp. 283–292. ACM (2010)
7. Baum, G., Gotsis, M., Chang, C., Drinkwater, R., Clair, D.S.: Synthecology: Sound use of audio in teleimmersion. In: Proceedings Stereoscopic Displays and Virtual Reality Systems XIII. vol. 6055. SPIE the Engineering Reality of Virtual Reality (2006)
8. Benali-khoudja, M., Hafez, M., marc Alex, J., Kheddar, A.: Tactile interfaces: a state-of-the-art survey. In: Int. Symposium on Robotics. pp. 721–726 (2004)
9. Bertin, J.: Sémiologie graphique: Les diagrammes - Les réseaux - Les cartes. Editions de l'Ecole Hautes Etudes en Sciences, Paris, France, les réimpressions edn. (1967)
10. Bezerianos, A., Isenberg, P.: Perception of visual variables on tiled wall-sized displays for information visualization applications. IEEE Transactions on Visualization and Computer Graphics 18(12), 2516–2525 (2012)
11. Bloomfield, A., Badler, N.I.: Virtual training via vibrotactile arrays. Presence: Teleoperators and Virtual Environments 17(2), 103–120 (2008)
12. Bogue, R.: Exoskeletons and robotic prosthetics: a review of recent developments. Industrial Robot: An International Journal 36(5), 421–427 (2009)
13. Bowman, D.A., Kruijff, E., LaViola, J., Poupirev, I.: User Interfaces - Theory and Practice. Addison Wesley, Boston, USA (2005)
14. Brown, C., Hurst, A.: Viztouch: automatically generated tactile visualizations of coordinate spaces. In: Proceedings of the Sixth International Conference on Tangible, Embedded and Embodied Interaction. pp. 131–138. ACM (2012)
15. Brown, L.M., Brewster, S.A., Ramloll, S., Burton, R., Riedel, B.: Design guidelines for audio presentation of graphs and tables (2003)
16. Burdea, G.C.: Force and Touch Feedback for Virtual Reality. John Wiley & Sons, Inc., New York, NY, USA (1996)
17. Calvert, G., Spence, C., Stein, B.E.: The Handbook of Multisensory Processes. MIT Press (2004)
18. Card, S.K., Mackinlay, J.D., Shneiderman, B. (eds.): Readings in Information Visualization: Using Vision to Think. Morgan Kaufmann Publishers, San Francisco (1999)
19. Carpendale, M.: Considering visual variables as a basis for information visualisation (2003)
20. Carter, T., Seah, S.A., Long, B., Drinkwater, B., Subramanian, S.: Ultrahaptics: multi-point mid-air haptic feedback for touch surfaces. In: Proceedings of the 26th Annual ACM Symposium on User Interface Software and Technology. pp. 505–514. ACM (2013)
21. Chen, H., Wu, W., Sun, H., Heng, P.A.: Dynamic touch-enabled virtual palpation. Computer Animation and Virtual Worlds 18(4-5) (2007)
22. Cini, G., Frisoli, A., Marcheschi, S., Salsedo, F., Bergamasco, M.: A novel fingertip haptic device for display of local contact geometry. In: Proceedings of the First Joint Eurohaptics Conference and Symposium on Haptic Interfaces for Virtual Environment and Teleoperator Systems. pp. 602–605. IEEE Computer Society (2005)
23. Cirio, G., Marchal, M., Hillaire, S., Lecuyer, A.: Six degrees-of-freedom haptic interaction with fluids. IEEE Transactions on Visualization and Computer Graphics 17(11), 1714–1727 (2011)
24. Cleveland, W.S., McGill, R.: Graphical perception: Theory, experimentation and application to the development of graphical methods. Journal of the American Statistical Association 79(387), 531–554 (1984)

25. Coles, T.R., Meglan, D., John, N.W.: The role of haptics in medical training simulators: A survey of the state of the art. IEEE Transactions on Haptics 4(1), 51–66 (2011)
26. Cordeil, M., Dwyer, T., Hurter, C.: Immersive solutions for future air traffic control and management. In: Proceedings of the 2016 ACM Companion on Interactive Surfaces and Spaces. pp. 25–31. ISS Companion '16, ACM, New York, NY, USA (2016)
27. Crider, M., Bergner, S., Smyth, T.N., Möller, T., Tory, M.K., Kirkpatrick, A.E., Weiskopf, D.: A mixing board interface for graphics and visualization applications. In: Proceedings of Graphics Interface. pp. 87–94 (2007)
28. Cunningham, J.P., Ghahramani, Z.: Linear Dimensionality Reduction: Survey, Insights, and Generalizations (2015)
29. Dargar, S., De, S., Sankaranarayanan, G.: Development of a haptic interface for natural orifice translumenal endoscopic surgery simulation. IEEE Transactions on Haptics 9(3), 333–344 (2016)
30. Dingler, T., Brewster, S., Butz, A.: Audiofeeds - a mobile auditory application for monitoring online activities. In: In Proceedings of ACM Multimedia (Florence, Italy), ACM Press (2010)
31. Engel, D., Hüttenberger, L., Hamann, B.: A survey of dimension reduction methods for high-dimensional data analysis and visualization. In: VLUDS (2011)
32. Few, S. (ed.): Information Dashboard Design: The Effective Visual Communication of Data. Analytics Press (2006)
33. Flowers, J.H., Buhman, D.C., Turnage, K.D.: Cross-modal equivalence of visual and auditory scatterplots for exploring bivariate data samples. Human Factors: The Journal of the Human Factors and Ergonomics Society 39(3), 341–351 (1997)
34. Foley, H., Matlin, M.: Sensation and Perception. Psychology Press (2015)
35. Follmer, S., Leithinger, D., Olwal, A., Hogge, A., Ishii, H.: inFORM: dynamic physical affordances and constraints through shape and object actuation. In: ACM Symposium on User Interface Software and Technology. vol. 13, pp. 417–426 (2013)
36. Franklin, K.M., Roberts, J.C.: Pie chart sonification. In: Proceedings of the Seventh International Conference on Information Visualization. pp. 4–9. IEEE Computer Society, Washington, DC, USA (2003)
37. Gaver, W.W.: What in the world do we hear?: An ecological approach to auditory event perception. Ecological Psychology 5(1), 1–29 (1993)
38. Goncu, C., Marriott, K.: GraVVITAS: generic multi-touch presentation of accessible graphics. In: IFIP Conference on Human-Computer Interaction. pp. 30–48. Springer (2011)
39. Goodwin, A.W., Wheat, H.E.: Physiological mechanisms of the receptor system. In: Grunwald, M. (ed.) Human Haptic Perception: Basics and Applications. pp. 93–102. Birkhäuser Basel (2008)
40. Grey, J.M.: Multidimensional perceptual scaling of musical timbres. Journal of the Acoustical Society of America 61(5), 1270–1277 (1977)
41. Hallowell, E.M.: Overloaded circuits. Harvard business review p. 11 (2005)
42. Hayward, V., Maclean, K.E.: Do it yourself haptics: part i. IEEE Robotics Automation Magazine 14(4), 88–104 (2007)
43. Heng, P.A., Cheng, C.Y., Wong, T.T., Xu, Y., Chui, Y.P., Chan, K.M., Tso, S.K.: A virtual-reality training system for knee arthroscopic surgery. Trans. Info. Tech. Biomed. 8(2), 217–227 (2004)
44. Heng, P.A., Wong, T.T., Yang, R., Chui, Y.P., Xie, Y.M., Leung, K.S., Leung, P.C.: Intelligent inferencing and haptic simulation for chinese acupuncture learning

and training. IEEE Transactions on Information Technology in Biomedicine 10(1), 28–41 (2006)

45. Hensel, H.: Cutaneous Thermoreceptors. In: Iggo, A. (ed.) Somatosensory System. pp. 79–110. Springer Berlin Heidelberg, Berlin, Heidelberg (1973)
46. Hermann, T., Hunt, A., Neuhoff, J.G.: The Sonification Handbook. Logos Publishing House, Berlin, Germany (2011)
47. Hermann, T.: Taxonomy and definitions for sonification and auditory display. International Community for Auditory Display (2008)
48. Hevner, K.: Experimental studies of the elements of expression in music. The American Journal of Psychology 48(2), 246–268 (1936)
49. Hoggan, E., Brewster, S.: Crosstrainer: Testing the use of multimodal interfaces in situ. In: Proceedings of the ACM Conference on Human Factors in Computing Systems. pp. 333–342. ACM Press (2010)
50. Hoshi, T., Takahashi, M., Iwamoto, T., Shinoda, H.: Noncontact tactile display based on radiation pressure of airborne ultrasound. IEEE Transactions on Haptics 3(3), 155–165 (2010)
51. Howes, D.: Cross-talk between the senses. The Senses and Society 1(3), 381–390 (2006)
52. Hu, M.: Exploring new paradigms for accessible 3D printed graphs. In: Proceedings of the 17th International ACM SIGACCESS Conference on Computers & Accessibility. pp. 365–366. ACM (2015)
53. Jang, S., Kim, L.H., Tanner, K., Ishii, H., Follmer, S.: Haptic edge display for mobile tactile interaction. In: Proceedings of the 2016 CHI Conference on Human Factors in Computing Systems. pp. 3706–3716. CHI '16 (2016)
54. Jansen, Y., Dragicevic, P., Isenberg, P., Alexander, J., Karnik, A., Kildal, J., Subramanian, S., Hornbæk, K.: Opportunities and challenges for data physicalization. In: Proceedings of the 33rd Annual ACM Conference on Human Factors in Computing Systems. pp. 3227–3236. CHI 15, ACM (2015)
55. de Jesus Oliveira, V.A., Brayda, L., Nedel, L., Maciel, A.: Designing a vibrotactile head-mounted display for spatial awareness in 3D spaces. IEEE Transactions on Visualization and Computer Graphics 23(4), 1409–1417 (2017)
56. Jones, L.A., Berris, M.: The psychophysics of temperature perception and thermal-interface design. In: Proceedings of 10th Symposium on Haptic Interfaces for Virtual Environment and Teleoperator Systems. p. 137. IEEE Computer Society (2002)
57. Keim, D., Andrienko, G., Fekete, J.D., Görg, C., Kohlhammer, J., Melançon, G.: Visual analytics: Definition, process, and challenges. In: Kerren, A., Stasko, J.T., Fekete, J.D., North, C. (eds.) Information Visualization: Human-Centered Issues and Perspectives. pp. 154–175. Springer Berlin Heidelberg, Berlin, Heidelberg (2008)
58. Keim, D.A., Mansmann, F., Schneidewind, J., Thomas, J., Ziegler, H.: Visual analytics: Scope and challenges. Lecture Notes in Computer Science, Visual Data Mining 4404, 76–90 (2008)
59. Kendrew, J.C., Bodo, G., Dintzis, H.M., Parrish, R., Wyckoff, H., Phillips, D.C.: A three-dimensional model of the myoglobin molecule obtained by x-ray analysis. Nature 181(4610), 662–666 (1958)
60. Klapperstueck, M., Czauderna, T., Goncu, C., Glowacki, J., Dwyer, T., Schreiber, F., Marriott, K.: ContextuWall: peer collaboration using (large) displays. In: 2016 Big Data Visual Analytics (BDVA). pp. 1–8 (2016)
61. Klatzky, R.L., Lederman, S.J., Metzger, V.A.: Identifying objects by touch: An "expert system". Perception & Psychophysics 37(4), 299–302 (1985)

62. Klingberg, T.: The Overflowing Brain: Information Overload and the Limits of Working Memory. Oxford University Press (2009)
63. Köbben, B., Yaman, M.: Evaluating dynamic visual variables. In: Proceedings of the Seminar on Teaching Animated Cartography, ACI/ICA, Madrid. pp. 45–51 (1996)
64. Kolarik, A.J., Cirstea, S., Pardhan, S., Moore, B.C.: A summary of research investigating echolocation abilities of blind and sighted humans. Hearing Research 310, 60–68 (2014)
65. Koulakov, A.: In search of the structure of human olfactory space. Flavour 3(1), O1 (2014)
66. Kramer, G.: Mapping a single data stream to multiple auditory variables: A subjective approach to creating a compelling design. In: International Conference on Auditory Displays (1996)
67. Kramer, G.: Auditory display: Sonification, audification, and auditory interfaces. Perseus Publishing (1993)
68. Kramer, G., Walker, B., Bonebright, T., Cook, P., Flowers, J., Miner, N., Neuhoff, J.: Sonification report: Status of the field and research agenda (1999)
69. Kramer, G., Walker, B., Bonebright, T., Cook, P., Flowers, J.H., Miner, N., Neuhoff, J.: Sonification report: Status of the field and research agenda (2010)
70. van Krevelen, R., Poelman, R.: A survey of augmented reality: Technologies, applications and limitations. The International Journal of Virtual Reality 9(2), 1–20 (2010)
71. Landau, S., Gourgey, K.: Development of a Talking Tactile Tablet. Information Technology and Disabilities 7(2) (2001)
72. Lederman, S.J., Campbell, J.I.: Tangible graphs for the blind. Human Factors 24(1), 85–100 (1982)
73. Ludovico, L.A., Presti, G.: The sonification space: A reference system for sonification tasks. International Journal of Human-Computer Studies 85, 72–77 (2016)
74. Mackinlay, J.: Automating the design of graphical presentations of relational information. ACM Transactions On Graphics (ToG) 5(2), 110–141 (1986)
75. Maclean, K.E., Hayward, V.: Do it yourself haptics: Part ii [tutorial]. IEEE Robotics Automation Magazine 15(1), 104–119 (2008)
76. Madhyastha, T.M., Reed, D.A.: Data sonification: do you see what I hear? IEEE Software 12(2), 45–56 (1995)
77. Massie, T.H., Salisbury, J.K.: The phantom haptic interface: A device for probing virtual objects. In: Proceedings of the ASME Winter Annual Meeting, Symposium on Haptic Interfaces for Virtual Environment and Teleoperator Systems. vol. 55(1), pp. 295–302 (1994)
78. Mazza, R. (ed.): Introduction to Information Visualization. Springer (2009)
79. McGookin, D., Robertson, E., Brewster, S.: Clutching at straws: Using tangible interaction to provide non-visual access to graphs. In: Proceedings of the ACM Conference on Human Factors in Computing SystemsI. pp. 1715–1724. ACM Press (2010)
80. McGookin, D., Brewster, S.: MultiVis: Improving Access to Visualisations for Visually Impaired People. In: ACM Conference on Human Factors in Computing Systems: Extended Abstracts. pp. 267–270. ACM (2006)
81. McGurk, H., MacDonald, J.: Hearing lips and seeing voices (1976)
82. Miles, H.C., Wilson, A.T., Labrosse, F., Tiddeman, B., Griffiths, S., Edwards, B., Ritsos, P.D., Mearman, J.W., Möller, K., Karl, R., Roberts, J.C.: Alternative representations of 3D-reconstructed heritage data. J. Comput. Cult. Herit. 9(1), 4:1–4:18 (2015)

83. Miller, G.A.: The magical number seven, plus or minus two: some limits on our capacity for processing information. Psychological Review 63(2), 81 (1956)
84. Munzner, T.: Visualization Analysis and Design. CRC Press (2014)
85. Murray, A.M., Klatzky, R.L., Khosla, P.K.: Psychophysical characterization and testbed validation of a wearable vibrotactile glove for telemanipulation. Presence: Teleoperators and Virtual Environments 12(2), 156–182 (2003)
86. Nakamoto, T., Yosihioka, M., Tanaka, Y., Kobayashi, K., Moriizumi, T., Ueyama, S., Yerazunis, W.: Colorimetric method for odor discrimination using dye-coated plate and multiLED sensor. Sensors and Actuators B: Chemical 116(1-2), 202–206 (2006)
87. Nakamoto, T., Kinoshita, M., Murakami, K., Yossiri, A.: Demonstration of improved olfactory display using rapidly-switching solenoid valves. IEEE Virtual Reality Conference pp. 301–302 (2009)
88. Neuhoff, J.G., Kramer, G., Wayand, J.: Sonification and the interaction of perceptual dimensions: can the data get lost in the map? (2000)
89. Panëels, S., Roberts, J.C.: Review of designs for haptic data visualization. IEEE Transactions on Haptics 3(2), 119–137 (2010)
90. Petermeijer, S.M., Abbink, D.A., Mulder, M., de Winter, J.C.F.: The effect of haptic support systems on driver performance: A literature survey. IEEE Transactions on Haptics 8(4), 467–479 (2015)
91. Petrie, H., Schlieder, C., Blenkhorn, P., Evans, G., King, A., O'Neill, A.M., Ioannidis, G.T., Gallagher, B., Crombie, D., Mager, R., Alafaci, M.: TeDUB: a system for presenting and exploring technical drawings for blind people. In: Miesenberger, K., Klaus, J., Zagler, W. (eds.) International Conference ICCHP 2002, Computers Helping People with Special Needs. pp. 537–539. Springer Berlin Heidelberg, Berlin, Heidelberg (2002)
92. Post, D.L., Greene, E.: Color name boundaries for equally bright stimuli on a CRT: Phase I. Society for Information Display - Digest of Technical Papers 86, 70–73 (1986)
93. Purves, D., Augustine, G.J., Fitzpatrick, D., Hall, W.C., LaMantia, A.S., McNamara, J.O., Williams, S.M. (eds.): Neuroscience: Third Edition. Sinauer Associates, Inc., Sunderland, MA, USA (2004)
94. Ramloll, R., Yu, W., Brewster, S., Riedel, B., Burton, M., Dimigen, G.: Constructing sonified haptic line graphs for the blind student: first steps. In: Proceedings of the Fourth International ACM Conference on Assistive Technologies. pp. 17–25. ACM (2000)
95. Razzaque, S., Swapp, D., Slater, M., Whitton, M.C., Steed, A.: Redirected walking in place. In: Proceedings of the workshop on Virtual environments 2002. pp. 123–130. Eurographics Association (2002)
96. Reed, S., Kreylos, O., Hsi, S., Kellogg, L., Schladow, G., Yikilmaz, M., Segale, H., Silverman, J., Yalowitz, S., Sato, E.: Shaping watersheds exhibit: An interactive, augmented reality sandbox for advancing earth science education. In: AGU Fall Meeting Abstracts. vol. 1, p. 01 (2014)
97. Rincon-Gonzalez, L., Warren, J.P., Meller, D.M., Tillery, S.H.: Haptic interaction of touch and proprioception: Implications for neuroprosthetics. IEEE Transactions on Neural Systems and Rehabilitation Engineering 19(5), 490–500 (2011)
98. Risset, J.C.: Pitch and rhythm paradoxes: Comments on "Auditory paradox based on fractal waveform" [J. Acoust. Soc. Am. 79, 186-189 (1986)]. Acoustical Society of America Journal 80, 961–962 (1986)

99. Roberts, J.C., Franklin, K.: Haptic glyphs (hlyphs) - structured haptic objects for haptic visualization. In: First Joint Eurohaptics Conference and Symposium on Haptic Interfaces for Virtual Environment and Teleoperator Systems. World Haptics Conference. pp. 369–374 (2005)
100. Robinett, W.: Interactivity and individual viewpoint in shared virtual worlds: The big screen vs. networked personal displays. SIGGRAPH Computer Graphics 28(2), 127–130 (1994)
101. Robinson, S., Coutrix, C., Pearson, J., Rosso, J., Torquato, M.F., Nigay, L., Jones, M.: Emergeables: Deformable displays for continuous eyes-free mobile interaction. In: Proceedings of the 2016 CHI Conference on Human Factors in Computing Systems. pp. 3793–3805. CHI '16, ACM (2016)
102. Rohn, H., Junker, A., Hartmann, A., Grafahrend-Belau, E., Treutler, H., Klapperstück, M., Czauderna, T., Klukas, C., Schreiber, F.: VANTED v2: a framework for systems biology applications. BMC Systems Biology 6(1), 139.1–13 (2012)
103. Salisbury, C., Gillespie, R.B., Tan, H., Barbagli, F., Salisbury, J.K.: Effects of haptic device attributes on vibration detection thresholds. In: Proceedings of the World Haptics 2009 - Third Joint EuroHaptics conference and Symposium on Haptic Interfaces for Virtual Environment and Teleoperator Systems. pp. 115–120. IEEE Computer Society (2009)
104. Saue, S.: A model for interaction in exploratory sonification displays. In: Proceedings of the International Conference on Auditory Display (2000)
105. Scaletti, C., Craig, A.B.: Using sound to extract meaning from complex data. In: Proceedings of SPIE 1459 (Extracting Meaning from Complex Data: Processing, Display, Interaction II). pp. 207–219 (1991)
106. Shams, L., Kamitani, Y., Shimojo, S.: Illusions: What you see is what you hear. Nature 408(6814), 788–788 (2000)
107. Shepard, R.N.: Circularity in judgements of relative pitch. Journal of the Acoustical Society of America 36(12), 2346–2353 (1964)
108. Shneiderman, B.: The eyes have it: A task by data type taxonomy for information visualizations. In: Proceedings of the IEEE Symposium on Visual Languages. pp. 336–343 (1996)
109. Shull, P.B., Damian, D.D.: Haptic wearables as sensory replacement, sensory augmentation and trainer – a review. Journal of NeuroEngineering and Rehabilitation 12(1), 59 (2015)
110. Sounds, S.: Iraq body count. https://soundcloud.com/somatic-sounds/iraq-body-count-guillaume-potard (2010)
111. Spirkovska, L.: Summary of Tactile User Interfaces Techniques and System. NASA Ames Research Center (2005)
112. Stroop, J.R.: Studies of interference in serial verbal reactions. Journal of Experimental Psychology pp. 643–662 (1935)
113. Takahashi, C., Watt, S.J.: Optimal visual–haptic integration with articulated tools. Experimental Brain Research 235(5), 1361–1373 (2017)
114. Tanaka, Y., Nakamoto, T., Moriizumi, T.: Study of highly sensitive smell sensing system using gas detector tube combined with optical sensor. Sensors and Actuators B: Chemical 119(1), 84–88 (2006)
115. Tory, M., Moller, T.: Human factors in visualization research. IEEE Transactions on Visualization and Computer Graphics 10(1), 72–84 (2004)
116. Vidal-Verdu, F., Hafez, M.: Graphical tactile displays for visually-impaired people. IEEE Transactions on Neural Systems and Rehabilitation Engineering 15(1), 119–130 (2007)

117. Ware, C.: Information Visualization: Perception for Design. Morgan Kaufmann Publishers Inc., San Francisco, CA, USA, 3 edn. (2013)
118. Wertheimer, M.: Untersuchungen zur lehre von der gestalt. Psychological Research 1(1), 47–58 (1922)
119. Wilson, D.A., Stevenson, R.J.: Learning to smell: olfactory perception from neurobiology to behavior. JHU Press (2006)
120. Winfield, L., Glassmire, J., Colgate, J.E., Peshkin, M.: T-pad: Tactile pattern display through variable friction reduction. In: Second Joint EuroHaptics Conference and Symposium on Haptic Interfaces for Virtual Environment and Teleoperator Systems (WHC'07). pp. 421–426. IEEE (2007)
121. Xi, H., Kelley, A.: Sonification of time-series data sets. Bulletin of the American Physical Society 60 (2015)
122. Yim, S., Jeon, S., Choi, S.: Data-driven haptic modeling and rendering of viscoelastic and frictional responses of deformable objects. IEEE Transactions on Haptics 9(4), 548–559 (2016)
123. Zarzo, M., Stanton, D.T.: Understanding the underlying dimensions in perfumers' odor perception space as a basis for developing meaningful odor maps. Attention, Perception, & Psychophysics 71(2), 225–247 (2009)
124. Zhao, H., Plaisant, C., Shneiderman, B., Lazar, J.: Data sonification for users with visual impairment: A case study with georeferenced data. ACM Transactions on Computer-Human Interaction 15(1) (2008)

4. Interaction for Immersive Analytics

Wolfgang Büschel[1], Jian Chen[2], Raimund Dachselt[1], Steven Drucker[3], Tim Dwyer[4], Carsten Görg[5], Tobias Isenberg[6], Andreas Kerren[7], Chris North[8], and Wolfgang Stuerzlinger[9]

[1] Technische Universität Dresden, Germany
[bueschel,dachselt]@acm.org
[2] The Ohio State University, USA
chen.8028@osu.edu
[3] Microsoft Research, USA
sdrucker@microsoft.com
[4] Monash University, Australia
tim.dwyer@monash.edu
[5] University of Colorado, USA
carsten.goerg@ucdenver.edu
[6] Inria & Université Paris-Saclay, France
tobias.isenberg@inria.fr
[7] Linnaeus University, Växjö, Sweden
kerren@acm.org
[8] Virginia Tech, USA
north@vt.edu
[9] Simon Fraser University, Canada
w.s@sfu.ca

Abstract. In this chapter, we briefly review the development of natural user interfaces and discuss their role in providing human-computer interaction that is *immersive* in various ways. Then we examine some opportunities for how these technologies might be used to better support data analysis tasks. Specifically, we review and suggest some interaction design guidelines for immersive analytics. We also review some hardware setups for data visualization that are already archetypal. Finally, we look at some emerging system designs that suggest future directions.

Keywords: natural user interfaces, embodied interaction, post-WIMP interfaces, visual analytics, data visualization

4.1. Introduction

Just as being able to interact with your environment is critical to your sense of 'being in' the environment, interaction is critical in immersive analytics systems. Donald Norman introduced the notion that the primary challenges in interactive system design were to reduce the *Gulf of Execution* (the barriers preventing people from completing actions when working with a computer interface) and also the *Gulf of Evaluation* (the aspects of the interface that make it difficult

K. Marriott et al. (Eds.): Immersive Analytics, LNCS 11190, pp. 95–138, 2018.
https://doi.org/10.1007/978-3-030-01388-2_4

for people to understand the output of the system) [63, 118]. It is arguable that the primary focus of visualization systems historically has been on minimizing the Gulf of Evaluation, that is, making visualizations as understandable as possible and that the Gulf of Execution in this domain is less well explored. However, supporting the fundamental tasks of visual analytics (e. g., exploring the visualization, filtering data, and adjusting parameters) with appropriate, intuitive interaction techniques is necessary for the development of efficient and pleasurable visualization systems.

We would further argue that reducing the Gulf of Execution (for example, through direct manipulation of elements of an information display [63]) and bringing the input and output spaces closer (or even uniting them) strongly contributes to a sense of immersion. Before embarking on an investigation of this premise with any degree of specificity, however, it is worth noting that display and interaction technologies are developing very rapidly, making it difficult to assess the practicability of interaction mechanisms, or indeed to predict what interaction with computers will look like in a few years. Thus, we take a moment to reflect on the history of human-computer interaction, and how the interaction devices and techniques that have been developed have been adopted by visual data analytics systems currently in use.

We can identify three broad and separate generations of interactive computing, characterized by distinct interface styles, each optimized to the available hardware capacity during the same period:

Online computing – beginning in the 1960s;

Graphical user interfaces – spearheaded by research in the 1960s but achieving popular use in the 1980s;

Natural user interfaces – again there is much earlier research, including research for 3D user interfaces, but this movement has garnered widespread attention since the 2000s, with the mainstream adoption of touch computing.

At the dawn of computing, communicating with computers was achieved through very low-bandwidth modalities, such as commands punched on paper tape. In the early 60s, computers "came online" with video, keyboard and (occasionally) light-pen interaction allowing operators to edit programs and documents directly in the systems' memory [113]. Most fundamental elements of interaction, as they are currently used in visual data analysis software, were demonstrated at this time. Examples include mouse control and the window metaphor (introduced by Engelbart and others in 1968[1]) and direct interaction with graphical objects (Sutherland's seminal SketchPad in 1963 [143]). The first commercially successful graphical user interfaces – as we know them today – appeared in the early 80s. Since then, their WIMP (Windows/Icons/Menus/Pointer) interaction paradigm has become mainstream. It has proved successful in the workplace and more specifically in visual analytics software. In fact, most current visualization and analytics applications still rely on classical desktop interfaces.

[1] At "The Mother of All Demos" https://www.youtube.com/watch?v=yJDv-zdhzMY

Meanwhile, innovation on alternative interface technologies has been ongoing. These post-WIMP interfaces do not use traditional menus, toolbars, and windows, but rely on, e. g., touch input, gestures, speech, or tangible interaction. Specifically, the *Natural User Interface* (NUI) movement has sought to teach computers to respond to peoples' gestures on multi-touch screens or in midair following very literal physical metaphors for "natural" interaction (see also Section 4.4.). While gesture control has been investigated for a long time, since at least the 1980s [29], the NUI movement has in recent years gained momentum with the massive popularity of touch-screen phones and tablets [10]. NUI also becomes more important in computing environments where a mouse or keyboard is impractical, such as extremely portable devices or in Augmented or Virtual Reality [98]. In addition, for the last few years, there have been efforts to open up (information) visualization to new devices making use of natural interaction techniques [100]. It clearly follows that such natural interaction techniques are promising for immersive analytics.

Incorporating NUIs into specific applications, however, is not trivial [117]. In general, the goal we aim for with any user interfaces is to minimize the potentially cumbersome mechanics of input and the cognitive distance between users' intent and the execution of that intent as provided by the system, i. e., reducing the Gulf of Execution. Despite already receiving strong emphasis in virtual environment research, interaction in immersive analytics brings in new challenges: How interaction augments insight discovery in large, dense, spatial and non-spatial data is still an active area of research (e. g., [47, 83, 138]). While speculation has begun regarding how this translates to immersive environments (e. g., [128]) there remains a great deal of fundamental research to be done to better understand the challenges of "immersing people in their data."

In Section 4.2. we look at some of the exciting developments in immersive human-computer interaction technologies, both systems that are already commercially available, and ones that are only now emerging in research labs; we list the benefits of immersion that we see for various data analytics applications; and, we motivate some requirements and challenges to be met to create effective immersive interaction devices and techniques.

In Section 4.3. we break down the key tasks that must be supported by any interactive visual analytics system. Then, in Section 4.4., we explore the novel interaction modalities in emerging immersive interaction techniques and discuss their viability in terms of these tasks. Then, in Section 4.5. we look in more detail at how these visual analytics tasks map to immersive interactions and we consider design guidelines for interaction for immersive analytics.

In Section 4.6. we describe in more detail some setups for immersive data visualization that have become 'archetypal' in the sense of being widely investigated, at least in research labs. Then, in Section 4.7. we look at new setups and use-cases for immersive analytics that may indicate future directions. Section 4.8. concludes with some research opportunities.

4.2. Opportunities and Requirements

Our vision for immersive analytics is to augment human cognition when working with data using immersive technologies. Since at least the work of Sutherland [144], the assumption has been that the "ultimate display" technology can take advantage of a broader range of senses and capabilities than traditional WIMP interfaces. In the early days of formal information visualization research, pioneers such as Card, Robertson, and Mackinlay painted a long-term vision for an ultimate "Information Visualizer" that was exploiting 3D graphics and made use of the *information workspace* metaphor [30]. While they discussed interaction at a high-level, basically acknowledging that the system needed to be fluid and performant in response to user actions in order to support workflow and user cognition, they gave little indication of what the mechanics (and the devices) for interaction might look like. Arguably, at the time (1991), while 3D graphics rendering technology was making rapid progress, there was little appreciation generally of the challenges that lay ahead in creating more natural and effective ways to interact with these immersive spaces.

We have come a long way since the early 1990s and there exists a plethora of promising technology for interacting with the surfaces and spaces in our environments rather than interaction with computers via a fixed workstation (see, e. g., [100]). Thus, before exploring specific immersive interaction techniques for data analytics, we look in Subsection 4.2.1. at some general motivating examples of the state of the art in immersive interaction techniques. In light of these examples, we consider in Subsection 4.2.2. some of the potential benefits of immersive interaction and then in Subsection 4.2.3. some desirable interface qualities for immersive analytics, hopefully being more specific than Card *et al.* were able to be in their vision from a quarter of a century ago.

4.2.1. Motivating Examples of Immersive Interaction

A lot of the current excitement around immersion and Virtual Reality (VR) is centered around the new generation of VR headsets, their relatively low cost, and their potential for entertainment in the home. Among the rush of new software for these devices, there are some interesting examples of natural interaction design. For example, *Tilt Brush*[2] is a VR paint app for the HTC Vive from Google. Tilt Brush features an intuitive "palette" interface. The operator holds the virtual palette in their left hand and uses their right to select different brushes, colors, and other functionality. Different faces of the palette have different suites of tools.

Still in the consumer space, we now have examples of a commodity, functional Augmented Reality (AR) headset systems. The most prominent of them is the Microsoft *HoloLens* (see Figure 1). The HoloLens represents a significant advance on previous systems in being a fully self-contained (no tether) wearable computing device with sufficient computing power to render stereo 3D graphics and to provide accurate optical spatial and gesture tracking through on-board

[2] https://www.tiltbrush.com/

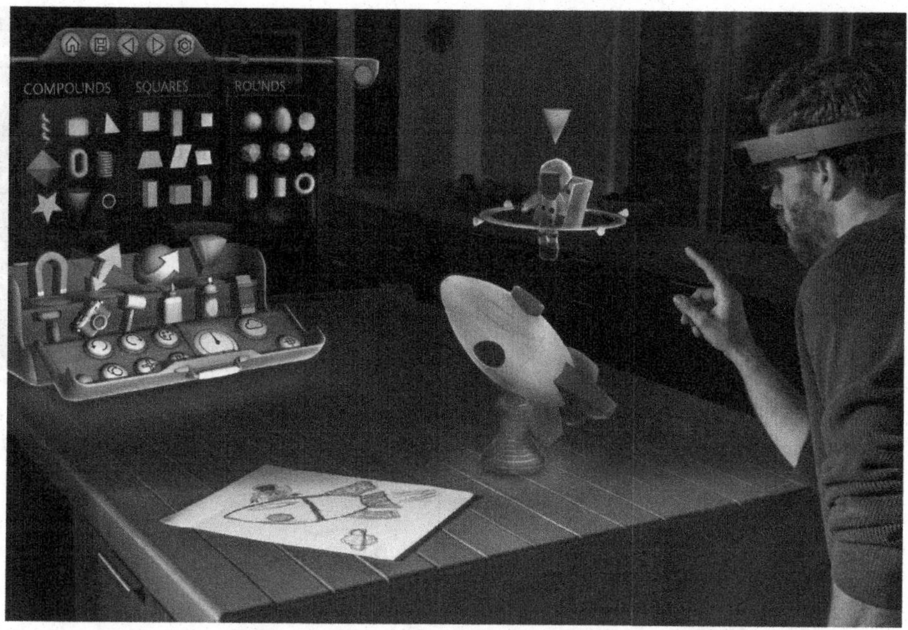

Fig. 1: Microsoft HoloLens is among a new generation of consumer-level Augmented Reality devices that feature interaction through gesture and voice recognition. *Courtesy Microsoft - used by permission.*

cameras and image processing. Other systems include Epson's *Moverio* and the *Meta* AR headsets.

Moving to more experimental interface devices, researchers are beginning to create fully dynamic physical display and interaction devices. MIT Media Lab's *InForm* system [50] is one compelling example, featuring a table mounted array of vertically actuated pins (see Figure 2). Potentiometers used for actuation can also detect input forces, and additional optical tracking of users' gestures is achieved via a Microsoft Kinect sensor. The creators give a number of mixed-reality and embodied interaction use-cases for such a system, including actuation of physical objects and devices placed on the surface, haptic input, and also data display and interaction. Input and output space being so closely intertwined, a sense of directness and engagement is created.

Another glimpse of possible future interaction technologies is offered by Google's experimental *Project Soli* (Figure 3). A radar sensor is used to demonstrate the accurate identification of fine, in-air hand and finger gestures not limited by the usual constraints of optical systems. The Soli radar sensor has been miniaturized to a single chip that can easily be incorporated into many different devices. Such devices can potentially increase the vocabulary and the precision of control available for immersive analytics tasks as described below.

Fig. 2: MIT Media Lab's InForm system is a fully dynamic tangible display and interaction device with many applications. *Courtesy Daniel Leithinger, Creative Commons License.*

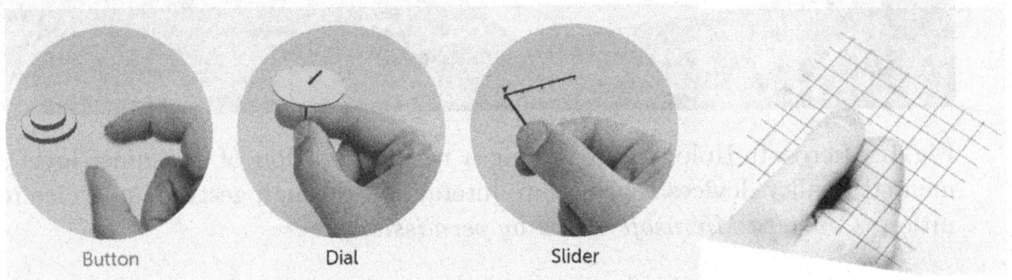

Fig. 3: Project Soli from Google is developing an experimental hardware device that uses radar to identify precise gestures. *Courtesy Ivan Poupyrev - used with permission.*

4.2.2. What Are Some Benefits of Immersion?

Talking about interaction for immersive analytics, one should not only ask how interaction can support visual analytics but also how *immersion* may improve interaction. In the following we look into some of these potential benefits.

Immersion → Presence → Engagement. Since at least the time of Slater and Wilbur's [135] work, the VR literature has made a distinction between *immersion* and *presence* (See Chapter 1). Presence is the user's sense of "being in" the virtual environment. Immersion is used to describe the technological affordances of the system that determine the degree of presence experienced by the user (*technological immersion*, see also the extended discussion on immersion and engagement in the introduction to this book). It is then assumed that greater immersion (or alternatively, "immersiveness") leads to a stronger sense of presence in the user, which leads to them being more engaged in the virtual experience [42].

In computer game design (psychological) "immersion" is used more freely as a synonym for "engagement," for example, as discussed by McMahan [110].

Further, it is understood to apply not only in games that are *spatially immersive* (by providing the user a first-person 3D view of the world), but in any game that is highly engaging. Games researchers differentiate additional dimensions of immersion independent of the spatial setting. For example, sensory-motoric immersion as identified by Bjork and Holopainen [16] is a function of the degree of ease with which the user can direct or interact with the game such that their motor skills are rewarded by immediate and appropriate feedback.

It is such questions of immersion related specifically to interaction, and ultimately how they affect people's presence and engagement with data analysis tasks, that are the concern of this chapter.

Embodiment. In his 2001 treatise [45], Paul Dourish gives a phenomenological motivation for exploring human-computer interaction paradigms that are *embodied.* Embodiment may be through physical affordances encoded in the design of the interface or the realization of the computing interface as a part of the built or social environment. While this is largely a philosophical argument rather than psychological, it is a compelling thesis that, since we are creatures evolved to thrive in a physical world, we are most engaged and effective when acting physically. Closely related to this are themes such as *proprioception* and *spatial memory* that describe how we perceive and understand our bodies and our environment. We will revisit this in Section 4.4. when we look into *Reality Based Interaction* and *Physical Navigation.*

Mobility. Until relatively recently, immersive and natural user interfaces were characterized by large, heavy lab equipment such as tethered AR and VR headsets, projected large walls (such as CAVE), or tabletops supporting multitouch interaction. The breakout technology for multitouch turned out not to be tables or walls, but small portable devices like smartphones and tablets. Most recently, untethered (in fact, fully self-contained) AR headsets like the HoloLens offer the promise of a new type of portable immersive computing. Long imagined scenarios for Augmented Reality are finally achievable with commercially available technology. An example is offering mechanics X-ray vision by overlaying a CAD model directly over the machine they are repairing [112], wherever they are, even outdoors or down a mine. In the future, AR headsets might also allow immersive information retrieval for serendipitous, context-aware search interfaces [25] and, in general, the possibility of *in-situ* data analytics in all kinds of new situations, as described in Chapter 7 on situated analytics.

With Augmented Reality and high-quality hand and environment tracking, every surface can become an interactive display. For example, where currently operations centers require workstations with large and expensive screens and interaction is typically done via conventional keyboard and mouse, in future all that may be required is for an operator to wear a headset. They can then surround themselves with arbitrarily large display "walls" and, for example in the case of emergencies, work from anywhere. Thus, the advantage in this example scenario is not primarily immersion but simply cost and convenience.

Collaborative visualization. One of the most exciting aspects of new display and interaction technologies is that they can potentially make it easier for people to work together. For example, head and body tracking offers remote collaborators the possibility of much greater presence in a shared environment. In the context of collaborative data exploration tasks, immersive display and interaction technologies offer users new ways to share and interact with information displays or to have their own private views and work areas. On the other hand, social interactions that follow from collaboration and make use of our social awareness and skills [73] can also increase user engagement and the feeling of presence in comparison to isolated desktop interfaces. However, many challenges remain for researchers in realizing this vision for collaborative data analytics, as described in Chapter 8 on collaboration.

Hands-free opportunities. Through voice or gaze control [115], for example, medical professionals can explore patient historical data, imagery or other records to better inform on the spot decisions, even during surgery. Similar hands-free interaction can offer machine operators or engineers additional diagnostic information via an HMD.

The 'ultimate display.' Sutherland's original vision imagined a distant future where: "The ultimate display would, of course, be a room within which the computer can control the existence of matter" [144]. While we have made advances in (for example) 3D printing, such technology remains out of reach. However, film-makers and animators (e. g., [19]) are beginning to imagine the potential of VR and AR that is indistinguishable from reality - which is now not such a remote future possibility.

4.2.3. Desirable Interface Qualities

There are many guidelines available for the design of user interfaces, probably the best known of which are those defined by Norman in his book "The Design of Everyday Things" [118]. While these are valuable design principles in general, the challenge is to reconsider them in the light of immersive and natural interaction. The focus of this section cannot be to state a complete list of requirements but only to suggest interface qualities that system designers may wish to consider.

For instance, *affordances* and *signifiers*, often misunderstood when talking about (virtual) user interfaces [116], become even more important when the user is interacting with an AR system that combines physical and virtual artifacts, and where the affordances of a real object may not always match the interface's signifiers. Similarly, in a system using VR headsets, *constraints* have to be designed with both the visualization itself in mind as well as the physical objects that naturally constrain the user's movement.

Elmqvist *et al.* [47] define fluidity in the context of visualization as an "elusive and intangible concept characterized by smooth, seamless, and powerful interaction; responsive, interactive and rapidly updated graphics; and careful, conscientious, and comprehensive user experience." They hypothesize that interactions that exhibit these types of characteristics will help users to stay in the flow, which is closely related to achieving a deeper sense of immersion. Thus, *Fluid Interaction* is particularly interesting in designing interaction for immersive analytics.

Elmqvist *et al.* present several design guidelines for creating visualization tools that support fluid interactions.

Use smooth animated transitions between states. Used appropriately, animated transitions can help the user maintaining a mental model of the system by avoiding abrupt switches between different modes. In the context of immersive systems, animations have to be handled with care. Forced viewport transitions, e. g., can easily lead to cybersickness.

Provide immediate visual feedback during interaction. Visual feedback should be provided in real-time for every interaction, including low-level interactions such as pressing a key or moving the mouse. This is especially true for continuous, direct input used in immersive analytics, such as head and body movement, gestures, or tracked 3D input devices.

Minimize indirection in the interface. In line with the concept of natural interaction, direct manipulation should be used whenever possible so that interaction operations become part of the visual representation instead of being separated out in control panels.

Integrate user interface components into the visual representation. If direct manipulation is not possible, try to integrate traditional user interface elements seamlessly. In immersive systems this also means to integrate 2D UIs in 3D environments. This poses challenges as to where to put them and how to cope with perspective distortion, occlusion, and text readability.

Reward interaction. Initially, the novelty of immersive systems may motivate users and thus "reward" them. However, this will quickly wear off with continued use. Interaction embodies a dialog between the user and system. Visual indications about how and when interactions can be performed can keep the user stimulated over the course of the exploration and act as rewarding effects.

Ensure that interaction never 'ends.' Continued exploration should always be possible and the user should never reach a dead end. At least regarding navigation, this is ensured in any immersive analytics systems in which the user freely moves through some virtual information space, e. g., in VR or AR environments.

Reinforce a clear conceptual model. Operations should be reversible to allow the user to return to a previous state and thus keep a clear idea of a system's state.

Avoid explicit mode changes. Mode changes may break the user's flow and should be avoided. If possible, all operations should be integrated and accessible in the same mode.

In addition, there are also *technical requirements* to immersive systems. These include a decent, real-time responsive tracking of the environment and, if applicable, good multi-modal interaction – voice, touch, gesture, eye-gaze, or head tracking. One area in which interaction technologies have seen major improvements that directly affect their immersion is in terms of *latency*, that is, the delay between the user initiating an action and receiving feedback from the system.

Other challenges include scalable interaction, issue of attention management and awareness, as well as unifying multiple device classes while coordinating interactions across devices.

4.3. Basic Tasks for Analytics

This section describes fundamental tasks for interactive visualizations and refers to existing task taxonomies in the literature. These tasks need to be supported by an immersive analytics user interface, and we will use them to anchor the discussion on designing interactions for immersive analytics in Section 4.5..

There exist several taxonomies that capture the individual activities users perform when using visualizations for exploring and understanding any kind of datasets. Most of these taxonomies cover a related set of concepts: Amar and Stasko [2], for instance, describe a set of low-level components gathered by observing students interacting with visualizations, while Heer and Shneiderman [55] break down that interaction into view specification and manipulation. In this chapter, we use the latter taxonomy as a basis for exploring the design of interactions for immersive analytics (see Section 4.5.) due to its focus on interactive dynamics in visual analytics. We review that taxonomy in the following paragraphs and refer the reader to the literature to learn more about alternative interaction taxonomies that range from more general (e. g., [98,154]) to more specific taxonomies (e. g., with a focus on multivariate network analysis [122]).

Heer and Shneiderman [55] distinguish between three high-level categories: (1) *data and view specification* that essentially corresponds to the data transformation and visual mapping steps in the Information Visualization Reference Model proposed by Card *et al.* [30], (2) *view manipulation* that is reflected by the view transformation step in the Information Visualization Reference Model, and finally (3) *process and provenance* for supporting analysis processes.

The category *data and view specification* can be further subdivided into the following lower-level tasks.

Encode/Visualize. Here, the analyst chooses a suitable visualization or visual representation for the data records, i. e., this is the actual creation of the visualization.

Filter. A visualization becomes more scalable by filtering out data records based on specific criteria. A popular interaction technique is dynamic queries, for example.

Sort. This task corresponds to the already mentioned basic interactions mentioned before. Sorting data items is good for many purposes, such as item lists ordered according to measurements (centrality measures, degree-of-interest, etc.).

Derive. The task of deriving information from the primary input data is more related to visual analytics than to pure visualization. For example, the analyst might want to integrate results from automatic computations (aggregations, clusterings, simulations, etc.) into the visual display.

Kerren and Schreiber [85] extended this category by two additional tasks that both address typical interactions needed in visual analytics:

Reconfigure. Changing or reconfiguring the graphical display for specific data records during the analysis process is a standard task performed by analysts.

Adjust. When deriving secondary data from the primary input data, the analyst usually has to modify parameter settings of automated analyses.

The second category discussed by Heer and Shneiderman is *view manipulation* as summarized below.

Select. Selection is a fundamental interaction concept that is often used prior to a filter operation.

Navigate/Explore. One of the core tasks that reflects very well the explorative character of Information Visualization. Navigation and exploration approaches often follow the information-seeking mantra *overview first, zoom and filter, then details on demand* [134] and encompass methods such as focus & context, zooming & panning, semantic zooming, etc.

Coordinate/Connect. In visual analytics systems, analysts are often enabled to relate views or even individual graphical entities to each other. Brushing and linking can then be used to build a bridge between connected views/items.

Organize. More complex visual analytics tools consist of many different components, views, or tabs. These components have to be arranged and grouped on the screen in such a way that the resulting arrangement supports the analysis process efficiently.

The last category on *process and provenance* goes beyond the most traditional information visualization taxonomies as it addresses typical issues that are more related to supporting the analysis process in general, and not tasks specifically related to interactive visualization. We briefly describe the tasks in this category here following that of Ragan *et al.* [124], but cover them in more detail in Chapter 5 where we discuss them in the context of *visual analytics*.

Record. Visualization tools should keep a *record* of the analysts' operations throughout the analysis process. Then, various interactions should be provided to allow them to step back through this record in order to understand the provenance of individual findings. At the very least such stepping is enabled by *undo/redo* operations, but more sophisticated analysis of the provenance, e. g., visualization of operations against a timeline, may also be beneficial.

Annotate. Adding labels, highlights or other annotations to visualizations allows analysts to keep track of significant insights in the context in which they were found. This is useful for explaining the results of an analysis to others, but also, again, to support the analyst's own working memory of the provenance of insights.

Share. Visualization can be a great aid to collaborative analysis, enabling communication about data as well as visual inspection. Thus, tools should support the sharing of various views together with the provenance history and annotations described above in order to make such collaboration as easy as possible. Collaborative visual analytics in the context of immersive systems is described in great detail in Chapter 8.

Guide. A particularly important use-case of shared visualization is guided explanation of insights within a dataset. To support this scenario, tools should enable generation of visualizations that are static yet self-explanatory (i. e., like the kind of infographics found in news-media reports), animated, or stepped interactions for guided presentation. Enabling such *storytelling* scenarios as effectively as possible is becoming a research area in its own right and is discussed in greater detail in Chapter 6.

We will instantiate a subset of these tasks for the concrete case of immersive analytics in Section 4.5.: select, filter, sort, navigate, reconfigure, and annotate. The next section introduces basic novel interaction modalities, their opportunities and limitations, and their contribution to engagement and immersion.

4.4. Natural User Interfaces (NUI) and Post WIMP Interaction

Interaction techniques for immersive analytics have to be powerful enough to support users in all the tasks mentioned in the previous section, while at the same time not distracting them from their work or breaking immersion. Techniques based on the WIMP metaphor or most classic 3D input devices (see, e. g., [98]) are usually not suitable for interaction in immersive environments. Several of their limitations were listed by van Dam [43]: WIMP interfaces are increasingly complex, can lead to screen clutter, and are inherently indirect, especially for 3D interaction. Maybe even more important for immersive analytics, they are primarily designed for use on desktop computers and do not make use of our rich senses and input capabilities. Novel post-WIMP interfaces are filling this gap. They are typically defined as containing at least one non-classical form of input (e. g., touch, gestures, speech, or tangibles), mostly process parallel input streams, and often support multiple users. They are closely connected to the concept of *Natural User Interfaces* (NUI) introduced earlier in Section 4.1.. Dachselt & Preim define NUIs as "those interfaces where people interact with by means of intuitive and mostly direct actions grounded in real-world, everyday human behavior. Natural does not mean innate but learned and familiar actions, which appear appropriate to the user in the moment of interaction." [121, p. 472] (translated by Dachselt & Preim). While there is certainly some overlap between the terms post-WIMP and NUI, post-WIMP is a term defined by the forms of input [43] but NUI is about creating an interface that "makes your user act and feel like a natural." [152, p. 14] It should also be noted that what makes an interface "natural" is debatable, and the term *Natural User Interface* itself has also been criticized, e. g., by Norman [117].

An overview of NUIs as well as guidelines on how to design them are given by Wigdor & Wixon [152] and Fikkert *et al.* [49]. One framework of post-WIMP interaction that is closely related to NUIs is the concept of *Reality Based*

Interaction [73], which was proposed by Jacob *et al.* in 2008. They identify four main themes from the real world that inform and inspire the design of post-WIMP interfaces:

- *Naïve Physics*, informal, common sense knowledge about the physical world, including aspects such as inertia, gravity, etc.
- *Body Awareness & Skills*, the user's ability to control and be aware of their own movement and the position of their limbs (proprioception).
- *Environment Awareness & Skills*, e. g., the ability to select or grasp objects, and estimate distances or sizes of objects.
- *Social Awareness & Skills*, knowledge about social protocols and the ability to collaborate with other people.

In the specific context of Information Visualization, post-WIMP interaction was analyzed both by Lee *et al.* [100] and Jansen & Dragicevic [78]. Lee *et al.* examined design considerations for "natural" information visualization interactions regarding the individual, the technology being used, social interactions between users, and the relation of technology and the user. Based on those considerations, they also identified opportunities and challenges for NUIs in information visualization. Jansen & Dragicevic adapted and extended the well-known information visualization pipeline for visualizations that go beyond the desktop. They also proposed a visual notation for interactive visualization systems that they applied to different case studies of post-WIMP visualization setups.

In the following, we describe different relevant interaction modalities in more detail. While we focus on NUI, it should be noted that there is also a large body of more "classical" 3D interaction research, including the fields of VR and AR. Here, more traditional 3D input devices such as ART's Flystick, VR controllers, or even Wii Remotes are being used. These input devices, especially when bundled and natively supported by commercial VR headsets, provide stable and tested means of input and are often well-suited for immersive 3D interaction. Besides the general overview of 3D user interfaces, including 3D input devices, by LaViola *et al.* [98], an overview of (non-immersive) 3D interaction is given by Jankowski and Hachet [76]. A recent survey of Augmented Reality, including a chapter on interaction, was written by Billinghurst *et al.* [15]. In Section 4.4.2., we discuss typical limitations of 3D interaction.

4.4.1. Interaction Modalities

Let us first introduce and discuss the major non-classical interaction methodologies that are commonly used in immersive visualization. Most of them are inspired by how we typically interact with everyday objects, hence the label "natural interaction techniques" sometimes attributed to them. In our case, however, we are interested mostly in how well they support immersion in the visualization task and how well they maintain (and do not interrupt) the flow.

Touch-based (tactile) interaction. Along with the surge of touch-sensing display technologies and hardware of the past two decades came a plethora of work on its application to interactive data exploration. Because a two-dimensional touch surface lends itself intuitively to the manipulation of 2D representations, a large number of touch interaction paradigms were explored for visualization subfields that represent data typically in the two-dimensional plane [100]. However, interaction techniques for inherently three-dimensional datasets have also been explored [67, 84], either for monoscopically (e. g., [52,105,155–157]) or stereoscopically displayed data (e. g., [38,72,103]). The benefits of haptic feedback are typically cited as a benefit supporting the use of touch interaction as opposed to traditional PC-based environments. In particular, somesthetic feedback [129] gives people the feeling that they actually are manipulating items and, thus, increases the immersion into the interaction with the data. A survey of touch interaction techniques, even if just for the application of data visualization, would be beyond the scope of this text, so we refer to the recent survey by Isenberg & Isenberg [66].

Sketching and pen Interaction. Pen interaction with computers actually predates mouse interaction. Widely regarded as a precursor to hyperlinking (and eventually, therefore, the web), Vannevar Bush's 1945 concept for an electromechanical document exploration machine (the *Memex*) featured a stylus for annotations [27]. Sutherland's Sketchpad system [143] was an early demonstration of interactive computer support for technical drawing built around a light-pen system. However, the practicality and ergonomics of holding a tethered pen up to a vertical screen for extended periods of time meant that pen computing took a long time to find favor. Chen *et al.* studied the use of a hand-held tablet as a remote control for viewpoint control and search tasks in an immersive CAVE environment [36]. They found that the tablet's mobility helps reduce context switching cost due to the form factor of the tablet input. In more recent years, the development of tabletop and smart board computing, smaller tablet devices, and the gradual advancement in machine recognition of hand-writing and drawings has led to renewed interest in pen-based interaction (e. g., [51, 59]).

Much more recently, information visualization researchers have begun examining how people communicate about data and complex systems by sketching on whiteboards. In a study of whiteboard sketches found throughout a large organization, Walny *et al.* found many instances of whiteboards being used to manually create quite sophisticated information visualizations, such as charts and diagrams [150]. Clearly, whiteboards are ubiquitous in workplaces and classrooms, but besides being cheap and convenient there are a number of other aspects that make them ideal in supporting people as they communicate complex ideas, for example, people seem very comfortable organizing their thoughts spatially on a whiteboard in a very freeform way. The observation that people routinely think and communicate about data visually by sketching has led to automated systems for integrating computer-generated charts into people's hand-drawn sketches.

Tangible interaction and data physicalization. As an alternative to touch interaction, tangible user interfaces, first introduced in the 1990s [70,133], have also been explored for the control of data exploration. Early examples focused, in particular, on tangible controls for traditional interfaces (e. g., [58,71]) and on geographical visualization (e. g., [69,119]). For the exploration of spatial data, in particular data defined in 3D space, several approaches demonstrated that tangible interaction can be useful by maintaining the spatial mapping between the exploration tool and a physical representation of the data (e. g., [13, 53, 94, 95]). Some recent work has even demonstrated the use of shape(-changing) displays (e. g., [102]). Beyond spatial data, however, a number of authors has also demonstrated the usefulness of tangible interaction with abstract data representations (e. g., [37, 77, 93, 137]). A closely related form of interaction is the exploration of physical visualizations [79]. In fact, it can be argued that there is a continuum from completely virtual/digital, via tangible interaction, to physical interaction [77].

The advantages of tangible interaction over, in particular, touch interaction lie in the physical nature of the manipulated tokes, facilitating a richer expression of interaction intents than touch interfaces. On the other hand, most tangible interfaces are highly specific, inferior to the flexibility offered by fully digital touch interfaces. The previously mentioned shape displays [50, 102] as well as recent micro-robotic technology (e. g., [99]), however, promise to make tangible or physical data displays more flexible.

Gestural interaction. Gestures are a form of non-verbal communication, often accompanying or sometimes even replacing speech. We use them, for example, to point at objects, to illustrate concepts, or to support cadence. Many taxonomies for gestures exist, such as by McNeill [111] or Karam & schraefel [82]. With gestures being part of our daily lives, gestural interaction systems can feel natural and intuitive. As such, gestures have been proposed for HCI at least since the 1980s [17]. An advantage of such interfaces is that they allow manipulation from a distance without physical contact or the use of any hand-held input device. Hence, they lend themselves for settings such as large display installations [109], public displays [151], or medical applications demanding sterility [80].

An early example in the field of data visualization is the *Information Cube* by Rekimoto & Green [126], a cuboid visualization of hierarchical data. Users wearing datagloves can rotate the visualization to inspect it from all sides and select nodes using hand gestures. Kirmizibayrak *et al.* [87] used gestures to control a visualization of medical volume data. Their studies show that gestures can outperform mouse interaction in rotation tasks. Chen *et al.* designed a set of numerical input techniques to model architectural modeling process [34], ranged from virtual sliders [35] to virtual keypad and gestural input [33]. Hybrid interfaces that combine 2D multi-touch and 3D gestural interaction have been examined by Benko *et al.* [12]. New and affordable depth-sensing cameras such as the *Kinect* or the *Leap Motion* allow gestural interaction to be included in consumer products and, at the same time, also provide researchers with the means to develop low-cost prototypes for this interaction modality. Despite this, several challenges remain. Gestural interaction is often perceived as unergonomic and can easily lead to fatigue (casually called the gorilla-arm effect [57], see also Subsection 4.4.2.). Similar to touch gestures, free-hand gestures also lack discoverability and usually have to be learned and trained for effective use. Finally, one has to acknowledge that gesture recognition accuracy affects user performance and is also negatively affected by the strategies that users adopt to deal with recognition errors [5].

While we often associate it with hand gestures, the term "gesture" can be applied to many other forms of input. For example, foot gestures [106], touch gestures (see above), and even gestures made with physical props, pens, 3D controllers, or other devices (part of tangible interaction, see above) can be found. However, the use of the term "gestural interaction"—in particular in the context of data visualization—has also been criticized [68]: both the task specification and the parameter manipulation during exploration can and are specified using gestural interaction, but both have different constraints. In particular, for immersive interaction, the specification of the task should happen in an instance in order to not interrupt a user's thought processes, and the transition from task specification to parameter control needs to be fluid. An example for this are the *MultiLenses* by Kister *et al.* [89]. There, graph lenses are instantiated with a gesture and the main parameter can be immediately manipulated by continuing this gesture in a fluid way.

Gaze interaction. Eye-tracking systems are often used for psychological studies or to evaluate user interfaces; an overview of eye tracking specifically for the *evaluation of visual analytics* is given in [97]. However, already in the 1980s, the first *gaze interaction* interfaces were presented. One such system is Bolt's *Gaze-Orchestrated Dynamic Windows* [18]. In this system, several video streams were presented on a single large display. By looking at a particular video, the user could start or stop the playback.

The main advantage of gaze interaction is that it does not rely on the user's hands. As such, gaze interaction is regularly used in systems for the physically disabled (e. g., [64]). However, as Bolt's system shows, gaze can also be used as a natural interaction technique to indicate a person's attention or simply keep their hands free for other tasks.

Early eye trackers were cumbersome and required the user to be stationary. However, advances in mobile eye tracking hardware now make it possible to, e. g., integrate them into commercial VR headsets[3], enabling their use in immersive analytics applications. Measuring (and reacting to) the user's attention is a key aspect of *Attentive User Interfaces* [148], an interface strategy that tries to address information overload. Also, visualizing a user's awareness can be helpful in collaborative systems. For example, coarse eye tracking is used by Dostal *et al.* [44] to measure awareness in a collaborative visualization system using large, wall-sized displays.

When gaze interaction is used directly as an input method, it is often combined with other modalities. While it is possible to design interfaces that solely or mainly use gaze (e. g., Adams *et al.* [1] presented techniques to explore large 2D information spaces using gaze), both precision and efficiency can be hampered by gaze interaction. Rapid, small eye movements (saccades) limit the precision of the eye gaze. The duality of using eyes as an input channel versus their normal task as

[3] See, e. g., https://www.tobiipro.com/product-listing/vr-integration/

the most important human sense is another limitation of gaze interaction, leading to problems such as the so-called *Midas Touch*: Do users of a gaze interaction interface look at an object or UI element to trigger an action after a certain dwell-time or just to visually inspect it? Additional modalities, e. g., touch, are used to circumvent these limitations. We call such interfaces *gaze-supported* [139]. Stellmach *et al.* [140] presented a system for the gaze-supported exploration of large image databases. Employing a large remote display, gaze was used to control a fisheye lens and fine target selection was done using a multitouch device. A combination of gaze and foot input was used by Klamka *et al.* [91] to explore zoomable information spaces, in this case Google Earth. Still, gaze-based pointing methods, including gaze-supported input with the (space) button for confirmation, can currently not match the performance achievable with a mouse for pointing tasks [107] on smaller screens.

An overview of eye tracking technology and applications including many more examples of gaze interfaces can be found in Majaranta & Bulling's survey [108]. Cernea and Kerren provide a survey article on technologies for emotion-enhanced interaction that also discusses basics of eye tracking technologies [32].

Physical navigation and locomotion. A key advantage of immersive analytics is the ability to display a large amount of information, potentially across multiple levels of scale. This provides the opportunity to navigate this information efficiently through physical or virtual means. Information foraging theory [120] models the cost of information access, and suggests office and computational metaphors in which frequently accessed information is kept nearby and can be accessed through quick operations, at the expense of less frequently used information stored at greater "distances". The concept of "information scent" models the visual hints that guide the user in finding and accessing targeted data in an information space.

Physical navigation exploits human embodiment to navigate the information space directly via body movement, such as head rotation to naturally control the view frustum. In contrast, virtual navigation uses some form of indirect interactive control to manipulate the viewpoint, such as a joystick. Beyond this binary categorization, a spectrum of fidelity of interaction ranges from high-fidelity that mimic real-world interactions to low-fidelity that do not attempt to mimic real-world behavior [98]. Jakobsen *et al.* [74] explored interaction techniques based on the spatial relationship of a user and large visualizations, including the adaptation of the visualization based on the user's position.

In immersive analytics, physical navigation spans two primary levels of scale. Micro-level physical navigation consists primarily of efficient rotational movements of the eyes, head, and body, to rotate the view frustum in the space, and can also include limited translational movements, such as leaning. These forms of physical navigation are very efficient and have been shown to be advantageous over virtual navigation, in terms of both access time as well as improving cognitive understanding of spatial relationships in the data [9]. This is typically implemented using head-mounted displays combined with head tracking, or large high-resolution fixed displays with or without head tracking.

Macro-level physical navigation deals with translational movement for locomotion in the space. Physical navigation for locomotion, such as walking, is typically limited due to the range of the tracked interaction space or the physical size of the display device. Exceptions include Augmented Reality methods based on GPS or computer vision in which users navigate the real world. Hence, longer range locomotion in immersive environments often requires some form of simulated physical navigation, such as walking in place or treadmills, or virtual navigation methods such as teleportation or joystick control [98].

4.4.2. Challenges and Fundamental Limitations of 3D Interaction

In many cases, immersive analytics applications may involve 3D data sets or 3D input and output technology. While the idea of interacting directly in 3D is attractive, many currently available solutions are often not practical and/or inefficient. In this subsection, we list a couple of common issues around 3D interaction that affect interaction performance in non-trivial ways.

One commonly held thought posits that human or technology limits could be easily addressed through navigation or better interaction methods. Yet, this is rarely true in a general sense. For example, interaction-at-a-distance, i. e., ray-based pointing (e. g., [81]), is fundamentally limited by the fact that pointing accuracy is negatively affected by limitations of orientation tracking or human limits on hand stability. Then, any inaccuracies in orientation result in errors that increase with distance. While techniques such as snapping the ray to the nearest target [4] can compensate for this in some instances, such solutions do not scale to dense object arrangements or work for large distances. Moreover, the cost for undoing incorrect selections through snapping is also often ignored. Disambiguation interfaces that temporarily magnify content to facilitate selection achieve this through an increase in interaction cost. Another way to compensate for pointing inaccuracies is to navigate to a position where the problem becomes simpler, e. g., by moving closer to the desired objects. This is true, but this solution adds the cost of navigation to the interaction, which again increases time. The user may then also have to spend additional time to navigate back to the original position. For interfaces that mix interaction and navigation modes, there is also the insidious issue that the need to switch between interaction and navigation increases the potential for mode errors.

Spatial abilities, especially for 3D, are learned skills, which include spatial perception (important for 3D navigation), mental rotation (important for 3D rotation), spatial visualization (important for planning 3D operations), and spatial working memory (important for 3D creation). Such abilities correlate well with STEM (Science, Technology, Engineering, and Mathematics) performance [149], which is only high in a limited subset of the general population. As the spatial abilities of the general population are below the levels observed in the STEM subpopulation, this fundamentally affects the potential generalizability of any interface that requires good spatial interaction skills.

Another fundamental issue is that one cannot interact with occluded content with any degree of precision, as the feedback loop that is central to human actions (and HCI) is disrupted. This is commonly visible in the real world, where only highly-trained users can manipulate things they cannot see directly with precision. Again, one can compensate for this through interaction or navigation techniques, but only at additional cost.

The human visual system can only focus on a single plane at any given time. In practice this means that one can either focus on the finger/hand or on a display, but not both simultaneously (unless they are close in depth), e. g., [23]. This fundamentally limits interaction accuracy that is achievable away from a display surface, including common stereo display and Augmented Reality systems. A related issue is the vergence-accommodation conflict, e. g., [60], which is the inability of commonly used stereo display systems, including head-mounted displays for Virtual Reality, to allow correct eye-vergence and focal distance for the perceived objects. This conflict affects depth perception, which in turn impacts interaction performance negatively. An easily observable symptom is that users start to "search" for the correct depth of a target in stereo display systems or that the distributions of hit points for 3D target shows an elongated profile in the depth dimension [24], which affects pointing performance [22]. Finally, any form of human stereo vision deficiency also affects interaction performance with systems that rely on accurate depth perception through stereo. Some researchers estimate that more than 30% of the population may have some form of stereo deficiency [56]. Moreover, as people age, average stereo acuity decreases, too [160]. This puts some limits on stereo-based systems being a general form of user interface mechanism.

Throughput is a good measure to characterize interaction performance, as it takes both speed and accuracy in pointing tasks in to account. Thus, throughput enables comparisons across different user strategies, such as slow and accurate vs. fast and sloppy. In terms of throughput, a mouse or touchscreen is significantly better than any currently available 3D interaction device (see, e. g., [20,21,23,146]). While interaction speed in 3D is usually not much affected, interaction accuracy is typically much worse. The list of reasons for this include the lack of human hand stability in mid-air interaction, 3D tracking limitations, depth perception limitations, or any combination thereof. Thus, it is a particular challenge to achieve interaction that feels natural yet is accurate enough.

Interaction in 3D typically involves more than two degrees of freedom (DOF). One good option to address this issue is to reduce the number of degrees of freedom through the use of constraints [132,141,142]

Another issue affecting interaction with 3D is the "gorilla-arm" syndrome, i. e., the fact that holding one's hands in the air for extended periods of time leads to fatigue and all its associated side-effects [57,75].

Finally, interaction through a single cursor, pen-tip or even multiple touch point(s) on a touch screen is much less rich compared to the interaction capabilities posed by human hands. One illustrative example is achieving the task of tying one's shoe-laces with any computer-based system.

4.5. Designing Interactions for Immersive Analytics

After describing the typical tasks associated with visual analytics in Section 4.3. and discussing different interaction modalities and their limitations in Section 4.4., we can now combine them and map techniques to tasks. Guidelines such as presented in Section 4.2.3., e. g., Elmqvist's fluid interaction concepts [47], can be used to inform the design of these interactions. This section outlines a first attempt at matching tasks to interaction techniques. Where appropriate, we explain how fluid interaction can be supported by these mappings. It should be noted that the following should only be seen as initial proposals, showing the opportunities of rich, fluid interaction for immersive analytics.

Selection: Selection is the basis for determining on what elements many subsequent analytic tasks operate. These tasks can include selection of data for more information, reconfiguring of elements, or sorting along a dimension. In immersive environments, techniques such as mouse interaction are not appropriate. Gestural interaction (e. g., pointing to and circling an element) can be used, though mid-air gesturing can be fatiguing. Great care should be taken to minimize strain on the user, e. g., by designing comfortable gestures [57] or providing alternative forms of input. For example, voice along with Natural Language Processing (NLP) can be used to indicate attributes and ranges of interest (e. g., 'Select all elements with negative profit') but is itself less suitable for selecting or deselecting individual elements. Eye-gaze, on the other hand, is well suited to indicate the user's point of regard and can be used to choose an object of interest, though *Midas Touch* usually means that other modalities would need to be engaged to choose the appropriate interaction (e. g., a button press on a VR controller or a voice command). Multi-selection techniques such as lasso selection can in principle be used with each modality that provides a form of pointer, e. g., touch, pen, mid-air pointing, or to some extent gaze. These techniques can provide *immediate, continuous feedback* [104]. It may not be enough to just separate out selections from the subsequent activity since some interactions may involve combining the act of selecting with that subsequent activity to design more fluid interactions [46]. Some work has also been done in combining multiple devices (touch displays, tablets) with immersive displays for more fine-tuned control.

Filter: If items to be filtered are already known, filtering is simply the triggering of an operation and can be accomplished through a semantic gesture (e. g., a wave of the hand), or voice. Filtering often is either used to filter out selected objects, or filter out all non-selected objects. The act of specifying the query may be combined with the interaction itself (e. g., from voice, we might filter out all values less than the average or focus only on outliers). On the other hand, in some cases, filtering needs to be dynamic. For example, a user would like to remove outliers to remove visual clutter in a complex dataset but does not yet have a clear understanding of what constitutes outliers in the specific data. In such use cases, *continuous* changes of the filter threshold and *smooth transitions* between filtered and unfiltered views may be required to keep the *flow of interaction.* Many natural interaction techniques, like hand or body movements, support continuous input with, however, varying degrees of precision.

Sort: Typically, a sort action is specified by an attribute upon which the data is to be sorted. This attribute may already be selected (see above), or selected during the sort. Some work involved a gesture on a surface or in mid-air, by starting the gesture on a particular axis [46]. Voice can be used as well. Sorting typically involves specifying whether the order is ascending or descending by value, or in some other order (e. g., alphabetical). Using *smooth transitions* to the new order can help users to track both individual items and the general arrangement. While these animations can also easily be triggered after discrete input events (such as a voice command or a button press), continuous input techniques allow for immediate, continuous feedback and may help users to abort erroneous sorting operations.

Navigation: There is a wide history of research on navigating through virtual environments (e. g., [98]) and many of these techniques apply here. Physical navigation, i. e., the user literally moving to change the view on the data, has been examined, e. g., for wall-sized display setups [9, 90]. Walking closer to data in a space can allow precise inspection of details while walking back allows for an overview. Additionally, Rädle *et al.* [123] studied the effect of physical navigation in zoomable user interfaces on large display walls and found not only benefits for navigation performance but also evidence of improved spatial memory. Limited space can be problematic for physical navigation in large datasets. Especially in VR, techniques such as teleporting the user to a new position can help to increase the apparent size of the interaction volume. These techniques, however, are potentially immersion breaking and can negatively affect the user's *mental model.* Gestural interactions can be used such as to shrink or zoom the overall world, or rotate it to a more appropriate view. Maps can be used in conjunction with a visualization to assist in navigating a large visualization.

Proxies that represent the data and make it more tangible can be used if orienting the data is of particular use. For example, Beaudouin-Lafon *et al.* [11] used a prop of a human brain to rotate MRI data on a large display wall, similar to those used by Hinckley *et al.* [58]. Similarly, hand-held devices that serve as peepholes into the virtual scene (e. g., [26, 137]) can be moved around to navigate the visualization.

Reconfiguration: Reconfiguration often includes assigning attributes to visual variables, e. g., to the axes of a visualization. While voice interaction can in principle be used for this task, this requires the correct recognition of spoken, previously unknown data attribute names. A good example of gestural reconfiguration is the ImAxes [39] project. In this HMD-based VR system, users can rearrange data axes with the VR controllers to compose different visualizations, e. g., scatterplots or parallel coordinates. This demonstrates how a close coupling between the user interface and the visual representation can be beneficial: Instead of *explicitly* switching between modes, users can *directly manipulate* the type of visualization and get *immediate system feedback*.

Labeling and annotating: Annotating data, assigning labels or highlighting parts of a visualization are important actions supporting the discussion and analysis of the data. Text input can be supported by voice recognition. Alternatively and depending on the setup, touch keyboards on personal mobile devices or displayed on a shared interactive display can be used as well. Pen input has also been proposed to annotate visualizations directly, e. g., using tangible lenses with Anoto technology [137]. An overview and a taxonomy of annotations in (outdoor) Augmented Reality has been presented by Wither *et al.* [153].

Given the mappings above, we can identify some fundamental interaction types that can be combined to create higher order interactions. We need to support selection of data and visualization elements. Similarly, we need to support discrete choices from lists. Whenever these items are graphically represented in the system, some form of *pointing* can be used to indicate/choose them, with options such as 3D input devices, touch, gaze, or mid-air pointing. Confirmation can then either use the same modality or a different form of interaction in multi-modal interfaces, e. g., gaze selection with voice confirmation. On the other hand, discrete items (including mode switches) can also be selected by more *symbolic, discrete input methods* such as voice commands, symbolic mid-air gestures, etc. Examples such as multi-selection or camera manipulation show the need for *continuous interaction*. Clearly, voice commands do not lend themselves for this type of interaction. Instead, touch, tracked 3D input devices, some forms of gestures, and physical navigation are good examples for continuous control.

4.6. Archetypal Setups

Systems for immersive analytics can take many and varied forms, including, for example, differences in the number, size, and types of displays used as well as input devices. In this section, some typical setups (i. e., combinations of output and input technology) that showcase this variety are described along with example research applications and upcoming trends. It is worth noting that many of these systems have, to date, seen more active use in Scientific Visualization applications than in the visualization of abstract data, i. e., Information Visualization.

4.6.1. Large Screen Collaborative Space

Large screens, especially wall-sized vertical displays and to lesser degree tabletops, provide the space needed to show complex datasets in their entirety. Their size also gives room for several people to interact with them at once. Therefore, setups of one or more large displays have been used extensively for collaborative visual analytics tasks.

This archetype has several challenges both regarding interaction and perception. One issue is that metaphors for interaction close to the display, e. g.,

Fig. 4: Distribution of a visual analytics system across different display geometries [92].

using touch, often cannot be applied directly to interaction from afar using, e. g., gestures. Another interaction challenge of such systems is to differentiate between the input of individual users. Different methods for touch user identification have been proposed, such as optical tracking in front of display walls [159], capacitive fingerprinting [54], or active IR beacons [130]. Awareness, both in regard to the display content and the collaborators' actions, is more of a perceptional challenge: While standing close to the display, other users and parts of the display can be blocked or simply outside the user's field of view. Stepping back to get an overview, on the other hand, prevents users from direct interaction with the display and may limit inspection of small details in the data as well.

In the last decade, the costs of display panels have fallen sharply. In 2007, LCD panels larger than 40" were not available commercially. Plasma panels larger than 50" cost in excess of USD 5,000 and weighed as much as a person (e. g., [131]). In 2017, full HD 50" LCD panels can be bought for only a few hundred dollars and weigh only a few kilograms. Ultra High Definition (UHD) panels with $3,840 \times 2,160$ resolution are only a little more expensive. Further, multiple software solutions now exist to provide *cluster rendering*, the capability to split the responsibility of rendering a continuous 2D desktop or 3D environment across a number of networked machines, each driving its own set of display panels.[4] Thus, the cost and difficulty of creating tiled display walls with arrays of such panels have fallen dramatically and with this increased convenience, researchers

[4] Popular cluster rendering software includes OmegaLib [48], Unity [147], and Sage2 [127].

have begun to investigate the opportunities for visual analytics using such display walls.

In an experimental study evaluating tiled vertical displays of various sizes for visual analytics tasks, Ball and North [8] found that small targets could be acquired and compared significantly more quickly on larger walls. A later, more qualitative study by Andrews *et al.* [3], found that analysts change their approach to managing documents and information when moving from a standard desktop display to a larger, tiled display. Basically, they use a more spatial approach to document organization, structuring the display space to externalize their analysis process.

In addition to the physical area, the other important property of display walls (compared to, for example, large projected displays) is their resolution. Ni *et al.*'s work is among the first to empirically demonstrate the benefits of high-resolution display for information search with text in spatial data [114]. With clustered rendering, resolution is theoretically unlimited. In practice, the cluster architecture has to provide a scalable way to distribute the data to the nodes and, from each node, to render only the part of the view needed for that node. Using this method researchers have been able to investigate new ideas to take advantage of massive resolution spread across a large wall. For example, Isenberg *et al.* [65] create static visualizations that allow inspection of very fine-grained detail when standing close to the wall, but on stepping further back, gross details (labels for larger regions and so forth that were blurred and therefore "hidden in plain sight" when standing close) become apparent (see Figure 5).

These results suggest that high-resolution, large-area display walls can change the interaction paradigm for data analytics, especially with respect to the task of navigation as described in Section 4.3.. That is, to some degree, the user(s) of large display walls are able to navigate by changing their physical position with respect to the data displayed, rather than changing the viewpoint through an interaction device. Arguably, the most "natural" user interface is no interface at all.

4.6.2. Personal Displays + Large Screen Collaborative Space

Setups consisting of one or more large displays can be combined with individual, personal displays. Typically, these personal displays come in the form of handheld smartphones or tablets. For example, several scenarios (and infrastructure to support those scenarios) are explored by Klapperstuck *et al.* [92] for multi-site collaboration, using a shared large area display wall together with handheld and tabletop devices for interaction. However, arguably any additional display (e. g., AR glasses or smartwatches) used by one person in addition to the main display(s) fits this category. An example is the system presented by Butscher *et al.* [28], which combines a large multitouch table with several HMDs for the collaborative analysis of multidimensional data.

This combination can help to address some of the challenges of large display immersive analytics systems: The use of personal devices and their own interaction capabilities provides an additional, independent view for the user and also allows

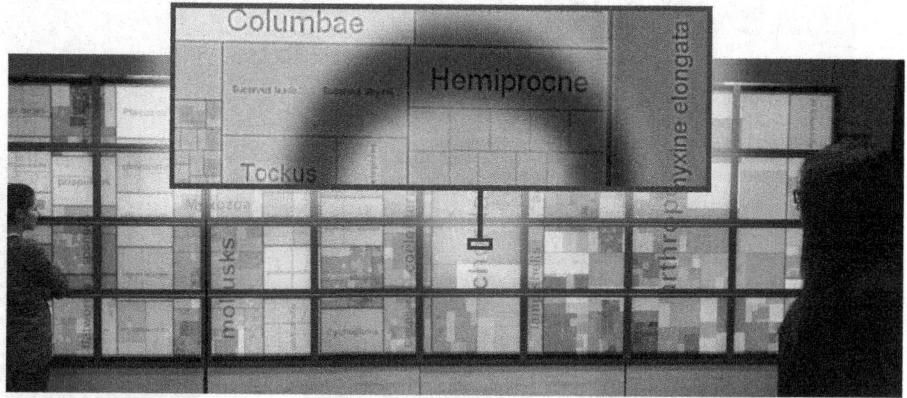

Fig. 5: Use of Hybrid-Image techniques to create combined overview and detail views in static large-wall visualization [65]. *Used by permission. Copyright Petra Isenberg.*

her to interact from a greater distance. For example, with a tablet used as a handheld lens into the data, a user could explore a visualization even if another user stands directly in front of the main display, blocking the view [88]. A user could also utilize the mobility of the tablet to reduce the context switching cost with multiple screens [36]. Additionally, as described above, these personal devices can be used to facilitate tracking and identification of the users, e. g., with RFID technology or using optical tracking such as in Google's *Project Tango* (https://get.google.com/tango/). An overview of current technologies for mobile device localization is given by Horak *et al.* [61].

Still, challenges remain and new issues emerge. One problem of multi-display environments in general and for the combination with handhelds specifically are gaze shifts, i. e., frequent changes of attention between multiple displays. They can interrupt the workflow and affect task performance [36,125]. Minimizing gaze shifts should, therefore, be one of the design goals during the development of such systems. To this end, one can also consider setups that only consist of personal devices (Figure 6). Without the use of shared displays, screen space is limited and the common context that would otherwise be given by the display needs to be defined differently, e. g., by virtually placing the scene on a physical surface [26].

4.6.3. CAVE

The "cave automatic virtual environment" or CAVE (for cleverness) was originally demonstrated in 1992 by Cruz-Neira *et al.* [41] as a VR system using five rear-projected surfaces covering three walls, floor, and ceiling. The CAVE concept has since spawned many variants, including the YURT [158] which features 360° wall, domed-ceiling, and floor projection; and CAVE2 [31], which replaces projection with LCD panels for higher resolution, but eschews ceiling and floor projection.

Fig. 6: Tracked tablet used as a peephole into a 3D information space that is located on a table [26].

Interaction in CAVE-style environments is usually done through optically tracked devices such as hand-held controllers and the primary user's tracked head position. Modern variants such as the CAVE2 and the YURT are large enough to accommodate a reasonable group of people. They would, therefore, be ideal for collaborative use, but a technological limitation is that usually only one user has a correct, undistorted stereoscopic perspective. However, there are experimental methods for multiplexing projected displays that could be used to create true multiuser caves, e. g., [96].

Historically, CAVEs have been used to visualize complex 3D models from domains such as mechanical engineering, architecture, or urban planning as well as scientific visualization applications. They provide a large field-of-view and their size often makes them suitable to display content such as cars, machinery or architectural models at their actual size, or to show small molecular structures at a larger scale for knowledge discovery. On the other hand, a CAVE is usually a major investment of both money and floor space. This limits their use to larger companies or research labs.

Thus, there remains room for improvement in technology for CAVE-style VR setups, but such technology now has to compete with self-contained head-mounted displays that offer comparable experiences at a fraction of the cost.

4.6.4. Head-Mounted Displays (AR/VR)

While head-mounted displays (HMDs) are nearly as old as Virtual Reality research itself [145], technological advances and resulting consumer systems such as the HTC Vive, Oculus Rift, or Microsoft's HoloLens now make VR and AR headsets widely available (and affordable) for immersive analytics. The systems are usually easy to set up and some HMDs even allow untethered use in non-instrumented environments. In a recent study comparing collaborative network visualization tasks in CAVE2 and HMD conditions, Cordeil *et al.* found participants were able to work more quickly and communicate just as well in the HMD setup [40]. However, the great advantage of the latter is cost.

Compared to using, e. g., mobile devices, such HMDs are usually more immersive. Virtual Reality headsets, however, can easily cause a feeling of disembodiment, negatively influencing presence and limiting collaboration. In any case, an HMD is inherently a single user device. Thus, multiuser setups need to provide an HMD for each user and scalability of HMD based setups is still a challenge – although Facebook and Samsung have demonstrated massively shared HMD VR environments for social computing [136]. Also compare the limitations explained in Subsection 4.4.2., many of which particularly apply to HMDs. Light-field displays [62] are a potential solution to the vergence-accommodation conflict described in Subsection 4.4.2..

4.6.5. Other Setups and Combinations

Besides the archetypes already described, other form factors exist that may also play a role in future immersive analytics systems. For example, wearables such as smart watches or even computers integrated into clothing could allow for personal tool palettes and clipboards, provide notifications, or act as additional input devices. Combinations of different form factors, such as using a display wall in conjunction with mobile devices which has been discussed above, generally allow a "best of both worlds" approach, addressing issues present with each device class. Today's AR headsets, for example, have only very limited input capabilities that can be extended with additional personal controllers.

The wide range of the archetypes discussed in this section shows that a universal solution does not exist. For example, in-the-wild analytics (see Chapter 7) could hardly be supported by stationary CAVE setups. Instead, advantages and limitations of the different form factors need to be carefully weighed depending on the requirements of the system and are key part of the immersive analytics design space (see Chapter 9).

4.7. Example Systems

This section identifies recent systems that are representative of an emerging class of immersive data visualization systems that feature natural interaction techniques, as explored in this chapter, as a central design philosophy.

4.7.1. Immersive Axes as Embodied Affordances for Interactive Multivariate Data Visualization

ImAxes [39] is a concept for immersive interactive tabular data exploration. It is a prototype system demonstrated with the HTC Vive HMD and controllers, that treats a data "axis" as an artifact in an immersive space. Depending on how individual axes are brought together, they are composed into different visualization idioms (e. g., 2- or 3-D scatterplots, scatterplot matrices, parallel coordinates, or linked scatterplots). Figure 7 shows some immersive data visualizations created with the system. ImAxes is motivated by ideas of Embodied Interaction, as discussed in Section 4.2.2.. In particular, the axes are rendered by the ImAxes system as rigid, but movable objects. Bi-manual interaction through tracked controllers, coupled with a declarative spatial grammar results in an intuitive, fluid interaction style for composing the simple axes objects into useful data visuals. The system naturally supports a number of existing data visualization idioms as above, but it is also possible to create a number of combinations of axis into data visualizations that are novel and interesting. Furthermore, a number of useful interaction mechanisms also emerge in the system, for example, the composed elements (e. g., scatterplots) configured with filters then picked up by the user and applied as "brushes" to other data visualizations, with transient links appearing between similar elements across the visualizations. In other words, the compound data visualizations can themselves become embodied query tools.

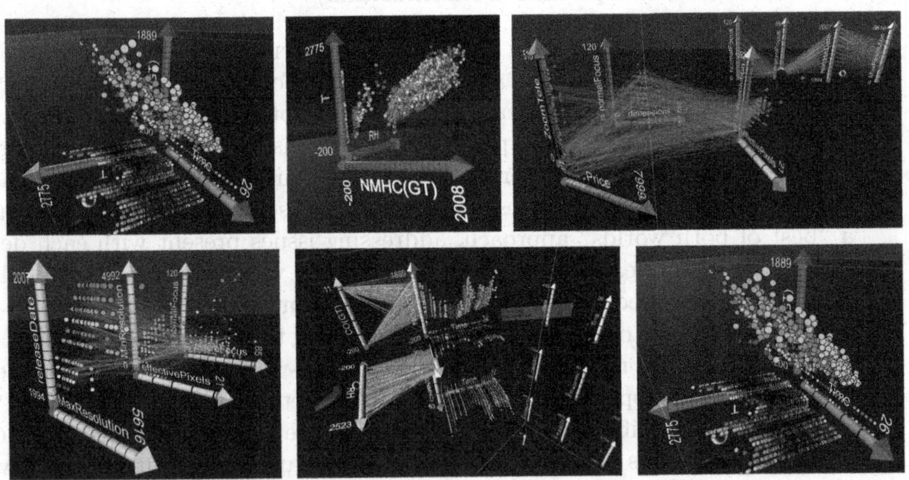

Fig. 7: The ImAxes system: data axes are composed into different visualizations in an immersive VR environment.

Through its spatial compositional rules and a number of direct interaction affordances built into the axes (such as filtering and rescaling), the system manages to avoid modal or WIMP interactions entirely. As with BodyLenses

(Section 4.7.2.) and the pen-based SketchStory system where the task was data-storytelling (Lee *at al.* [101], see Chapter 6), the modality of the interaction device lends itself to a very "task-focused" interaction paradigm for data exploration; focused in the sense that the user is able to get on with the activity at hand without being distracted by the arcana of the interface, such as hunting through menus.

Data analysis with ImAxes is demonstrated for one type of data (multivariate/tabular). However, the general idea of reusable, reconfigurable and composable, embodied data visualization elements should be applicable to many other types of data.

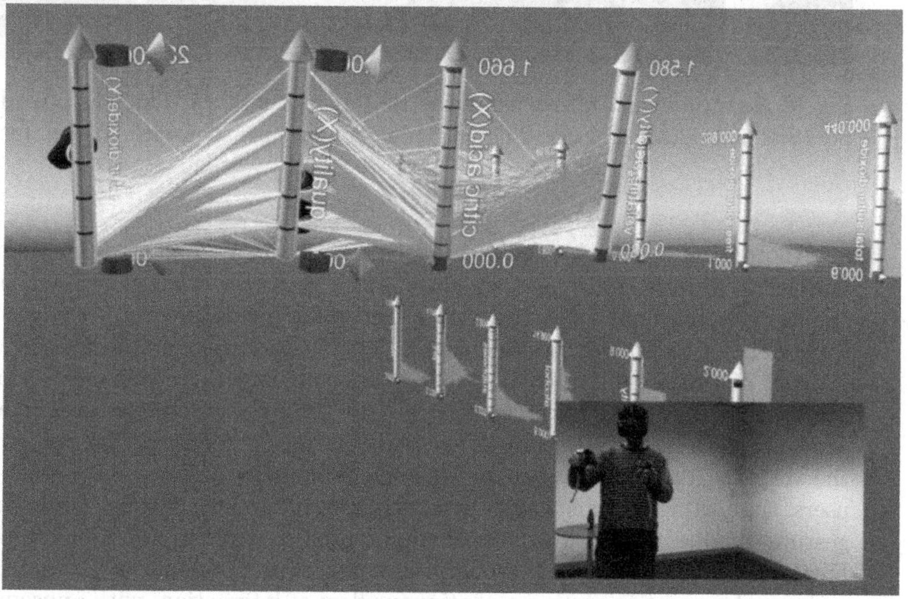

Fig. 8: A user working with the ImAxes system. Here, the user has arranged four axes to form parallel coordinates.

4.7.2. BodyLenses

Magic lenses, introduced by Bier *et al.* [14], are a focus and context technique that is often used in visualization systems. They provide localized (and in collaborative settings: personalized) alternative views into the data. Besides their use in traditional, desktop-based systems, tangible lenses on tabletops have also been proposed, for example by Kim & Elmqvist [86]. Spindler *et al.* [137] even presented *spatially tracked* tangible magic lenses, which are used in the space above a tabletop.

Fig. 9: A graph visualization using the BodyLenses system. The lens provides a personal embodied territory. The user can configure her lens with a touch menu.

Another novel concept for magic lenses, specifically for the use in front of interactive wall-sized displays, are *BodyLenses* by Kister *et al.* [90]. BodyLenses are flexible, personal work territories that can provide diverse functions and tools. They are body-controlled magic lenses appearing on the display wall in front of the users. "Body-controlled" encompasses three different forms of interaction: (a) body movement relative to the display, (b) gestures, mainly arms and hands, but also any other body part, and (c) direct interaction on the display, using touch, pen or tangible input. BodyLenses move with the users, supporting implicit navigation within an information space. Additionally, gestures or direct input on the wall can be used to explicitly manipulate them. Furthermore, they serve as personal territories and support mutual awareness of co-located users. Supporting a continuous flow of interaction, with appropriate interaction techniques depending on the distance to the display wall, BodyLenses aim to make data exploration an immersive and engaging experience.

The authors explored the design space by examining design aspects such as appearance, function, interaction, and multi-user contexts. They present different shapes of lenses including classic, geometries such as circles and rectangles; body-centric lenses like shadows; and content-aware, data-driven shapes.

The shape of the lens can either be continuously changed depending on the user' movement and posture (e. g., for shadow-like lenses) or can explicitly be controlled by the user. In addition to changing the lens' position, the user's distance to the display can also control other parameters. For example, users can move through time in a time-series visualization or control the properties of the lens function, e. g., a zoom level, abstraction, or displacement factor. Distance-based interaction can also address the notion of *proxemics*, a concept describing the spatial relationships governing social interactions. Thus, the distance between

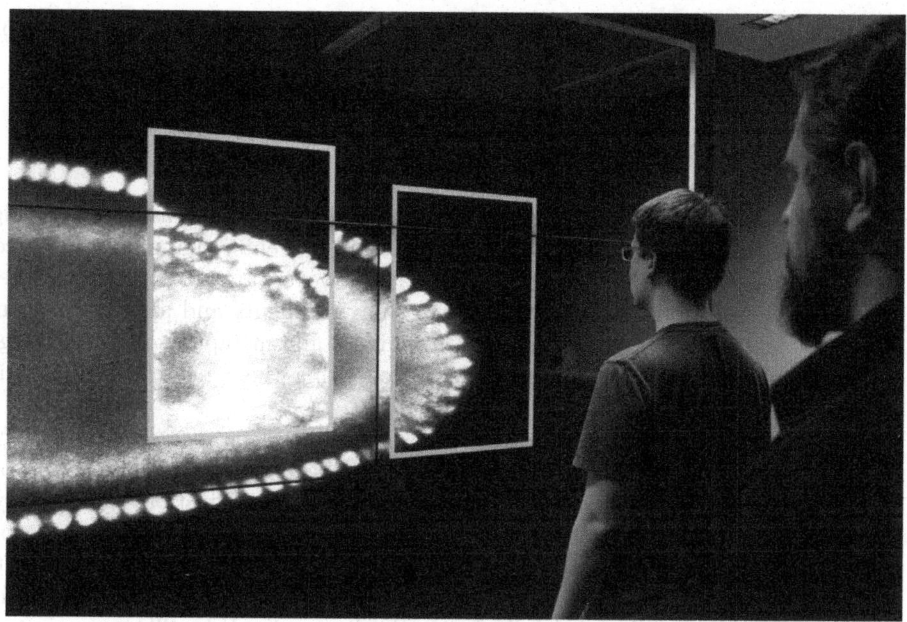

Fig. 10: BodyLenses allows for multiple lenses at the same time. Here, two users inspect a time series of a biological data set.

a user and the wall can indicate the degree of engagement and can influence the lens accordingly, e. g., fading it out after some threshold.

Wall-sized displays are suitable for multiple users, therefore, BodyLenses support several lenses at a time. Overlapping lenses (and their effects) can be combined and separated to create common embodied territories sharing the same properties and elements (see also [7]). They also continuously convey which part of the data a user is currently investigating, providing mutual awareness.

Kister *et al.* implemented several example applications that address visualization use cases. The first is a graph explorer and includes domain-specific lens functions specific, e. g., local edge, bring neighbors, and fish-eye lenses. This application can be seen in Figure 9, which also shows the concept of using personal menus around the lens that allow changing lens parameters.

Figure 10 shows the second application. It allows the exploration of time series of, e. g., microscopy image sets. The distance to the wall is mapped to time, consequently, the users can easily "step" through time by moving in front of the wall.

ImAxes gives users "presence" in the data, and gives the data an embodied "presence" in the users' physical space. BodyLenses, on the other hand, show that presence is not limited to fully immersive virtual experiences. The emergent quality of these systems, as well as the minimal interference they place between the user and the data analysis task, are compelling evidence that immersive environments can create truly new ways for users to experience as well as explore data.

4.8. Conclusion

Modern analysts are well-versed in the specific devices, as well as interface widgets such as the WIMP desktop metaphor used in current visual analytics systems. These hardware and interface components, however, are often inappropriate for the non-traditional immersive analytics environments and applications under development today. New interaction techniques and metaphors must be designed and we must also provide guidance in choosing these new designs based on empirical evidence.

Visualization and virtual reality researchers have been successful in identifying user tasks and some interaction metaphors, are beginning to evaluate the usability of 3D interaction techniques for immersive analytics applications, and are trying to improve the usability of techniques for analytics tasks. However, the usability of 3D interfaces in real-world applications is still not at a desirable level. Scientists perhaps often perceive these technologies as good for demonstrations but without sufficient benefit to be used daily for insight discoveries. It is still an open question under which circumstances immersive analytics interfaces should be 2D or 3D (see Chapter 2) and how these interfaces need to be designed to be intuitive and engaging. Therefore, it is vital to focus on the use and to understand the design and evaluation of interface and interaction techniques to show how immersive analytics can actually increase efficiency, facilitate team collaboration, and reduce cost.

This chapter serves as an early step in this direction. We examined opportunities for the use of natural user interfaces to support immersive data analysis. To this end, we discussed typical analysis tasks and how natural user interfaces can be used to support these tasks. It is clear that no single input method is 'perfect' and suitable for all tasks. Instead, trade-offs between them have to be explored to choose techniques based on the specific requirements regarding, e. g., precision or physical demand. We also reviewed different, archetypal hardware setups for data visualization, which suggest that we will see a multitude of system designs in future immersive analytics systems. Finally, we looked at two example system designs that suggest such possible future directions.

One particular challenge is to integrate techniques designed for a single display type, a single task type, or a single user group into a seamless cross-display, cross-task, and cross-use multi-sensory environment. In such a system, realism is perhaps not the key but the magic interactivity integrated with visuals to understand what are the best mappings between these system factors to facilitate scientists' and users' decision making and insight discovery process.

A next step toward quantifying the benefits of interaction could be the creation of a taxonomy that separates all variables related to factors such as head tracking, immersion, display sizes, users, and tasks, to classify which characteristics are truly beneficial. There are multiple efforts to advance these frontiers, as discussed in this chapter. A recent study by Bach *et al.* [6] evaluated what they considered to be the state-of-the-art for mixed-reality data visualization. However, their findings, while generally favorable for the mixed-reality condition, were inconclusive. They describe a number of limitations to their study: the fact that they were testing only one immersive interaction design from a huge space of possibilities; rapidly evolving capabilities of the current technology; and, the limited experience of their participants with immersive environments. In a way, this work neatly summarizes the current state of interaction for immersive analytics. There is considerable potential but precisely what form interaction with immersive analytics will ultimately take is uncertain.

In this chapter, we have surveyed the various technologies that currently enable immersive experiences and how these can be used for data visualization. While there have been immersive VR interfaces in the past, with current technological developments, access to these technologies becomes easier. For more and more domain experts, immersive analytics is within reach. Even everyday users will be able to afford future systems, enabling immersive, personal analytics. As the technologies improve and the costs come down, there will surely be a convergence or at least clearer winners in terms of which technologies are adopted in both the professional and the consumer space. Similarly, particular interaction techniques will emerge as standard as people's familiarity with these environments grows. The interaction techniques that we propose now and the studies that we perform to evaluate and refine them have the opportunity to influence these emerging standards, and hence, significantly impact and shape the future of data analytics in immersive environments.

Acknowledgements

Büschel acknowledges funding by the German Federal Ministry of Education and Research, grant no. 03ZZ0514C and Dwyer acknowledges support by the Australian Research Council Discovery Scheme, project DP180100755.

References

1. Adams, N., Witkowski, M., Spence, R.: The inspection of very large images by eye-gaze control. In: Proceedings of the Working Conference on Advanced Visual Interfaces (AVI). pp. 111–118. ACM, New York (2008) doi: 10.1145/1385569.1385589
2. Amar, R., Eagan, J., Stasko, J.: Low-level components of analytic activity in information visualization. In: Proceedings of the IEEE Symposium on Information Visualization (InfoVis). pp. 111–117. IEEE Computer Society, Los Alamitos (2005) doi: 10.1109/INFVIS.2005.1532136
3. Andrews, C., Endert, A., North, C.: Space to think: Large high-resolution displays for sensemaking. In: Proceedings of the SIGCHI Conference on Human Factors in Computing Systems (CHI). pp. 55–64. ACM, New York (2010) doi: 10.1145/1753326.1753336

4. Argelaguet, F., Andujar, C.: A survey of 3D object selection techniques for virtual environments. Computers & Graphics 37(3), 121–136 (2013) doi: 10.1016/j.cag.2012.12.003
5. Arif, A.S., Stuerzlinger, W.: User adaptation to a faulty unistroke-based text entry technique by switching to an alternative gesture set. In: Proceedings of Graphics Interface (GI). pp. 183–192. Canadian Information Processing Society, Toronto (2014) doi: 10.20380/GI2014.24
6. Bach, B., Sicat, R., Beyer, J., Cordeil, M., Pfister, H.: The hologram in my hand: how effective is interactive exploration of 3D visualizations in immersive tangible augmented reality? IEEE Transactions on Visualization and Computer Graphics 24(1), 457–467 (2018) doi: 10.1109/TVCG.2017.2745941
7. Badam, S.K., Amini, F., Elmqvist, N., Irani, P.: Supporting visual exploration for multiple users in large display environments. In: Proceedings of the IEEE Conference on Visual Analytics Science and Technology (VAST). pp. 1–10. IEEE Computer Society, Los Alamitos (2016) doi: 10.1109/VAST.2016.7883506
8. Ball, R., North, C.: Effects of tiled high-resolution display on basic visualization and navigation tasks. In: Extended Abstracts on Human Factors in Computing Systems (CHI EA). pp. 1196–1199. ACM, New York (2005) doi: 10.1145/1056808.1056875
9. Ball, R., North, C., Bowman, D.A.: Move to improve: Promoting physical navigation to increase user performance with large displays. In: Proceedings of the SIGCHI Conference on Human Factors in Computing Systems (CHI). pp. 191–200. ACM, New York (2007) doi: 10.1145/1240624.1240656
10. Ballmer, S.: CES 2010: A transforming trend–the natural user interface. The Huffington Post (2010), http://www.huffingtonpost.com/steve-ballmer/ces-2010-a-transformingt_b_416598.html/
11. Beaudouin-Lafon, M., Huot, S., Nancel, M., Mackay, W., Pietriga, E., Primet, R., Wagner, J., Chapuis, O., Pillias, C., Eagan, J., Gjerlufsen, T., Klokmose, C.: Multisurface interaction in the WILD room. Computer 45(4), 48–56 (Apr 2012) doi: 10.1109/MC.2012.110
12. Benko, H., Ishak, E.W.: Cross-dimensional gestural interaction techniques for hybrid immersive environments. In: Proceedings of the IEEE Conference on Virtual Reality (VR). pp. 209–216, 327. IEEE Computer Society, Los Alamitos (2005) doi: 10.1109/VR.2005.1492776
13. Besançon, L., Issartel, P., Ammi, M., Isenberg, T.: Hybrid tactile/tangible interaction for 3D data exploration. IEEE Transactions on Visualization and Computer Graphics 23(1), 881–890 (Jan 2017) doi: 10.1109/TVCG.2016.2599217
14. Bier, E.A., Stone, M.C., Pier, K., Fishkin, K., Baudel, T., Conway, M., Buxton, W., DeRose, T.: Toolglass and magic lenses: The see-through interface. In: Conference Companion on Human Factors in Computing Systems. pp. 445–446. ACM, New York (1994) doi: 10.1145/259963.260447
15. Billinghurst, M., Clark, A., Lee, G.: A survey of augmented reality. Foundations and Trends® in Human–Computer Interaction 8(2–3), 73–272 (2015) doi: 10.1561/1100000049
16. Bjork, S., Holopainen, J.: Patterns in Game Design (Game Development Series). Charles River Media, Inc., Rockland, MA, USA (2004)
17. Bolt, R.A.: "Put-that-there": Voice and gesture at the graphics interface. ACM SIGGRAPH Computer Graphics 14(3), 262–270 (Jul 1980) doi: 10.1145/965105.807503
18. Bolt, R.A.: Gaze-orchestrated dynamic windows. ACM SIGGRAPH Computer Graphics 15(3), 109–119 (1981) doi: 10.1145/965161.806796

19. Branit, B.: World Builder. Online video (2009), https://vimeo.com/3365942
20. Brown, M.A., Stuerzlinger, W.: Exploring the throughput potential of in-air pointing. In: Proceedings of the International Conference on Human-Computer Interaction (HCI). pp. 13–24. Springer, Berlin/Heidelberg (2016) doi: 10.1007/978-3-319-39516-6_2
21. Brown, M.A., Stuerzlinger, W., Mendonça Filho, E.J.: The performance of un-instrumented in-air pointing. In: Proceedings of Graphics Interface (GI). pp. 59–66. Canadian Information Processing Society, Toronto (2014) doi: 10.20380/GI2014.08
22. Bruder, G., Steinicke, F., Stuerzlinger, W.: Effects of visual conflicts on 3D selection task performance in stereoscopic display environments. In: Proceedings of the IEEE Symposium on 3D User Interfaces (3DUI). pp. 115–118. IEEE Computer Society, Los Alamitos (2013) doi: 10.1109/3DUI.2013.6550207
23. Bruder, G., Steinicke, F., Stuerzlinger, W.: To touch or not to touch? Comparing 2D touch and 3D mid-air interaction on stereoscopic tabletop surfaces. In: Proceedings of the 1st Symposium on Spatial User Interaction (SUI). pp. 9–16. ACM, New York (2013) doi: 10.1145/2491367.2491369
24. Bruder, G., Steinicke, F., Stuerzlinger, W.: Touching the void revisited: Analyses of touch behavior on and above tabletop surfaces. In: Proceedings of Human-Computer Interaction (INTERACT). pp. 278–296. Springer, Berlin/Heidelberg (2013) doi: 10.1007/978-3-642-40483-2_19
25. Büschel, W., Mitschick, A., Dachselt, R.: Here and now: Reality-based information retrieval. In: Proceedings of the 2018 Conference on Human Information Interaction & Retrieval. pp. 171–180. CHIIR '18, ACM, New York, NY, USA (2018) doi: 10.1145/3176349.3176384
26. Büschel, W., Reipschläger, P., Langner, R., Dachselt, R.: Investigating the use of spatial interaction for 3D data visualization on mobile devices. In: Proceedings of the 2017 ACM International Conference on Interactive Surfaces and Spaces. pp. 62–71. ISS '17, ACM, New York, NY, USA (2017) doi: 10.1145/3132272.3134125
27. Bush, V.: As we may think. The Atlantic Monthly 176(1), 101–108 (July 1945), https://www.theatlantic.com/magazine/archive/1945/07/as-we-may-think/303881/
28. Butscher, S., Hubenschmid, S., Müller, J., Fuchs, J., Reiterer, H.: Clusters, trends, and outliers: How immersive technologies can facilitate the collaborative analysis of multidimensional data. In: Proceedings of the 2018 CHI Conference on Human Factors in Computing Systems. pp. 90:1–90:12. CHI '18, ACM, New York, NY, USA (2018) doi: 10.1145/3173574.3173664
29. Buxton, B.: Multi-touch systems that I have known and loved. Tech. rep., Microsoft Research (2007), http://www.billbuxton.com/multitouchOverview.html
30. Card, S.K., Robertson, G.G., Mackinlay, J.D.: The information visualizer, an information workspace. In: Proceedings of the SIGCHI Conference on Human Factors in Computing Systems (CHI). pp. 181–186. ACM, New York (1991) doi: 10.1145/108844.108874
31. EVL CAVE2 homepage, https://www.evl.uic.edu/entry.php?id=2016
32. Cernea, D., Kerren, A.: A survey of technologies on the rise for emotion-enhanced interaction. Journal of Visual Languages and Computing 31, Part A, 70–86 (Dec 2015) doi: 10.1016/j.jvlc.2015.10.001
33. Chen, J., Bowman, D.A.: Effectiveness of cloning techniques for architectural virtual environments. In: IEEE Virtual Reality Conference. pp. 103–110. IEEE (2006) doi: 10.1109/VR.2006.57

34. Chen, J., Bowman, D.A.: Domain-specific design of 3D interaction techniques: An approach for designing useful virtual environment applications. Presence: Teleoperators and Virtual Environments 18(5), 370–386 (2009) doi: 10.1162/pres.18.5.370
35. Chen, J., Bowman, D.A., Lucas, J.F., Wingrave, C.A.: Interfaces for Cloning in Immersive Virtual Environments. In: Eurographics Symposium on Virtual Environments. The Eurographics Association (2004) doi: 10.2312/EGVE/EGVE04/091-098
36. Chen, J., Narayan, M.A., Manuel, Pérez-Quiñones, A.: The use of hand-held devices for search tasks in virtual environments. The IEEE Symposium on 3D User Interfaces pp. 15–18 (2005)
37. Claes, S., Moere, A.V.: The role of tangible interaction in exploring information on public visualization displays. In: Proceedings of the International Symposium on Pervasive Displays (PerDis). pp. 201–207. ACM, New York (2015) doi: 10.1145/2757710.2757733
38. Coffey, D., Malbraaten, N., Le, T., Borazjani, I., Sotiropoulos, F., Erdman, A.G., Keefe, D.F.: Interactive Slice WIM: Navigating and interrogating volume datasets using a multi-surface, multi-touch VR interface. IEEE Transactions on Visualization and Computer Graphics 18(10), 1614–1626 (2012) doi: 10.1109/TVCG.2011.283
39. Cordeil, M., Cunningham, A., Dwyer, T., Thomas, B.H., Marriott, K.: ImAxes: Immersive axes as embodied affordances for interactive multivariate data visualisation. In: Proceedings of the 30th Annual ACM Symposium on User Interface Software and Technology. pp. 71–83. UIST '17, ACM, New York, NY, USA (2017) doi: 10.1145/3126594.3126613
40. Cordeil, M., Dwyer, T., Klein, K., Laha, B., Marriott, K., Thomas, B.H.: Immersive collaborative analysis of network connectivity: CAVE-style or head-mounted display? IEEE Transactions on Visualization and Computer Graphics 23(1), 441–450 (2017) doi: 10.1109/TVCG.2016.2599107
41. Cruz-Neira, C., Sandin, D.J., DeFanti, T.A., Kenyon, R.V., Hart, J.C.: The CAVE: audio visual experience automatic virtual environment. Communications of the ACM 35(6), 64–72 (Jun 1992) doi: 10.1145/129888.129892
42. Cummings, J.J., Bailenson, J.N.: How immersive is enough? A meta-analysis of the effect of immersive technology on user presence. Media Psychology 19(2), 272–309 (2016) doi: 10.1080/15213269.2015.1015740
43. van Dam, A.: Post-WIMP user interfaces. Communications of the ACM 40(2), 63–67 (Feb 1997) doi: 10.1145/253671.253708
44. Dostal, J., Hinrichs, U., Kristensson, P.O., Quigley, A.: Spidereyes: Designing attention- and proximity-aware collaborative interfaces for wall-sized displays. In: Proceedings of the International Conference on Intelligent User Interfaces (IUI). pp. 143–152. ACM, New York (2014) doi: 10.1145/2557500.2557541
45. Dourish, P.: Where the Action Is: The Foundations of Embodied Interaction. MIT Press (2001)
46. Drucker, S.M., Fisher, D., Sadana, R., Herron, J., schraefel, m.c.: TouchViz: A case study comparing two interfaces for data analytics on tablets. In: Proceedings of the SIGCHI Conference on Human Factors in Computing Systems (CHI). pp. 2301–2310. ACM, New York (2013) doi: 10.1145/2470654.2481318
47. Elmqvist, N., Vande Moere, A., Jetter, H.C., Cernea, D., Reiterer, H., Jankun-Kelly, T.J.: Fluid interaction for information visualization. Information Visualization 10(4), 327–340 (Oct 2011) doi: 10.1177/1473871611413180

48. Febretti, A., Nishimoto, A., Mateevitsi, V., Renambot, L., Johnson, A., Leigh, J.: Omegalib: A multi-view application framework for hybrid reality display environments. In: Proceedings of the IEEE Conference on Virtual Reality (VR). pp. 9–14. IEEE Computer Society, Los Alamitos (2014) doi: 10.1109/VR.2014.6802043
49. Fikkert, W., D'Ambros, M., Bierz, T., Jankun-Kelly, T.: Interacting with visualizations. In: Kerren, A., Ebert, A., Meyer, J. (eds.) Human-Centered Visualization Environments, LNCS, vol. 4417, chap. 3, pp. 77–162. Springer, Berlin/Heidelberg (2007) doi: 10.1007/978-3-540-71949-6_3
50. Follmer, S., Leithinger, D., Olwal, A., Hogge, A., Ishii, H.: inFORM: Dynamic physical affordances and constraints through shape and object actuation. In: Proceedings of the Annual ACM Symposium on User Interface Software and Technology (UIST). pp. 417–426. ACM, New York (2013) doi: 10.1145/2501988.2502032
51. Frisch, M., Heydekorn, J., Dachselt, R.: Diagram editing on interactive displays using multi-touch and pen gestures. In: Proceedings of the International Conference on Diagrammatic Representation and Inference (Diagrams). pp. 182–196. Springer, Berlin/Heidelberg (2010) doi: 10.1007/978-3-642-14600-8_18
52. Fu, C.W., Goh, W.B., Ng, J.A.: Multi-touch techniques for exploring large-scale 3D astrophysical simulations. In: Proceedings of the SIGCHI Conference on Human Factors in Computing Systems (CHI). pp. 2213–2222. ACM, New York (2010) doi: 10.1145/1753326.1753661
53. Gillet, A., Sanner, M., Stoffler, D., Olson, A.: Tangible interfaces for structural molecular biology. Structure 13(3), 483–491 (Mar 2005) doi: 10.1016/j.str.2005.01.009
54. Harrison, C., Sato, M., Poupyrev, I.: Capacitive fingerprinting: Exploring user differentiation by sensing electrical properties of the human body. In: Proceedings of the Annual ACM Symposium on User Interface Software and Technology (UIST). pp. 537–544. ACM, New York (2012) doi: 10.1145/2380116.2380183
55. Heer, J., Shneiderman, B.: Interactive dynamics for visual analysis. Communications of the ACM 55(4), 45–54 (Apr 2012) doi: 10.1145/2133806.2133821
56. Hess, R.F., To, L., Zhou, J., Wang, G., Cooperstock, J.R.: Stereo vision: The haves and have-nots. i-Perception 6(3) (Jun 2015) doi: 10.1177/2041669515593028
57. Hincapié-Ramos, J.D., Guo, X., Moghadasian, P., Irani, P.: Consumed endurance: a metric to quantify arm fatigue of mid-air interactions. In: Proceedings of the SIGCHI Conference on Human Factors in Computing Systems (CHI). pp. 1063–1072. ACM, New York (2014) doi: 10.1145/2556288.2557130
58. Hinckley, K., Pausch, R., Goble, J.C., Kassell, N.F.: Passive real-world interface props for neurosurgical visualization. In: Proceedings of the SIGCHI Conference on Human Factors in Computing Systems (CHI). pp. 452–458. ACM, New York (1994) doi: 10.1145/191666.191821
59. Hinckley, K., Yatani, K., Pahud, M., Coddington, N., Rodenhouse, J., Wilson, A., Benko, H., Buxton, B.: Pen + touch = new tools. In: Proceedings of the Annual ACM Symposium on User Interface Software and Technology (UIST). pp. 27–36. ACM, New York (2010) doi: 10.1145/1866029.1866036
60. Hoffman, D.M., Girshick, A.R., Akeley, K., Banks, M.S.: Vergence–accommodation conflicts hinder visual performance and cause visual fatigue. Journal of Vision 8(3), 33:1–33:30 (2008) doi: 10.1167/8.3.33
61. Horak, T., von Zadow, U., Kalms, M., Dachselt, R.: Discussing the state of the art for "in the wild" mobile device localization. In: Proceedings of the ISS Workshop on Interacting with Multi-Device Ecologies "in the wild" (2016), http://cross-surface.com/papers/Cross-Surface_2016-2_paper_2.pdf

62. Huang, F.C., Chen, K., Wetzstein, G.: The light field stereoscope: immersive computer graphics via factored near-eye light field displays with focus cues. ACM Transactions on Graphics 34(4), 60:1–60:12 (2015) doi: 10.1145/2766922
63. Hutchins, E.L., Hollan, J.D., Norman, D.A.: Direct manipulation interfaces. Human–Computer Interaction 1(4), 311–338 (1985) doi: 10.1207/s15327051hci0104_2
64. Hutchinson, T.E., White, K.P., Martin, W.N., Reichert, K.C., Frey, L.A.: Human-computer interaction using eye-gaze input. IEEE Transactions on Systems, Man, and Cybernetics 19(6), 1527–1534 (1989) doi: 10.1109/21.44068
65. Isenberg, P., Dragicevic, P., Willett, W., Bezerianos, A., Fekete, J.D.: Hybrid-image visualization for large viewing environments. IEEE Transactions on Visualization and Computer Graphics 19(12), 2346–2355 (Dec 2013) doi: 10.1109/TVCG.2013.163
66. Isenberg, P., Isenberg, T.: Visualization on interactive surfaces: A research overview. i-com 12(3), 10–17 (Nov 2013) doi: 10.1524/icom.2013.0020
67. Isenberg, T.: Interactive exploration of three-dimensional scientific visualizations on large display surfaces. In: Anslow, C., Campos, P., Jorge, J. (eds.) Collaboration Meets Interactive Spaces, chap. 6, pp. 97–123. Springer, Berlin/Heidelberg (2016) doi: 10.1007/978-3-319-45853-3_6
68. Isenberg, T., Hancock, M.: *Gestures* vs. postures: 'Gestural' touch interaction in 3D environments. In: Proceedings of the CHI Workshop on "The 3rd Dimension of CHI: Touching and Designing 3D User Interfaces" (3DCHI). pp. 53–61 (2012), https://hal.inria.fr/hal-00781237
69. Ishii, H., Ratti, C., Piper, B., Wang, Y., Biderman, A., Ben-Joseph, E.: Bringing clay and sand into digital design—Continuous tangible user interfaces. BT Technology Journal 22(4), 287–299 (Oct 2004) doi: 10.1023/B:BTTJ.0000047607.16164.16
70. Ishii, H.: The tangible user interface and its evolution. Communications of the ACM 51(6), 32–36 (Jun 2008) doi: 10.1145/1349026.1349034
71. Ishii, H., Ullmer, B.: Tangible bits: Towards seamless interfaces between people, bits and atoms. In: Proceedings of the ACM SIGCHI Conference on Human Factors in Computing Systems (CHI). pp. 234–241. ACM, New York (1997) doi: 10.1145/258549.258715
72. Jackson, B., Schroeder, D., Keefe, D.F.: Nailing down multi-touch: Anchored above the surface interaction for 3D modeling and navigation. In: Proceedings of Graphics Interface (GI). pp. 181–184. Canadian Information Processing Society, Toronto (2012) doi: 10.20380/GI2012.23
73. Jacob, R.J., Girouard, A., Hirshfield, L.M., Horn, M.S., Shaer, O., Solovey, E.T., Zigelbaum, J.: Reality-based interaction: A framework for post-WIMP interfaces. In: Proceedings of the SIGCHI Conference on Human Factors in Computing Systems (CHI). pp. 201–210. ACM, New York (2008) doi: 10.1145/1357054.1357089
74. Jakobsen, M.R., Haile, Y.S., Knudsen, S., Hornbæk, K.: Information visualization and proxemics: Design opportunities and empirical findings. IEEE Transactions on Visualization and Computer Graphics 19(12), 2386–2395 (Dec 2013) doi: 10.1109/TVCG.2013.166
75. Jang, S., Stuerzlinger, W., Ambike, S., Ramani, K.: Modeling cumulative arm fatigue in mid-air interaction based on perceived exertion and kinetics of arm motion. In: Proceedings of the SIGCHI Conference on Human Factors in Computing Systems (CHI). pp. 3328–3339. ACM, New York (2017) doi: 10.1145/3025453.3025523
76. Jankowski, J., Hachet, M.: Advances in interaction with 3D environments. Computer Graphics Forum 34(1), 152–190 (Jan 2015) doi: 10.1111/cgf.12466

77. Jansen, Y.: Physical and tangible information visualization. Ph.D. thesis, Université Paris Sud - Paris XI, France (Mar 2014), https://tel.archives-ouvertes.fr/tel-00981521
78. Jansen, Y., Dragicevic, P.: An interaction model for visualizations beyond the desktop. IEEE Transactions on Visualization and Computer Graphics 19(12), 2396–2405 (Dec 2013) doi: 10.1109/TVCG.2013.134
79. Jansen, Y., Dragicevic, P., Isenberg, P., Alexander, J., Karnik, A., Kildal, J., Subramanian, S., Hornbæk, K.: Opportunities and challenges for data physicalization. In: Proceedings of the SIGCHI Conference on Human Factors in Computing Systems (CHI). pp. 3227–3236. ACM, New York (2015) doi: 10.1145/2702123.2702180
80. Johnson, R., O'Hara, K., Sellen, A., Cousins, C., Criminisi, A.: Exploring the potential for touchless interaction in image-guided interventional radiology. In: Proceedings of the SIGCHI Conference on Human Factors in Computing Systems (CHI). pp. 3323–3332. ACM, New York (2011) doi: 10.1145/1978942.1979436
81. Jota, R., Nacenta, M.A., Jorge, J.A., Carpendale, S., Greenberg, S.: A comparison of ray pointing techniques for very large displays. In: Proceedings of Graphics Interface (GI). pp. 269–276. Canadian Information Processing Society, Toronto (2010) doi: 10.20380/GI2010.36
82. Karam, M., schraefel, m.c.: A taxonomy of gestures in human computer interactions. Tech. Rep. 261149, University of Southampton (2005), http://eprints.soton.ac.uk/261149/, ISBN 0854328335
83. Keefe, D.F.: Integrating visualization and interaction research to improve scientific workflows. IEEE Computer Graphics and Applications 30(2), 8–13 (Mar/Apr 2010) doi: 10.1109/MCG.2010.30
84. Keefe, D.F., Isenberg, T.: Reimagining the scientific visualization interaction paradigm. IEEE Computer 46(5), 51–57 (May 2013) doi: 10.1109/MC.2013.178
85. Kerren, A., Schreiber, F.: Toward the role of interaction in visual analytics. In: Proceedings of the Winter Simulation Conference (WSC). pp. 420:1–420:13. Winter Simulation Conference (2012), http://dl.acm.org/citation.cfm?id=2429759.2430303 doi: 10.1109/WSC.2012.6465208
86. Kim, K., Elmqvist, N.: Embodied lenses for collaborative visual queries on tabletop displays. Information Visualization 11(4), 319–338 (Apr 2012) doi: 10.1177/1473871612441874
87. Kirmizibayrak, C., Radeva, N., Wakid, M., Philbeck, J., Sibert, J., Hahn, J.: Evaluation of gesture based interfaces for medical volume visualization tasks. In: Proceedings of the International Conference on Virtual Reality Continuum and Its Applications in Industry (VRCAI). pp. 69–74. ACM, New York (2011) doi: 10.1145/2087756.2087764
88. Kister, U., Klamka, K., Tominski, C., Dachselt, R.: GRASP: Combining spatially-aware mobile devices and a display wall for graph visualization and interaction. Computer Graphics Forum 36(3), 503–514 (Jun 2017) doi: 10.1111/cgf.13206
89. Kister, U., Reipschläger, P., Dachselt, R.: MultiLens: Fluent interaction with multi-functional multi-touch lenses for information visualization. In: Proceedings of the ACM Conference on Interactive Surfaces and Spaces (ISS). pp. 139–148. ACM, New York (2016) doi: 10.1145/2992154.2992168
90. Kister, U., Reipschläger, P., Matulic, F., Dachselt, R.: BodyLenses: Embodied magic lenses and personal territories for wall displays. In: Proceedings of the International Conference on Interactive Tabletops & Surfaces (ITS). pp. 117–126. ACM, New York (2015) doi: 10.1145/2817721.2817726

91. Klamka, K., Siegel, A., Vogt, S., Göbel, F., Stellmach, S., Dachselt, R.: Look & pedal: Hands-free navigation in zoomable information spaces through gaze-supported foot input. In: Proceedings of the International Conference on Multimodal Interaction (ICMI). pp. 123–130. ACM, New York (2015) doi: 10.1145/2818346.2820751
92. Klapperstuck, M., Czauderna, T., Goncu, C., Glowacki, J., Dwyer, T., Schreiber, F., Marriott, K.: ContextuWall: Peer collaboration using (large) displays. In: Proceedings of the International Symposium on Big Data Visual Analytics (BDVA). pp. 1–8. IEEE, Red Hook, NY, USA (2016) doi: 10.1109/BDVA.2016.7787047
93. Klum, S., Isenberg, P., Langner, R., Fekete, J.D., Dachselt, R.: Stackables: Combining tangibles for faceted browsing. In: Proceedings of the International Working Conference on Advanced Visual Interfaces. pp. 241–248. AVI '12, ACM, New York, NY, USA (2012), http://doi.acm.org/10.1145/2254556.2254600 doi: 10.1145/2254556.2254600
94. Konchada, V., Jackson, B., Le, T., Borazjani, I., Sotiropoulos, F., Keefe, D.F.: Supporting internal visualization of biomedical datasets via 3D rapid prototypes and sketch-based gestures. In: Proceedings of the Symposium on Interactive 3D Graphics and Games (I3D). pp. 214–214. ACM, New York (2011) doi: 10.1145/1944745.1944794
95. Kruszyński, K.J., van Liere, R.: Tangible props for scientific visualization: Concept, requirements, application. Virtual Reality 13(4), 235–244 (Nov 2009) doi: 10.1007/s10055-009-0126-1
96. Kulik, A., Kunert, A., Beck, S., Reichel, R., Blach, R., Zink, A., Froehlich, B.: C1x6: a stereoscopic six-user display for co-located collaboration in shared virtual environments. ACM Transactions on Graphics 30(6), 188:1–188:12 (2011) doi: 10.1145/2070781.2024222
97. Kurzhals, K., Fisher, B., Burch, M., Weiskopf, D.: Evaluating visual analytics with eye tracking. In: Proceedings of the Workshop on Beyond Time and Errors: Novel Evaluation Methods for Visualization (BELIV). pp. 61–69. ACM, New York (2014) doi: 10.1145/2669557.2669560
98. LaViola, J., Kruijff, E., Bowman, D., McMahan, R., Poupyrev, I.: 3D user interfaces: theory and practice. Usability Series, Pearson Education, Limited (2017)
99. Le Goc, M.: Supporting versatility in tangible user interfaces using collections of small actuated objects. Ph.D. thesis, Université Paris-Saclay, France (Dec 2016), https://tel.archives-ouvertes.fr/tel-01453175
100. Lee, B., Isenberg, P., Riche, N.H., Carpendale, S.: Beyond mouse and keyboard: Expanding design considerations for information visualization interactions. IEEE Transactions on Visualization and Computer Graphics 18(12), 2689–2698 (Dec 2012) doi: 10.1109/TVCG.2012.204
101. Lee, B., Kazi, R.H., Smith, G.: SketchStory: Telling more engaging stories with data through freeform sketching. IEEE Transactions on Visualization and Computer Graphics 19(12), 2416–2425 (2013) doi: 10.1109/TVCG.2013.191
102. Leithinger, D., Lakatos, D., DeVincenzi, A., Blackshaw, M., Ishii, H.: Direct and gestural interaction with relief: A 2.5D shape display. In: Proceedings of the Annual ACM Symposium on User Interface Software and Technology (UIST). pp. 541–548. ACM, New York (2011) doi: 10.1145/2047196.2047268
103. López, D., Oehlberg, L., Doger, C., Isenberg, T.: Towards an understanding of mobile touch navigation in a stereoscopic viewing environment for 3D data exploration. IEEE Transactions on Visualization and Computer Graphics 22(5), 1616–1629 (May 2016) doi: 10.1109/TVCG.2015.2440233

104. Lucas, J., Bowman, D., Chen, J., Wingrave, C.: Design and evaluation of 3D multiple object selection techniques. In: ACM Interactive 3D graphics (2005)
105. Lundström, C., Rydell, T., Forsell, C., Persson, A., Ynnerman, A.: Multi-touch table system for medical visualization: Application to orthopedic surgery planning. IEEE Transactions on Visualization and Computer Graphics 17(12) (Dec 2011) doi: 10.1109/TVCG.2011.224
106. Lv, Z., Halawani, A., Feng, S., Li, H., Réhman, S.U.: Multimodal hand and foot gesture interaction for handheld devices. ACM Transactions on Multimedia Computing, Communications, and Applications 11(1s), 10:1–10:19 (Sep 2014) doi: 10.1145/2645860
107. MacKenzie, I.S.: Evaluating eye tracking systems for computer input. In: Majaranta, P., Aoki, H., Donegan, M., Hansen, D.W., Hansen, J.P., Hyrskykari, A., Räihä, K.J. (eds.) Gaze Interaction and Applications of Eye Tracking: Advances in Assistive Technologies: Advances in Assistive Technologies, pp. 205–225. IGI Global, Hershey, PA, USA (2011) doi: 10.4018/978-1-61350-098-9.ch015
108. Majaranta, P., Bulling, A.: Eye tracking and eye-based human–computer interaction. In: Fairclough, S.H., Gilleade, K. (eds.) Advances in Physiological Computing, pp. 39–65. Springer, London (2014) doi: 10.1007/978-1-4471-6392-3_3
109. Malik, S., Ranjan, A., Balakrishnan, R.: Interacting with large displays from a distance with vision-tracked multi-finger gestural input. In: Proceedings of the Annual ACM Symposium on User Interface Software and Technology (UIST). pp. 43–52. ACM, New York (2005) doi: 10.1145/1095034.1095042
110. McMahan, A.: Immersion, engagement, and presence: A method for analyzing 3-D video games. In: Wolf, M., Perron, B. (eds.) The Video Game Theory Reader, chap. 3, pp. 67–86. Routledge (2003), http://www.alisonmcmahan.com/node/277
111. McNeill, D.: Hand and mind: What gestures reveal about thought. University of Chicago Press (1992), http://press.uchicago.edu/ucp/books/book/chicago/H/bo3641188.html
112. Mohr, P., Kerbl, B., Donoser, M., Schmalstieg, D., Kalkofen, D.: Retargeting technical documentation to augmented reality. In: Proceedings of the SIGCHI Conference on Human Factors in Computing Systems (CHI). pp. 3337–3346. ACM, New York (2015) doi: 10.1145/2702123.2702490
113. Myers, B.A.: A brief history of human-computer interaction technology. ACM Interactions 5(2), 44–54 (Mar/Apr 1998) doi: 10.1145/274430.274436
114. Ni, T., Bowman, D.A., Chen, J.: Increased display size and resolution improve task performance in information-rich virtual environments. In: Proceedings of Graphics Interface. pp. 139–146 (2006)
115. Nilsson, S., Gustafsson, T., Carleberg, P.: Hands free interaction with virtual information in a real environment: Eye gaze as an interaction tool in an augmented reality system. PsychNology Journal 7(2), 175–196 (2009)
116. Norman, D.A.: THE WAY I SEE IT: Signifiers, not affordances. ACM Interactions 15(6), 18–19 (Nov/Dec 2008) doi: 10.1145/1409040.1409044
117. Norman, D.A.: Natural user interfaces are not natural. interactions 17(3), 6–10 (May/Jun 2010) doi: 10.1145/1744161.1744163
118. Norman, D.A.: The design of everyday things: Revised and expanded edition. Basic books, New York (2013), https://www.jnd.org/books/design-of-everyday-things-revised.html
119. Piper, B., Ratti, C., Ishii, H.: Illuminating clay: A 3-D tangible interface for landscape analysis. In: Proceedings of the SIGCHI Conference on Human Factors in Computing Systems (CHI). pp. 355–362. ACM, New York (2002) doi: 10.1145/503376.503439

120. Pirolli, P., Card, S.: Information foraging. Psychological review 106(4), 643–675 (Oct 1999) doi: 10.1037/0033-295X.106.4.643
121. Preim, B., Dachselt, R.: Interaktive Systeme – Band 2: User Interface Engineering, 3D-Interaktion, Natural User Interfaces, vol. 2. Springer/Vieweg, Berlin/Heidelberg (2015) doi: 10.1007/978-3-642-45247-5
122. Pretorius, A.J., Purchase, H.C., Stasko, J.T.: Tasks for multivariate network analysis. In: Kerren, A., Purchase, H.C., Ward, M.O. (eds.) Multivariate Network Visualization: Dagstuhl Seminar #13201, Dagstuhl Castle, Germany, May 12–17, 2013, Revised Discussions, pp. 77–95. Springer International Publishing, Cham, Switzerland (2014) doi: 10.1007/978-3-319-06793-3_5
123. Rädle, R., Jetter, H.C., Butscher, S., Reiterer, H.: The effect of egocentric body movements on users' navigation performance and spatial memory in zoomable user interfaces. In: Proceedings of the International Conference on Interactive Tabletops and Surfaces (ITS). pp. 23–32. ACM, New York (2013) doi: 10.1145/2512349.2512811
124. Ragan, E.D., Endert, A., Sanyal, J., Chen, J.: Characterizing provenance in visualization and data analysis: An organizational framework of provenance types and purposes. IEEE Transactions on Visualization and Computer Graphics 22(1), 31–40 (Jan 2016), https://doi.org/10.1109/TVCG.2015.2467551 doi: 10.1109/TVCG.2015.2467551
125. Rashid, U., Nacenta, M.A., Quigley, A.: The cost of display switching: A comparison of mobile, large display and hybrid UI configurations. In: Proceedings of the International Working Conference on Advanced Visual Interfaces (AVI). pp. 99–106. ACM, New York (2012) doi: 10.1145/2254556.2254577
126. Rekimoto, J., Green, M.: The information cube: Using transparency in 3D information visualization. In: Proceedings of the Annual Workshop on Information Technologies & Systems (WITS). pp. 125–132 (1993), https://www.sonycsl.co.jp/person/rekimoto/cube/
127. Renambot, L., Marrinan, T., Aurisano, J., Nishimoto, A., Mateevitsi, V., Bharadwaj, K., Long, L., Johnson, A., Brown, M., Leigh, J.: SAGE2: a collaboration portal for scalable resolution displays. Future Generation Computer Systems 54, 296–305 (2016) doi: 10.1016/j.future.2015.05.014
128. Roberts, J.C., Ritsos, P.D., Badam, S.K., Brodbeck, D., Kennedy, J., Elmqvist, N.: Visualization beyond the desktop—The next big thing. IEEE Computer Graphics and Applications 34(6), 26–34 (Nov/Dec 2014) doi: 10.1109/MCG.2014.82
129. Robles-De-La-Torre, G.: The importance of the sense of touch in virtual and real environments. IEEE MultiMedia 13(3), 24–30 (Jul 2006) doi: 10.1109/MMUL.2006.69
130. Roth, V., Schmidt, P., Güldenring, B.: The IR ring: Authenticating users' touches on a multi-touch display. In: Proceedings of the Annual ACM Symposium on User Interface Software and Technology (UIST). pp. 259–262. ACM, New York (2010) doi: 10.1145/1866029.1866071
131. Samsung introduces 2007 LCD, plasma, DLP and CRT lineup (2007 (accessed 11th April 2017)), https://www.engadget.com/2007/01/07/samsung-introduces-2007-lcd-plasma-dlp-and-crt-lineup/
132. Scheurich, D., Stuerzlinger, W.: A one-handed multi-touch method for 3D rotations. In: Human-Computer Interaction – INTERACT 2013. pp. 56–69. Springer (2013) doi: 10.1007/978-3-642-40483-2
133. Shaer, O., Hornecker, E.: Tangible user interfaces: past, present, and future directions. Foundations and Trends® in Human–Computer Interaction 3(1–2), 4–137 (2010) doi: 10.1561/1100000026

134. Shneiderman, B.: The eyes have it: A task by data type taxonomy for information visualizations. In: Proceedings of the IEEE Symposium on Visual Languages (VL). pp. 336–343. IEEE Computer Society, Los Alamitos (1996) doi: 10.1109/VL.1996.545307
135. Slater, M., Wilbur, S.: A framework for immersive virtual environments (FIVE): Speculations on the role of presence in virtual environments. Presence: Teleoperators and virtual environments 6(6), 603–616 (1997) doi: 10.1162/pres.1997.6.6.603
136. Facebook shows how it's gonna make virtual reality social, https://www.cnet.com/au/news/facebook-mark-zuckerberg-shows-off-live-vr-virtual-reality-chat-with-oculus-rift/
137. Spindler, M., Tominski, C., Schumann, H., Dachselt, R.: Tangible views for information visualization. In: Proceedings of the International Conference on Interactive Tabletops and Surfaces (ITS). pp. 157–166. ACM, New York (2010) doi: 10.1145/1936652.1936684
138. Stasko, J., Görg, C., Liu, Z.: Jigsaw: Supporting investigative analysis through interactive visualization. Information Visualization 7(2), 118–132 (Apr 2008) doi: 10.1145/1466620.1466622
139. Stellmach, S., Dachselt, R.: Look & touch: Gaze-supported target acquisition. In: Proceedings of the SIGCHI Conference on Human Factors in Computing Systems (CHI). pp. 2981–2990. ACM, New York (2012) doi: 10.1145/2207676.2208709
140. Stellmach, S., Stober, S., Nürnberger, A., Dachselt, R.: Designing gaze-supported multimodal interactions for the exploration of large image collections. In: Proceedings of the Conference on Novel Gaze-Controlled Applications (NGCA). pp. 1:1–1:8. ACM, New York (2011) doi: 10.1145/1983302.1983303
141. Stuerzlinger, W., Wingrave, C.: The value of constraints for 3D user interfaces. In: Virtual Realities: Dagstuhl Seminar 2008. pp. 203–224. Springer (2011) doi: 10.1007/978-3-211-99178-7
142. Sun, J., Stuerzlinger, W., Shuralyov, D.: Shift-sliding and depth-pop for 3D positioning. In: Proceedings of the 2016 Symposium on Spatial User Interaction. pp. 69–78. ACM (2016)
143. Sutherland, I.E.: Sketchpad: A man-machine graphical communication system. In: Proceedings of the Spring Joint Computer Conference (AFIPS, Spring). pp. 329–346. ACM, New York (1963) doi: 10.1145/1461551.1461591
144. Sutherland, I.E.: The ultimate display. In: Proceedings of the IFIP Congress. pp. 506–508 (1965)
145. Sutherland, I.E.: A head-mounted three dimensional display. In: Proceedings of the Fall Joint Computer Conference (AFIPS, Fall, part I). pp. 757–764. ACM, New York (1968) doi: 10.1145/1476589.1476686
146. Teather, R.J., Stuerzlinger, W.: Pointing at 3D targets in a stereo head-tracked virtual environment. In: Proceedings of the IEEE Symposium on 3D User Interfaces (3DUI). pp. 87–94. IEEE Computer Society, Los Alamitos (2011) doi: 10.1109/3DUI.2011.5759222
147. Cluster rendering, Unity user manual, https://docs.unity3d.com/Manual/ClusterRendering.html
148. Vertegaal, R.: Attentive user interfaces. Communications of the ACM 46(3), 30–33 (Mar 2003) doi: 10.1145/636772.636794
149. Wai, J., Lubinski, D., Benbow, C.P.: Spatial ability for STEM domains: aligning over 50 years of cumulative psychological knowledge solidifies its importance. Journal of Educational Psychology 101(4), 817 (2009) doi: 10.1037/a0016127

150. Walny, J., Carpendale, S., Henry Riche, N., Venolia, G., Fawcett, P.: Visual thinking in action: Visualizations as used on whiteboards. IEEE Transactions on Visualization and Computer Graphics 17(12), 2508–2517 (Dec 2011) doi: 10.1109/TVCG.2011.251
151. Walter, R., Bailly, G., Valkanova, N., Müller, J.: Cuenesics: Using mid-air gestures to select items on interactive public displays. In: Proceedings of the International Conference on Human-computer Interaction with Mobile Devices & Services (MobileHCI). pp. 299–308. ACM, New York (2014) doi: 10.1145/2628363.2628368
152. Wigdor, D., Wixon, D.: Brave NUI world: designing natural user interfaces for touch and gesture. Elsevier/Morgan Kaufmann, Amsterdam (2011) doi: 10.1016/B978-0-12-382231-4.00037-X
153. Wither, J., DiVerdi, S., Höllerer, T.: Annotation in outdoor augmented reality. Computers & Graphics 33(6), 679–689 (Dec 2009) doi: 10.1016/j.cag.2009.06.001
154. Yi, J.S., Kang, Y.a., Stasko, J., Jacko, J.: Toward a deeper understanding of the role of interaction in information visualization. IEEE Transactions on Visualization and Computer Graphics 13(6), 1224–1231 (Nov/Dec 2007) doi: 10.1109/TVCG.2007.70515
155. Ynnerman, A., Rydell, T., Antoine, D., Hughes, D., Persson, A., Ljung, P.: Interactive visualization of 3D scanned mummies at public venues. Communications of the ACM 59(12), 72–81 (Dec 2016) doi: 10.1145/2950040
156. Yu, L., Efstathiou, K., Isenberg, P., Isenberg, T.: Efficient structure-aware selection techniques for 3D point cloud visualizations with 2DOF input. IEEE Transactions on Visualization and Computer Graphics 18(12), 2245–2254 (Dec 2012) doi: 10.1109/TVCG.2012.217
157. Yu, L., Svetachov, P., Isenberg, P., Everts, M.H., Isenberg, T.: FI3D: Direct-touch interaction for the exploration of 3D scientific visualization spaces. IEEE Transactions on Visualization and Computer Graphics 16(6), 1613–1622 (Nov/Dec 2010) doi: 10.1109/TVCG.2010.157
158. Brown University YURT homepage, https://web1.ccv.brown.edu/viz-yurt
159. von Zadow, U., Reipschläger, P., Bösel, D., Sellent, A., Dachselt, R.: YouTouch! Low-cost user identification at an interactive display wall. In: Proceedings of the International Working Conference on Advanced Visual Interfaces (AVI). pp. 144–151. ACM, New York (2016) doi: 10.1145/2909132.2909258
160. Zaroff, C.M., Knutelska, M., Frumkes, T.E.: Variation in stereoacuity: Normative description, fixation disparity, and the roles of aging and gender. Investigative Ophthalmology & Visual Science 44(2), 891 (Feb 2003) doi: 10.1167/iovs.02-0361

5. Immersive Human-Centered Computational Analytics

Wolfgang Stuerzlinger[1], Tim Dwyer[2], Steven Drucker[3], Carsten Görg[4], Chris North[5], and Gerik Scheuermann[6]

[1] School of Interactive Arts + Technology (SIAT), Simon Fraser University, Canada
w.s@sfu.ca
[2] Monash University, Australia
tim.dwyer@monash.edu
[3] Microsoft Research, USA
sdrucker@microsoft.com
[4] University of Colorado, USA
carsten.goerg@ucdenver.edu
[5] Virginia Tech, USA
north@vt.edu
[6] Leipzig University, Germany
scheuermann@informatik.uni-leipzig.de

Abstract. In this chapter we seek to elevate the role of the human in human-machine cooperative analysis through a careful consideration of immersive design principles. We consider both strategic immersion through more accessible systems as well as enhanced understanding and control through immersive interfaces that enable rapid workflows. We extend the classic sensemaking loop from visual analytics to incorporate multiple views, scenarios, people, and computational agents. We consider both sides of machine/human collaboration: allowing the human to more fluidly control the machine process; and also allowing the human to understand the results, derive insights and continue the analytic cycle. We also consider system and algorithmic implications of enabling real-time control and feedback in immersive human-centered computational analytics.

Keywords: human-in-the-loop analytics, visual analytics, data visualization

5.1. Introduction

In Chapter 4, we reviewed the basic tasks that immersive analytics systems need to support. The tasks considered in that chapter were mostly 'low-level' in the sense that each task corresponded to a single conceptual action supporting data analysis. These types of tasks were categorized in Heer and Shneiderman's task taxonomy for information visualization [24] as *data and view specification* and *view manipulation* tasks. However, we also reviewed the third category of tasks from this taxonomy on so-called *process and provenance*. These latter tasks were

K. Marriott et al. (Eds.): Immersive Analytics, LNCS 11190, pp. 139–163, 2018.
https://doi.org/10.1007/978-3-030-01388-2_5

still fairly finely grained in terms of corresponding to concrete actions but they related to "doing things" with insights gleaned from the data (e. g., *record*, *share*, *annotate*, *guide*) rather than tasks required to make these individual insights in the first place. Thus, these process and provenance tasks were required to support a full workflow around data analytics – not simply identifying particular features of data, but *making sense* of data in a more holistic way. We review these 'traditional views' of the analytics process in Section 5.2. This chapter focuses squarely on this more holistic process or workflow, also known as the *sensemaking loop* of visual analytics [44], and the various ways in which *human immersion* can play a role in this loop, and the way that that immersion can be supported by machine guidance. The sense-making loop is considered again briefly in Chapter 9 of this book along with a model for the Immersive Analytics process as part of a broader discussion of a general design framework for immersive analytics.

Also in Chapter 4, we described the opportunities for visualization researchers and designers to take advantage of the different kinds of immersion and increased user presence afforded by natural user interfaces and immersive display technologies. We described how spatial and sensory-motoric immersion can help to increase the engagement of the users in their data analysis tasks.

In this chapter, in considering more broadly the higher-level concerns of the data analytics process, the type of immersion we are seeking could be more accurately described as *Strategic Immersion*. This follows a concept from game design that—compared to other types of immersion—is more closely related to high-level problem solving, or literally, a game player's strategy for succeeding in the game [1].

Another aspect of the data analytics workflow that we begin to consider in this chapter is the integration of automatic processes, such as machine optimization and learning, into the workflow. Thus, we consider the role of a user in a larger-scale collaborative analytics process, which includes both other people and machine assistance. It is timely to consider this now because, in addition to the rapidly emerging display and interaction technologies described throughout this book, we are also in the midst of a step-change in the capability of machine learning (ML). We want to make sure that the rapid advances in deep-learning, for instance, do not close the door on interaction.

We can summarize the various considerations of this chapter as follows:

- To leverage the advantages of immersive environments for problem-solving tasks in Visual Analytics (VA) (Section 5.2.).
- We want to elevate the role of the human in human-machine cooperative analysis (over perhaps the ML or DataMining Human in the Loop perspective) (Section 5.3.).
- How do the above considerations affect algorithm/system/platform design and what are the challenges for the future? (Section 5.4.).

5.2. Analytics Process

In this section, we discuss the analytics process, including models for how people analyze data. Then we analyze which parts of this process can be augmented by immersive technologies. We also discuss how human collaborators and automatic "intelligent" processing can be integrated into the immersive analytics process. Finally, we develop an overview of the requirements for keeping an analytics system responsive enough to be used in an interactive immersive environment.

5.2.1. Example Scenario for Immersive Analytics Processes

To date, there are few compelling examples of systems that use immersion for information seeking analytical activities. An intriguing scenario proposed as a demonstration game for the Microsoft Hololens is the Fragments game (see Figure 1), which explores many aspects of immersive analytics. In the scenario, the user plays a detective that examines multiple crime scenes and gathers evidence to inform subsequent search criteria. Different 'lenses' can be used so that different aspects of the real world are highlighted – in the case of the game, x-ray lenses for seeing inside or underneath the surface of objects, infrared for exploring heat and recently manipulated objects, or audio lenses that play certain sounds triggered by examining objects in the environment.

This information is then used to filter both map-based geographic visualizations and lists of facts. Hypotheses can be formed and tested within the scenario and when a hypothesis is confirmed, the user moves on to deeper challenges. The scenario exemplifies many potential immersive visual analytics activities: gathering evidence, forming hypotheses, refining queries, and organizing information. It further shows how the system can facilitate both manual interaction—where the user is completely controlling the exploration based on their gaze—and automated interaction, where the system takes a combination of observations and generates a model of the results that is visualized for appropriate subsequent actions.

5.2.2. Sensemaking as the Analytics Process

There are several different models that help describe the way by which humans understand and process information. Depicted below are two models (from among many) that are commonly cited in the visual analytics literature. Specifically, in Figure 2 we have one of the earliest (1999) attempt at a visualization "reference model" by Card *et al.* [5] and then in Figure 3, the more recent (2005) and sophisticated *Sensemaking Loop* by Pirolli and Card [44]. Both of these models incorporate stages for taking in data, transforming the data into a representation convenient for interaction, and an iterative process by which we refine through successive interactions.

We have chosen to use the Pirolli-Card Sensemaking Loop (Figure 3) as a basis for this chapter in part because of its wide popularity, and in part because it breaks down the process in a more fine-grained fashion than many other models. For each of the stages, we can explore how that stage might be transformed by

Fig. 1: The Hololens Fragments game allows deeper exploration of a scene using alternate 'lenses'. *Courtesy Microsoft - used with permission.*

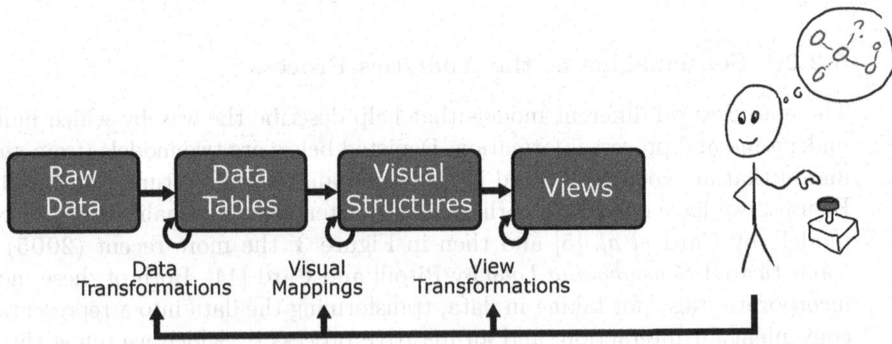

Fig. 2: The traditional reference model for visualisation, after Card *et al.* [5]

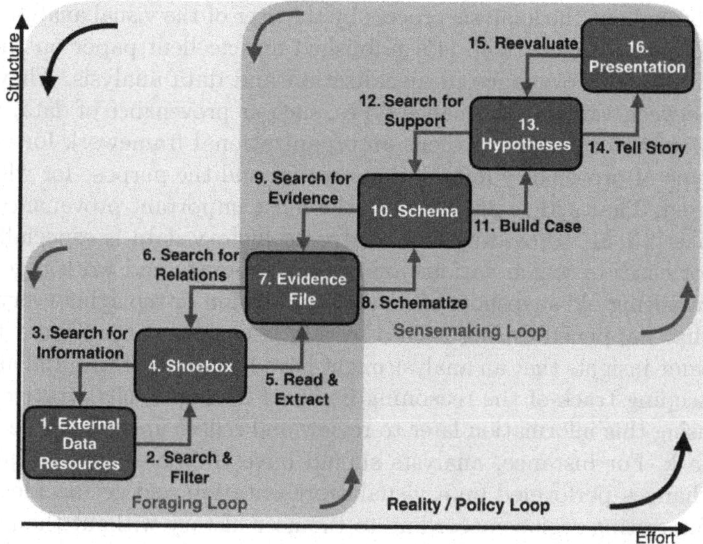

Fig. 3: Pirolli and Card's sensemaking loop (courtesy Jie Liu, 2017).

immersive capabilities. In particular, the Pirolli-Card model has a series of steps for both:

Creating a model (bottom-up) where those steps involve finding information, extracting meaning, schematizing, building a case, and subsequently communicating that information.

Evaluating the model (top-down) where those steps involve re-evaluation, finding supporting evidence, finding relations in the information or finding basic information itself.

Each stage can loop back down or move upwards in the chain.

5.2.3. Tasks in the Analytic Process

In Chapter 4 we described three categories of tasks that need to be supported by immersive analytics systems. Here we describe how those tasks fit into the Sensemaking Loop model.

The first two categories of tasks, *data/view specification* and *view manipulation*, describe fairly low-level operations that mostly fall within the "foraging" portion of the Pirolli and Card model. The last category, *process and provenance*, goes beyond most traditional visualization task taxonomies as it addresses typical issues that are more related to supporting the analysis process in general, and not tasks specifically related to interactive visualization. As described below, the *process and provenance* tasks are more the domain of the "sensemaking" portion of the Pirolli and Card model.

Record: Provenance research is mostly interpreted as the development of methods and tools to improve awareness of the history of changes and advances throughout the analysis process by the user of the visual analytics tool. Quite recently, Ragen *et al.* [45] published an excellent paper on the characterization of provenance in visualization and data analysis. They distinguish between various provenance types, such as provenance of data, visualization, or interaction, and present an organizational framework for clarifying the type of provenance information capture and the purpose for which it will be used. That article also surveys the most important provenance approaches like [23, 51]. Providing and analyzing history data is especially important for cases in which various analysts collaborate and work together. Simply revisiting old snapshots of an analytic session or replaying every single event that happened during such a session is usually not sufficient to reveal the same insights that an analyst might have had during the initial analysis. Thus, keeping track of the reasoning involved during a collaborative process and using this information later to review and reflect upon it can be a challenging task. For instance, analysts should have the possibility to quickly review changes performed on a visual representation and get an idea of the most interesting regions according to the user history without the need to replay every single action that was performed by previous users.

Share: Collaboration is an important aspect in practice, but still not very well researched or supported by visualization tools. "A VA system has to support discussions, dissemination of results, or interactions of several analysts at the same place and the same time (co-located) or at different places and not necessarily at the same time (distributed). Sharing views or publication of visualizations are examples of important requirements for efficient collaboration between many analysts." [30]. Isenberg *et al.* [28] provide an excellent overview of definitions, tasks and examples for collaborative visualization (also see 8). They also provide an excellent summary of ongoing challenges in this field. A recent visualization system that supports the distributed (synchronous and asynchronous) analysis of networks is OnGraX [59]. It even makes data-aware annotations available as discussed in the next item.

Annotate: Pointing to interesting elements or giving comments to individual graphical features or patterns discovered within a visualization are important for any analytical process and also for potential discussions within a collaborative setting. As a visualization is not a static image or diagram, such annotations must be stable/persistent with respect to the represented data as well as to the actual visible graphical elements. Both can and will change over the period a visual analysis is performed. An example of such a dynamic situation is the analysis of a social network where network nodes might appear/disappear, and the layout may change due to a reconfiguration by the analyst (e. g., by using another layout algorithm). In consequence, annotations should be viewable in their historical context. Thus, it should be possible for analysts to review old visualization states where the annotation took place (cf. the provenance and history discussion above). As an example, the OnGraX network visualization system [59] makes it possible to link textual annotations and chat messages to specific network elements. Those annotations are permanently tracked and stored in a database.

Guide: Analytics processes are typically non-linear, i. e., the representation of workflows is challenging. Guiding the user through workflows for shared activities would be clearly beneficial, for instance. The first approach to a more detailed characterization schema for guidance in visual analytics has been recently proposed by Ceneda *et al.* [8]. Another related conceptual approach for guidance was proposed by Streit *et al.* [53], but there the authors only focus on previously defined workflow-driven approaches for concrete biomedical use cases. Besides the previously mentioned works, there is only a little work done to understand or define the process of user guidance in general, and there are also only a few practical realizations. Guidance provided by the VA system can be based on several inputs (individually used or all together), such as the input data itself, interaction when using the VA system, user/domain knowledge, or it may even be based on emotion tracking or similar sources [9]. The exact way in which a system supports guidance and to what extent (more proposing or more decisive) can be varied too.

5.2.4. The Analytics Process in an Immersive Environment

We now discuss the potential for integrating the analytic process with immersive environments. In particular, we examine specific components of the sensemaking process that could be enhanced by immersive technologies.

The first half of Pirolli and Card's sensemaking process is about foraging for information. We can envision using attributes of both Augmented Reality (AR) and Virtual Reality (VR) technologies to help find and access appropriate information on an as-needed basis. In an AR setting, we can associate information sources with objects in the real world by taking advantage of their spatial context (see Chapter 7). In an application on a factory floor, for example, simply looking at a particular machine could provide usage and maintenance statistics associated with that machine. Traffic patterns throughout the factory could be shown by patterns superimposed on the floor. In a VR setting, we can use models in a fashion similar to icons to represent data sources, but those models could have additional semantic meaning associated with them–so that a model of an engine might serve as a gateway for information about emissions, maintenance, power output, etc. This type of semantic association could entail both advantages and disadvantages for the sensemaking process: on the positive side, it could help remind people what is available; but, on the negative side, more abstract measures and data might be difficult to associate with concrete representations.

The second half of the sensemaking process is about synthesizing information–organizing collected information, formulating hypotheses and arranging supporting and contradictory evidence. It has been shown that space (a physical interaction space or relatively large display space) can play an important role in this process and assist in task completion by allowing greater space for organization [2, 60]. Analysts can use the space to organize and structure not only collected information but also their analytical workflow and thought processes.

As a simple example of combining these two portions of the sensemaking process, an immersive environment can serve as a huge canvas where information can be accessed relative to the user. Furthermore, as a user moves around the space, information can be organized using spatial position and relative proximity between data representations to imply a relationship between them. Another potential advantage of immersion is the possibility to provide a physical instantiation of the 'memory palace' mnemonic device so that parts of a complex model can be compartmentalized to different spatial locations–virtual in the case of VR or physical in the case of AR.

5.2.5. Support for Analytics Steps in Immersive Environments

Next, we discuss how well specific types of interactions in the various steps of the sensemaking process may be supported by immersive environments. In the following, **bold numbers** refer to the individual steps in Pirolli and Card's Sensemaking Loop model in Figure 3.

The sensemaking loop contains a variety of different search processes (see steps **2,3,6,9,12**). These could be supported through easier visual access to large amounts of information, e. g., by rotating the head. As long as the cost of navigation is small, say due to a one-to-one mapping between user and viewpoint, accessing large amounts of information through physical navigation is beneficial [2]. Yet, if navigation becomes challenging, e. g., in large-scale environments or due to the use of more complex interaction schemes for navigation, the cost of navigation can become a bottleneck. Given strong spatial memory, we can re-find information more easily when it has been associated with a spatial position. Furthermore, automated search can reveal information 'in-context' by highlighting the results while preserving their spatial positions, reinforcing spatial memory. There are still obstacles in using immersive environments for search. One notable example is that current resolutions in both VR and AR are extremely limited in comparison to the real world. Experiments with foveated displays may assist, but especially when working with textual data, we need large, high-resolution displays for effective interaction.

For schematizing (steps **8,10**), it is possible to use the immersive environment to bridge the gap between data embedded in the real world and abstract data, for example, by augmenting a real-world scene with an abstract data display. This can help to create stronger associations, that further support visual search. This can also support aspects of distributed cognition, enabling analysts to readily offload cognitive activities into the environment.

Sensemaking tasks that are focused on data manipulation (steps **8,11,10,13**) rather than data retrieval may be harder to accomplish in immersive environments as detailed interaction (especially with textual information) may pose more usability challenges (at least with current technologies). Whereas, interacting with large amounts of information may be made easier by exploiting greater degrees of freedom. Pointing and selecting data objects in immersive environments is often not as efficient as on the desktop. Thus, the trade-off between input modalities is different in immersive environments. Speech, gesture, and other input modalities might counterbalance the shortcomings of interactions in other modalities. Some interactions are easier because they are naturally supported

(e. g., panning head). Others might become more difficult (e. g., selection), and require the use of gestures or voice (see Chapter 4).

The presentation of analysis results at the end of the sensemaking loop (step **16**) can be augmented through immersive environments, including overlaying results on the real world. However, a potential downside is that the potential for deception might be even stronger than in more abstract representations since abstraction might require more verification of the substance of the arguments. Early experiments with augmented presentation techniques in which gestures and speech trigger 3D visual animations are promising in helping to convey complex concepts. One current difficulty is in the complexity of authoring such experiences. Another difficulty is in viewing them. Do viewers need for themselves to be in a virtual environment? How do differing viewpoints affect the presentation?

Sensemaking Step	**IA Support**	**Comments**
1. External Data Sources	−	not well suported
2. Search & Filter	∼	filtering not well supported
3. Search for Information	+	visual search
4. Shoebox	+	large display space
5. Read & Extract	+	access to much information
6. Search for Relations	+	visual search
7. Evidence File	+	large display space
8. Schematize	+	easy to organize with more space
9. Search for Evidence	+	visual search
10. Schema	+	distributed cognition
11. Build Case	−	interaction-heavy
12. Search for Support	+	visual search
13. Hypotheses	−	interaction-heavy
14. Tell Story	−	storytelling not well supported
15. Reevaluate	∼	comparisons easier
16. Presentation	+	immersive displays

Table 1: Summary of support of sensemaking activities through immersive analytics systems. '+' indidates good, '∼' partial, and '−' little or no support.

In Table 1 we list all steps in the sensemaking process and defined how well they are supported by current immersive systems. Steps that rely mostly on visual perception or scanning (e. g., steps **3,6,9,12,15,16**) and/or can benefit from large interactive display spaces to organize information (e. g., steps **4,5,7,8,9**) are already reasonably well supported by immersive systems. On the other hand, steps that are interaction-heavy, potentially require substantial amounts of text to be entered, or require the user to externalize complex thoughts "through" the system (e. g., steps **1,11,13,14**) are less well supported. This highlights the potential need for complementary methods to support such steps.

Moreover, the fact that some steps are better supported than others also poses the question of whether immersion is needed for all parts of an analysis process? Given that current systems do not support all sensemaking steps well, we believe that it is prudent to support easy, rapid and seamless switching in and out of immersion. An illustrative example is that an analyst may want to switch out of an immersive system to write up a page of a report about the insights gained from the current immersive session in a word processor and then go back into the immersive system to hunt for additional insights. Similarly for switching out of the immersive system to ask a colleague to bounce ideas around for the exact formulation of a hypothesis. Or someone who has to engage with a long, complex text document and (due to individual preferences) wants to read it on a tablet in a more comfortable setting. All these scenarios point out that the transition into and out of, or between different forms of, immersive analytics systems needs to be well supported, too.

Overall, some parts become easier, some parts are harder in immersive environments. Thus, there is no clear win-win situation, but there are many trade-offs that pose challenges to user interface and system designers. Interestingly, the difficulties identified here match, at least to some degree, the challenges that occur in other types of visual analytics systems. This highlights again major avenues for future work.

Below we discuss a new lens on the Pirolli-Card model, which incorporates automatic processes into the sensemaking process. In general, collaboration is an essential component of data analytics, and we discuss this in the following section.

5.3. Collaboration between Humans and Automated Processes

In this section, we discuss how immersive analytics systems can assist with sensemaking at larger scales. In particular, we target situations where multiple people are working together and are assisted by multiple automatic processes. The (potentially infinite) space available in immersive environments provides an appropriate "canvas" for all intermediate results in such a collaboration.

At this point, we consider an extended sensemaking loop, where multiple people interact with an evolving (intermediate) set of computationally generated/refined and human-mediated analysis results and insights. Much of the work discussed in the Chapter 8, such as maintaining awareness, applies to both human and machine actors. Here we discuss only aspects that are central to immersive analytics.

A tenet of successful collaborations is that the actions of any single actor (be they humans or algorithms) should never destroy other actors' work (without their consent). This means that multiple, potentially parallel, analyses and/or scenarios need to co-exist and the system needs to support them and their management [61]. Moreover, it should be possible to merge advances of work on a given analysis/scenario into other analyses/scenarios to avoid re-doing of work.

While source-code control systems are a traditional way to handle branching and merging of text documents, the visual nature of immersive analytics makes it necessary to explore graphical user interfaces for branching and merging. Here it is important to point out that structured code documents are fundamentally different from free-flowing text or graphical content and that source-code control systems are not necessarily the best way to handle such content. A recent exploration in this direction presented a graphical user interface for parallel work in the domain of generative design [58] and these ideas seem directly applicable to immersive analytics.

One of the primary reasons for sensemaking tools is to help people deal with more information than can comfortably be managed by an individual. Thus, it seems intuitive (and is also supported by research [2,19]) that larger displays can enhance people's sensemaking abilities.

Maintaining awareness of the activities of others in the system (both human and automated) is a challenge. With multiple actors, it becomes necessary to keep track of who did and modified what, i. e., maintaining provenance of data and annotations about the data need to be supported

An interesting facet of the challenge to maintain awareness is that changes by other actors can impact an individual's sensemaking activities. In the foraging loop, either another individual or the computer can augment the search for information based on the currently gathered information. When new information is thus retrieved, this information can be added at the appropriate level of abstraction. For example, new raw data could be added to the shoebox, new relational data could be inserted into the evidence file, or a strong correlation could be added as a potential hypothesis. The system can use visual cues such as spatial organization or representation to help distinguish such new information from previously examined information. As more of the models are built, the system could automatically flag information that supports or contradicts any given conclusion–again using spatial or visual representation to help distinguish the material.

As we scale a system to deal with more people and more automated processes, the challenge of maintaining awareness of the activities of others increases. While this is not unique to immersive environments, we can use certain aspects of immersive environments to help manage that scale. In particular, we can move from overviews of the data to focal areas while maintaining context. We can use visual attributes in different ways to show who (or what) has contributed new information or what information may have changed since last viewed.

Just as we change the level of detail at which we might observe the information, we can choose to have private views of the information in addition to a shared view. In this way, we can locally modify information without destroying the work of others. This poses yet more challenges with respect to version control of the information, rolling the system back to previous organizations and models of the data.

5.3.1. Human-in-the-loop Analytics

Immersive analytics seeks to broaden the bandwidth of communication between machine and human through more complete engagement of human sensorial perception (in the machine-to-human direction) and more fluid interaction (in the human-to-machine direction). We have discussed in previous sections and chapters the challenges involved in designing improved multisensory displays and more natural and expressive interaction devices and techniques. However, even assuming these challenges can be met to create a higher-bandwidth communication channel between machine and human, there remain a number of technical challenges in order to create completely immersive data analytics experiences. In particular, we focus in this section on the algorithmic and system architecture requirements that must be met to:

1. open algorithms to the possibility of human-in-the-loop control;
2. ensure responsiveness of algorithms in the face of the dynamic changes to parameters or the underlying data.

These challenges can arise in scenarios such as:

- large quantities of data, i. e. *scalability*;
- data changing in real-time, e. g., from *streaming data* feeds;
- prediction and optimization that can deal with uncertainty;
- synchronizing and scheduling long-running processes.

These challenges are not unique to immersive analytics scenarios and progress has been made in these areas in a number of fields, such as data mining. However, it is arguable that the focus on user-engagement in immersive analytics systems and the potential for this higher-bandwidth communication channel, make these requirements for interactive data analysis systems more pressing than ever. Thus, this section provides a survey of the state-of-the-art in the area of design patterns and issues involved in engineering algorithms to be responsive.

Immersive Algorithms (Live feedback and control) The research field of Human-Computer Interaction has long recognized the importance of minimizing delay. For example, in 1968 Miller described this not only as an "operational need" (the computer has to respond to a command before the plane crashes into the mountain) but also as a "psychological need" [38]. Card *et al.* later quantified the desirable limits on delay in an information visualization system [6], identifying three distinct time constants that a system must meet:

Perceptual processing - 0.1 second was the time they considered acceptable for a screen refresh.

Immediate response - 1 second was nominated as the time a human takes to acknowledge (not necessarily answer) a question. This was therefore suggested as a reasonable upper limit on the time an automated agent in an information visualization system might reasonably take to respond.

Unit task - 10 seconds was considered a reasonable time limit on completing a basic task or operation in the system.

These three basic time constants have become "rules-of-thumb" for user interface design [40, Chapter 5] and lore around acceptable latency for asynchronous interfaces, for example in web design [41]. However, advances in technology have arguably made some of these time limits seem generous. For example, predictive interfaces such as autocomplete (originally conceived as an accessibility feature for keyboards [15]) are now an integral part of both web and desktop search and routinely offer results to queries in significantly less than a second.

Similarly, advances in display and interaction hardware have shown that users of multitouch displays not only perceive but can be adversely affected by latencies of significantly less than 0.1 seconds [39]. In VR, latencies of more than about 20 milliseconds, from tracking of head-position movement to re-rendering the view, not only ruin immersion but can make users ill [7].

This section describes what conditions analytics algorithms have to fulfill to allow for immersive analytics. A potential metaphor is that immersive analytics means human and machine co-processing. We survey classes of data analysis and data production algorithms and name necessary requirements as well as enhancing properties for data analytics. Furthermore, we give examples of algorithms that are close to fulfilling the minimal requirements of immersive analytics. Typical requirements are:

(1) Immediate, or seemingly immediate, feedback in the sense that there is no human impression of latency. This includes situations where the human triggers the rerun of an analysis of a larger subset of the data or reruns a simulation that may necessarily take time, but where the human still needs feedback indicating the status of the computation.
(2) Possibilities for the human to control, steer or interfere with the algorithm.
(3) Allowance for human reasoning about the algorithmic results, e. g., allow for human co-processing. This requires mechanisms for the human to look behind the curtain, i. e. any black box method must allow for human inspection on request if the human questions the computer.

While a complete fulfillment of these requirements provides an open challenge, in many cases there are algorithmic developments in recent years heading in the right direction. Some examples by field:

Data Mining: There already exist data mining algorithms that support streaming results. As an example, there is work on data stream clustering, for example, Silva *et al.* [50]. However, taking the human back into the loop is an open challenge.

Clustering: Other classes of clustering algorithms allow users to manually steer the clustering process. Such algorithms use strategies like semi-supervised clustering where must-link and cannot-link constraints are added by the user as in BoostCluster [32]. Another class of such algorithms are subspace search and grouping of similar subspaces that incorporate the user into the clustering, see [54].

Optimization: Optimization and operations research are discovering the importance of human-in-the-loop operation, recognizing that not every optimization problem can be completely modeled and then solved in isolation [37]. In multi-objective optimization, strategies like exploring Pareto frontiers allow for human co-processing [55]. Goodwin *et al.* [22] explore requirements for visual profiling of Constraint Programming solvers. Liu *et al.* [31] explore the relationship between interactive optimization and visual analytics, proposing a "problem-solving loop" for optimization, analogous to the sensemaking loop.
Text Analytics: Interactive topic modeling enables users to view and refine analyses of large document collections [11]. Some existing systems allow the user to define relations between documents spatially to the machine so algorithms can take this into account to incrementally update topic models, for example [20].
Dimension Reduction: With respect to dimension reduction techniques, there are ideas like probing [52] allowing human analysts to gain an understanding of the projections using interaction, or direct manipulation of the projection output to explore projection parameter spaces [17].
Scientific Simulation: For flow simulations, there are some methods that allow the interactive study of particle traces including interactive seeding of additional particles [48]. In similar scientific contexts, some feature detection systems allow for interactive feature definition [16]. While this has been explored for point-based feature detection, this may also be beneficial for particle-based feature extraction [47]. Even topological data analysis algorithms have important parameters with respect to simplification and interactive presentation, as well as further inspection [25]. Here, immersive interaction opens the way for a deeper human understanding of structural data properties.
Information Theory: There are also ideas to use information theory to find unusual data, e. g., by measuring entropy [29]. However, methods that allow the human to indicate which part of the data has highly informative content are missing to date.

Some general questions have not been addressed appropriately, for example, how can an algorithm explain to the human how its conclusions are reached?

5.4. Challenges

From the extended sensemaking loop we identify some aspects that can be improved through immersive design principles. In the following we identify some examples for existing paths through–and potential for new extensions of–the sensemaking loop.

5.4.1. The Role of Alternatives

Good analysis practice considers alternative explanations for any given observation, often in the form of more or less explicit hypotheses. Another form of alternatives occurs in the visual analytics process through different views of the same data, including comparisons and multi-scale views. Yet, such alternatives are not just a part of the process to arrive at insights, they can also play a central role to enable collaborative work between humans while also integrating algorithmic assistance.

Consider a group working asynchronously together. To avoid the potential for destruction of each other's work, it is necessary that any visual analytics system can support parallel, independent alternative views and interactions. If multiple people work independently on the same content, such as a dashboard, it is appropriate for the system to support such parallel work, e. g., by keeping people aware of other changes. But as network connections cannot always be taken as granted, the support for post hoc integration of changes (aka post hoc merging), is also highly beneficial.

Full support for asynchronous work also enables more seamless integration of machine assistance. A notable issue here is that machine processes can take indeterminate amounts of time to finish. Having (multiple) humans wait on a machine is not appropriate for modern workflows, especially if the results provided by the algorithmic assistance are not part of the core thread of work, such as speculative machine optimization building on human-derived results. This can be addressed by supporting alternatives and thus alternative threads of work as first-class citizens directly in the system [35]. Then one could start an ensemble solver, any form of optimization process, or some system that automatically explores the solution space, and be assured that the results of that computation are, once they are available, easily integrated into the whole workflow as a separate alternative or have the option to merge these results (wholly or partially) into the work by humans or other algorithms, as appropriate or needed.

5.4.2. Human Control of Computational Analytical Processes

Immersive analytics offers new opportunities for human-centered interactive analytics. By focusing on the sensemaking loop, we make clear that human sensemaking tasks are the central considerations around which computational analytics can be designed and situated [20]. Immersive analytics whole-heartedly takes this point of view by immersing the user in the sensemaking process and contextualizing computational support in the immersive sensemaking space. This leads to new challenges in the design of immersive interactive controls for computational analytics.

The large physical and/or virtual spaces offered by immersive environments can be exploited to support the synthesis portion of sensemaking, such as schematizing, by giving analysts "space to think" [2] (Figure 4). Analysts use the space to interactively externalize cognitive schemas by organizing information into series, clusters, and other spatial structures. Over time, analysts "incrementally formalize" their hypotheses via course- or fine-grained adjustments to these spatial structures [49]. These immersive interactions can be exploited as human-in-the-loop feedback for computational analytics and semi-supervised machine learning algorithms that support the sensemaking process, such as user-guided dimension reduction for spatialization of text corpora [18].

Fig. 4: Space to think: An analyst is immersed in a large sensemaking space, organizing a schema of textual data in collaboration with machine learning algorithms [2, 4].

A key challenge is designing immersive interactions that provide relevant input to computational analytics and designing computational analytics that appropriately support such user feedback [35]. One of the principles of Semantic Interaction [18] is to exploit existing cognitive operations that sensemakers naturally apply in physical environments, such as organizing and annotating, and re-casting these cognitive-level interactions into low-level feedback required by computational algorithms. Since these interactions are likely to be incremental in nature, it is important that the algorithms are designed such that they (1) do not require complete specification of all parameters up front, and (2) support incremental model learning [49].

Immersive environments offer opportunities for rich, multi-modal interactions, through many kinds of input devices and tracking many kinds of human analytic behaviors, to control computation. Subtle cues can be recognized and used to steer computational analytics. For example, big data computation can be steered onto areas of human focus of attention in the space, such as via gaze tracking, to provide just-in-time results [26]. Multiple degrees of freedom in the interaction space can offer more fluent control for parallel input. This enables the possibility for more efficiently steering multidimensional parameter spaces of complex analytics, manipulating multiple parameters and constraints for ensembles, or simultaneously specifying operations and target data. Immersive analytics can also support interaction with larger amounts of data at multiple levels of scale, such as manipulating many data objects via multi-touch [42] or physical-navigation aware cone-casting [43] methods. Multiple input devices can be used to exploit the most appropriate interactive affordances for each sensemaking task [13]. These complex interactions, such as simultaneously controlling several parameters, are typically a skill that requires training and thus create new usability challenges.

However, immersive environments also pose some difficulties for user input to computation. Immersive environments may have less precise input controls that would need to be supplemented with computational support. Also, text input in immersive systems is a notable challenge. Text input is useful for many tasks that cannot easily be solved when using pointing, such as annotating, formulating a hypothesis, or building a case. Speech recognition is a potential solution, but error recovery (after either the speech recognizer or the human makes a mistake) typically requires a surprisingly large amount of time with speech recognition.

Another design challenge is supporting transitions into and out of the immersive environment or between forms of immersive environments. For example, a user takes off an HMD to sketch on a tablet for designing a new computationally-generated visualization and then goes back into the HMD to see how the final result looks. Such transitions might be necessary due to the limited display resolution of the HMD or the limited tracking of pen-based input in an HMD environment. Similar transitions need to be considered for transitioning between individual and collaborative sensemaking tasks.

A final challenge is recording interaction history for provenance purposes, such as computational checkpointing. This is already a challenge in current visual analytics systems but becomes an even bigger challenge in immersive analytics systems due to the need to consider the current viewpoint and/or location in space of the users at any given time. For augmented reality applications, provenance systems may also need to take snapshots of how the world looked at each point in time, for example, to determine if a given person or object was present.

5.4.3. Computational Output in Immersive Analytics

There are a number of challenges and opportunities that arise in embedding computational analytical results in interactive immersive environments in ways that support the collaborative sensemaking process.

Holistic approach to the collaborative sensemaking loop: Rather than treating each step in the sensemaking process as a distinct tool, immersive analytics seeks to integrate the processes in a common space with common operations. A holistic approach can help to better support the many interconnections between the looping steps of the sensemaking process. This is important because analysts make many rapid iterations through portions of the sensemaking loop during the course of an analysis. This is exacerbated by the presence of multiple collaborating human and computational agents, each potentially working at different stages within the sensemaking loop. For example, in the sensemaking concept of "dual search", analysts must seek to simultaneously find hypotheses that explain the given evidence and also find evidence that supports their hypotheses [44]. An integrated approach can help analysts to more efficiently propose, and confirm or refute hypotheses.

A challenge for immersive analytics is the design of such unified spaces, and the design of the visual representations, interactive links, and computational processes that connect the steps of the sensemaking process. Designs should seek to minimize breaks in immersion across task boundaries. For example, with "synthesis driven foraging" (e. g., Starspire [4], as in Figure 4), human interactions in the later synthesis-oriented stages of sensemaking, such as schematizing and hypotheses generation, can automatically drive computational re-foraging for supporting evidence in the earlier stages of sensemaking. Results would then be immediately visualized for their impact on the hypotheses and enable further synthesis operations by the analysts. A particular opportunity with the holistic approach is overcoming confirmation bias. Since human analysts frequently suffer this problem, computational agents can be utilized to specifically seek and display refuting information.

Embedding users in computational workflows: An important opportunity in immersive analytics is to exploit the large physical and/or virtual spaces offered by immersion to visually represent complex analytical workflows, along with concomitant parameters and results at each stage. Increasingly complex computational analytic workflows lead to an overload of human short-term memory and difficulties in human understanding of the results. As an initial solution, visualization researchers have explored the use of visual representations of computational workflows, such as iconic representations of process steps (e. g., VisTrails [3]). This is particularly important in human-in-the-loop analytics, where the computational workflows are designed to reflect the steps of the human sensemaking loop.

A challenge of immersive analytics is the design of representations that visually embed the user and the computational results directly into the workflow representation. This approach can simultaneously represent the parameters and full outputs of multiple stages of the workflow, potentially enabling the user to navigate and compare results along the computational pipeline, thus supporting rapid progress through the sensemaking loop [46]. Multiple users can be simultaneously embedded to analyze different portions of the workflow while maintaining awareness of each other, similar to analogous physical organizations of collaborative human activity such as air traffic control [33].

With these methods, immersive analytics can help to open the analytical black-box by enabling users to see inside the workflow, participate in various steps of the workflow, and directly relate inputs to process to outputs. Such an introspection capability could lead to better user control of computational analytics and increased trust in algorithmically generated results [12]. Additional opportunities arise in annotating and examining the provenance of process and results, such as visualizing which source data contributed to certain output results throughout the entire analytical workflow [45].

Contextualizing computational feedback in human sensemaking: To support human sensemaking, computational analytic results can be contextualized directly within the human sensemaking process. Previously we have described how sensemakers exploit immersive spaces to externalize their cognitive process and construct organized schemas of information. Supervised learning algorithms can use such input to compute relevant results, and then display these results directly in connection to the inputs. A principle of Semantic Interaction [18] is to represent computational feedback within the context of the cognitive constructs in the immersive space. This can help analysts to better connect computational results to their own cognitive work than if the results were displayed separately elsewhere. The resulting space is a blending of computational and human-created schemas, representing a collaborative effort between cognition and computation.

Immersive environments provide meaningful space for such computational enrichment of the user input. In a sense, the large spaces offered by immersive environments provide a form of common ground between cognition and computation. The principles of spatial and distributed cognition emphasize the role of the physical spatial environment in human cognition [27]. Meanwhile, many data analytic methods exploit spatial metaphors such as distance metrics and triangle inequalities. Thus, space offers a rich medium for interaction between the computer and human.

A challenge is designing visual representations that re-cast computational output into task-oriented elements in the human sensemaking process. For example, in StarSpire [4], the user interest model that is learned by the computational algorithms in the form of keyword weights is visualized to the user by highlighting those keywords directly in the documents that they are reading with a color brightness that is proportional to their weight in the model. This explicitly supports the human sensemaking task of foraging for relevant information in the documents, but also implicitly gives the user feedback about the model state.

Managing user attention: A particular challenge in immersive analytics is managing users' attention in the immersive space in the presence of new or changing information that results from computational processes. For example, computational processes can be used to suggest regions of particular interest in a large space of results (e. g., Voyager [57]), to find latent connections between spatially distant information on the display (e. g., VisLink [14]), or to progressively refine streaming data or large computations on big data (e. g., [21]).

When small or non-obvious changes take place, such as new computational results appearing out of the user's current viewing frustum, the notification problem arises [36]. The question is how to alert users to the new information in a clear and yet unobtrusive fashion. Immersive environments can exploit additional human embodied resources such as peripheral vision or sonification to subtly notify users of changes [26].

At the other end of the spectrum, when very large changes take place, such as a complete re-organization of the space based on the results of a dimension reduction algorithm, they can be overwhelming and disorienting to an immersed user. This leads to the need for methods analogous to "smooth and efficient zoom and pan" [56] that attempts to minimize optical flow during navigation by zooming out before significant panning, making use of the larger frame of reference. Similarly, incremental approaches such as incremental learning algorithms or animated force-directed layouts, combined with landmark persistence, can help users maintain orientation while exploring new results (e. g., ForceSpire [18]).

Representing sensemakers: In immersive analytics, actors in the sensemaking process can be visually represented in the sensemaking space to make the collaboration more clear. A challenge is creating avatars or other forms of representations of both human and computational agents, enabling collaborators to see what part of the data or sensemaking process activities others are working on and potentially share perspectives [34]. With augmented reality, actors might be represented physically. For example, "Be the Data" [10] enables collaborating students to take on the perspectives of individual data points as they are manipulated by dimension reduction algorithms, and directly visualize distances between points as distances between people in the space.

5.5. Conclusion

In this chapter, we discussed higher-level concerns of the sensemaking process around data, corresponding to *Strategic Immersion*, similar to high-level problem-solving in games [1], and analyzed how immersive environments can help here. We also looked at how immersive environments can help with the integration of automatic processes, such as machine optimization and learning, into the analytics workflow and the user's role in a large-scale collaborative analytics process with both other people and machine assistance. This is a natural step in the integration of interactive data analytics capabilities with modern machine learning methods. Such integration also satisfies the growing need to be able to explain data analytics results to others. Consider having to defend the choices made–by human or algorithmic data analyst–to a superior or a judge. Finally, we also looked at some of the technical requirements associated with doing data analytics in immersive environments.

There are a variety of avenues for future research. These include:

- Can–and if so, how can–immersive environments enable users to think about, and deal with, more complex problems than is currently possible on desktop platforms. This is especially a challenge when one considers that it may be necessary to employ multiple actors, both human and automatic, working together to solve such problems.
- How can we use immersion to amplify human intelligence, intuition, and creativity? Specifically, this targets the higher-level process and provenance tasks described in Section 5.2., schematization and hypothesis generation (and testing). These high-level cognitive processes remain relatively poorly understood and thus this is a significant research challenge.
- How can immersion be used to advance human collaboration with computational processes? In particular, what new opportunities do immersive environments provide to enable human interaction with the inputs and outputs of computational analytics?
- Many of the current limitations for immersive analytics are technological. Research needs to provide an understanding of human capabilities for understanding analytics, given future technological capabilities. For example, by lifting the arbitrary limitation imposed by the display space of current desktop environments, can we imagine or prototype environments that overcome those limitations in order to discover where the next challenges lie?
- How can we minimize artificial breaks in immersion/engagement–especially across task boundaries? And if we require users to break their immersion, e. g., when switching from an HMD to keyboard input and back, how can we keep their engagement intact?

- One of the premises of this chapter has been that ideas from game design which promote immersion, engagement, and flow, can be beneficially brought to data analytics and sensemaking. Are there additional opportunities in this vein? For example, another potential avenue of future work is to explore the gamification of the immersive analytics process.
- A final future consideration is the evaluation of sensemaking activities in immersive analytics environments. There are opportunities for evaluation of immersive systems, for example, in many such systems gesture control and immersive rendering necessitate head and body position tracking. Thus, we can collect a fairly complete model of user interaction which could be further enriched with other biometric data collection, e. g., pulse-rate, affective measures or even cortisol levels. With such a complete model we can study peoples' patterns of interaction during sensemaking and ultimately better understand this complex activity.

Acknowledgements

Dwyer acknowledges support by the Australian Research Council Discovery Scheme, project DP180100755.

References

1. Adams,E.:Thedesigner'snotebook:Postmod-ernismandthe3typesofimmersion(2004), http://www.gamasutra.com/view/feature/130531/the_designers_notebook_.php
2. Andrews, C., Endert, A., North, C.: Space to think: large high-resolution displays for sensemaking. In: Proceedings of the SIGCHI Conference on Human Factors in Computing Systems. pp. 55–64. ACM (2010)
3. Bavoil, L., Callahan, S.P., Crossno, P.J., Freire, J., Scheidegger, C.E., Silva, C.T., Vo, H.T.: Vistrails: enabling interactive multiple-view visualizations. In: VIS 05. IEEE Visualization, 2005. pp. 135–142 (Oct 2005) doi: 10.1109/VISUAL.2005.1532788
4. Bradel, L., North, C., House, L., Leman, S.: Multi-model semantic interaction for text analytics. In: 2014 IEEE Conference on Visual Analytics Science and Technology (VAST). pp. 163–172 (Oct 2014)doi: 10.1109/VAST.2014.7042492
5. Card, S.K., Mackinlay, J.D., Shneiderman, B.: Readings in information visualization: using vision to think. Morgan Kaufmann (1999)
6. Card, S.K., Robertson, G.G., Mackinlay, J.D.: The information visualizer, an information workspace. In: Proceedings of the SIGCHI Conference on Human Factors in Computing Systems. pp. 181–186. ACM (1991)
7. Carmack, J.: Latency mitigation strategies (2013), https://www.twentymilliseconds.com/post/latency-mitigation-strategies/
8. Ceneda, D., Gschwandtner, T., May, T., Miksch, S., Schulz, H.J., Streit, M., Tominski, C.: Characterizing guidance in visual analytics. IEEE Transactions on Visualization and Computer Graphics 23(1), 111–120 (Jan 2017), https://doi.org/10.1109/TVCG.2016.2598468 doi: 10.1109/TVCG.2016.2598468

9. Cernea, D., Ebert, A., Kerren, A.: A study of emotion-triggered adaptation methods for interactive visualization. In: UMAP 2013 Extended Proceedings: Late-Breaking Results, Project Papers and Workshop Proceedings of the 21st Conference on User Modeling, Adaptation, and Personalization. CEUR workshop proceedings, vol. 997, pp. 9–16. CEUR-WS.org (2013)
10. Chen, X., Self, J.Z., House, L., North, C.: Be the data: a new approach for immersive analytics. In: IEEE Virtual Reality Workshop on Immersive Analytics (2016)
11. Choo, J., Lee, C., Reddy, C.K., Park, H.: Utopian: User-driven topic modeling based on interactive nonnegative matrix factorization. IEEE Transactions on Visualization and Computer Graphics 19(12), 1992–2001 (Dec 2013)
12. Chuang, J., Ramage, D., Manning, C., Heer, J.: Interpretation and trust: Designing model-driven visualizations for text analysis. In: Proceedings of the SIGCHI Conference on Human Factors in Computing Systems. pp. 443–452. ACM (2012)
13. Chung, H., North, C., Joshi, S., Chen, J.: Four considerations for supporting visual analysis in display ecologies. In: 2015 IEEE Conference on Visual Analytics Science and Technology (VAST). pp. 33–40 (Oct 2015)
14. Collins, C., Carpendale, S.: Vislink: Revealing relationships amongst visualizations. IEEE Transactions on Visualization and Computer Graphics 13(6),1192–1199 (Nov 2007) doi: 10.1109/TVCG.2007.70521
15. Darragh, J.J., Witten, I.H.: Adaptive predictive text generation and the reactive keyboard. Interacting with Computers 3(1), 27–50 (1991)
16. Doleisch, H.: SimVis: Interactive visual analysis of large and time-dependent 3d simulation data. In: Proceedings of the 39th Conference on Winter Simulation: 40 years! The best is yet to come. pp. 712–720. IEEE Press (2007)
17. Endert, A., Han, C., Maiti, D., House, L., Leman, S., North, C.: Observation-level interaction with statistical models for visual analytics. In: 2011 IEEE Conference on Visual Analytics Science and Technology (VAST). pp. 121–130 (Oct 2011)
18. Endert, A., Fiaux, P., North, C.: Semantic interaction for sensemaking: inferring analytical reasoning for model steering. IEEE Transactions on Visualization and Computer Graphics 18(12), 2879–2888 (2012)
19. Endert, A., Fox, S., Maiti, D., North, C.: The semantics of clustering: analysis of user-generated spatializations of text documents. In: Proceedings of the International Working Conference on Advanced Visual Interfaces. pp. 555–562. ACM (2012)
20. Endert, A., Hossain, M.S., Ramakrishnan, N., North, C., Fiaux, P., Andrews, C.: The human is the loop: new directions for visual analytics. Journal of intelligent information systems 43(3), 411–435 (2014)
21. Fisher, D., Popov, I., Drucker, S., schraefel, m.: Trust me, I'm partially right: Incremental visualization lets analysts explore large datasets faster. In: Proceedings of the SIGCHI Conference on Human Factors in Computing Systems. pp. 1673–1682. ACM (2012)
22. Goodwin, S., Mears, C., Dwyer, T., de la Banda, M.G., Tack, G., Wallace, M.: What do constraint programming users want to see? Exploring the role of visualisation in profiling of models and search. IEEE Transactions on Visualization and Computer Graphics 23(1), 281–290 (2017)
23. Heer, J., Mackinlay, J., Stolte, C., Agrawala, M.: Graphical histories for visualization: Supporting analysis, communication, and evaluation. IEEE Transactions on Visualization and Computer Graphics 14(6),1189–1196 (Nov 2008), http://dx.doi.org/10.1109/TVCG.2008.137 doi: 10.1109/TVCG.2008.137

24. Heer, J., Shneiderman, B.: Interactive dynamics for visual analysis. Communications of the ACM 55(4), 45–54 (Apr 2012), http://doi.acm.org/10.1145/2133806.2133821 doi: 10.1145/2133806.2133821
25. Heine, C., Leitte, H., Hlawitschka, M., Iuricich, F., De Floriani, L., Scheuermann, G., Hagen, H., Garth, C.: A survey of topology-based methods in visualization. Computer Graphics Forum 35(3), 643–667 (2016)
26. Heun, V., von Kapri, A., Maes, P.: Perifoveal display: Combining foveal and peripheral vision in one visualization. In: Proceedings of the 2012 ACM Conference on Ubiquitous Computing. pp. 1150–1155. UbiComp '12, ACM (2012)
27. Hollan, J., Hutchins, E., Kirsh, D.: Distributed cognition: Toward a new foundation for human-computer interaction research. ACM Transactions on Computer-Human Interaction 7(2), 174–196 (Jun 2000)
28. Isenberg, P., Elmqvist, N., Scholtz, J., Cernea, D., Ma, K.L., Hagen, H.: Collaborative visualization: Definition, challenges, and research agenda. Information Visualization 10(4), 310–326 (Oct 2011), http://dx.doi.org/10.1177/1473871611412817 doi: 10.1177/1473871611412817
29. Jänicke, H., Böttinger, M., Tricoche, X., Scheuermann, G.: Automatic detection and visualization of distinctive structures in 3D unsteady multi-fields. Computer Graphics Forum 27(3), 767–774 (2008)
30. Kerren, A., Schreiber, F.: Toward the role of interaction in visual analytics. In: Proceedings of the Winter Simulation Conference. pp. 420:1–420:13. WSC '12, Winter Simulation Conference (2012), http://dl.acm.org/citation.cfm?id=2429759.2430303
31. Liu, J., Dwyer, T., Marriott, K., Millar, J., Haworth, A.: Understanding the relationship between interactive optimisation and visual analytics in the context of prostate brachytherapy. IEEE Transactions on Visualization and Computer Graphics 24(1), 319–329 (2018)
32. Liu, Y., Jin, R., Jain, A.K.: Boostcluster: Boosting clustering by pairwise constraints. In: Proceedings of the 13th ACM SIGKDD international conference on Knowledge discovery and data mining. pp. 450–459. ACM (2007)
33. MacKay, W.E.: Is paper safer? The role of paper flight strips in air traffic control. ACM Transactions on Computer Human Interaction 6(4), 311–340 (Dec 1999)
34. Mahyar, N., Tory, M.: Supporting communication and coordination in collaborative sensemaking. IEEE Transactions on Visualization and Computer Graphics 20(12), 1633–1642 (Dec 2014) doi: 10.1109/TVCG.2014.2346573
35. Makonin, S., McVeigh, D., Stuerzlinger, W., Tran, K., Popowich, F.: Mixed-initiative for big data: The intersection of human+ visual analytics+ prediction. In: 2016 49th Hawaii International Conference on System Sciences (HICSS). pp. 1427–1436. IEEE (2016)
36. McCrickard, D.S., Chewar, C.M., Somervell, J.P., Ndiwalana, A.: A model for notification systems evaluation—assessing user goals for multitasking activity. ACM Transactions on Computer-Human Interaction (TOCHI) 10(4), 312–338 (2003)
37. Meignan, D., Knust, S., Frayret, J.M., Pesant, G., Gaud, N.: A review and taxonomy of interactive optimization methods in operations research. ACM Transactions on Interactive Intelligent Systems (TiiS) 5(3), 17 (2015)
38. Miller, R.B.: Response time in man-computer conversational transactions. In: Proceedings of the December 9-11, 1968, Fall Joint Computer Conference, part I. pp. 267–277. ACM (1968)

39. Ng, A., Lepinski, J., Wigdor, D., Sanders, S., Dietz, P.: Designing for low-latency direct-touch input. In: Proceedings of the 25th annual ACM symposium on User interface software and technology. pp. 453–464. ACM (2012)
40. Nielsen, J.: Usability engineering. Elsevier (1994)
41. Nielsen, J.: Web-based application response time (2014), https://www.nngroup.com/articles/response-times-3-important-limits/
42. North, C., Dwyer, T., Lee, B., Fisher, D., Isenberg, P., Robertson, G., Inkpen, K.: Understanding multi-touch manipulation for surface computing. In: Proceedings of the 12th IFIP TC 13 International Conference on Human-Computer Interaction: Part II (INTERACT). pp. 236–249. Springer-Verlag (2009)
43. Peck, S.M., North, C., Bowman, D.: A multiscale interaction technique for large, high-resolution displays. In: 2009 IEEE Symposium on 3D User Interfaces. pp. 31–38 (March 2009)
44. Pirolli, P., Card, S.: The sensemaking process and leverage points for analyst technology as identified through cognitive task analysis. In: Proceedings of International Conference on Intelligence Analysis. vol. 5, pp. 2–4 (2005)
45. Ragan, E.D., Endert, A., Sanyal, J., Chen, J.: Characterizing provenance in visualization and data analysis: An organizational framework of provenance types and purposes. IEEE Transactions on Visualization and Computer Graphics 22(1), 31–40 (Jan 2016), https://doi.org/10.1109/TVCG.2015.2467551 doi: 10.1109/TVCG.2015.2467551
46. Ragan, E.D., Sowndararajan, A., Kopper, R., Bowman, D.A.: The effects of higher levels of immersion on procedure memorization performance and implications for educational virtual environments. Presence: Teleoperators and Virtual Environments 19(6), 527–543 (2010)
47. Salzbrunn, T., Garth, C., Scheuermann, G., Meyer, J.: Pathline predicates and unsteady flow structures. The Visual Computer 24(12), 1039–1051 (2008)
48. Sauer, F., Zhang, Y., Wang, W., Ethier, S., Ma, K.L.: Visualization techniques for studying large-scale flow fields from fusion simulations. IEEE Computing in Science and Engineering 18(2), 68–77 (March/April 2016)
49. Shipman, F.M., Marshall, C.C.: Formality considered harmful: Experiences, emerging themes, and directions on the use of formal representations in interactive systems. Computer Supported Cooperative Work (CSCW) 8(4), 333–352 (1999)
50. Silva, J.A., Faria, E.R., Barros, R.C., Hruschka, E.R., de Carvalho, A.C., Gama, J.: Data stream clustering: A survey. ACM Computing Surveys (CSUR) 46(1), 13 (2013)
51. Simmhan, Y.L., Plale, B., Gannon, D., Marru, S.: Performance evaluation of the karma provenance framework for scientific workflows. In: Moreau, L., Foster, I. (eds.) Provenance and Annotation of Data: International Provenance and Annotation Workshop, IPAW 2006, Chicago, IL, USA, May 3-5, 2006, Revised Selected Papers, pp. 222–236. Springer Berlin Heidelberg, Berlin, Heidelberg (2006), http://dx.doi.org/10.1007/11890850_23 doi: 10.1007/11890850_23
52. Stahnke, J., Dörk, M., Müller, B., Thom, A.: Probing projections: Interaction techniques for interpreting arrangements and errors of dimensionality reductions. IEEE Transactions on Visualization and Computer Graphics 22(1), 629–638 (2016)
53. Streit, M., Schulz, H.J., Lex, A., Schmalstieg, D., Schumann, H.: Model-driven design for the visual analysis of heterogeneous data. IEEE Transactions on Visualization and Computer Graphics 18(6), 998–1010 (June 2012), https://doi.org/10.1109/TVCG.2011.108 doi: 10.1109/TVCG.2011.108

54. Tatu, A., Maaß, F., Färber, I., Bertini, E., Schreck, T., Seidl, T., Keim, D.: Subspace search and visualization to make sense of alternative clusterings in high-dimensional data. In: IEEE Conference on Visual Analytics Science and Technology (VAST). pp. 63–72. IEEE (2012)
55. Thieke, C., Küfer, K.H., Monz, M., Scherrer, A., Alonso, F., Oelfke, U., Huber, P.E., Debus, J., Bortfeld, T.: A new concept for interactive radiotherapy planning with multicriteria optimization: first clinical evaluation. Radiotherapy and Oncology 85(2), 292–298 (2007)
56. Van Wijk, J.J., Nuij, W.A.A.: Smooth and efficient zooming and panning. In: Proceedings of the Ninth Annual IEEE Conference on Information Visualization. pp. 15–22. INFOVIS'03, IEEE Computer Society (2003)
57. Wongsuphasawat, K., Moritz, D., Anand, A., Mackinlay, J., Howe, B., Heer, J.: Voyager: Exploratory analysis via faceted browsing of visualization recommendations. IEEE Transactions on Visualization and Computer Graphics 22(1), 649–658 (2016)
58. Zaman, L., Stuerzlinger, W., Neugebauer, C., Woodbury, R., Elkhaldi, M., Shireen, N., Terry, M.: Gem-ni: A system for creating and managing alternatives in generative design. In: Proceedings of the 33rd Annual ACM Conference on Human Factors in Computing Systems. pp. 1201–1210. ACM (2015)
59. Zimmer, B., Kerren, A.: Ongrax: A web-based system for the collaborative visual analysis of graphs. Journal of Graph Algorithms and Applications 21(1), 5–27 (2017), http://dx.doi.org/10.7155/jgaa.00399 doi: 10.7155/jgaa.00399
60. Cetin, G., Stuerzlinger, W., Dill, J.: Visual analytics on large displays: exploring user spatialization and how size and resolution affect task performance. In: IEEE Symposium on Big Data Visual Analytics (BDVA 2018), 10 p. (2018, to appear)
61. El Meseery, M., Wu, Y., Stuerzlinger, W.: Multiple workspaces in visual analytics. In: E EE Symposium on Big Data Visual Analytics (BDVA 2018), 12 p. (2018, to appear)

6. Immersive Visual Data Stories

Petra Isenberg[1], Bongshin Lee[2], Huamin Qu[3], and Maxime Cordeil[4]

[1] Inria, France
[2] Microsoft Research, USA
[3] Hong Kong University of Science and Technology, Hong Kong
[4] Monash University, Australia

Abstract. We discuss opportunities and challenges for making people experience immersion when interacting with visual data stories. Even though visual data stories are an important means for communicating information, the extent to which viewers feel immersed in such stories has so far been hardly explored. In this chapter, we explore the concept of immersion in visual data stories from the viewpoint of related disciplines in which narratives play an important role. We pay special attention to games research, which shares a focus on graphics and interactivity with our context of visual data stories. From this exploration we derive research opportunities and challenges for immersion in visual data stories.

Keywords: storytelling, immersion, data-driven narratives, narrative visualization, visualization

6.1. Introduction

Visual data-driven stories are a powerful means for communicating information to a broad range of audiences. Practitioners such as data journalists are increasingly creating popular data-driven stories that have been described as attractive, absorbing, engaging, or immersive. Examples include Hans Rosling's BBC performance [37] that has been viewed over eight million times on YouTube alone (as of December 2017). In the video, Hans Rosling narrates – with the help of active gestures, simple mixed-reality visuals, and a compelling script – the improvements of 200 countries in terms of average life expectancy and income over the past 100 years. This type of visual data story closely relates to movies and film in that the audience can watch but not interact but feels nevertheless "immersed" despite a lack of mouse or touch-based interaction.

Others have explored hybrid approaches allowing the audience to get involved in a scripted data story. For example, in "The Fallen of World War II" [20], a data story in the form of a narrated movie, the viewer can interrupt the story and interact with a chart that shows the deaths that occurred in WWII. With the advancement of mixed or virtual reality technology, practitioners have also started to tell stories by incorporating or mimicking real and virtual worlds. In 2015, Roger Kenny and Ana Asnes Becker (working for *The Wall Street Journal* at the time), for example, created a Virtual Reality (VR) visualization tour of

K. Marriott et al. (Eds.): Immersive Analytics, LNCS 11190, pp. 165–184, 2018.
https://doi.org/10.1007/978-3-030-01388-2_6

the financial crisis of 2007 [25]. This story uses a roller coaster metaphor to convey the variation of the stock market value; the viewer is sitting on a virtual carriage on top of the ridge of the stock market values and follows the narration as the carriage moves forward in time. The ride starts during the pre-2000 boom and goes up and down through the chart from March 10 2000, when the Bubble Bursts, to November 2015. At this point, the ridge is very thin, reflecting low share prices. The ride continues with a big fall and passes through the terror attack of 2001 and rides to 2015. The authors aimed to create a data story that conveyed the data by evoking different feelings and experiences in the viewers [6]. The story unfolds as the viewer moves forward in time but stops at key moments on the Nasdaq variations. As in this piece, it is relatively common that immersive journalism uses 360° videos to immerse their audience into a documentary. The aim of such techniques is to provide the audience with an auditory and visual experience that evokes people's belief to be *within the situation*.

While these visual data stories above, as well as many others, have been described as immersive, the exact characteristics of an immersive data story remain elusive. In particular, it is most often not even clear what the experience of immersion into a data story would encompass. Do immersed viewers lose their sense of time when consuming data stories, feel particularly connected to the data, feel more broadly engaged, start to care about the data more, or any combinations of characteristics that have in the past been associated with an immersive experience?

While researchers and practitioners are actively exploring the challenges and opportunities of narrative visualization, the challenge of creating an immersive data-driven story or narrative has so far received very little research attention. Yet, the concept of immersion has been extensively discussed in the context of different storytelling media. Unfortunately, these discussions often use different meanings and definitions of the term immersion itself, which leads to confusion with related terms including presence, engagement, perception of realism, addiction, suspension of disbelief, and flow [14].

In this chapter, we discuss how we can understand immersion in the context of visual data stories after briefly describing related work on storytelling with data-driven narratives. It is important to note that in these discussions we do not focus on any specific technology such as virtual or augmented reality. Instead, we discuss immersion as a concept that involves cognitive and emotional involvement, and derive a set of goals and research challenges based on this view of immersion.

6.2. Visual Data-Driven Stories

Data-driven storytelling–also called narrative visualization–has become an active research direction within the domain of visualization [40]. Specifically, instead of focusing only on providing means for effective exploration and analysis of data, narrative visualization concerns effective explanation and presentation of data using visualization. The goal of visual data-driven stories (in short, visual data stories) is generally to reach a wide or targeted audience by putting together visualized findings or messages with connections such as temporal or causal relations [27,29]. In the past, there have been conceptual and theoretical research papers on the topic, work on specific storytelling techniques and methods, as well as work dedicated to specific storytelling genres or data types.

6.2.1. Understanding Data-Driven Narratives

Dedicated research on storytelling with visualizations does not yet have a very long tradition. In 2010, Segel and Heer presented the first systematic study of the design space of narrative visualizations and categorized different genres, design elements, and narrative structures [40]. Similarly, the work by Hullman and Diakopolous focused on describing techniques for communicating an intended message with a visualization – with a focus on visualization rhetoric [22]. Both of these papers did not use a clear definition for a "visual story" or "data-driven visual narrative," a point critiqued later by Lee *et al.* [29].

In their work, Lee *et al.* looked more closely at the process of creating data stories. The authors began by proposing three defining characteristics of a visual data story: visual data stories must include a set of facts backed by data (i. e., facts must be data-driven), most of these facts must be visualized to support an intended message (i. e., representation must be visual), and the visualization must include a meaningful order or connections that support the intended message (i. e., a story). As such, the presence of underlying data, an intended message, and a logical collection of supporting visualizations are key to distinguishing a visualization that is meant to tell a story from others that are meant to be used primarily for exploration and analysis. Lee *et al.* then proposed a working model for visual data storytelling process consisting of three main phases – explore data, make a story, and tell a story – to encompass the entire process of transforming data into visually shared stories. Chevalier *et al.* [15] later revised Lee *et al.*'s process grounded by interviews with nine professionals who create visual data stories. The authors identified new roles including data collector and director as well as additional external factors including time and ethics.

Researchers have also studied existing visual data stories to derive insights helpful for developing storytelling techniques and authoring tools. To better understand the effect of sequences in narrative visualization in order to develop an automatic sequencing algorithm, Hullman *et al.* conducted a focused analysis of transitions between scenes in 42 linear, slide-show-style presentations [23]. Stolper *et al.* [43] performed a qualitative analysis of 45 popular data stories and identified 20 data-driven storytelling techniques grouped under four categories: Communicating Narrative and Explaining Data, Linking Separated Story Elements, Enhancing Structure and Navigation, and Providing Controlled Exploration. In proposing the concept of "visual narrative flow," McKenna *et al.* [32] systematically investigated 80 stories found on popular websites, and identified seven "flow-factors" that can shape the flow of visual data-driven stories: navigation input, level of control, navigation progress, story layout, role of visualization, story progression, and navigation feedback.

6.2.2. Techniques and Authoring Tools for Data-Driven Visual Stories

Several researchers have proposed design considerations for visual data-driven stories of a particular style or for particular types of data. Amini *et al.* [1], for example, systematically studied 50 professionally designed data videos to understand the structure and sequence designers commonly use to construct narrative visualization. After that, through a further analysis of an extended set of data videos, Amini *et al.* [2] identified a library of data clips that cover major components for creating compelling data videos. Similarly, Wang *et al.* [46] studied the use of animated narrative visualization for the presentation of video clickstream Data. Animation can also be used to highlight critical information in data stories. For example, Waldner *et al.* [45] studied how to guide the audience's attention through a flicker in dynamic visualization.

Bach *et al.* [3] studied comic-strip-style narrative visualizations to show changes in dynamic networks. The authors propose eight different design factors for creating this particular type of visual story, involving, for example, the visual representation of graph items, changes over time, or characters. Brehmer *et al.* [9] performed a survey of 263 timelines to identify a design space for storytelling with timelines. The authors show that 20 combinations of 14 design choices lead to viable timeline designs that can be integrated into visual stories together with smooth animation.

While the research presented above mostly focused on survey-style or theoretical contributions for proposing design considerations for data-driven visual stories, several others focused on contributing authoring tools. For example, Lee *et al.* [30] introduced a new storytelling system, *SketchStory*, a data-enabled digital whiteboard that extends the narrative storytelling attributes of whiteboard animation with pen and touch interactions (Figure 1).

Hullman *et al.* [21], for example, described a technique, *contextifier*, that focuses on the generation of annotated charts. By analyzing a set of news articles related to the chart, contextifier can generate narrative visualization in an annotated chart style. Similarly, Ren *et al.* [35] focused on chart annotations in their survey of 106 annotated chart images published by prominent news graphics. The authors' survey led to the design of a system *ChartAccent* (Figure 2) that helps authors quickly and easily augment basic charts through a set of annotation interactions that generate manual and data-driven annotations. Wang *et al.* [47] proposed a narrative visualization system that helps researchers read academic papers by turning research paper into interactive slides.

Researchers have also started to investigate ways to integrate exploration and presentation processes in narrative visualization tools. Gratzl *et al.* [19] propose the CLUE (Capture, Label, Understand, Explain) model that allows people to create a visual data story based on the history of the exploration; they can extract key steps, add annotations, and construct a story using the provenance data captured during the exploration process. Bryan *et al.* [12] present an approach that automatically creates and ranks data-driven annotations during the analysis to help people synthesize a coherent narrative with a temporal data summary.

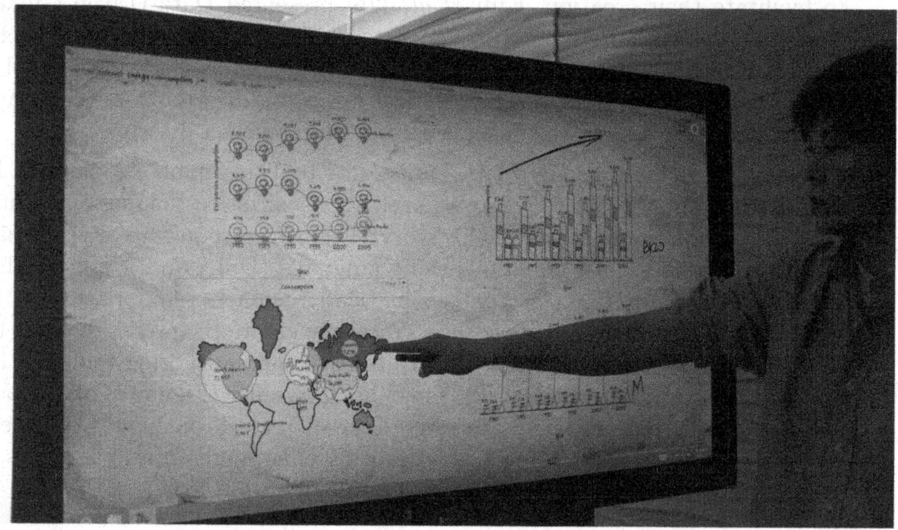

Fig. 1: SketchStory attracts attention and creates anticipation using a real-time approach to content creation with pen and touch interaction.

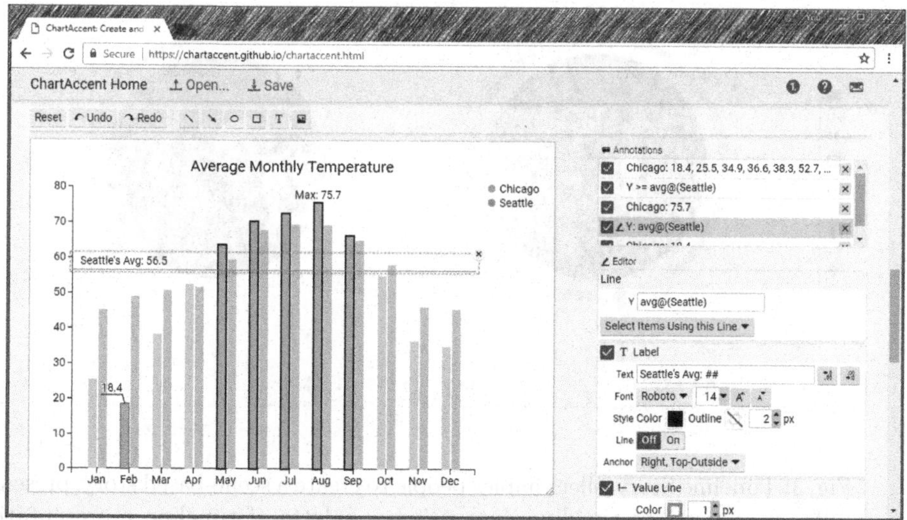

Fig. 2: ChartAccent is a web-based authoring tool that enables people to augment charts using a palette of annotation interactions.

Due to the popularity of infographics, we are seeing an emergence of tools to facilitate their creation. Kim *et al.* [26] presented Data-Driven Guides, a technique to enable designers to generate guides from data and use them to accurately place and measure custom shapes. Hanpuku uses a bridge model that allows designers to bring their work back from the drawing tool (e. g., Adobe Illustrator) to re-edit in the generative tool (e. g., using D3 scripts) [7].

Researchers have also developed authoring tools to enable people with little or no programming skills to create a narrative visualization that supports interactions and animations. *Ellipsis* helps storytellers generate narrative visualization using templates with a domain-specific language (DSL) and a graphical user interface [39]. *TimeLineCurator* automatically extracts temporal events from freeform text and enables people to interactively curate the events, helping them easily generate a linear timeline [18]. DataClips is an authoring tool that helps non-experts create data videos [2]. Timeline Storyteller (Figure 3) allows people to present different aspects of timeline data such as chronology, sequence and the periodicity of events using a palette of timeline representations, scales, and layouts, along with controls for filtering and annotation [10].

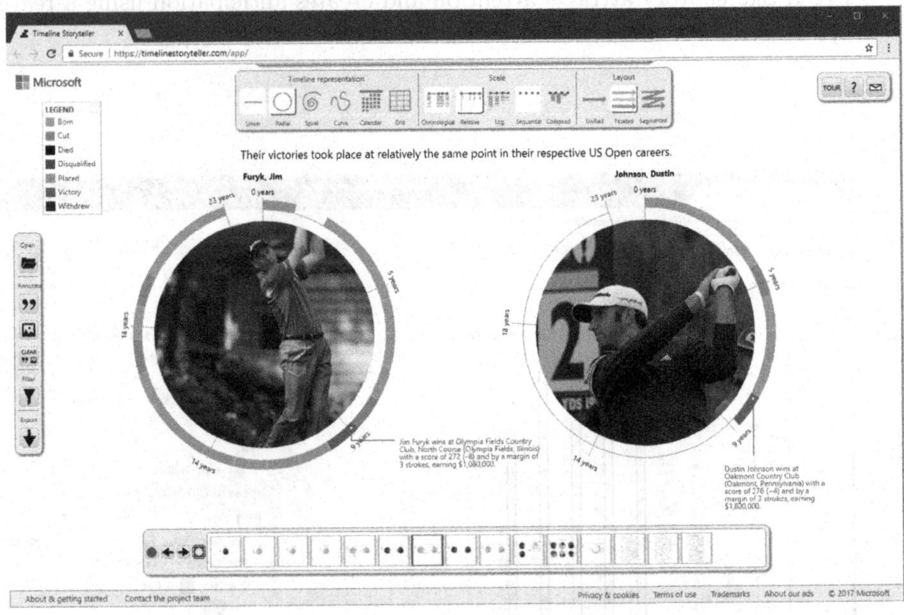

Fig. 3: Timeline Storyteller enables people to create a scene-based story, presenting different aspects of timeline data using a palette of timeline representations, scales, and layouts. It provides people with controls for filtering, highlighting, and annotation.

6.3. Defining Immersion in Visual Data Stories

In the previous section, we introduced a large number of projects dedicated to narrative visualization or the creation of data-driven visual stories. None of these papers have specifically focused on immersive data-driven stories – in the general definition of immersion that we use in this book. So let us now more concretely discuss what we exactly mean by an immersive visual data story.

In previous work, the term immersion has been used with various definitions depending on many factors such as the type of media referred to, the research domain, or the individual researchers who used it [14]. Much of this past work, however, has in common that immersion refers to a specific phenomenon that describes the experience a person has when engaging with a specific medium, such as a book, a movie, or a game. Immersion in the domain of visualization – narrative visualization in particular – has, however, not been clearly defined as a term that describes an experience. When "immersion" is used with the term "visualization" it most often refers to the fact that 3D visualizations are generated for viewing in virtual reality environments (e. g. [17, 28, 44]) and the focus of the work is more technical on how to achieve smooth renderings for these more complex technical setups or a multi-sensory experience. For example, previous work has investigated how virtual reality technology affects persuasion in data-driven storytelling [5]. The definition of immersion used in this paper followed Sanchez-Vives & Slater as [41]: "the technical capability of the system to deliver a surrounding and a convincing environment with which the participant can interact." No evidence was found in this paper to support the benefits of using an immersive environment given this definition.

We argue here, that this narrow view of immersion in visualization misses to point out many design opportunities and does not help us explain why some visualizations may capture viewers more than others. Before discussing how we use the term in this chapter and describing the experiences an immersive data story may want to create, we will take a look at the difficulty of defining the term in a related discipline: games research. We chose to focus on this particular context as it shares several characteristics with the specific data storytelling environments that we are ultimately interested in: both games and visual data stories are interactive and inherently graphical, they (often, but not always [13]) attempt to engage the player/viewer in a narrative, involve either open-ended or prescribed tasks to be accomplished that are often challenging, and mostly focus on non-stereoscopic presentation outside of VR – a technical focus we want to avoid in this book chapter. By relating our definition to games research, we do not, however, exclude experiences such as the Hans Rosling and Fallen of WWII examples described in the introduction, which both are less interactive and more movie-like. We will describe these data-driven stories using the same definition of immersion that we will choose for more interactive and open-ended data stories.

6.3.1. Immersion in Games

For games research, Calleja [14] discusses how the almost interchangeable use of the terms *immersion* and *presence* has been detrimental for research. The author details the varying uses of the term and proposes to distinguish between the *absorption-sense of immersion* and *transportation-sense of immersion*.

The *absorption-sense* of immersion refers to what Lombard and Ditton [31] call "psychological immersion:" a sense of involvement, absorption, engagement, and engrossment in a game. For example, someone could become fully absorbed in playing a simple game such as Tetris – or one could say "immersed" in the absorption-sense of the term.

In contrast, the *transportation-sense* of immersion refers to viewers, readers, or players feeling they have been transported into a different world. This sense of transportation can be graphically created or internally generated, for example, when reading a story. A game such as Tetris, for example, cannot provide immersion in the transportation sense since its game world is not meant to be spatially navigated and besides the falling building-blocks, no other game objects can react freely to the player's actions. Thus, the capability to provide immersion as transportation is effectively different for different media. When readers feel transported into the world of a book, this world does not provide feedback. An interactive storytelling medium, on the other hand, can provide a very different form of transportation by reacting to a user's actions.

Brown and Cairns [11] added an important aspect to the discussion of the term immersion by introducing three degrees of immersion: engagement, engrossment, and total immersion. According to Brown and Cairns, players first need to invest time, effort, and attention to become engaged and interested in a game to want to keep playing. As immersion increases, players can become engrossed in a game. They become less aware of their real surroundings and establish an emotional connection to the game. Plots, tasks, and visuals are particularly important to create a sense of engrossment [11]. Brown and Cairns equate total immersion, the most highly immersed state of a player, with the term presence, a situation in which one feels completely present in the game world and reality and sense of time are cut off. Similar to engrossment, total immersion includes an emotional component–empathy and attachment with game characters–and a technical and storytelling component: atmosphere, which includes the graphics, plot, and sound of the game. Calleja [14] argues that Brown and Cairns [11] merge the absorption and transportation senses of immersion. Both engagement and engrossment follow the absorption-sense of immersion while total immersion uses the transportation-sense of immersion. Cairns *et al.* [13] themselves state in a later book chapter that equating presence with total immersion was confusing as presence and immersion are not the same. They now more simply describe immersion in a game as "the engagement or involvement a person feels as a result of playing a digital game." The authors, in particular, describe immersion as a cognitive and emotional state or experience that players achieve which makes them feel like they are "in the game." The distinctions between presence and immersion are further complicated by the fact that the term "presence" is not coherently used in the literature either [14, 42].

Yet, Calleja [14] agrees with previous work that immersion is not a single experience that can be easily measured and it is never just present or not, it exists on a continuum and is the result of various forms of involvement with a medium. These forms of involvement, Calleja [14] argues, must be understood first before immersion can be studied. He proposes that immersion, together with a sense of transportation (presence), is a component of the larger concept of incorporation; incorporation describes how a player incorporates/assimilates the game into their consciousness and at the same time becomes incorporated into the game world as an avatar. Calleja goes on to distinguish and discuss six dimensions of involvement: kinesthetic involvement (control of character or game pieces), spatial involvement (navigation, exploration), shared involvement (with other game agents), narrative involvement (with story elements), affective involvement (emotional engagement), and ludic involvement (making game choices). One or more of these types of involvement can together be precursors to the experience of immersion. Cairns *et al.* [13] argue that there is another precursor to the first level of immersion that was missed in Calleja's work: the external context of playing the game such as the room the game is played in. This argument is based on the results of a study in which the authors found that physical lighting conditions, for example, influence the experience of immersion.

In summary and most importantly, however, Cairns *et al.* and Calleja both describe immersion from an experiential perspective and as an experience that includes different levels of involvement and cognitive absorption.

Others have proposed types of immersion that are more closely related to narrative or storytelling. Games research, similar to visualization, has controversial discussions about the role of narrative. Adams [6] previously proposed consideration of three different types of immersion, one of which he called narrative immersion (the other two being tactical and strategic immersion). According to Adams, a player has reached narrative immersion when he or she starts to care about the game characters and wants to see the end of the game story. Important precursors to such immersion in a narrative are a good plot, dialogue, and believable or relatable characters. As such, narrative immersion is closely related to the emotional involvement with a game mentioned by Cairns [13]. Similarly, Calleja [14] argues that one reason games are often extremely absorbing is that they affect players' emotions. In addition, Calleja [14] discusses narrative involvement as a pre-cursor to immersion and tries to understand how narrative is experienced in game environments. Calleja proposes to distinguish between the *alterbiography*, or the story generated by the player as he/she interacts with the game, and *scripted narrative* which are the scripted story events that the game designers included in the game. In citing Iser's work [24] Calleja brings up the concept of (internal) *synthesis* which describes how a reader/gamer/user of any representational medium forms a mental image of their experience with or understanding of the medium. Synthesis, thus, becomes an important part of experiencing a game narrative. In addition, when players are kept wondering "what will happen next?" or "what will happen when I make a certain choice" they may become quickly engaged with a scripted narrative and their current alterbiography.

In contrast to the ways of discussing immersion presented above, immersion can also be described as closely related to the concept of presence in a virtual environment. Some definitions of presence relate closely only to the availability of sensory input and output parameters. Zeltzer [48], for example, referred to it as a "lumped measure of the number and fidelity of available sensory input and output channels" – which is a much more technical definition than the "feeling of transportation" that other parts of the literature use. Slater [42] also argues that immersion reflects technical capabilities of a system: " The more that a system delivers displays (in all sensory modalities) and tracking that preserves fidelity in relation to their equivalent real-world sensory modalities, the more that it is immersive." Presence, for Slater, on the other hand, is the human reaction to immersion. Slater's proposal seems to be widely adopted in the VR literature and is also sometimes referred to as "perceptual immersion" [31]. It is also the sense in which immersive visualization is most often used (e. g., [5]).

Cairns *et al.* [13] also discuss definitions for presence and their relationship to immersion in detail. The authors specifically differentiate between social presence and spatial presence. Social presence is defined by social factors of the game environment (the social character of the interaction, the feeling of being a social actor in the environment, and social actions/reactions from the game environment) which relate to the concept of a narrative or story. Spatial presence, on the other hand, includes a sense of realism of the virtual environment, a sense of transportation into the game world, and sensory immersion, which is a more technologically oriented view on presence. The authors conclude that "immersion is influenced by social presence but not necessarily by spatial presence" in particular since they define immersion as a cognitive phenomenon.

6.3.2. Immersion in Visual Data-Driven Stories

Unfortunately, researchers do not yet know much about how models of immersion from games (or other) research transfer to visual data-driven stories. As discussed above, there are similarities between the two environments, in particular their primarily graphical nature, ability for interaction, and possibility for communicating a narrative–but there are also large differences. Viewers of a visual data story, for example, typically will not approach a visualization with the same incentives and goals; they will consequently have different expectations and preconceptions of a visualization than they would of a game. The two most important differences are, however, the frequent lack of a central character in a visual story to identify with and the story's data being frequently based on not alterable non-fiction in contrast to the narratives of games that–even if based on historical events–can typically be influenced by the player to deviate from what truly happened in the past (changing their alterbiography). As such, we can be inspired by the discussions of immersion in game narratives when trying to define what it means for visual data stories but the relationships will be non-trivial.

In general, the main goal for constructing a data story in the first place is effective communication of information or an intended message backed by data. We do not know how an immersive experience would affect the perception and retention of the depicted information. In order to begin studying the effects of immersion or designing for immersion, we need to be clear about the definition of immersion for data-driven visual stories. Following our discussions from above, we will begin by considering what it would mean if we considered immersion for visual data stories using the absorption- or transportation-sense of the term.

Describing immersive data stories in the transportation-sense would require the data story to be spatially navigated or interacted with in an almost physical (or pseudo-physical) way. A few visualizations exist that allow this type of experience but generally, they are rarely built, distributed, and adopted.

The roller coaster example from the Introduction Section is one example of a visualization that has been specifically built for storytelling and an immersive experience in the transportation-sense. There has been little past work on how setting up these types of environments affects a potentially immersive experience of a viewer or user.

If we discuss immersive data stories using the absorption-sense of the term, we expect an immersive data story to engage and involve viewers or users to different degrees in the data story. These types of data stories can be two-dimensional visualizations found in online journalism, blogs, or newspaper articles, similar to the examples surveyed in the past [32, 40, 43]. Past research on narrative visualization has to a large extent focused on these types of data stories. Understanding immersion according to the absorption-sense will ultimately require understanding how a viewer (or "user" if the stories are designed for interaction) cognitively experiences or synthesizes their experience with a narrative visualization. This experience, unfortunately, is something researchers still know very little about. Past research (see Section 6.2.) on storytelling with data has to a large extent considered the means by which a story can be communicated with data or the process by which data-driven stories can be created and largely only conjectured on the effects of storytelling elements on effective communication. The related work on immersive virtual reality visualizations has, perhaps, put the most emphasis on creating a specific absorption experience – primarily through effective rendering techniques and sensory input. However, as we discussed above, many more factors than the display environment can contribute to an immersive experience according to the absorption-sense.

Previous research on immersion in narratives in other disciplines has, in addition, considered what makes a narrative immersive and even attempted to measure immersion. Qin *et al.* [34], for example, take narrative as a broad term in their work on a questionnaire for measuring immersion in game narratives. Their questionnaire includes seven dimensions of questions, three of which are targeted specifically at user immersion in the absorption-sense: comprehension of the structure and content of the story/plot, empathy or a feeling of being in the game world or emotionally involved in the game, and familiarity with the game story. The other four dimensions seem more targeted to measuring precursors to immersion: curiosity to explore the game narrative, concentration on the game, challenge and skills offered and required by the game, as well as a sense of control over the game narrative.

Outside of games research, several authors have tried to extract what makes other types of media narratives immersive. In "The Art of Immersion" [36], Rose discusses how media has been changing and evolved to form new types of narratives and immersive experiences. The type of immersion he describes is different from the ones we discussed above. Rose, in particular, refers to new methods for readers to engage deeply with stories that have previously not been interactive. His book includes many examples of movies such as Star Wars that describe a whole universe – which through books, games, websites, etc. can now be experienced deeply outside the original medium – the movie theatre. For Rose, immersion in a narrative can be reached by giving viewers the ability to "drill down as deeply as you like about anything you care to" [36, p.3].

In her work on "Narrative as Virtual Reality" [38], Ryan explores theories of immersion for literary texts. She shows that the concept of immersion as "feeling like one is part of another world while reading" has been discussed by authors and literary scholars for a long time for narrative texts. For such an immersion to take place while reading, the text must offer a "textual world" that readers can imagine as a reality with objects and characters and build a mental model of. When a reader feels transported into the world of a book, the textual world becomes present in the mind of the reader. How well this representation can be established depends on many features of the text such as its plot, the narrative presentation, images, and style; but it also depends on how effortlessly the world can be accessed or how much concentration is necessary. Ryan further distinguishes four levels of absorption in a text: concentration on the text while still being easily distracted, imaginative involvement where the reader follows the narrative but still is able to assess the author's writing skills, entrancement in the textual world and minor dissociation from the physical world, and addiction in which the reader devours a book without assessing it while being completely dissociated from the physical world.

At this point we have seen that immersion is an elusive concept. It is an emotional and cognitive experience, with multiple levels of involvement and many influencing factors. Given how others have attempted to define and describe immersion or immersion in narratives above, we can now begin by describing a set of goals we may want to achieve by an immersive visual data story. The following list is meant to expand upon other similar immersive experiences that can be evoked by a visualization or analysis environment – such as dissociation from the presence or feeling of being "in the data" – see for example Chapter 1. Concentrating solely on immersion in a data story, we may want to achieve:

- A feeling of being closely connected to the data story and its intended message.
- An emotional reaction to the message. This emotional reaction can be a positive or negative one, including anger or sadness about the depicted content, or a feeling of surprise and joy about the data;

- An urge to deeply explore and "get lost" in the data story, a deep engagement or engrossment with the components of the data story.

Given what we have reviewed above, we advocate to take a wide view of the term immersion in visualization and follow Cairns *et al.* [13] in proposing a wide definition for the field of visualization: *Immersion in visualization is the engagement or involvement someone feels as the result of looking, exploring, or analyzing a visual data representation.* Given their goals and ours, we propose to, in particular, consider immersion in visual data stories as an experience that involves a sense of *absorption* leading to deep involvement, engagement, and engrossment with the data. Many additional factors discussed above can lead to this kind of immersion, such as a social presence, internal synthesis, emotional connection, or a feeling of transportation into the data-world. It will have to be explored which factors influence immersion in visual data stories and the list of research projects to engage in this realm is still vast.

6.4. Research Opportunities in Immersive Visual Storytelling with Data

The three goals listed in the previous section are central to what immersion in visual data stories can aim to achieve but other goals are certainly possible. In this section, we describe several opportunities and challenges that arise when we want to design immersive visual data stories that achieve these three goals. We present what we believe to be some of the most interesting research questions on this topic, but many more are possible and our list is certainly not complete. Each research question posed is also purposefully broad leading to a wide number of possible future research projects.

How much reality is necessary? Traditional definitions of immersion in the field of virtual reality have focused on immersion from a technological perspective, focusing on creating sensory experiences that are as close as possible to the real world and involve more than the visual sense and include audio or even tactile stimulation. Game development similarly has long striven for realistic graphics, sound, and character animation. Yet, as we have discussed immersion above, realism might not be necessary for people to become immersed in the absorption-sense of the term. When a game like Tetris can be described as immersive, so should a 2D infographic have possible immersive capabilities. When we move away from realism as a purely sensory experience we may ask the question what other "real" elements a 2D visual story could incorporate to make the experience of looking at or interacting with the data more immersive? For example, the Hans Rosling example from the Introduction included a real narrator, the Fallen of WWII included references to real-world characters as well as voice narration, and the roller coaster example had the viewer virtually following up-and-down movements with the up and downs of the financial data.

Perhaps storytelling elements that make connections to the "real-world" or the context of the data can help to make visual data-driven stories more immersive?

For example, many infographics contain images related to the context of the data, such as the four images of baseball players in the New York Time's piece on steroid use in baseball: "Steroids Or Not, the Pursuit is On" reprinted by Segel and Heer [40]. Past research has shown that some form of embellishments to data charts can be helpful, e. g. for memorability [8]. Yet, how embellishments such as images, or pictograms can aid in storytelling and immersion has not yet been deeply researched. In addition, many other forms of connecting abstract data to the real-world data context are certainly possible as described in the three examples from the introduction. Which connection techniques exist, how and if they are effective, and what kinds of immersion they support will be a challenging but undoubtedly interesting research problem to tackle.

What is the role of the visual storytelling medium and context? Visualizations can be shown using many different media: visualization can be printed on paper, shown on computer screens, projected on physical environments, or printed into 3D physical shapes. Related to the question of realism above, it is interesting to understand to which extent the presentation medium and its physical context play a role in creating an immersive experience. Previous work has shown that context such as lighting can play a role in facilitating immersion. To which extent would the same be true for visual data stories? Also can, as previously conjectured, different types of displays such as large displays or CAVEs aid immersion in a visual story? Even if their goal is not to necessarily create a feeling of physical realism?

What is the role of interaction in creating or hindering immersion? Many experiences described as immersive in other media such as watching a scary movie or reading a captivating book require little interaction from the viewer. Rose's [36] discussion on immersion by "drilling down as deeply as you like on anything that you care to" is related to this question of the role of interaction for immersion–and in particular the type of cognitively absorbing experience that we focus on here. In his book he looks at interaction as a more global concept that involves viewers or fans creating content of their own (such as the Lostpedia[5] for the TV series Lost) or adapting and remixing content from their favorite shows. As Rose points out, this type of interactivity with the content has the advantage of people becoming experts on the content but also allows the audience to run away with a story and change it as they please. With a data-driven story this is potentially dangerous as it may allow people to insert rumors, personal beliefs and other non-data-driven content around an existing data story.

Yet, the role of interaction can also be considered at a much lower level for individual data stories in which the type of interaction techniques need to be considered (e. g. mouse vs. touch), how much of the data can be manipulated, or which interaction hardware will be offered. Data visualizations often offer interactive capabilities to help people drill down on details that interest them. This type of free exploration can both help in creating an immersive experience of "getting lost in the data" but it can also break an emerging immersion when people have to search for interactions or cannot find their way back from detail

[5] http://lostpedia.wikia.com

views and undo their past exploration steps. What the right balance between fully interactive experiences, guided walkthroughs, or no interaction at all is for the creation of an immersive data exploration experience is so far unclear.

How can we emotionally involve viewers? As discussed above, an emotional reaction to a visual data story can be an important pre-cursor to immersion. Yet, how a deep emotional connection can be achieved for visualizations and in particular for data-driven visual stories is yet unclear. It can become in particular difficult since visualizations–unlike games–typically do not include specific characters that viewers/users can attach to or feel empathy with or a "world" that they can be part of. It also needs to be considered what kinds of emotions one might want to evoke in the first place. For example, we may want to create feelings of empathy when showing data on deaths, fear when seeing visualizations of the results of climate change, joy in seeing personal visualizations of past travels, surprise in how much money the government spends, anxiety to change behavior when seeing one's own energy consumption, or pride when looking at personal visualizations of fitness data.

Emotions are a very complex phenomenon and so studying the role of emotion for immersive data-drive visual stories will be challenging. Past work on memorability [8] or sustainability/persuasion [33] have laid some groundwork for studying concepts related to emotion and immersion in visualization. Recently, Bartram *et al.* [4] studied affective color for visualization which is one step towards design elements for visualizations that can influence visual storytelling with data. More dedicated work in this direction could re-examine already proposed storytelling techniques for visualization and their potential influence on emotion, for example, how can the presentation of annotations lead to emotional involvement, would fonts, font sizes, and the type of writing influence how people emotionally react? Similarly, other storytelling techniques could be re-examined.

What are levels of immersion in visual data stories? As discussed above, immersion is not a binary experience that is either present or not. Immersion has been described as an experience along a continuum, for example, from people feeling simply engaged, to feeling fully absorbed in the medium. It is not clear to which extent this continuum will be present in immersive experiences around data visualization. Which past definitions of the immersion continuum would most relate to how people experience visual data stories? Would Brown and Cairns' [11] engagement, engrossment, and total immersion in games research make sense to apply? Or would Ryan's [38] immersion continuum from concentration, imaginative involvement, entrancement, to addiction in literary texts make more sense? In general, more research is necessary to see how concepts of immersion from other research fields apply to visual stories. While we have outlined a large body of past work on the topic in games as well as a few discussions from other fields in this book chapter, the remaining literature is vast and certainly more can be extracted and learned from it. For the visualization practitioner, the most useful goal will be to derive design considerations for immersive visual stories. In addition to theoretical assessment of the remaining literature, it is, thus, important to derive ways for measuring immersion.

What are the effects of immersion on the viewer? All research questions above hinge to some or even a large extent on the question of how to measure immersion for visual data stories. Some related work has attempted to study immersion through questionnaires, and there is related work in brain-computer interfaces that has looked at studying components of immersion such as concentration or emotion/affect (e. g. [16]). This past work may be a good starting point to attempt to measure immersion in visualization before more dedicated research methodologies can be developed or adapted from existing techniques. Studying immersion is important as many interesting questions are open as to the effects of immersion on the viewer. Will an immersive visual data story aid visualizations to be more memorable, will viewers retain more information, will they learn better, will they be better persuaded to act? In addition, the research questions raised above hinge to a large extent on the possibilities to measure immersion.

What are potential dangers for immersive visual stories? Finally, it is not clear to which extent it is even desirable to create an immersive visual data story. If viewers become so immersed that they stop to question the data, where it comes from, and what it might want to say, this can be potentially dangerous. In addition, it is possible that people want to make a visual story their own and synthesize it as they please. Could immersion help to lead people on the right path? Or drive them down even further in the wrong direction? In addition, attention has to be paid to the blurring of fiction and fact in particular when specific storytelling elements are added to potentially create immersion but which hinder the interpretation of the data. In general, negative side-effects of immersion have to be considered side-by-side with measuring positive effects of an immersive experience.

6.5. Conclusion

Visual data stories bring us a powerful means for communicating information to a range of audiences. In this chapter, we discussed immersion in the context of visual data stories. We first presented an overview of how immersion has been discussed in the related literature, focusing on a definition of immersion for visual data stories that is inspired by previous descriptions of the absorption-sense of immersion. We propose to begin research on the concept of immersion in visualization with a broad definition: *Immersion in visualization is the engagement or involvement someone feels as the result of looking, exploring, or analyzing a visual data representation.* This type of immersion can involve many factors such as a deep sensory experience in VR environments, an emotional connection to the data and its main message, a feeling of social presence, or even transportation into the data world. Not all of these factors will be necessary to create this feeling of immersion and much research has to be conducted to understand the role of these and other factors in creating immersive data visualization experiences. In this book chapter, we focused in particular on challenges and opportunities for immersive data stories. We hope that our work will inspire others to start their own projects in this direction as the research questions on this topic are still wide open.

Acknowledgements

We would like to thank the following members of the storytelling working group at the the Dagstuhl seminar on Immersive Analytics: Mark Hancock, Todd Margolis, and Steffen Oeltze-Jafra. Their ideas and input have helped to shape this chapter. Maxime Cordeil acknowledges support by the Australian Research Council Discovery Scheme, project DP140100077.

References

1. Amini, F., Henry Riche, N., Lee, B., Hurter, C., Irani, P.: Understanding data videos: Looking at narrative visualization through the cinematography lens. In: Proceedings of Conference on Human Factors in Computing Systems (CHI). pp. 1459–1468. ACM, New York, NY, USA(2015) doi: 10.1145/2702123.2702431
2. Amini, F., Henry Riche, N., Lee, B., Monroy-Hernandez, A., Irani, P.: Authoring data-driven videos with dataclips. IEEE Transactions on Visualization & Computer Graphics 23(1), 501–510(2017) doi: 10.1109/TVCG.2016.2598647
3. Bach, B., Kerracher, N., Hall, K.W., Carpendale, S., Kennedy, J., Henry Riche, N.: Telling stories about dynamic networks with graph comics. In: Proceedings of the Conference on Human Factors in Information Systems (CHI). pp. 3670–3682. ACM, New York, NY, USA(2016) doi: 10.1145/2858036.2858387
4. Bartram, L., Patra, A., Stone, M.: Affective color in visualization. In: Proceedings of the Conference on Human Factors in Computing Systems (CHI). pp. 1364–1374. ACM, New York, NY, USA(2017) doi: 10.1145/3025453.3026041
5. Bastiras, J., Thomas, B.H.: Combining virtual reality and narrative visualisation to persuade. In: Proceedings of the Symposium on Big Data Visual Analytics (BDVA). IEEE, Los Alamitos, CA, USA(2017) doi: 10.1109/bdva.2017.8114623
6. Becker, A.A.: Designing virtual reality data visualizations. Talk at the OpenVis Conference 2016, Available Online(May 2016), https://www.youtube.com/watch?v=EEN_sNXMyko, last visited: May, 2018
7. Bigelow, A., Drucker, S., Fisher, D., Meyer, M.: Iterating between tools to create and edit visualizations. IEEE Transactions on Visualization & Computer Graphics 23(1), 481–490(2017) doi: 10.1109/TVCG.2016.2598609
8. Borkin, M.A., Vo, A.A., Bylinskii, Z., Isola, P., Sunkavalli, S., Oliva, A., Pfister, H.: What makes a visualization memorable? IEEE Transactions on Visualization & Computer Graphics 19(12), 2306–2315(2013) doi: 10.1109/TVCG.2013.234
9. Brehmer, M., Lee, B., Bach, B., Henry Riche, N., Munzner, T.: Timelines revisited: A design space and considerations for expressive storytelling. IEEE Transactions on Visualization and Computer Graphics 23(9), 2151–2164(2017) doi: 10.1109/TVCG.2016.2614803
10. Brehmer, M., Lee, B., Henry Riche, N.: Microsoft timeline storyteller. Open Source Software(2017), https://timelinestoryteller.com, last visited: May 2018
11. Brown, E., Cairns, P.: A grounded investigation of game immersion. In: Extended Abstracts on Human Factors in Computing Systems (CHI). pp. 1297–1300. ACM, New York, NY, USA(2004) doi: 10.1145/985921.986048

12. Bryan, C., Ma, K.L., Woodring, J.: Temporal summary images: An approach to narrative visualization via interactive annotation generation and placement. IEEE Transactions on Visualization & Computer Graphics 23(1), 511–520(2017) doi: 10.1109/TVCG.2016.2598876
13. Cairns, P., Cox, A., Nordin, A.I.: Immersion in digital games: Review of gaming experience research. In: Handbook of Digital Games, pp. 337–361. John Wiley & Sons, Inc.(2014) doi: 10.1002/9781118796443.ch12
14. Calleja, G.: In-Game: From Immersion to Incorporation. MIT Press (2011)
15. Chevalier, F., Tory, M., Lee, B., van Wijk, J., Santucci, G., Dörk, M., Hullman, J.: From analysis to communication: Supporting the lifecycle of a story. In: Data-Driven Storytelling, pp. 151–184. A K Peters / CRC Press (2018)
16. Crowley, K., Sliney, A., Pitt, I., Murphy, D.: Evaluating a brain-computer interface to categorise human emotional response. In: Proceedings of the Conference on Advanced Learning Technologies (ICALT). pp. 276–278. IEEE, Los Alamitos, CA, USA(2010) doi: 10.1109/ICALT.2010.81
17. Donalek, C., Djorgovski, S.G., Cioc, A., Wang, A., Zhang, J., Lawler, E., Yeh, S., Mahabal, A., Graham, M., Drake, A., Davidoff, S., Norris, J.S., Longo, G.: Immersive and collaborative data visualization using virtual reality platforms. In: Proceedings of the Conference on Big Data (Big Data). pp. 609–614. IEEE, Los Alamitos, CA, USA(2014) doi: 10.1109/BigData.2014.7004282
18. Fulda, J., Brehmel, M., Munzner, T.: Timelinecurator: Interactive authoring of visual timelines from unstructured text. IEEE Transactions on Visualization and Computer Graphics 22(1), 300–309(2016) doi: 10.1109/TVCG.2015.2467531
19. Gratzl, S., Lex, A., Gehlenborg, N., Cosgrove, N., Streit, M.: From visual exploration to storytelling and back again. Computer Graphics Forum 35(3), 491–500(2016) doi: 10.1111/cgf.12925
20. Halloran, N.: The Fallen of World War II. Website, http://www.fallen.io/ww2, last visited: May 2018
21. Hullman, J., Diakopoulos, N., Adar, E.: Contextifier: Automatic generation of annotated stock visualizations. In: Proceedings of the Conference on Human Factors in Computing Systems (CHI). pp. 2707–2716. ACM, New York, NY, USA(2013) doi: 10.1145/2470654.2481374
22. Hullman, J., Diakopoulos, N.: Visualization rhetoric: Framing effects in narrative visualization. IEEE Transactions on Visualization and Computer Graphics 17(12), 2231–2240(2011) doi: 10.1109/TVCG.2011.255
23. Hullman, J., Drucker, S., Henry Riche, N., Lee, B., Fisher, D., Adar, E.: A deeper understanding of sequence in narrative visualization. IEEE Transactions on Visualization and Computer Graphics 19(12), 2406–2415(2013) doi: 10.1109/TVCG.2013.119
24. Iser, W.: The Act of Reading: A Theory of Aesthetic Response. Johns Hopkins University Press (1991)
25. Kenny, R., Becker, A.A.: Is the Nasdaq in Another Bubble? Website(2015), http://graphics.wsj.com/3d-nasdaq, last visited: May 2018
26. Kim, N.W., Schweickart, E., Liu, Z., Dontcheva, M., Li, W., Popovic, J., Pfister, H.: Data-driven guides: Supporting expressive design for information graphics. IEEE Transactions on Visualization and Computer Graphics 23(1), 491–500(2017) doi: 10.1109/TVCG.2016.2598620
27. Kosara, R., Mackinlay, J.: Storytelling: The next step for visualization. Computer 46(5), 44–50(2013) doi: 10.1109/MC.2013.36

28. Kreylos, O., Bawden, G.W., Kellogg, L.H.: Immersive visualization and analysis of LiDAR data. In: Bebis, G., Boyle, R., Parvin, B., Koracin, D., Remagnino, P., Porikli, F., Peters, J., Klosowski, J., Arns, L., Chun, Y.K., Rhyne, T.M., Monroe, L. (eds.) Advances in Visual Computing: 4th International Symposium, ISVC 2008, Las Vegas, NV, USA, December 1-3, 2008. Proceedings, Part I. pp. 846–855. Springer, Berlin, Heidelberg(2008), https://doi.org/10.1007/978-3-540-89639-5_81 doi: 10.1007/978-3-540-89639-5_81
29. Lee, B., Henry Riche, N., Isenberg, P., Carpendale, S.: More than telling a story: Transforming data into visually shared stories. IEEE Computer Graphics and Applications 35(5), 84–90(Sep/Oct 2015) doi: 10.1109/MCG.2015.99
30. Lee, B., Kazi, R.H., Smith, G.: Sketchstory: Telling more engaging stories with data through freeform sketching. IEEE Transactions on Visualization and Computer Graphics 19(12), 2416–2425(2013) doi: 10.1109/TVCG.2013.191
31. Lombard, M., Ditton, T.: At the heart of it all: The concept of presence. Journal of Computer-Mediated Communication 3(2)(2006) doi: 10.1111/j.1083-6101.1997.tb00072.x
32. McKenna, S., Henry Riche, N., Lee, B., Boy, J., Meyer, M.: Visual narrative flow: Exploring factors shaping data visualization story reading experiences. Computer Graphics Forum 36(3), 377–387(Jun 2017) doi: 10.1111/cgf.13195
33. Pandey, A.V., Manivannan, A., Nov, O., Satterthwaite, M., Bertini, E.: The persuasive power of data visualization. IEEE Transactions on Visualization and Computer Graphics 20(12), 2211–2220(Dec 2014) doi: 10.1109/TVCG.2014.2346419
34. Qin, H., Rau, P.L.P., Salvendy, G.: Measuring player immersion in the computer game narrative. International Journal of Human–Computer Interaction 25(2), 107–133(2009) doi: 10.1080/10447310802546732
35. Ren, D., Brehmer, M., Lee, B., Höllerer, T., Choe, E.K.: Chartaccent: Annotation for data-driven storytelling. In: Proceedings of the Pacific Visualization Symposium (PacificVis). pp. 230–239. IEEE, Los Alamitos, CA, USA(2017) doi: 10.1109/PACIFICVIS.2017.8031599
36. Rose, F.: The Art of Immersion: How the Digital Generation is Remaking Hollywood, Madison Avenue, and The Way We Tell Stories. W. W. Norton & Company (2011)
37. Rosling, H.: Hans Rosling's 200 Countries, 200 Years, 4 Minutes. Video Presentation(November 2010), https://www.youtube.com/watch?v=jbkSRLYSojo, last visited: December, 2017
38. Ryan, M.L.: Narrative as Virtual Reality: Immersion and Interactivity in Literature and Electronic Media. The Johns Hopkins University Press (2003)
39. Satyanarayan, A., Heer, J.: Authoring narrative visualizations with ellipsis. Computer Graphics Forum 33(3), 361–370(2014) doi: 10.1111/cgf.12392
40. Segel, E., Heer, J.: Narrative visualization: Telling stories with data. Transactions on Visualization and Computer Graphics 16(6), 1139–1148(2010) doi: 10.1109/TVCG.2010.179
41. Slater, M.V.S.V..M.: From presence to consciousness through virtual reality. Nature Reviews Neuroscience 6, 332–339(2005) doi: 10.1038/nrn1651
42. Slater, M.: A note on the presence terminology (2017), retrieved from: https://www.researchgate.net/publication/242608507_A_Note_on_Presence_Terminology, Dec. 2017
43. Stolper, C.D., Lee, B., Henry Riche, N., Stasko, J.: Emerging and recurring data-driven storytelling techniques: Analysis of a curated collection of recent stories. In: Data-Driven Storytelling, pp. 85–105. CRC Press (2018)

44. Tufo, H.M., Fischer, P.F., Papka, M.E., Blom, K.: Numerical simulation and immersive visualization of hairpin vortices. In: Proceedings of the Conference on Supercomputing (SC). ACM, New York, NY, USA(1999) doi: 10.1145/331532.331594
45. Waldner, M., Le Muzic, M., Bernhard, M., Purgathofer, W., Viola, I.: Attractive flicker—guiding attention in dynamic narrative visualizations. IEEE Transactions on Visualization and Computer Graphics 20(12), 2456–2465(2014) doi: 10.1109/TVCG.2014.2346352
46. Wang, Y., Chen, Z., Ma, X., Luo, Q., Qu, H.: Animated narrative visualization for video clickstream data. In: SIGGRAPH ASIA Symposium on Visualization. ACM, New York, NY, USA(2016) doi: 10.1145/3002151.3002155
47. Wang, Y., Liu, D., Qu, H., Luo, Q., Ma, X.: A guided tour of literature review: Facilitating academic paper reading with narrative visualization. In: Proceedings of the Symposium on Visual Information Communication and Interaction (VINCI). pp. 17–24. ACM, New York, NY, USA(2016) doi: 10.1145/2968220.2968242
48. Zeltzer, D.: Autonomy, interaction, and presence. Presence: Teleoperators and Virtual Environments 1(1), 127–132(1992) doi: 10.1162/pres.1992.1.1.127

7. Situated Analytics

Bruce H. Thomas[1], Gregory F. Welch[2], Pierre Dragicevic[3], Niklas Elmqvist[4], Pourang Irani[5], Yvonne Jansen[6], Dieter Schmalstieg[7], Aurélien Tabard[8], Neven A. M. ElSayed[9], Ross T. Smith[1], and Wesley Willett[10]

[1] University of South Australia
[bruce.thomas,ross.smith]@unisa.edu.au
[2] University of Central Florida
welch@ucf.edu
[3] Inria, France
pierre.dragicevic@inria.fr
[4] University of Maryland, College Park
elm@umd.edu
[5] University of Manitoba
irani@cs.umanitoba.ca
[6] Sorbonne University, Paris
jansen@isir.upmc.fr
[7] Graz University of Technology
schmalstieg@tugraz.at
[8] University Lyon
atabard@liris.cnrs.fr
[9] Banha University
neven.elsayed@mymail.unisa.edu.au
[10] University of Calgary
wesley.willett@ucalgary.ca

Abstract. This chapter introduces the concept of *situated analytics* that employs data representations organized in relation to germane objects, places, and persons for the purpose of understanding, sensemaking, and decision-making. The components of situated analytics are characterized in greater detail, including the users, tasks, data, representations, interactions, and analytical processes involved. Several case studies of projects and products are presented that exemplify situated analytics in action. Based on these case studies, a set of derived design considerations for building situated analytics applications are presented. Finally, there is a an outline of a research agenda of challenges and research questions to explore in the future.

Keywords: situated analytics,immersive analytics,immersion,human-computer interaction,augmented reality, data visualisation

7.1. Introduction

People are increasingly interested in understanding data directly associated with objects, locations, or persons in their everyday life. For example, imagine hunting

K. Marriott et al. (Eds.): Immersive Analytics, LNCS 11190, pp. 185–220, 2018.
https://doi.org/10.1007/978-3-030-01388-2_7

for a house by walking through the neighborhood in which you want to live. Your search could be informed by social media posts about the area appearing in virtual signs on the ground, dynamic census data rising above the houses, and historical traffic data rendered on the street in a way that reflects the ebb and flow throughout a typical day. In an industrial context, imagine a team of professionals collaboratively reorganizing machines and stations on a factory floor. As they walk around together, dynamic data would appear embedded in and around the floor. To demonstrate this concept, the data could be related to physical space, safety, economics (e. g., layout constraints related to past manufacturing data), power, ventilation, ergonomics and worker preferences, past accidents, and legal concerns.

In these examples, the individuals would be interested in discovering, interpreting, and communicating meaningful patterns in data that is directly relevant to, and integrated into, the physical space all around them. For the first time both the technology—such as sensors, wearable displays, natural user interfaces, and augmented reality devices—as well as the data sources—such as dynamically updating social media, ubiquitous sensor information, and large-scale movement data—exist to make this vision a reality. To cope with this massive quantity of data, analytics techniques are required to help the user, much in the same way visual analytics grew out of the visualization research domain. Visual Analytics (VA) has been defined as *"the science of analytical reasoning facilitated by visual interactive interfaces"* [58].

Analogously, the concept of *Situated Analytics* [18] (SA) is the use of data representations organized in relation to relevant objects, places, and persons in the physical world for the purpose of understanding, sensemaking, and decision-making. For example, virtual labels on a physical container provide semantic information for the analyst, as does the proximity of different objects. Situated analytics allows users to access the power of the cloud (data and analysis) seamlessly analyzing virtual data situated in the physical world simultaneously.

Imagine walking into a pharmacy and placing an order for your prescriptions. While you are waiting for your order, you browse the shop for other purchases. Through the use of Internet of Things technology [2] and situated analytics, you will be reminded of items you might wish to replenish. This is performed by highlighting items in your field of view using augmented reality to draw your attention. You notice a natural supplement you have not tried that looks interesting. Situated analytics can provide a number of supporting functions for you. First, it can recognize the supplement and determine if the ingredients are compatible with your prescription and if you are allergic to the item. Second, you can compare different brands of the supplement by placing them next to one another. The system will automatically perform an analysis and compare the products. Third, a visualization summarizing the reviews, keywords, and ratings can be embedded on the store shelf right next to the supplement. Finally, the user can inspect more detailed information about the product by selecting portions of the label to bring up Augmented Reality (AR) [54] information in greater detail.

Situated analytics and immersive analytics are complementary techniques that have emerged at similar times. Situated analytics draws from the domains of Visual Analytics and Augmented Reality to support a new form of in-situ interactive visual analysis. First published as a novel interaction and visualization concept for reasoning support, situated analytics incorporates four primary elements: situated information, abstract information, augmented reality interaction, and analytical interaction [19]. Meanwhile immersive analytics [14] covers a broad range of display techniques and technologies [32, 54, 64].

The degree of immersion you might associate with an instance of situated analytics depends on your definition of the word *immersion*. If one considers immersion to reflect deep mental involvement, it is unclear that situated analytics would be any different (from an immersion standpoint) from non-situated analytics In other words, the situated nature of the analytical task would not necessarily bring any new immersion-related considerations or affects to the task. If one considers immersion to reflect the degree to which the analyst is surrounded by an engrossing total environment—including the real environment, virtual data, and analytics—then situated analytics could be considered inherently immersive, as the environment where the virtual data and analytics are situated surrounds the analyst. If instead one considers immersion to be associated solely with the virtual data and analytics (not including the real environment), then one's sense of the degree of immersion might depend on the degree to which the virtual data and analytics surround the analyst, i. e., the degree of immersion is proportional to the spatial extents of the virtual data and analytics.

In 1997, Slater and Wilbur defined the concept of *immersion* as being more generally related to the characteristics of a *system*, and in particular to the *sensorimotor contingencies* that the system supports [55]. Sensorimotor contingencies refer to the available actions humans employ to perceive things using vision and other sensory modalities, for example moving one's body, head, or eyes to obtain a better visual or aural perspective [47, 48]. This notion of immersion has been widely used in the Virtual Reality and Augmented Reality communities. If one adopts this perspective, then the degree of immersion is related to the sensorimotor contingencies afforded by the system presenting the virtual data and analytics to the user. If, for example, a person is using an AR system with a relatively narrow visual field of view, the user might not be able to see the complete virtual data and analytics without scanning their view left-right or up-down. From a Slater and Wilbur perspective, such a system would be less immersive than a system that presented the virtual data and analytics completely (in the same resolution) without the need for explicit movement on the part of the user. This same concept would apply beyond vision to other senses including sound, smell, and touch (haptic senses). In this view, the degree of immersion is essentially proportional to the sensorimotor contingencies.

7.1.1. Comparison to Other Fields and Concepts

Situated analytics has a close relationship with a number of fields. Table 1 compares a number of fields from low to high of their *Situatedness* versus their

Analytic Level. Where *situatedness* is the degree the information and person are connected to the task, location, and/or another person, and the *analytic level* is the quantity of analytic processing of the information. You will notice situated analytics requires high levels of both situatedness and analytics.

Situatedness	Analytic Level Low	Analytic Level High
High	Situation Awareness	Situated Analytics
Low	Information Displays Ambient Displays	Visual Analytics Traditional Analytics

Table 1: Situatedness versus Analytic Level

Below is a set of brief overviews of some of the related fields and concepts:

1. **Augmented/Mixed reality** [9, 54] is a dominant form of presentation of information in situated analytics, and interaction techniques from these fields can inform new interaction techniques for situated analytics.
2. **Wearable and mobile computing** [56] support the user operating in unprepared physical locations and leverages such technologies as interaction, device form factor, and display techniques. This mobile nature is required by many situated analytics applications.
3. **Situated computing** [26] investigates computational devices that detect, interpret and respond to aspects of the user's local environment.
4. **Situated visualization** [63, 64] refers to data representations that are related to and portrayed in their physical environment. Sensemaking is achieved through the combination of the visualization and the relationship of that visualization to the immediate physical environment.
5. **Embedded data representations** [64] focus on the use of visual and physical representations of data that are deeply integrated in the physical spaces, objects, and entities the data refers to. This closer association with physical objects and virtual information is critical for situated analytics.
6. **Contextual computing** overlaps with situated analytics; Chen and Kotz [15] defines context as a set of environmental states and settings that 1) determines an application's behavior or 2) when an application event arises then is of interest to the user.
7. **Ambient displays** [65] employ the user's complete physical environment as an interface to their virtual information space. Situated analytics endeavors to bring the users analytic information space to be in-situ to physical objects and spaces of interest.
8. **Ubiquitous computing**, according to Mark Weiser's [62] vision, consists of embedding numerous computers in the user's physical environment, and as such make the computation device fade into the user's background. The goal of SA is to bring visual analytics to bear on problems away from the user's workstation and into the physical world. This can be performed through either ubiquitous computing or wearable computer or even mobile computing.

9. **Visualization beyond the desktop** [28,38,53] is a broad research agenda of which situated analytics and situated visualization is a component. Instead of the ubiquitous mouse and keyboard, such visualization systems focus on touch-based, pen-based, or gestural interaction methods with multiple form factors (smartphones, smartwatches, tablets) and both large and small displays (HMDs, powerwalls, wearable displays, etc.).
10. **Ubiquitous analytics** [17] is "*... amplif[ying] human cognition by embedding the analytical process into the physical environment to enable sensemaking of big data anywhere and anytime.*" Several tools and toolkits have been proposed to support this practice [3, 4]. Situated analytics builds on this concept by focusing on place as an index.
11. **Personal visual analytics** (PVA) is concerned with assisting visual analytics with a personal context [25]. The aim of personal visual analytics is to support people with the ability to acquire an awareness of, explore, and learn from data around them and from their personal context. This is a similar goal for situated analytics, yet again without the immersive aspect.

7.1.2. Visual Analytics and Augmented Reality

Situated analytics leverages two research domains—VA and AR—to deliver analytical reasoning in the world around the user [21]. VA is a multidisciplinary research domain spanning analytical reasoning techniques with visualization, while AR enhances the physical worldview with a visual overlay of registered contextual information in real-time. Most of situated analytics combines VA techniques with AR techniques for in-situ registration of information onto the physical space.

AR has been shown to be a useful tool for visualization [57]. Kalkofen *et al.* [33] considered three types of AR visualization techniques: 1) data integration, 2) scene manipulation and 3) context-driven. Data integration techniques enhance the smooth mixing of the virtual information with the physical world [23, 32]. Scene manipulation techniques manipulate the real scene to augment information. A few examples of this smooth mixing are as follows: the relocation of physical objects [34], color corrections [23], and diminished reality techniques [39]. To incorporate some of the user's influence on the visual presentation of information, context-driven techniques have been employed [63].

A major research challenge remains with the limitations of current AR display technologies [36]. AR display technologies and techniques primarily fall into two categories: Visual Augmented Reality (VAR) and Spatial Augmented Reality (SAR). In the case of VAR the virtual content is overlaid into the user's visual field, for example via a head-worn (head-mounted) display (HMD) device, a handheld device such as a mobile phone, and—some day—special AR contact lenses [44], see the example in Figure 1. This is the most common form of AR, and thus often the implied form when someone refers to AR.

In the case of SAR, virtual content is displayed directly on objects in the user's physical space [11, 50, 51]; typically using digital projectors and a mapping technique initially known as *shader lamps* [49, 52]. More recently this concept is

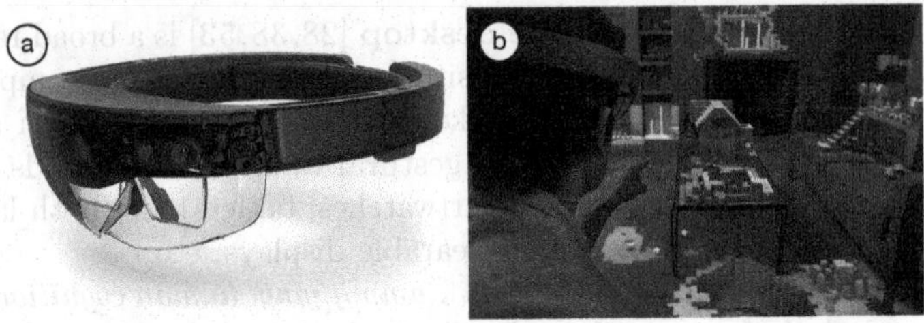

Fig. 1: An example of Visual Augmented Reality (VAR), where the virtual imagery is overlaid onto the user's visual field. The left image (a) shows a Microsoft HoloLens device. The right image (b) shows a person wearing a Microsoft HoloLens device, and a depiction of what they would see—Minecraft [43] game objects visually overlaid onto the real world table, couch, etc.

referred to as *projection mapping*, see examples in Figure 2. When the virtual content is not associated directly with any physical object, e. g., as would be the case with air flow visualization information or floating virtual labels attached to physical objects, then VAR would be more appropriate. When the virtual content is to appear (or is intended to appear) directly on the surface of a physical object, SAR becomes an option. Some advantages of SAR in such situations include the natural coincidence of vergence and accommodation of the human visual system (a problem with VAR), and not requiring devices to be worn or held—a particular advantage in group settings, where one would like to see other individuals naturally as they discuss the issues at hand.

7.1.3. Motivation

Why do we need situated analytics? This method of sensemaking has a great potential to have a major impact on people's use and application of Big Data in their everyday lives. The significance of this method of sensemaking is a new research domain that provides the intersection of many research concepts. Situated analytics can be beneficial for data exploration and information comprehension. There are three ways situated analytics can enhance sensemaking:

1. more understandable information presentation by immediately associating information with the germane physical objects (i. e., place acting as a *spatial index*),
2. more natural method for information exploration interactions by allowing the user to touch and manipulate the germane physical objects (i. e., the use of *natural interaction*), and
3. more comprehensive information analysis providing contextual and overview information (i. e., *contextual synthesis* of data).

Critical to the success of situated analytics for the appropriate application of this new technique for casual and expert users with real world tasks in actual physical settings are techniques that enhance the user's ability and increase their

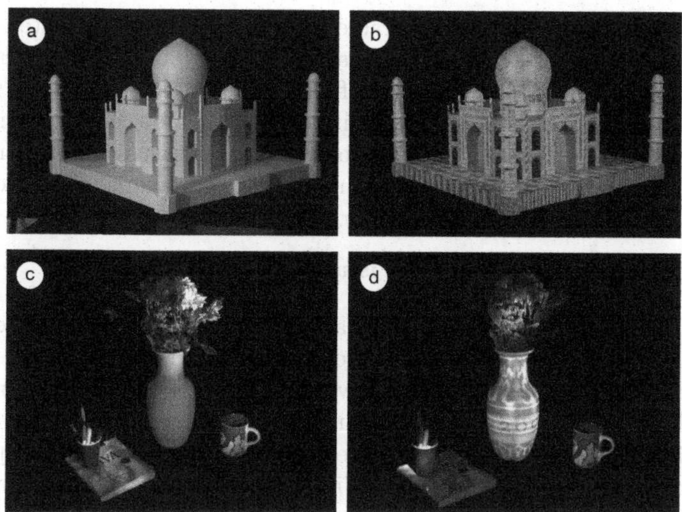

Fig. 2: Examples of Spatial Augmented Reality (SAR) [11, 50, 51]. The upper pair of images show a one meter square physical model of the Taj Mahal (a) before and (b) after augmentation via the *shader lamps* technique [49, 52]. The lower pair of images similarly show a vase (c) before and (d) after augmentation.

effectiveness. There are limitations to the current technologies (displays [41] and computer vision [9] for example). Barring these limitations, people increasingly want to base their decisions on data at the location of the decision, such as a purchase.

7.1.4. Structure of the Chapter

This chapter starts by characterizing situated analytics in greater detail, including the users, tasks, data, representations, interactions, and analytical processes involved. A set of case studies of projects and products are examined that exemplify best practice situated analytics in action. Extending the interaction technologies of SA are the presented blended situated analytics controls with a set of example applications. Based on these case studies, a set of derived design considerations for building situated analytics applications are presented. Finally, there is a an outline of a research agenda of challenges and research questions to explore in the future.

7.2. Characterization of Situated Visualizations

While *visual analytics* aims at supporting analytic reasoning through the use of visualisations, *situated analytics* aims at supporting analytic reasoning through the use of *situated* visualizations. This section introduces a conceptual framework and a terminology that help characterize and reason about situated visualizations, while temporarily leaving out the analytic aspects. This framework is based largely on Willett *et al.* [64][1]. The section first starts by explaining what it means for a data visualization to be spatially situated. It then discusses physically-situated vs. perceptually-situated visualizations, embedded visualizations, and temporally-situated visualizations. Finally, a model of interaction is presented.

7.2.1. Spatially-Situated Visualizations

Since situated analytics involves data visualizations that are integrated in the physical environment, a model of data visualization is required that accounts for the existence of the physical world. The most widely used model of data visualization, i. e., the information visualization reference model (or "visualization pipeline") [12,16], essentially ignores the physical world. A conceptual model is described that unifies two recently introduced models that capture the physical world around visualizations: the embedded data representation model from Willett *et al.* [64], and the beyond-desktop pipeline model from Jansen *et al.* [28].

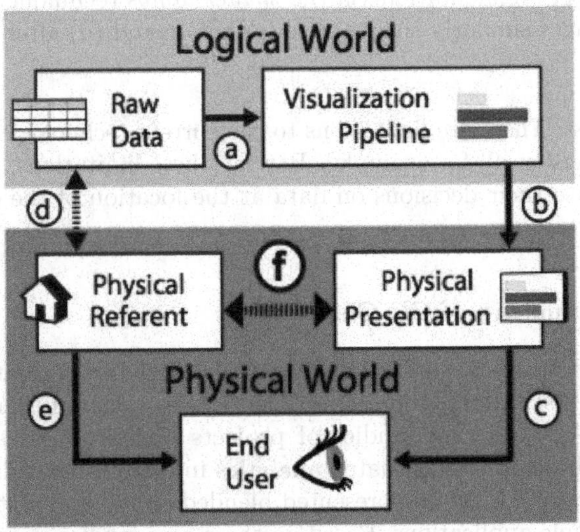

Fig. 3: Conceptual model of a spatially-situated visualization and analytics (adapted from Willett *et al.* [64]).

The conceptual model is illustrated in Figure 3. It covers both the logical world (top) and the physical world (bottom). Black arrows show information

[1] While the basic model is the same (Figure 3), the text and definitions have been fully reworked, and an illustration has been added to clarify the notion of embedded visualization (Figure 4). The interaction model (Figure 5) is new.

flows, while dashed arrows refer to conceptual relationships. Only information that flows from the data to the end user is shown here—other information flows will be covered in Subsection 7.2.5. on interaction.

The flow of information starts with the raw data, on the top left. The conceptual model assumes that a visualization system turns this raw data into a visual form that humans can understand (a→b). In information visualization, this process is generally computer-automated and can be characterized by a *visualization pipeline.* The visualization pipeline applies a sequence of transformations to the raw data until a final image is produced. The different stages of the pipeline have been covered extensively in the past [12, 16, 28], but for the sake of simplicity, Figure 3 shows the entire visualization pipeline as a single block.

Both the raw data and the visualization pipeline exist in a logical world. This logical world relates to the physical world in two major ways [64]: through the data's *physical presentation* (b) and through the data's *physical referent* (d).

A *physical data presentation* (or physical presentation for short) is *"the physical object or apparatus that makes the visualization observable"* [28]. For example, suppose a person is viewing data about a house for sale. The data consists of information such as the house's size, number of bedrooms, price, or energy efficiency. The visualization pipeline (Figure 3, a→b) describes the process by which this data is turned into a visual form (e. g., a bar chart representation, a numerical table or a starplot). For the observer to be able to see it (c), the visual form needs to be brought into existence in the objective world (b). A physical presentation can be an image displayed on a particular computer screen or projected on a particular physical surface, or ink on the surface of a newspaper page. It can also be a physical artifact, e. g., a data physicalization [29]. Virtual presentations as seen in AR systems will be discussed in Subsection 7.2.2..

The second way in which data is connected to the physical world is through *physical referents* (Figure 3-d). A physical referent is a *physical object or physical space to which the data refers* [64]. In the case of our house buyer, the dataset refers to a particular house that exists in the physical world. As the relationship (d) is a conceptual relationship, a dataset can have many possible referents [64]. For example, one can decide that the house dataset refers to the house owner, or to the headquarters of the real estate company that manages it. Both exist in the physical world and could be at a very different location than the house. Finally, the physical referent may or may not be visible to the observer (e).

Whether the physical referent and the physical presentation are simultaneously observable largely depends on whether they share the same space, i. e., on the physical distance that separates them (Figure 3-f). For example, our house buyer can choose to visualize the house data on a laptop in her own house, in which case the house of interest will likely be visually inaccessible. If in contrast, the user stands in front of the house of interest and visualizes the data on her smartphone, or if the data is visualized on a sign placed on the house, the distance (f) will be small enough that both the data and its referent can be examined (c,e). In such a case, the visualization is referred to as *spatially situated.*

A visualization is *spatially situated* if its physical presentation is close to the data's physical referent.

The term "close" is left vague on purpose, as spatial situatedness lies on a continuum: the visualization shown on a sign placed on the house is spatially more situated than the visualization shown on a bystander's smartphone, which is spatially more situated than the visualization shown on a desktop computer.

Although the definition presented here is far from capturing the full richness of the term "situated" (see, e. g., [6, 26]), it has the merit of clarifying what is situated with respect to what. It also clarifies that spatial situatedness cannot be a property of the data, since data is a purely logical entity. Similarly, when a visualization is referred to as being spatially situated or non-situated, this is really referring to the *physical presentation* of a visualization system, not to the visualization as a representation. For example, two different smartphones can display the same bar chart about car consumption data, with one smartphone being far from the car and the other one being inside. While the two smartphones show the *same* visualization, one is situated and the other one is not. For similar reasons, it would be meaningless to ask whether a bar chart is a more situated visualization than a scatterplot, at least within the present framework of spatial situatedness. Other forms of situatedness will be discussed later in the chapter.

Finally, the conceptual model makes it clear that situated visualizations do not need to assume a particular technology. A situated visualization can be created with rudimentary means, e. g., by printing a visualization of a house's data and bringing the printout to the house. Conversely, an AR visualization system can be non-situated, e. g., when two users interact with a 3D visualization that shows data about a physical entity located far away. It is clear, however, that new and emerging technologies make it possible to create elaborate forms of situated visualizations.

7.2.2. Physically- vs. Perceptually-Situated Visualizations

The *physical distance* separating a physical presentation and its physical referent may not necessarily match the *perceived distance* between them [64]. One reason is that distances are perceived in a relative manner. Thus, a one-meter separation may appear large if both the physical presentation and the physical referent are small and the observer is standing close to them (e. g., visualizing data about a rare stone), while the same distance could be negligible in the opposite case (e. g., visualizing data about a distant mountain).

Discrepancies between physical and perceived distances are very common in AR setups [54]. For example, consider a person wearing an HMD who stands in front of a house and sees a data visualization overlaid on the house. The physical data presentation is literally the array of pixels on the surface of the physical display worn by the observer, and could be dozens of meters away from the data's physical referent (the house). However, the AR system could be designed in such a way that the visualization appears to physically coincide with the house.

The previous definition of spatial situatedness can be either left ambiguous on purpose or refined to distinguish between physical and perceptual distance:

A visualization is *physically situated in space* if its physical presentation is physically close to the data's physical referent.

A visualization is *perceptually situated in space* if its (physical or virtual) presentation appears to be close to the data's physical referent.

As stated by the last definition, perceptual situatedness can refer to virtual presentations. For example, if a visualization is rendered next to a house using an HMD, the visualization seen by the user is virtual rather than physical. Since the physical/virtual distinction is not without conceptual difficulties [42], it is often easier to consider the *percept* elicited by the physical presentation rather than the presentation itself [28]. Thus, an alternative definition is as follows:

A visualization is *perceptually situated in space* if its percept appears to be close to the percept of the data's physical referent.

This last definition works for all setups, irrespective of the display technology.

7.2.3. Embedded Visualizations

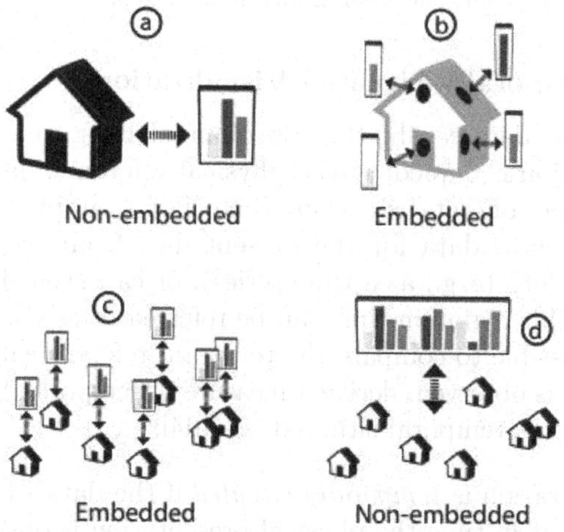

Fig. 4: Examples of embedded and non-embedded visualizations (all situated).

Embedded visualizations are situated visualizations that are deeply integrated within their physical environment [64]. Figure 4 shows examples of embedded and non-embedded situated visualizations. If data about a house is shown on a single visualization placed next to (or inside) the house as in Figure 4-(a), the visualization is simply situated. If, however, different sub-elements of the visualization align with different sub-elements of the physical house (b), the visualization becomes embedded. For example, energy consumption data could be displayed within each room of the house, or next to every power socket. Thermal isolation data could even be visualized as "heat maps" on the walls themselves using AR displays or simply thermochromic paint. Willett *et al.* [64] discuss several such examples of highly-embedded data representations, while Hanrahan [24] and Offenhuber [45, 46] specifically discuss physical implementations.

A visualization is *spatially embedded* if each of its physical sub-presentations is close to its corresponding physical sub-referent.

Embedded visualizations assume multiple sub-presentations that are aligned with their corresponding sub-referents. Thus, if energy consumption is displayed near each power socket, as proposed before, but a house only has a single power socket, the visualization ceases to be embedded and becomes a regular situated visualization. Conversely, it is possible to create an embedded visualization simply by duplicating situated visualizations. For example, if the setup in Figure 4-(a) is duplicated across an entire neighborhood, the entire set of physical presentations becomes an embedded visualization, as shown in Figure 4-(c). The physical referent becomes the set of all houses for sale, and each house becomes a sub-referent. If, however, the same data is shown on a single visualization placed somewhere in the neighborhood (e. g., as a map of all houses for sale), as shown in Figure 4-(d), then the visualization would be situated but not embedded.

7.2.4. Temporally-Situated Visualizations

The same way data can be thought of as referring to a concrete region in space (i. e., the region occupied by the physical referent), data can be thought of as referring to a concrete region in time. For example, an energy consumption display can show data for the present day, from the day before, for several consecutive days (e. g., as a time series), or can even show forecast data about the future. This region in time can be referred to as the data's *temporal referent*. It is then possible to compare the temporal referent with the moment in time a visualization is observed, derive a measure of temporal distance, and characterize a visualization's temporal situatedness [64]:

A visualization is *temporally situated* if the data's temporal referent is close to the moment in time the physical presentation is observed.

An example of a visualization that is highly situated both spatially and temporally is a car's speedometer, because it is located within the data's physical referent (the car) and shows real-time data. A car's mileage display is similarly highly situated spatially but less so temporally, since it shows data about the present but also about a large segment of the past.

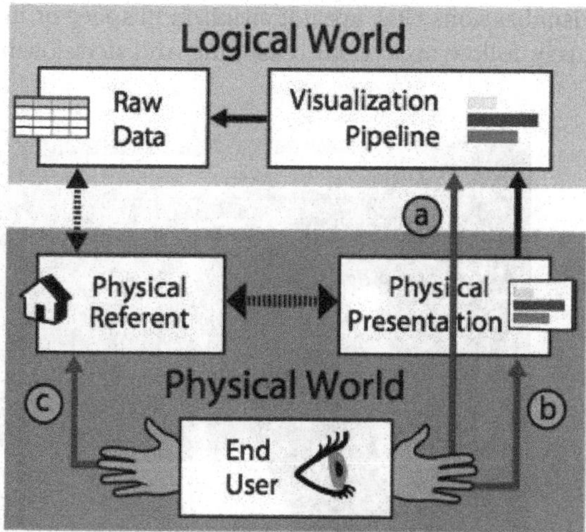

Fig. 5: Interaction with a spatially-situated visualization. Red arrows represent possible flows of information from the user to the system. The flows (a) and (b) are supported by any interactive visualization system (situated or not), while the flow (c) is specific to situated visualizations.

7.2.5. Interaction

Figure 5 shows the different ways a user can interact with a spatially-situated visualization. On any interactive visualization system (situated or not), an analyst can generally interact with the visualization by altering its pipeline (a). Operations such as filtering data, changing the visual representation, highlighting data points, or zooming, are all modifications to the visualization pipeline and have been extensively discussed by Jansen and Dragicevic [28]. Usually, these interactions are implemented through *instruments*, i. e. combinations of software and hardware elements that interpret users' actions into changes in the pipeline [5, 28].

A second way of interacting with a visualization system is by directly altering its physical presentation (b). While desktop visualization systems generally offer limited interaction possibilities at this level, physical visualizations can let users filter, compare or reorder data by rearranging physical elements [28, 29]. In addition, users can alter their percept of a physical presentation by moving it or by moving around [27, 28]. Thus, a rich set of interactions can take place in the real world outside the visualization pipeline. Some of these physical interactions can be sensed and reflected back to the pipeline (right black arrow on Figure 5).

A situated visualization system offers a third mode of interaction through the physical data referent (c). Not only does a situated visualization make the physical referent observable, but it also generally makes it reachable and manipulable [64]. Thus, an analyst can use insights gained from the visualization to take immediate action, such as fixing a thermal leak in a room or removing cancerous cells. In contrast to visualizations that are not situated in space or in time, physical action can immediately follow analytical reasoning and decision-making.

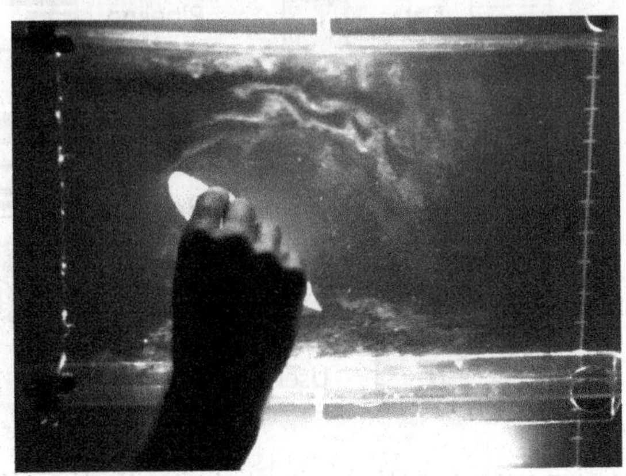

Fig. 6: A water tunnel visualization where a wing model can be rotated to examine the impact of orientation on aerodynamism [31]. Here the physical referent is the wing and the physical presentation is the set of water bubbles.

In case the physical referent is the data source and the system implements real-time sensing (see Figure 3-d), analysis and action can be intertwined. For example, a thermal leak visualization could dynamically update itself as thermal leaks are fixed, and assuming a sufficiently advanced technology, a 3D body scan visualization could update itself as cancerous tissue is removed. In these examples, the end user interacts with a visualization *by modifying the data itself*, a mode of interaction that classical visualization systems generally do not support. Although in these examples the ultimate task is to take action on the physical referent, this mode of interaction is also compatible with purely epistemic tasks. For example, an airplane designer could use a physical or virtual wind tunnel visualization on a malleable or articulated model of an airplane, and physically manipulate the model to explore how different shapes or orientations impact aerodynamism (Figure 6).

7.2.6. Levels of Situatedness

In situated analytics, *situatedness* is a multidimensional property, with each dimension lying on a continuum. As previously discussed, a key element to consider is the *spatial situatedness* of the data visualization employed, i. e., to what extent its physical presentation is close to (or appears to be close to) the data's physical referent. When this distance is sufficiently low for the visualization to qualify as spatially situated, a finer way of assessing its situatedness is by considering its level of *spatial embedding*. As discussed in Section 7.2.3., spatial embedding captures to what extent the geometry of the visualization's physical presentation *aligns* with the geometry of the physical referent. Since spatial situatedness is a necessary condition for being spatially embedded, spatial embedding can be seen as a stronger form of spatial situatedness. For example, in Figure 4, the setups a) and d) are spatially situated but not spatially embedded, while the setups b) and c) are spatially embedded. The level of spatial embedding lies on a continuum and depends on several factors such as the number of physical sub-presentations and their distance to their physical sub-referent. For example, a system that overlays a continuous heat map on a physical surface to display its temperature at every single point (e.g. using AR techniques or thermochromic paint) [46, 64] is more deeply embedded than a system that uses an array of thermometers.

There are also non-spatial forms of situatedness. For example, the level of *temporal situatedness* is a non-spatial form of situatedness, i.e., to what extent the data's temporal referent matches the time of observation. The interactions supported (especially when the physical referent can be directly manipulated for pragmatic or for epistemic purposes, as discussed in Section 7.2.5.) also likely participate in the observer's subjective impression of situatedness. Section 7.4. will cover more specific examples of interaction styles involving the manipulation of physical referents for epistemic purposes. For now we will go through simpler and more classical examples of situated analytics systems.

7.3. Examples of Situated Analytics

This section presents examples of situated analytics used in real world applications. Key characteristics include situated virtual data and associated analytics.

7.3.1. Pollution Monitoring

NoxDroid is a sensor system aimed at monitoring air quality in cities. As shown in Figure 7, NoxDroid is a small mobile sensor device built and mounted on bicycles by volunteers. The sensor provides low fidelity real-time feedback on air quality as people ride their bicycles (green: Nox level are well below the official limit; yellow: Nox level are just below the limit; red: Nox level is around or above the limit). The sensor connects to an Android application to upload its data, share it with others, and offer other advanced functionality. This enables cyclists to analyze pollution level and navigate in the sensor history through their mobile-phones, in situation, and chose cycling routes accordingly.

7.3.2. Personal Protective Equipment (PPE) Donning/Doffing

During 2014-2015, Prof. Greg Welch directed a small group of graduate computer science students at the University of Central Florida in the development of a system to allow volunteers around the world to help check the integrity of personal protective equipment (PPE) being worn by healthcare providers caring for patients with deadly viruses such as Ebola, before the providers come into contact with any patients. See Figure 8(a) for an example of a provider in their

Fig. 7: NoxDroid situated analytics. Left: sensor with embedded pollution indicators. Right: smartphone application with contextual measures.

PPE. The system, called *SterilEyes*, consists of a smartphone app and a back-end server system that allows the provider to quickly capture video imagery of themselves in their PPE, that is instantly made available to certified volunteer observers from around the world who can instantly check the provider's PPE and vote on the quality of the protection over the entire body.

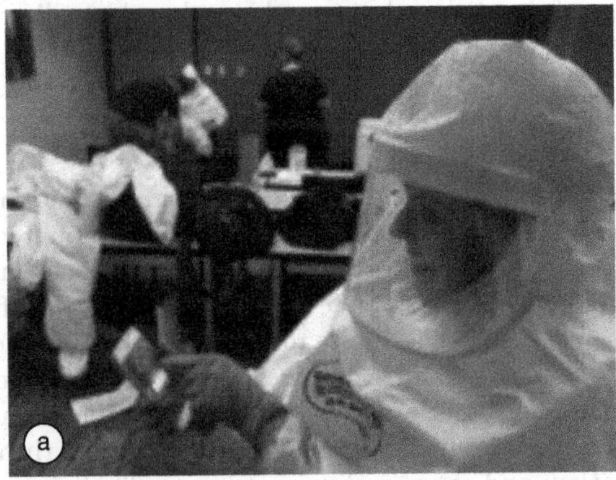

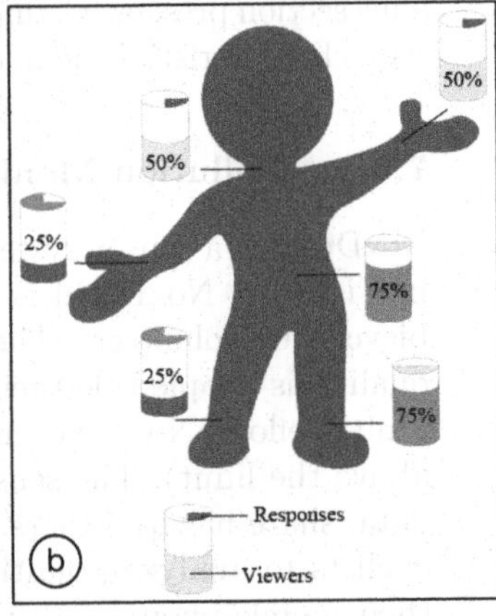

Fig. 8: Left (a): Example of healthcare provider wearing personal protective equipment (PPE) such as would be used when caring for patients during an outbreak of a deadly contagious disease such as Ebola. Right (b): Example observer (crowd) analytics situated on the appropriate body parts.

The smartphone app would be used in two different circumstances and corresponding modes: the provider mode and the observer mode. After donning the PPE, and before entering the potentially contagious space around the patient, the provider or a colleague would capture video of the PPE on the provider—in particular in locations known to be problematic such as the neck, wrist, and ankle connections/seals. Each observer would be notified and if possible/willing would respond by selecting each video—associated (situated) with a part of the body—and rating it. Progressively, as the observers around the world respond, the back-end system would calculate and update the displayed confidences associated with each critical body location. See Figure 8(b) for an early example of a visualization presented to the provider as the observer votes evolve.

7.3.3. Future Farming

In a recent TechCrunch article [35], contributor Jeff Kavanaugh discussed a futuristic (but not far off) vision for farming where sensors collect data about plant and soil health for example, machine learning or approaches continually perform some analytical analyses, and Mixed (Augmented) Reality is used to allow a farmer to see and interact with the data in place to "help both farmers and gardeners to monitor and manage crop health." Kavanaugh also described an Infosys open-source digital farming project called Plant.IO.[2] Kavanaugh describes the vision where PVC pipes provide a frame for devices such as sensors and plant growth lights, a remote server continually analyzes and predicts plant health, and "AR-capable glasses" like the HoloLens could be used to both visualize crop analytics in place and affect plant health via AR actuator interfaces that control fertilizer, water flow, growth lights and more.

There are additional elaborations on these ideas. For example, on the heels of the TechCrunch article, Rob LaPointe of SDI presented some related ideas [37]. LaPointe pointed out how sensors for monitoring crops, weather stations, satellite information, etc. can be cross-referenced to specific crops, and analyzed by AI algorithms that are informed by the latest agricultural publications, with the results being "wirelessly transmitted to a set of AR Goggles" that provide the farmer with information about water, light, and fertilizer needs for each plant in (or region of) the field.

Fig. 9: Blended user interface.

[2] http://plantio.de (website in German)

7.4. Blended Situated Analytics Controls

This section explores a particular style of situated analytics interaction methodology, *Blended Situated Analytics Controls* [20]. Existing solutions for AR interaction techniques provide users with a limited number of predefined interaction perspectives for the presented data and the input controls are either static for all objects or have a limited number of controls that can be associated. Working with abstract information in AR requires more methods of interaction than the traditional approach, allowing the user to manipulate the data freely and explore relationships between data in two different spaces: physical and virtual.

The blended user interface is a promising SA tool, which fuses the controls into the physical referents (physical objects), and derives the controls' appearance from the physical context, affording dynamic widget appearance and layout techniques [18, 21] (see Figure 9). The appearance of the controls is dynamic depending on their placement and function on the physical object. The novelty of the techniques is their context-aware dynamic blending of physical/virtual user interface controls allowing seamless transition between the physical and information spaces. The blended user interface has three main components: blended controls, blended views, and the blended model.

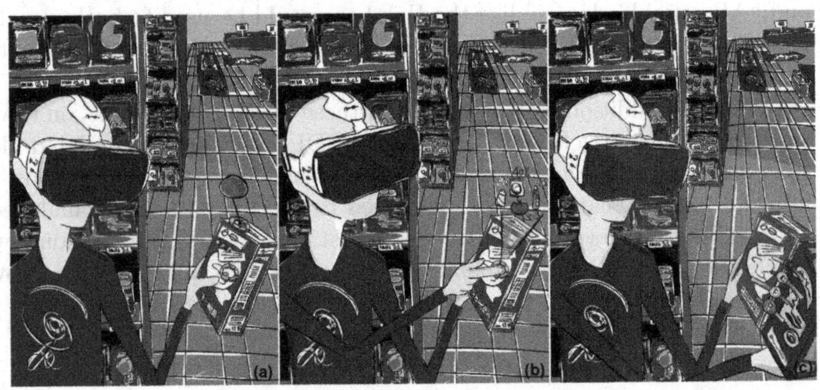

Fig. 10: Situated analytics blended controls. (a) Users can view the attached information, (b) interact with physical objects to explore more information, (c) and view/compare the information associated with multiple physical objects.

7.4.1. Overview of Blended Controls

The blended controls allow users to 1) view in a meaningfully fashioned abstract data with their relationships and 2) apply operations such as select, zoom, search, filter, and analyze. Figure 10 demonstrates the blended controls within the context of a shopping task, enabling user exploration and interaction with information in novel ways. In Figure 10-a, a user explores a product's overall information, presented to them as a virtual annotation overlayed on the top of the physical box. Information of interest is highlighted—for example, if the user is searching for Australian-made products, the Australian logo can be highlighted. Figure 10-b shows a user interacting with the physical referent to explore more information (Details-on-Demand). The user can explore information, such as touching the ingredients listing printed on the product's box, and the SA system will display additional detailed visual analytical information as an AR overlay. This information representation is based on the product's ingredients (for example, the percentage of the user's daily recommended intake (RDI) for a nutritional category such as sugar or fat that the product contains). SA also allows a user to analyze and compare information between products (seen in Figure 10-c). As an example, when a user selects two products and places them side-by-side, the SA system presents a comparison of the two products to the user.

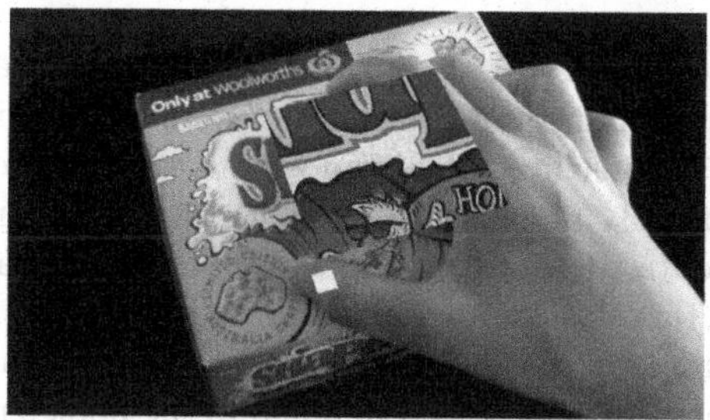

Fig. 11: Blended zoom.

Blended interactions differ in that the user is not restricted to the planar screen of a tablet device, keyboard, or an indirect pointing device. Instead, the user is guided by the form factor of the underlying physical referent such as a product box, physical lever or button, or tangible artifact. The user is therefore not disconnected from the physical referent as in the mid-air interactions. In this scenario, the haptic feedback is given through the product while an HMD provides the overlay of visual information. Figure 11 depicts the user employing the pinch gesture, zooming on a supermarket product to provide an easier to read portion of the label. Using context-aware blended controls alters the assigned UI control. For instance, a blended selection can be altered based on the ratio between the width and the height of the tracked image. Figure 12-a shows a calculation of the percentage of the juice in the cup, computing the calorie content by using the one-dimensional slider. In the box scenario, the type of slider for the same operation has been changed; a two-dimensional slider has been used due to the physical shape of the box (Figure 12-b). This shape adaptation feature reduces the complexity of UI design, enabling the storing of the UI properties and constraints, which will automatically blend the relevant UI components to the physical referents.

(a) (b)

Fig. 12: Blender sliders changing their appearance based on the physical object's shape.

Blended interaction can also provide intuitive interaction with the physical space, such as proximity and collision. Proxemics is an interaction based on the user's view, by calculating the distance between the user's view and the tactile physical referents. By moving the referent nearer and further to the user's view, the amount of data presented changes. Where holding a physical referent closer the user's view, this closer view reflects an interest in the object. Figures 13-a and 13-b show an implementation of proximity exploration, between overview and detailed representations. The overview shows the book's ranking, and the detailed view shows the book's table of content. Through an AR display, the user can see the virtual overview annotation (see Figure 13-a), and by bringing the book nearer to the user's view, this will invoke the detailed view. The registered table of contents is color-coded based on the user's query and preferences, as the green shows highly related book sections moving towards red for the least preferable ones. The white text means that the section title is not about the user's entered query (see Figure 13-b). Another example is shown in Figures 13-c and 13-d demonstrating depth-level adaptation to override the small FOV challenge of the optical see-through devices. The technique arranges the data into multi-layers controlled by the distance between the user and the physical referents. Proxemic interactions invoke the visualization based on the cue's ratio to the physical referent's size. When the physical object is near to the user, its size will increase, which will invoke more visual cues.

Collision is an interaction based on the spatial relationship of multiple objects to provide information pertinent to the objects' combination. Collision can be to aggregate the virtual data associated with the physical referents. Figure 14 depicts a collision-based example, allowing the user to calculate the total calorie intake of two products by aligning the physical objects side-by-side. As the user calculates the total star point of two products, by putting them side-by-side. When the user holds the chips by the crackers box, it shows a low star point value, a low nutrition outcome. Then the user checked the juice with the cracker

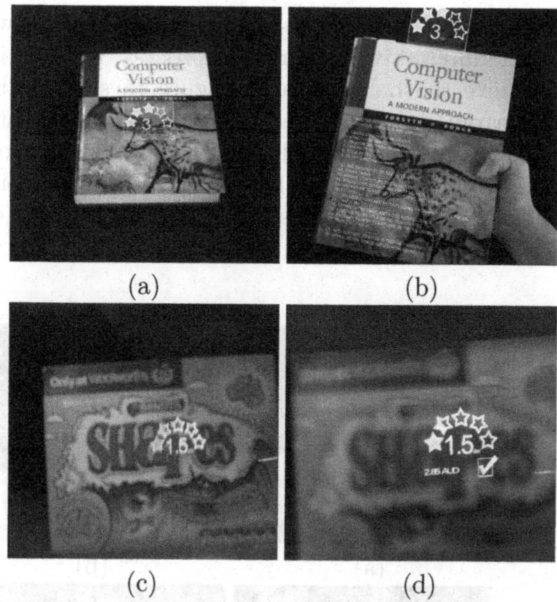

Fig. 13: Proxemic interaction.

by aligning the juice by the crackers box, which showed a better star nutrition value than the chips combination.

Fig. 14: Collision interaction to combine products' nutritional value.

7.4.2. The Blended Views

The blended views hold the GUI elements and are responsible for generating the blended widgets. The uniqueness of the blended views is attaching the widgets and the visuals based on the physical context to leverage their meaning. The semantic fusion of the UI elements to the physical world allows physical referents to be part of the interactive information process, working in concert with the controls to achieve the blending aim. Figure 15 shows a blended menu that changes its appearance and items based on the physical context. The menu can be dragged and relocated to any place on the physical referents, with dynamic size, shape, and color of the menu based on the physical context. These menus use pre-stored regions' meta-values to restrict the location of the menu on the physical box.

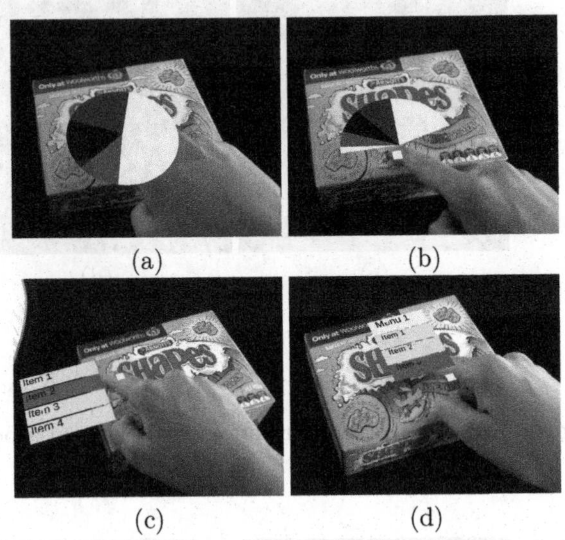

Fig. 15: Blended menu.

7.4.3. The Blended Model

The blended model allows a two-way, real-time association between the physical and the virtual information, enabling contextual and situation awareness for the interactive information process. Figure 16 depicts the user experience during a series of interaction states in the blended space for picking a meal. The user moves between the states based on the predefined parameters, defining the invoking trigger for each state, permissions, and parameters associated with the mapped contextual feature. In Figure 16-(a), the user moves the AR display with a camera to scan products on the shelf and select the product. The selected product is highlighted by a green frame. In Figure 16-(b), the user takes one of the products off the shelf, as they are interested in more detailed information about this particular product. This user's interaction will invoke a detailed view of the product; the user is holding, enabling region selection. The user selects the product's logo, then tilts the box to select the flavor region. Finally in Figure 16-(c), the user starts to interact with two fingers on the box surface, the interaction control changes to a magnifying pinch zoom.

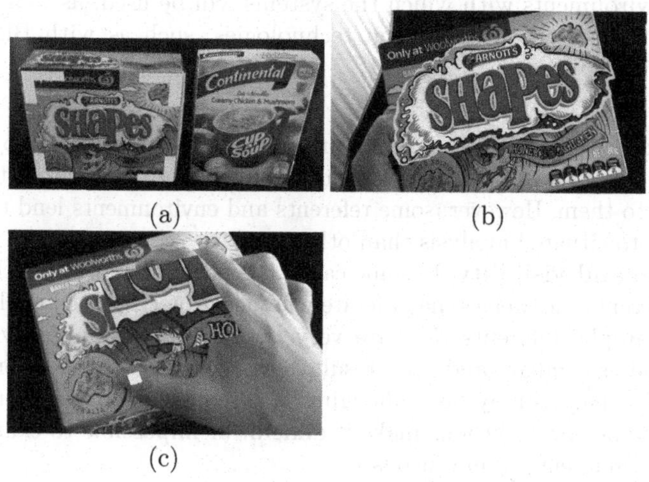

Fig. 16: Interaction states in the blended space.

7.5. Design Considerations for Situated Analytics Systems

This section discusses design considerations for SA. As usual when designing interactive systems, no single perfect solution that would fit all intended use cases exists. The design of SA systems must account for the physical environment, data, and viewers with which it will be used, as well as the presentation and sensing technology used to implement it. However, because only a small number of SA systems have been developed so far, few guidelines and best practices for situated tools currently exist. This section goes on to discuss a variety of practical design decisions that, based on the authors' experience, have important trade-offs and repercussions for situated tools. The discussions are structured around the components of situated analytics systems as introduced earlier in this chapter (see Section 7.2. Characterization of Situated Visualizations). The section starts by discussing components of the physical world—the physical referents, the physical presentation, and the users—and then discusses design considerations for components in the logical world—the data and the visualization pipeline.

7.5.1. Physical World

Situated analysis tools are characterized by their relationship to the physical world. As a result, these tools must account for the environments and physical referents to which the data are related. Moreover, the visual feedback from SA tools themselves must ultimately emanate from some source (typically an object, projector, or display) in the physical world. Therefore, the design of situated tools must take into account the physical characteristics of the referents and environments with which the systems will be used, as well as the physical limitations of the presentation technologies, such as with Blended Situated Analytics Controls.

Physical Referents and Environments. Essentially any object, person, or environment can potentially become a referent, given a dataset that somehow relates to them. However, some referents and environments lend themselves more readily to situated analysis than others.

Size and visibility. In some cases, the physical and visual characteristics of the referents themselves may dictate whether or not situated analysis is practical. For example, referents that are very large or very small may be difficult to examine or compare and, as a result, may not provide useful context. Similarly, situated analysis may be challenging in cases where environmental constraints like distance or occlusions make it difficult or impossible to examine important physical referents simultaneously.

Identifiability and dynamicity. Similarly, the viability of a situated analysis system may be dictated by how easy it is to distinguish, track, and connect physical referents with data about them. In order to display the appropriate data in context, it must be possible for either the system or the viewer to identify corresponding referents and environments. As a result, environments with many similar referents or high dynamicity (such as quickly moving swarms or crowds) may pose serious implementation challenges.

Safety and security. In other situations, the risks to the physical safety of viewers and those around them need to be considered. Situated analysis may not be viable in locations where visual augmentations might distract viewers' attention away from the environment and disrupt critical tasks like driving, flying, or operating machinery.

Physical Presentation. When considering the design of a situated system, one of the most important decisions is whether to display information virtually—using projection or overlays that are visually superimposed on top of the environment—or physically—via physical output mechanisms that are situated in the environment itself. This distinction is not strictly binary. For example, physical screens placed in an environment may be concrete objects, but provide largely virtual content. As a result, the choice to situate data displays via primarily physical or primarily virtual means will likely have a considerable impact on the scalability of the system, as well as the kind of observations and interactions it supports.

Virtual output. At one extreme are overlays produced by HMDs. While these kinds of hardware can make it possible for wearers to superimpose data on top of environments and objects, the relationship between the presentation and referent is purely visual and largely individualized. As a result, the physical presentation provides no tactile or physical feedback and has no direct physical relationship in the environment. Computer vision and other tracking techniques can be used to align virtual overlays and controls with specific physical referents (as with Blended Situated Analytics Controls [20]). However, correctly aligning presentations and referents can be challenging in complex environments, and providing appropriate depth cues and haptic feedback may be difficult.

This degree of independence may be useful in situations where an analytic system needs to display very large numbers of data points, or where data must be displayed in areas with no corporeal physical referents. Virtual displays can also deal with environments that contain dynamic referents whose form or identity may change over a short period of time. Tasks like displaying data about tens of thousands of parts in a manufacturing plant or visualizing air quality data in the center of an open space may benefit from these kinds of virtual presentation mechanisms. In fact, virtual presentations may be the only viable options if referents are physically very large or small, or if they are fragile, distant, or otherwise inaccessible.

Physical output. Alternatively, more concrete physical presentations may be beneficial when analyses are centered around a smaller number of stable referents. In these cases, presenting data via physical output in the real world may support a more direct coupling between the information and the referents it relates to. Displaying visual output via displays which are physically attached to their referents provides an immediate coupling between data and context, and can make it easier for viewers to examine the two simultaneously. Tight physical connections may also provide more physical affordances for interaction, making it easier for viewers to interact with the analytic tools using the referents themselves as input controls.

Physical output may also be helpful in collaborative situations where multiple viewers need to examine and interact with the analytics tools simultaneously. Because physical presentations preserve real-world visibility and interaction cues, they may make it easier for individuals to understand what their collaborators can see and manipulate, and what they cannot. However, physical outputs like these are also more difficult to secure, especially when displays are not dynamic or the identities of viewers cannot be determined. In these situations, systems may need to rely on restricting physical access to the space or encoding data displays to reduce their intelligibility.

More generally, physically attaching presentations of data to referents may be a practical technical solution—especially in situations where the set of referents is human-scale, small in number, and relatively static (small numbers of people, animals, tools, objects, rooms, etc.). In these cases, physically associating data presentations with their referents may eliminate or reduce the need to track the referents' locations in order to display data at the right place and time.

Embedded vs. Situated Output. When designing situated analysis tools, developers may also need to consider the degree to which the system is connected to individual physical referents. On one hand, systems may be only lightly situated—presenting data in a relevant environment, but ignoring the specific orientations and positions of related people, objects, and spaces. Alternatively, systems can be more deeply embedded, placing presentations of data on or near their referents. Determining what kind of embedding is appropriate may depend not only on the available presentation technologies but also on the complexity of the environment and viewers' likely tasks.

Embedded. Choosing to embed presentations of data directly alongside their corresponding referents may present a number of benefits. For example, embedding output on or near relevant objects, people, and environments can make it easier for viewers to understand the relationship between data and physical referents, and take action based on it. Doing so also increases the likelihood that viewers can correctly identify which referent the data corresponds to. Similarly, embedding makes it easier for viewers to perceptually integrate information from the dataset with relevant contextual information from the physical environment [40].

Situated. In contrast, situated views may often be less technically difficult to implement—as they only need to be presented in the appropriate environment at the right time, but do not need to be aligned with the individual referents in any particular fashion. In fact, simply placing an existing data display or analysis tool into an appropriate environment (for example, on a phone, tablet, or head-mounted display) can be enough to produce a situated analysis experience. Using a purely situated approach also ensures that the presentation of data is not limited by the physical positions of the referents. As a result, this strategy can make it easier to guarantee that viewers will be able to see and access the data, regardless of the environmental configuration.

Users. Important design decisions need to be made when considering who will be the end user(s) of the system. Will it be a single person or does the system need to be able to accommodate multiple users? If it is a multi-user system, will these users collaborate or work in parallel? Should all users be able to access the same data or are there restrictions on who can access what data? While some of these questions have already been mentioned above when considerations were discussed for choosing physical presentations, the discussion now focuses on considerations taking the users' point of view.

Privacy and collaboration. Situated analytics can be performed on many different types of data. Some of these data can be private or confidential and may need to remain hidden from other people sharing the same environment—a problematic shared with any "sensing system" [7]. Privacy can be assured implicitly by using an HMD instead of publicly visible displays. Yet such HMDs make collaboration more difficult as they require that each collaborator have their own device. Furthermore, content and changes need to be dynamically coordinated across all of the individual displays. As a result, this type of setup can make it more difficult for multiple users to determine whether they are seeing the same data. Thus, shared situated displays may be preferable for applications that involve collocated collaboration.

Access-controlled environments, for example in a corporate setting, present a special case, particularly if the SA system has access to information on who is allowed to view what data and who is currently in a room, for example, through tracked badges [60]. In such cases, a SA system could ensure confidentiality by adapting the visual output so that it shows only content accessible to all current viewers. In turn—with HMDs—data with different levels of detail can be shown to different people according to their access rights without requiring them to leave the physical environment before certain data can be viewed.

7.5.2. Logical World

When creating situated analysis tools, designers and developers must also consider the logical world—including the data and the visualization pipeline. While these underlying constructs are shared with other non-situated visualization systems, situated analysis tools introduce a number of new complexities.

Data. Data in an SA system are viewed in spatial proximity to the physical referents. Beyond spatial proximity, temporal proximity of the data can be relevant as well. For example, White and Feiner report a small field study where their users would have preferred to access real-time data about air pollution in a city instead of "stale", previously made measurements [63]. In cases where the intended purpose of the SA systems is to (possibly) take action in the physical environment, for example, to explore how such modifications affect sensor readings, live data become crucially important.

Tracking physical referents. In order to display data at the appropriate time and place, situated tools may require considerably more information about the environment in which they are used than traditional analysis tools. Desktop data analysis packages can render the same visual output on a wide variety of different commodity hardware regardless of their surroundings. In contrast, situated tools will typically display different information (often in different configurations) depending on where they are used. As a result, situated tools need mechanisms for uniquely identifying and tracking physical referents around them, and for associating referents with related data. This means that SA tools may often need more elaborate data models that can represent referents as logical objects within the system, as well as mechanisms for authoring and updating relationships between referents and data. Unless the visual output of an analysis system is physically connected to the referents, systems must also be able to track and process referents' position, movement, and visibility, and use this data to update the situated presentations in real time.

Visualization pipeline. The visualization pipeline transforms the data into a visual representation that can be displayed using physical presentations as was discussed earlier. The physical presentation and the physical referents need to be taken into account when designing the visualization pipeline. Particularly, the geometry of the physical referents and physical presentations are important to consider when choosing appropriate visual encodings to ensure that the SA system informs but not hinders users' actions.

Visual encodings. Most of previous work studying the perception of visual encodings focused on two-dimensional encodings which are best adapted to the presentation of 2D screens. With situated analytics, data are shown in physical, three-dimensional environments thus it may be beneficial to consider 3D encodings for such systems especially in the case of head-mounted displays or physical output. White and Feiner [63] gauged preferences from their field study users who expressed a preference for representations that facilitated making the link between the location of sensor readings and their value. For example, they preferred the use of spheres over cylinders to represent sensor readings associated to a particular position in 3D space.

A first study on size perception of physical 3D marks found that the size perception of 3D bars and spheres is not—as previously assumed—systematically biased if an appropriate transfer function is chosen [30]. However, if the physical referents feature flat 2D surfaces, then a 2D visual encoding matching these surfaces would be preferable. Yet prior work on the perception of two-dimensional visual marks displayed on large wall displays suggests that these are not accurately perceived when viewed at a non-perpendicular angle [8].

7.5.3. Summary

Situated analytics is an emerging theme and as of yet few empirical studies can give validated advice on how to best design such systems. This discussion refrains from making prescriptive design recommendations and instead focused on laying out the different aspects a designer of a situated analytics system should consider. At the same time the need for more empirical studies illustrates rich research opportunities within situated analytics. The open challenges are described in the next section.

7.6. Challenges and Research Agenda

Analytics moving into "the real world" raises challenges at multiple levels: technical ones, methodological ones, and conceptual ones. As has been seen in the previous sections, new typologies of analytical tasks are also emerging to account for a more "casual" approach to analytics. For example, people may conduct analysis in short situated bursts instead of long focused sessions in front of a computer. Supporting new analytical tasks should lead us to rethink how we design analytical tools, i. e., how do we prototype situated tools, and how we evaluate them. Besides new design methods, conceptual tools and technical frameworks will be needed to support development of these tools.

The envisioned pervasiveness of SA will require attention to new domains. Understanding expert tasks will not be enough, and designers will have to consider pleasure, engagement, or social acceptability. Finally, we should not forget to ask, what are the benefits and limitations of situated analytics, i. e., when is it worthwhile to offer such analytics, and when would people be better off with traditional analytics tools? There are clear trade-offs in terms of attention and information overload, privacy risks, and ethical concerns in case badly situated analytics could reinforce prejudices by only displaying a partial view of the situated data.

7.6.1. Visual Display

The emergence of novel display form factors and capabilities bears a direct impact on possibilities latent in situated analytics. From using HMDs to pico-projectors that facilitate group-based sense-making, necessary consideration needs to be placed on where to project information, how to embed content in the environment. There is a difference between personal and group-based displays. In terms of personal displays, attention is needed to issues involving color blending (for superimposing virtual content on physical objects) [36], on issues of environmental saliency to suitably embed content [32], as well as on placement strategies for effective interaction with content. In terms of group-based displays, attention is needed to identify how best to position the display to suit group work [13], offer shared displays with HMDs [10], and to facilitate group interaction. With current advances, many of the above areas can be further explored in more depth. For example, brighter displays affect how content can be fused into the environment and advances in steerable pico-projection can facilitate more fluid approaches to SA.

7.6.2. Interactions Techniques

One primary challenge that needs addressing is the design of novel interactive tools for SA. Unlike traditional desktop environments, where devices and tools have been entrenched in the fundamentals of areas such as visual analytics, interaction interfaces and devices for SA is uncharted territory. As described above, one approach could include the use of Blended Situated Analytics Controls that fuse the user's interaction onto the physical objects in the environment. Such an approach relies on no more than the sensors HMDs are already equipped with, and thus offers an attractive solution for SA interactivity. However, when the embeddings are loosely connected to the physical objects, such as an entire environment, novel approaches are necessary. Ens and Irani [22] offer a preliminary discussion into the types of interactive devices possible for situated analytics. These include finger-worn sensors [59], digital pens [1], on-body interactivity [61] and the use of physical objects, that can be tracked by the displays worn by users [22]. Such forms of devices have shown little application to SA, and therefore re-examining these from the standpoint of specific usage scenarios (see Section 7.3.) in SA is an important first step. Furthermore, such forms of interactivity have not been explored in the context of mobility or applications involving Augmented and/or Virtual Reality. Therefore pressing questions include:

"can such devices be appropriated for tasks in SA?", "what environment properties affect the use of such forms of interactivity?", "how can such interfaces be made more efficient and optimized in the context of SA?". These and other questions can formulate the basis of a new research agenda in situated analytics.

7.6.3. Rethinking the Design Cycle

Designing visual analytics tools has traditionally centered on answering the specialized needs of experts. Situated analytics shifts the focus from experts to a much broader user population. Moreover, the context for which to design is also much more ill-defined. If visual analytics is typically conducted on a desktop computer with mouse and keyboard, exceptionally on a large wall display, situated analytics is, by definition, associated with any possible context. This radically changes the way analytical tools should be designed. New methods are needed to better account for the situated aspect of visualisation: consider space, consider the unexpected, consider social acceptance, etc.

With ill defined tasks, the design process cannot rely as heavily on the collection of requirements, and the specification of needs. Designers will have to explore opportunities for design in a much more iterative way, sketching possible applications, testing them out and figuring whether they fit the needs of people. Such an iterative process requires new tools that enable quick sketch solutions to explore a design space.

Beyond sketches, developing fully functional situated analytics tools is still particularly complex, and costly. New frameworks guiding development, offering ready to use building blocks, could speed up development significantly.

Finally evaluation methods, whether it is for early sketches or fully fledged applications, must be refined. Because of the situated nature of tools, evaluations methods will have to incorporate some forms of field work to assess situated analytics applications on open-ended activities. This differs widely from well-defined tasks typically supported by visual analytics, for which methods to measure time, errors or insights have been developed.

7.7. Future Work

Situated analytics is a new and emerging research field. Investigations are required into new display technologies, application domains, forms of data, and interaction methodologies; just to name a few. Two particular research directions of interest are moving beyond spatial situatedness and tackling the ethical challenges this new research field presents.

7.7.1. Moving Beyond Spatial Situatedness

Situating analytics in the physical space, i. e., spatially close to the objects of interest, is the predominant strategy used for situated analytics. Section 7.2 discussed alternative dimensions, such as using time as the frame of reference.

However, these physical dimensions only account for a limited part of users' situation. In the field of ubiquitous computing, situatedness has often be modeled alongside several dimensions describing what is generally referred to as *context*. The notion of context helps to account for broader phenomena and people's activity.

For instance, while picking up a citybike at a station, the relevant information may not be the availability of bicycles in the pick-up spot since the user can already see whether there are free bicycles in its surrounding, but the number of free spots at the destination so that the user can adjust the travel goal, to the closest station with free parking spots. To develop a better understanding of people's intention, context should include information about the people involved in the activity, the set of devices available, the active applications, as well as sensor information such as light, noise, or temperature.

With such an understanding of context, it becomes possible to bring analytics relevant to users' activity rather than their location. For instance, a museum guide and visitors could benefit from SA about an art piece they stand in front of while touring the museum. But as the guide goes through the museum after hours with colleagues, to revise the guiding plan, they might get more relevant analytics about the time visitors spent in front of the piece, what other pieces they were interested in, etc. At the same location, situated analytics could take various forms depending on the activities people are involved in.

7.7.2. Ethical Challenges

Widespread use of SA raises a number of ethical concerns that we should be aware of and ideally consider in the early phase of any project. Situating analytics whether it is in space, time, or activities requires having rich datasets that have such detailed properties. Situated visualizations of the books borrowed in a library could be highly valuable to patrons, but could also lead to "leaks" revealing sensitive books rented by individuals. Similarly, SA of health related information could improve patients' understanding of treatments, their adherence, and their overall experience of illness, but capturing sensitive information about health and "projecting it into the world" should be done with extreme care to potential side effects.

Another concern of SA relates to the reinforcement of prejudices. Data collection is never exhaustive, and datasets offer a partial view of reality, however faithful we try to be. Selectively displaying data, is a way to introduce some prejudice by over-emphasizing some elements. For instance, designers working on urban situated analytics could decide to display information about criminality, but only display crimes against people or property, and not white-collar crimes which are harder to locate physically, leading to an emphasis on crime from one population, while ignoring another.

7.8. Conclusion

As discussed in Chapter 1 and described above, there are two ways in which analytical activities can be immersive: either perceptually or cognitively. Perceptually speaking, a situated visualization can be thought of as more immersive than a non-situated visualization because the user is exposed to extra perceptual (visual or otherwise) information from the *physical* world. Naturally, a user is *always* situated in a physical environment (e. g., a desktop computer user can be situated in an office space), and this environment can be extremely rich in perceptual information (e. g., a messy desktop, a loud office). However, in non-situated systems this information is irrelevant to the analytic task — it is either filtered out if the user is focused, or disruptive if the user is not. In contrast, for the user of a situated visualization, a larger portion of the physical environment is task-relevant, and therefore the user can be considered as perceptually more immersed in the task. This is all the more true if both the physical referent and the visualization occupy a large area (e. g., a tourist who walks in a city and explores city data using an AR display). This perceptual immersion and the relatively lower proportion of task-irrelevant stimuli can reduce the opportunities for distraction, and in turn increase the likelihood of being *cognitively* immersed in the analytic task.

This chapter defines a new method of immersive analytics referred to as situated analytics. The concept is characterized in greater detail, including the users, tasks, data, representations, interactions, and analytical processes involved. A set of case studies is examined in detail to elicited the best practices for situated analytics in action. Blended situated analytics controls are detailed as a particular method of developing situated analytics user interactions. A set of derived design considerations for building situated analytics applications is described. A research agenda of challenges and research questions to be explored in the future are presented.

References

1. Aliakseyeu, D., Irani, P., Lucero, A., Subramanian, S.: Multi-flick: an evaluation of flick-based scrolling techniques for pen interfaces. In: Proceedings of the SIGCHI Conference on Human Factors in Computing Systems. pp. 1689–1698. ACM (2008)
2. Atzori, L., Iera, A., Morabito, G.: The Internet of Things: A survey. Computer Networks 54(15), 2787–2805 (2010)
3. Badam, S.K., Elmqvist, N.: PolyChrome: A cross-device framework for collaborative web visualization. In: Proceedings of the ACM Conference on Interactive Tabletops and Surfaces. pp. 109–118. ACM(2014), http://dl.acm.org/citation.cfm?id=2669485
4. Badam, S.K., Fisher, E.R., Elmqvist, N.: Munin: A peer-to-peer middleware for ubiquitous analytics and visualization spaces. IEEE Transactions on Visualization and Computer Graphics 21(2), 215–228(2015), http://dx.doi.org/10.1109/TVCG.2014.2337337;http://doi.ieeecomputersociety.org/10.1109/TVCG.2014.2337337

5. Beaudouin-Lafon, M.: Instrumental interaction: an interaction model for designing post-wimp user interfaces. In: Proceedings of the ACM Conference on Human Factors in Computing Systems. pp. 446–453. ACM (2000)
6. Beaudouin-Lafon, M., Mackay, W.E.: Research directions in situated computing. In: Extended Abstracts on Human Factors in Computing Systems. pp. 369–369. ACM (2000)
7. Bellotti, V., Back, M., Edwards, W.K., Grinter, R.E., Henderson, A., Lopes, C.: Making sense of sensing systems: Five questions for designers and researchers. In: Proceedings of the SIGCHI Conference on Human Factors in Computing Systems. pp. 415–422. CHI '02, ACM, New York, NY, USA(2002), http://doi.acm.org/10.1145/503376.503450 doi: 10.1145/503376.503450
8. Bezerianos, A., Isenberg, P.: Perception of visual variables on tiled wall-sized displays for information visualization applications. IEEE Transactions on Visualization and Computer Graphics 18(12), 2516–2525 (2012)
9. Billinghurst, M., Clark, A., Lee, G.: A survey of Augmented Reality. Foundations and Trends in Human-Computer Interaction 8(2-3), 73–272 (2015)
10. Billinghurst, M., Kato, H.: Collaborative augmented reality. Communications of the ACM 45(7), 64–70 (2002)
11. Bimber, O., Raskar, R.: Spatial Augmented Reality: Merging Real and Virtual Worlds. A. K. Peters, Ltd., Natick, MA, USA (2005)
12. Card, S.K., Mackinlay, J.D., Shneiderman, B.: Readings in Information Visualization: Using Vision to Think. Morgan Kaufmann (1999)
13. Cauchard, J.R., Löchtefeld, M., Irani, P., Schoening, J., Krüger, A., Fraser, M., Subramanian, S.: Visual separation in mobile multi-display environments. In: Proceedings of the 24th Annual ACM Symposium on User Interface Software and Technology. pp. 451–460. ACM (2011)
14. Chandler, T., Cordeil, M., Czauderna, T., Dwyer, T., Glowacki, J., Goncu, C., Klapperstueck, M., Klein, K., Marriott, K., Schreiber, F., Wilson, E.: Immersive analytics. In: Proceedings of the IEEE Symposium on Big Data Visual Analytics. pp. 73–80. IEEE (2015)
15. Chen, G., Kotz, D., et al.: A survey of context-aware mobile computing research. Tech. Rep. TR2000-381, Department of Computer Science, Dartmouth College (2000)
16. Chi, E.H.h., Riedl, J.T.: An operator interaction framework for visualization systems. In: Proceedings of the IEEE Symposium on Information Visualization. pp. 63–70. IEEE (1998)
17. Elmqvist, N., Irani, P.: Ubiquitous analytics: Interacting with big data anywhere, anytime. IEEE Computer 46(4), 86–89 (2013)
18. Elsayed, N., Thomas, B., Marriott, K., Piantadosi, J., Smith, R.: Situated analytics. In: Proceedings of the IEEE Symposium on Big Data Visual Analytics. pp. 1–8. IEEE (2015)
19. Elsayed, N., Thomas, B., Smith, R., Marriott, K., Piantadosi, J.: Using augmented reality to support situated analytics. In: Proceedings of the IEEE Conference on Virtual Reality. pp. 175–176. IEEE (2015)
20. Elsayed, N.A.M., Smith, R.T., Marriott, K., Thomas, B.H.: Blended UI controls for situated analytics. In: Proceedings of the IEEE International Symposium on Big Data Visual Analytics. pp. 1–8. IEEE (2016)
21. Elsayed, N.A., Thomas, B.H., Marriott, K., Piantadosi, J., Smith, R.T.: Situated analytics: Demonstrating immersive analytical tools with Augmented Reality. Journal of Visual Languages & Computing 36, 13–23 (2016)

22. Ens, B.M., Finnegan, R., Irani, P.P.: The personal cockpit: a spatial interface for effective task switching on head-worn displays. In: Proceedings of the 32nd Annual ACM conference on Human Factors in Computing Systems. pp. 3171–3180. ACM (2014)
23. Gruber, L., Richter-Trummer, T., Schmalstieg, D.: Real-time photometric registration from arbitrary geometry. In: Proceedings of the IEEE International Symposium on Mixed and Augmented Reality. pp. 119–128. IEEE (2012)
24. Hanrahan, P.: Self-illustrating phenomena. In: Visualization, 2004. IEEE. p. xix. IEEE (2004)
25. Huang, D., Tory, M., Aseniero, B.A., Bartram, L., Bateman, S., Carpendale, S., Tang, A., Woodbury, R.: Personal visualization and personal visual analytics. IEEE Transactions on Visualization and Computer Graphics 21(3), 420–433 (2015)
26. Hull, R., Neaves, P., Bedford-Roberts, J.: Towards situated computing. In: Proceedings of the International Symposium on Wearable Computers. pp. 146–153. IEEE (1997)
27. Isenberg, P., Dragicevic, P., Willett, W., Bezerianos, A., Fekete, J.D.: Hybrid-image visualization for large viewing environments. IEEE Transactions on Visualization & Computer Graphics 19(12), 2346–2355 (2013)
28. Jansen, Y., Dragicevic, P.: An interaction model for visualizations beyond the desktop. IEEE Transactions on Visualization and Computer Graphics 19(12), 2396–2405 (2013)
29. Jansen, Y., Dragicevic, P., Isenberg, P., Alexander, J., Karnik, A., Kildal, J., Subramanian, S., Hornbæk, K.: Opportunities and challenges for data physicalization. In: Proceedings of the ACM Conference on Human Factors in Computing Systems. pp. 3227–3236. ACM (2015)
30. Jansen, Y., Hornbaek, K.: A Psychophysical Investigation of Size as a Physical Variable. IEEE Transactions on Visualization and Computer Graphics 22(1), 479–488(Jan 2016), http://dx.doi.org/10.1109/TVCG.2015.2467951 doi: 10.1109/TVCG.2015.2467951
31. Jordan, T.: Water Flow Visualization using Electrolysis Hydrogen Bubbles (youtube video. https://youtu.be/memvL8NG8jc (2013), [Online; accessed 17-November-2016]
32. Kalkofen, D., Mendez, E., Schmalstieg, D.: Interactive focus and context visualization for augmented reality. In: Proceedings of the 2007 6th IEEE and ACM International Symposium on Mixed and Augmented Reality. pp. 1–10. IEEE Computer Society (2007)
33. Kalkofen, D., Sandor, C., White, S., Schmalstieg, D.: Visualization techniques for Augmented Reality. In: Handbook on Augmented Reality, pp. 65–98. Springer (2011)
34. Kalkofen, D., Tatzgern, M., Schmalstieg, D.: Explosion diagrams in augmented reality. In: Proceedings of the IEEE Virtual Reality Conference. pp. 71–78. IEEE (2009)
35. Kavanaugh, J.: How mixed reality and machine learning are driving innovation in farming. https://techcrunch.com/2016/11/17/how-mixed-reality-and-machine-learning-are-driving-innovation-in-farming/ (November 2016)
36. Kruijff, E., Swan II, J.E., Feiner, S.: Perceptual issues in Augmented Reality revisited. In: Proceedings of the ACM/IEEE International Symposium on Mixed and Augmented Reality. vol. 9, pp. 3–12 (2010)
37. LaPointe, R.: How AI and AR apps can change agriculture. https://softwaredevelopersindia.com/blog/ai-ar-apps-can-change-agriculture/ (November 2016)

38. Lee, B., Isenberg, P., Riche, N.H., Carpendale, S.: Beyond mouse and keyboard: Expanding design considerations for information visualization interactions. IEEE Transactions on Visualization and Computer Graphics 18(12), 2689–2698(2012), http://dx.doi.org/10.1109/TVCG.2012.204;http://doi.ieeecomputersociety.org/10.1109/TVCG.2012.204
39. Lepetit, V., Berger, M.O.: An intuitive tool for outlining objects in video sequences: Applications to augmented and diminished reality. In: Proceedings of the International Conference on Mixed Reality (2001)
40. Marner, M.R., Irlitti, A., Thomas, B.H.: Improving procedural task performance with augmented reality annotations. In: 2013 IEEE International Symposium on Mixed and Augmented Reality (ISMAR). pp. 39–48. IEEE (2013)
41. McGill, M., Boland, D., Murray-Smith, R., Brewster, S.: A dose of reality: overcoming usability challenges in VR head-mounted displays. In: Proceedings of the ACM Conference on Human Factors in Computing Systems. pp. 2143–2152. ACM (2015)
42. Milgram, P., Kishino, F.: A taxonomy of Mixed Reality visual displays. IEICE Transactions on Information and Systems 77(12), 1321–1329 (1994)
43. Mojang: Minecraft. https://minecraft.net/en/ (December 19 2016)
44. Nguyen, M.: Augmented Reality: Will 2016 be the year of smart contact lens? https://www.wearable-technologies.com/2016/02/augmented-reality-will-2016-be-the-year-of-smart-contact-lens/ (December 2016)
45. Offenhuber, D., Bertini, E., Stefaner, M.: Indexical visualization with Dietmar Offenhuber – data stories podcast (2016), http://datastori.es/80-indexical-visualization-with-dietmar-offenhuber/
46. Offenhuber, D., Telhan, O.: Indexical visualization – the data-less information display. Ubiquitous Computing, Complexity and Culture p. 288 (2015)
47. O'Regan, J.K., Noë, A.: A sensorimotor account of vision and visual consciousness. Behavioral and Brain Sciences 24(05), 939–973 (2001)
48. O'Regan, J.K., et al.: What it is like to see: A sensorimotor theory of perceptual experience. Synthese 129(1), 79–103 (2001)
49. Raskar, R.: Projector-Based Three Dimensional Graphics. Ph.D., University of North Carolina at Chapel Hill (2001)
50. Raskar, R., Welch, G., Chen, W.C.: Table-top spatially-augmented reality: Bringing physical models to life with projected imagery. In: Proceedings of the IEEE and ACM International Workshop on Augmented Reality. IEEE Computer Society, Washington, DC, USA (1999)
51. Raskar, R., Welch, G., Fuchs, H.: Spatially augmented reality. In: Behringer, R., Klinker, G., Mizell, D. (eds.) Augmented Reality: Placing Artificial Objects in Real Scenes, pp. 63–72. A.K. Peters Ltd., San Francisco, CA, USA (1998)
52. Raskar, R., Welch, G., Low, K.L., Bandyopadhyay, D.: Shader lamps: Animating real objects with image-based illumination. In: Gortler, S.J., Myszkowski, K. (eds.) Rendering Techniques 2001, Proceedings of the Eurographics Workshop in London, United Kingdom, pp. 89–102. Springer, NewYork, University College London (UCL), London, England (2001)
53. Roberts, J.C., Ritsos, P.D., Badam, S.K., Brodbeck, D., Kennedy, J., Elmqvist, N.: Visualization beyond the desktop — the next big thing. IEEE Computer Graphics and Applications 34(6), 26–34(Nov/Dec 2014) doi: 10.1109/MCG.2014.82
54. Schmalstieg, D., Hollerer, T.: Augmented Reality: Principles and Practice. Addison-Wesley Professional (2016)

55. Slater, M.: Place illusion and plausibility can lead to realistic behaviour in immersive virtual environments. Philosophical Transactions of the Royal Society B: Biological Sciences 364(1535), 3549–3557 (December 2009)
56. Thomas, B.H.: Have we achieved the ultimate wearable computer? In: Proceedings of the International Symposium on Wearable Computers. pp. 104–107. IEEE (2012)
57. Thomas, B.H., Marner, M., Smith, R.T., Elsayed, N.A.M., Von Itzstein, S., Klein, K., Adcock, M., Eades, P., Irlitti, A., Zucco, J., Simon, T., Baumeister, J., Suthers, T.: Spatial augmented reality—a tool for 3D data visualization. In: Proceedings of the IEEE International Workshop on 3DVis. pp. 45–50. IEEE (2014)
58. Thomas, J.J., Cook, K.A.: Illuminating the Path: The Research and Development Agenda for Visual Analytics. IEEE Press (2005)
59. Wang, F., Cao, X., Ren, X., Irani, P.: Detecting and leveraging finger orientation for interaction with direct-touch surfaces. In: Proceedings of the 22nd Annual ACM Symposium on User Interface Software and Technology. pp. 23–32. ACM (2009)
60. Want, R., Hopper, A., Falcao, V., Gibbons, J.: The active badge location system. ACM Transactions on Information Systems (TOIS) 10(1), 91–102 (1992)
61. Weigel, M., Lu, T., Bailly, G., Oulasvirta, A., Majidi, C., Steimle, J.: Iskin: flexible, stretchable and visually customizable on-body touch sensors for mobile computing. In: Proceedings of the 33rd Annual ACM Conference on Human Factors in Computing Systems. pp. 2991–3000. ACM (2015)
62. Weiser, M.: Some computer science issues in ubiquitous computing. Communications of the ACM 36(7), 75–84 (1993)
63. White, S., Feiner, S.: SiteLens: situated visualization techniques for urban site visits. In: Proceedings of the ACM Conference on Human Factors in Computing Systems. pp. 1117–1120. ACM (2009)
64. Willett, W., Jansen, Y., Dragicevic, P.: Embedded data representations. IEEE Transactions on Visualization and Computer Graphics 23(1), 461–470 (2017)
65. Wisneski, C., Ishii, H., Dahley, A., Gorbet, M., Brave, S., Ullmer, B., Yarin, P.: Ambient displays: Turning architectural space into an interface between people and digital information. In: International Workshop on Cooperative Buildings. pp. 22–32. Springer (1998)

All links were last followed on October 20, 2016.

8. Collaborative Immersive Analytics

Mark Billinghurst[1], Maxime Cordeil[2], Anastasia Bezerianos[3], and Todd Margolis[4]

[1] School of ITMS, University of South Australia, Mawson Lakes, Australia
mark.billinghurst@unisa.edu.au
[2] Monash University, Australia
max.cordeil@monash.edu
[3] Univ. Paris-Sud, CNRS, Inria, Université Paris-Saclay, France
anastasia.bezerianos@u-psud.fr
[4] Qlik, California USA
tmargo@gmail.com

Abstract. Many of the problems being addressed by Immersive Analytics require groups of people to solve. This chapter introduces the concept of Collaborative Immersive Analytics (CIA) and reviews how immersive technologies can be combined with Visual Analytics to facilitate co-located and remote collaboration. We provide a definition of Collaborative Immersive Analytics and then an overview of the different types of possible collaboration. The chapter also discusses the various roles in collaborative systems, and how to support shared interaction with the data being presented. Finally, we summarize the opportunities for future research in this domain. The aim of the chapter is to provide enough of an introduction to CIA and key directions for future research, so that practitioners will be able to begin working in the field.

Keywords: collaborative immersive analytics, immersive analytics, immersion, human-computer interaction, visual analytics, collaboration, collaborative visualization, shared interaction

8.1. Introduction

In a world of increasing computing power and sensing, there is more data being generated than ever before. Over the last ten years Big Data [95] has become an important field of research with data scientists exploring many different ways to transform terabytes of information into valuable insights. One of the popular methods for creating understanding is to generate visual representations of the data, as explored in the area of Visual Analytics [125], defined as "the science of analytical reasoning facilitated by interactive visual interfaces". In this case a wide variety of visualization techniques are used to explore complex datasets. For example, 2D bar charts can be used to understand detailed election results and 3D graphics to show sensor data on terrain models. Visualization tools have been shown to improve performance time and productivity on a range of different tasks

K. Marriott et al. (Eds.): Immersive Analytics, LNCS 11190, pp. 221–257, 2018.
https://doi.org/10.1007/978-3-030-01388-2_8

such as software analysis [50], data analysis [118], and information retrieval [130], among others. Sun *et al.* [119] provide an excellent summary of visual analytics techniques and applications, and their benefits.

Most recently, researchers have begun to explore how novel immersive display technology can be used to enhance visual analytics solutions (Chapter 1). The term Immersive Analytics [20] was coined to describe "an emerging research thrust investigating how new interaction and display technologies can be used to support analytical reasoning and decision making". These display technologies range from room scale immersive CAVE projection systems [30] to Virtual Reality head mounted displays (HMDs) [31], and from interactive walls, tables and multi-display environments [124] to portable head worn Augmented Reality displays [3]. Klapperstück *et al.* [72] proposed ContextuWall, a system for interactive local and remote collaboration using touch and mobile devices as well as displays of various sizes. Emerging interaction technologies include devices like the Microsoft Kinect [71] or Leap Motion [74] which support natural gesture input, eye-tracking devices [99] for collecting awareness information, and even Brain Computer Interfaces that respond to thoughts [87].

Previous research has shown that using Immersive Analytics technologies can enable people to be significantly more effective at understanding data visualizations than more traditional interface technologies. For example, Belcher *et al.* found that using Augmented Reality (AR) improved user performance at finding node connections in complex graph visualizations compared to a 2D desktop presentation [8]. Similarly, Ware [135] found that using head-coupled stereo viewing enabled a person to understand an abstract graph three times the size of a graph viewed on a normal non-stereo monitor.

However, effective presentation on immersive displays is only one way to gain an understanding of complex data. Research stretching back over decades has found that collaborative decision making is often more effective than working on problems alone. Hill [51] provides a good review of early research comparing group versus individual performance on different tasks, finding that group performance is generally superior to that of an average individual. Similarly, in comparing collaborative to single user performance on an information visualization task, Mark *et al.* [83] found that groups worked slower, but produced more accurate results. Recently, Woolley *et al.* [137] have argued for a group collective intelligence factor that predicts performance on collaborative tasks, and could be improved by using collaborative tools. However, supporting effective collaboration can be challenging and was identified as one of the Grand Challenges for Visual Analytics [27].

Co-located collaboration provides important benefits. Sawyer *et al.* showed that team rooms supporting face-to-face activities helped focus the activities of work groups and removed them from interruptions [108]. Most recently, Teasley *et al.* found that co-located software teams working in "war rooms" with access to tools such as computers, whiteboards and flipcharts were twice as productive as the similar teams working in a traditional office environment [123]. Some visualization systems, such as CoVis [33] have specific tools for supporting co-located collaboration.

Significant benefits can be found from teams working together in an Immersive Analytics setting. Marai *et al.* [82] review three Immersive Analytics projects undertaken by research teams using the CAVE2 immersive projection environment (see Figure 1). The feedback was overwhelmingly positive, with the authors saying, "At the end of the meeting one of the team members said that the team got more done in 2 days than in 6 months of email, Skype, and Google Hangout." They were able to make such rapid progress because the CAVE2 environment enabled a group of people to work together face to face while seeing multiple representations of the data across a large amount of screen real-estate all at the same time. This research builds on their earlier work with the Cyber-Commons [76] which was a 100 megapixel tiled display wall that allowed small groups of multidisciplinary researchers to work together.

Fig. 1: EVL researchers at work in the CAVE2 at UIC, from [82]

In this chapter we provide an overview of and introduction to Collaborative Immersive Analytics. Although there has been a significant amount of research on how immersive technologies can support collaboration, there has been very little research in the newer area of Collaborative Immersive Analytics. Our aim is to provide an introduction to researchers to this field, describe some example applications, provide design guidelines, and clearly identify directions for future research. This should be helpful for guiding researchers wanting to enter this emerging field of research or for teams requiring new means of analysis for complex data.

In the remainder of the chapter we first provide a definition of Collaborative Immersive Analytics, and various roles people have when using collaborative systems. We then provide an overview of collaborative interaction methods, before identifying promising areas for research. Finally, we summarize the chapter and outside areas for future work. Overall, the aim of this chapter is to provide enough of an introduction to Collaborative Immersive Analytics that interested readers could begin to do their own work in the field.

8.2. Definition and Scope

Before we can discuss Collaborative Immersive Analytics (CIA) we need to define what the term means and describe the overall scope of the chapter. CIA is so new that there is no well accepted definition. However Collaborative Immersive Analytics is related to Collaborative Visualization, a term that Isenberg *et al.* [58] define as:

The shared use of computer-supported, (interactive,) visual representations of data by more than one person with the common goal of contribution to joint information processing activities.

Using this definition, Isenberg points out that collaborative visualization lies at the intersection of the two major research fields of visualization and computer supported collaborative work (CSCW), each of which have made significant research contributions that could benefit collaborative visualization.

Considering this and returning to the original definition of Immersive Analytics, we define Collaborative Immersive Analytics as: *The shared use of immersive interaction and display technologies by more than one person for supporting collaborative analytical reasoning and decision making.*

The main difference between Collaborative Immersive Analytics and Collaborative Visualization is the focus in CIA on the use of immersive interaction and display technologies. Hackathorn and Margolis [45] point out that Immersive Analytics environments can span most of Milgram's Reality-Virtuality (RV) continuum [86]. The RV continuum is a well-known way of classifying interface technologies in terms of how they connect the physical and virtual worlds, from the fully physical world (on the left) to the fully virtual world (on the right) (Figure 2). Within this continuum is the class of Mixed Reality technologies which merge real and virtual worlds. This ranges from tabletop displays and Augmented Reality environments to fully immersive virtual reality head mounted displays and rooms.

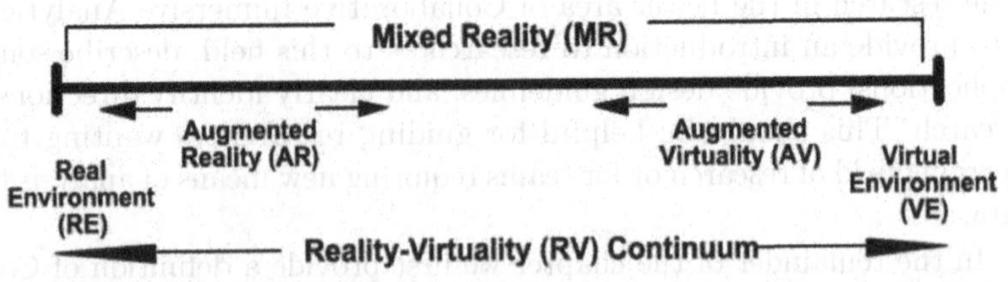

Fig. 2: Milgram's Mixed Reality Continuum, from [86].

Collaborative Immersive Analytics explores how Mixed Reality technologies such as these can be used in a collaborative setting. In contrast, Collaborative Visualization is concerned more with shared visualization in general, so the field of CIA can be viewed as a subset of the broader field of Collaborative Visualization. Just as Collaborative Visualization lies at the intersection of the field of visualization and CSCW, Collaborative Immersive Analytics lies at the intersection of Collaborative Visualization and Mixed Reality (see Figure 3).

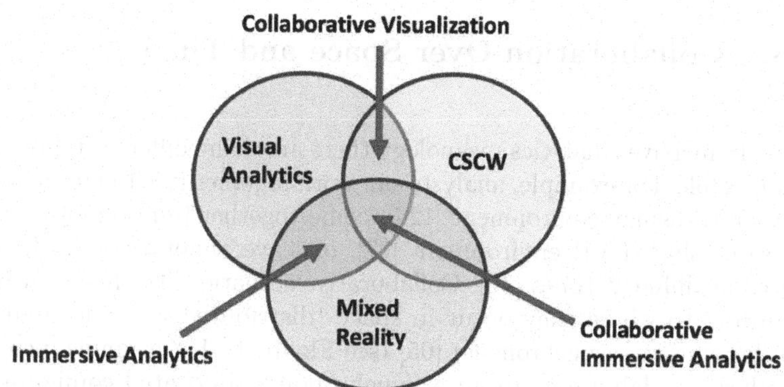

Fig. 3: The relationship between Collaborative Immersive Analytics, Collaborative Visualization and Immersive Analytics.

By its very nature, CIA is a multi-disciplinary research field. In addition to Collaborative Visualization, it is also related to the fields of Scientific Visualisation (SciVis) [68], Information Visualisation (InfoVis) [17] and Visual Analytics [125], all of which are well established with ongoing conferences and journals over the past 20 years. However, in these fields relatively little attention has been paid to the study of collaborative visualisation, especially using advanced interface tools. For example, Isenberg points out that of the nearly 1600 papers published in the three main IEEE visualization conferences from 1990 to 2010, only 34 focused on collaborative visualisation, less than three percent of the total [58]. According to Google Scholar, until now there have been no papers published using the term "Collaborative Immersive Analytics".

This lack of research means there are significant opportunities for research in the field of Collaborative Immersive Analytics. The focus of this chapter highlights these areas and provides some of the background material to help interested researchers. We provide some important background work in collaborative systems, discuss multi-user interaction modalities, highlight lessons learned from collaboration with immersive technologies such as Virtual and Augmented Reality displays and interactive walls and tables, and specifically identify important research topics. We should note that this chapter is not an exhaustive literature review, nor a tutorial on collaborative technologies or immersive interfaces in general.

In the next section we begin by introducing a taxonomy of collaborative systems based on space and time, and examples of collaborative immersive technologies that fit into this taxonomy. Then, we discuss the different roles that people have in collaborative systems and how they can interact with the datasets. Finally, we provide a high-level overview of some of the possible research opportunities that could be explored in the future.

8.3. Collaboration Over Space and Time

Using Immersive Analytics technology there are many different types of collaboration possible. For example, analysts can work together face to face in a CAVE [82] or a multi-display environment [124], come together from remote locations into the same shared VR environment [77], or leave annotations in datasets to be viewed at different times [35]. Collaborative scenarios like these can be classified according to where they occur in space (distributed vs. co-located) and time (synchronous vs. asynchronous) [65] (see Figure 4). For example, people working together in a lab space are in a Synchronous/Co-located configuration, while those exchanging email over time are working in a Distributed/Asynchronous configuration.

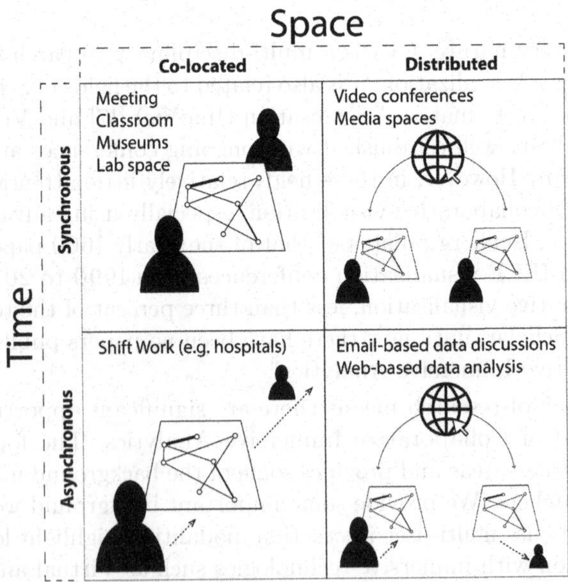

Fig. 4: A space-time taxonomy of collaborative visualisation, from [58].

In this section we describe this classification in more detail and review several examples of CIA systems at different points in the space/time collaborative matrix. We also describe some of the lessons that have been learned from previous research that can be used as guidelines for developing collaborative systems.

8.3.1. Co-Located Synchronous Collaboration

There are many examples of Immersive Analytics applications where collaborators are in the same physical space and working together at the same time. Marai *et al.* [82] describes three Immersive Analytics projects where a small group of researchers work face-to-face together inside the CAVE2 environment surrounded by immersive projection screens. In this case researchers brought their own laptop computers into the CAVE2 and were able to work on their private displays as well as use the shared immersive display. Other environments include shared visualizations on interactive tabletops where people stand around the table surface [70] [1], responsive wall displays that multiple people can interact with at the same time [23] [29] [2] [5], and face to face collaborative AR solutions [109] [12]. Figure 5 shows a typical use of interactive tables and walls to support face-to-face collaboration.

Fig. 5: Examples of using interactive wall displays and tabletops for co-located synchronous collaborative visualization.

Co-located synchronous collaboration has a number of advantages. Collaborators can directly see one another and work together at the same time and so changes they make to the data set can be easily seen by their co-workers [115]. This makes it very easy to have awareness of others which can improve communication, and to move between focusing on their individual work and group work. Collaborators can also easily bring their own externalisation tools (such as computers and notes) into the meeting and share them amongst each other, which helps establish a common ground.

The different immersive technologies available for face-to-face collaboration may also provide unique benefits. For example, with a co-located Augmented

Reality interface each user has their independent view into the shared dataset that can be customized according to their role [109]. A virtual terrain model could be overlaid with sensor data for an environmental engineer, but an urban designer looking at the same AR model might see traffic information overlaid on the terrain. Similarly, using a tablet at the same time as an interactive wall [97,140] or table [134] allows the user to have their own custom private view and input into the shared display space.

8.3.2. Distributed Synchronous Collaboration

Many collaborative analytics tasks are performed by distributed teams, so there can be a need for Collaborative Immersive Analytics applications that support remote synchronous collaboration. For example immersive virtual reality displays can be used to allow analysts working at different locations to come together in the same virtual space to jointly explore complex datasets. Donalek *et al.* [31] describes how the OpenSim framework was used to create an immersive collaborative visualization space that could be explored in VR head mounted displays (Figure 6). Similarly, high-speed networking can be used to bring remote collaborators into an environment with interactive walls or tabletop displays. For example, the Hugin framework [70] allows the creation of visualization systems where a group of people around an interactive table at one location can connect and collaborate with users around a similar table at a remote location. Other systems have explored the use of mobile devices [88], web browsers [5], CAVEs [66] and Augmented Reality [138] for supporting remote collaboration for information visualization.

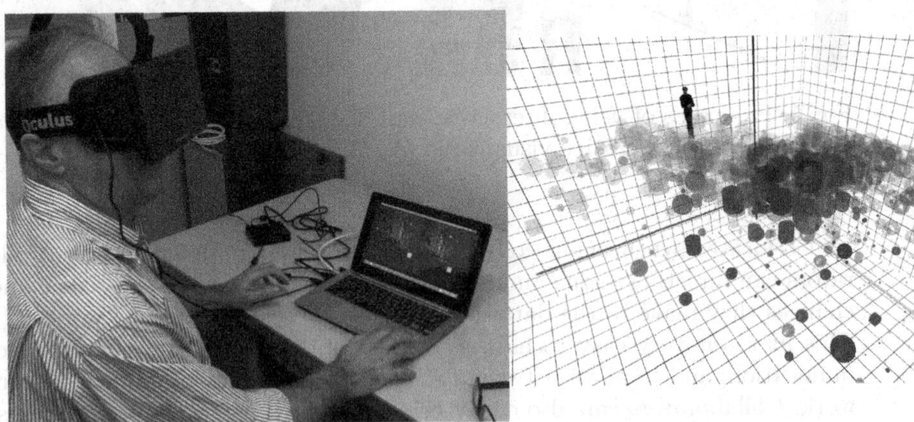

Fig. 6: Using VR to support remote collaborative data visualization, from [31]. User in VR HMD interacting with the system (b) VR view showing remote collaborator as virtual person.

The main advantage of synchronous remote collaboration tools is that they allow remote individuals to connect and collaborate together. In some cases this can produce a similar performance as face-to-face collaboration. For example, in a study comparing performance on a collaborative visual analytics task in a CAVE (face-to-face) or VR HMDs (remote), researchers found that searching in the HMD condition was as accurate as in the CAVE, and was completed faster [28].

However, there are significant challenges that need to be addressed around awareness and representation of each of the collaborators. For example, traditional video conferencing does not produce the same conversation style as face-to-face interaction [47]. This is because video conferencing cannot adequately transmit the rich non-verbal signals so vital in face-to-face communication and this introducing a communication seam between the participants [61]. In interactive walls and tables, the presence of remote collaborators are often reduced to a pointer icon [43], or virtual shadow of a hand [122]. Collaborative virtual environments immerse users in the same virtual space, but even here the remote participants may be reduced to simple video textures [46] or avatars that cannot convey subtle body motions [31].

Gutwin and Greenberg point out that designing for collaborative systems is difficult because of having to support two goals; designing for individual control over the application and designing for group awareness [43]. They say that collaboration in remote groupware tools is different from co-located collaboration for the following reasons: Groupware systems show far less of the workspace than what can be seen in a physical environment. Manipulation techniques in virtual workspaces are not bound by the physical constraints that exist in physical workspaces. Virtual workspaces can represent and display artifacts in more ways than physical workspaces allow.

8.3.3. Distributed Asynchronous Collaboration

For Immersive Analytics most collaborative applications involve synchronous collaboration. Viégas and Wattenberg point out that in general "synchronous collaborative scenarios have been much more widely explored than asynchronous visualization based communication" [131]. However, distributed asynchronous collaboration involves capturing input from people at different times and different places and so can provide some unique benefits. For example, Benbunan-Fich *et al.* found that asynchronous collaboration can produce broader discussions and more complete reports from group discussions than their face-to-face counterparts [9]. Other benefits include enabling people to contribute whenever they have time to provide input [104], they can work on the part of the problem that they feel most qualified to address [129], and can combine information from a variety of sources [52].

Some efforts have been made to add support for asynchronous collaboration to CAVE and immersive Virtual Reality experiences, mostly through simple recording and playing back of messages. For example, Imai's V-Mail system allows people to send and view asynchronous messages in VR [54]. In this case the user can record a voice message along with their virtual avatar body movements and gestures for later playback. Later, this was extended to include a VR-annotator tool for attaching 3D recordings to objects, and a VR-vcr streaming recorder for recording all actions occurring in a collaborative session [55]. Similarly, the Virtue immersive visualization environment provided support for multimedia annotations that allowed users to mark temporal and spatial points for later replay and sharing [111]. More recently, the vAcademia Virtual World shows how 3D recording can be used for asynchronous collaboration in desktop VR environments [89].

There are other examples of non-immersive asynchronous Analytics interfaces that can provide valuable lessons for extending this work. Zimmer and Kerren introduced OnGraX [143], a collaborative synchronous and asynchronous web based tool to support visual analysis of networks. Willet *et al.* have developed CommentSpace, a collaborative visual analysis tool that allows analysts to annotate information visualisations [136]. The tool allows analysts to add comments or view tags to the visualization over time and link the tags together to aid understanding of the document. In this way Collaborators gain the benefit of seeing the tagged classifications that people are applying to the text, and the semantic links being created. Similarly, Chen *et al.* [22] developed ManyInsights, a web-based tool for asynchronous collaborative analysis of multidimensional data (see Figure 7). Using this tool people can record their own insights from data, and read the insights of others over time. They found in an evaluation that this led to the generation of more shared insights, and being able to group insights by data similarity was a particularly powerful way to understand the data.

Heer and Agrawala [48] provide an excellent description of design characteristics for asynchronous collaborative visual analytics interfaces, drawing on web-based interfaces. In particular they list design considerations that should be taken into account, such as the value of supporting freeform annotations, using visualization bookmarks, linking to specific views, and clearly showing past actions that have taken place, among others. They designed the sense.us web application for social visual data analysis, showing how these design guidelines can be used [49]. In this case the interface supports view sharing, doubly linked discussions, graphical annotation, collecting and linking of views, awareness and social navigation, and unobtrusive collaboration. Figure 8 shows the sense.us interface and collaboration features.

Viegas and Wattenberg highlight the research opportunities available in the Distributed Asynchronous Collaboration Space [131]. They say "By not fully exploring asynchronous communication of visualization discoveries and processes, the research community is missing an opportunity to make important contributions to visualization research". In particular, they identify three features that are important; (1) Playback: Allowing users to edit a visualization session, picking out only a few key frames, and sharing it with someone else who can rewatch it. (2) Annotation: Enabling users to point to objects and add information. Tracking changes in annotations over time, and supporting group creation. (3) Information Foraging: Supporting how users spread their attention over the

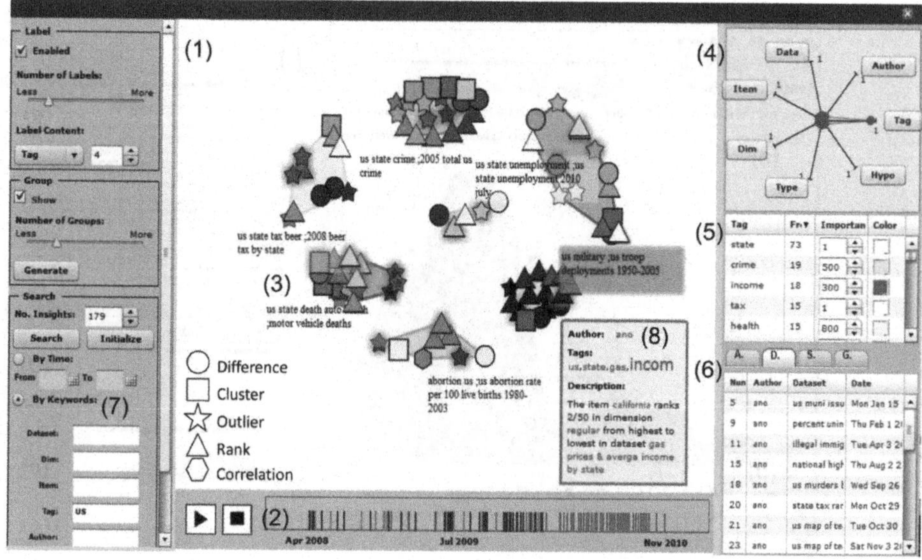

Fig. 7: ManyInsights User Interface [22].

data space, and encouraging users to look at little viewed parts of the dataset. We discuss more about the research opportunities in Distributed Asynchronous Collaboration in Section 8.6.

8.3.4. Co-Located Asynchronous Collaboration

Another area which has not been well studied for information visualization is co-located asynchronous collaboration. One common example of an asynchronous collaboration tool is a shared public display that people can view at different times. For example, Carter *et al.* [19] describe a public display interface that they developed for showing common topics of interest among emails and the current locations of the email writers. This display was designed to encourage more collaboration between co-workers. Other examples of using collaborative public displays include Groupcast [84], CWall [114], and the Notification Collage [40]. Figure 9 shows the Notification Collage interface with a variety of different media items (web pages, notes, video feeds, desktop views, etc.) posted on a shared public display.

The availability of public displays has prompted researchers to experiment with asynchronous, co-located visualizations, for example, in the form of ambient information displays [113]. In this case, public displays in the physical environment are used for information visualization. Pousman and Stasko [100] provide a good overview about how such systems can be used for casual information visualization in a public setting, such as showing bus timetable information, social networks,

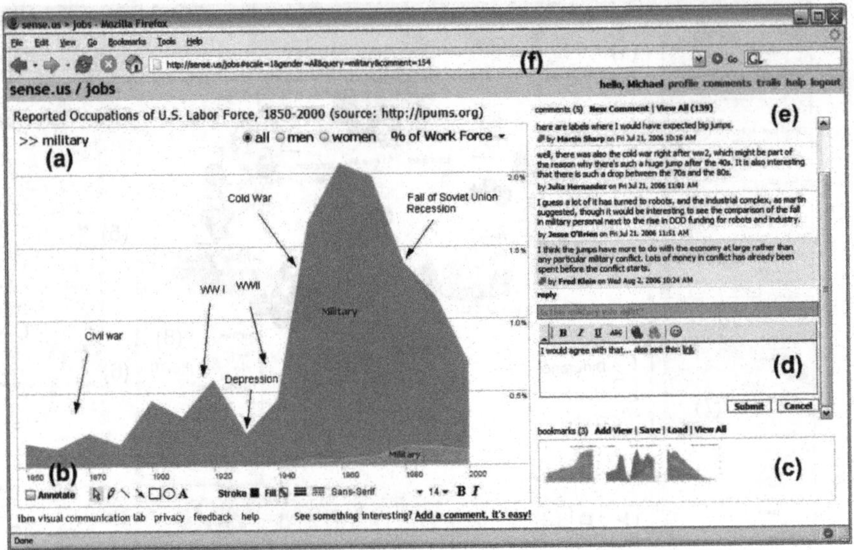

Fig. 8: Sense.us interface [49]; (a) an interactive visualization applet, (b) annotation tools, (c) a bookmark trail of saved views, (d) text-entry field for adding comments, (e) threaded comments attached to the current view, (f) URL for the current state of the application, updated automatically as the state changes.

or photo collections. Similarly, Vogel provides an overview and design guidelines for interacting with co-located displays [133].

Co-located asynchronous collaborative systems have many of the benefits of distributed systems, with the additional benefit of collaborators viewing the same physical space. Viegas and Wattenberg [131] mention that this offers some interesting design opportunities for the physical surroundings around the visualization, such as providing pens and paper for people to add their own notes around the display. Heer and Agrawala [48] point out the value of collaborators being able to see the same collaboration space, and other researchers have identified the value of having externalization tools that help people create and add their own insights [81]. Overall, having a common physical reference space with shared visualization and external objects should significantly help collaborators achieve common ground and shared contextual understanding [25].

8.3.5. Mixed-Presence Collaboration

So far we have talked about collaborative experiences that fit into only one quadrant of the time and space taxonomy. However, it is also possible to create experiences that link together two or more quadrants. For example, Mixed Presence Groupware (MPG) systems are collaborative systems that connect both co-located and distributed collaborators [53] [120]. As such Mixed-Presence

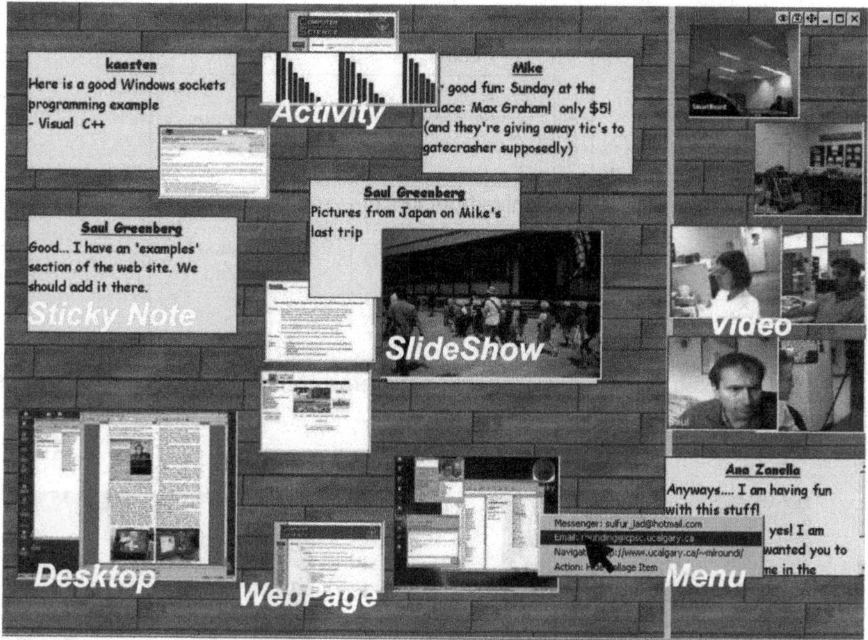

Fig. 9: The Notification Collage interface [40].

systems support synchronous collaboration between people in the same location and a remote location (see Figure 10). For example, the NICE Project supported collaboration between groups in one immersive CAVE with remote collaborators in other VR environments in an educational setting [67]. Other examples include interactive tables that include local and remote participants [106], and combining a VR conferencing space with a physical interactive table [103]. Figure 11 shows a typical mixed presence tabletop application where remote users are represented by video shadows of their arms (from [Tuddenham 2007]).

MPG systems combine the advantages of co-located and distributed synchronous collaborative interfaces, allowing distributed groups of people to work together. However there are a number of design challenges that need to be addressed. For example it can be challenging to enable co-located and remote users to have the same level of mutual awareness, and there is a need to provide some representation of the remote users into the local users space [98]. For example, video arms [121], as seen in Figure 11, can show where the remote users are reaching into the shared interactive space. It is also difficult to enable users to share notes, their own device screen and other local physical artifacts with remote users. Robinson and Tuddenham provides a list of design guidelines to address some of these challenges [106].

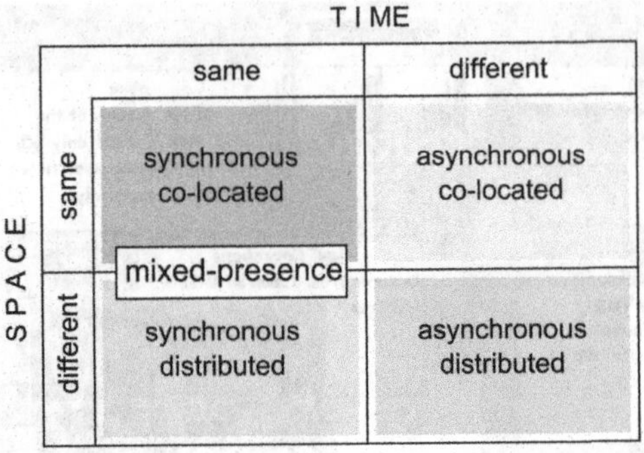

Fig. 10: Mixed Presence Groupware systems combining co-located and remote groups.

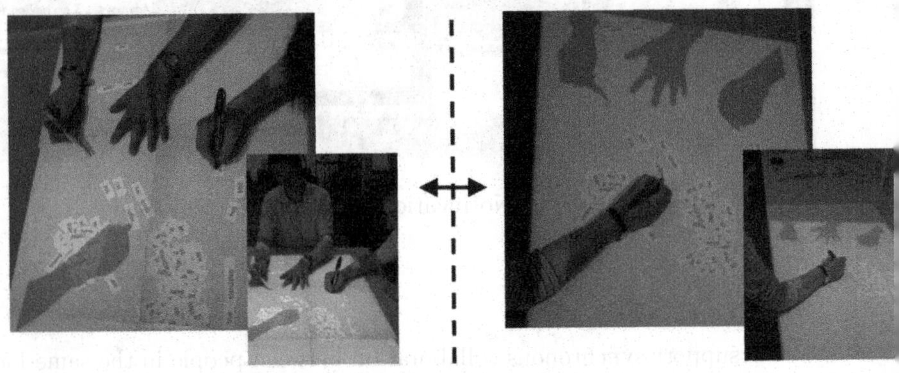

Fig. 11: Mixed Presence Tabletop System [106].

8.3.6. Lessons Learned

A number of lessons have been learned from this research. From the co-located synchronous research (e. g. [82]) the following features were found to be important:

- Supporting different independent viewpoints
- Enabling the use of different tools for different data
- Supporting face-to-face group work
- Using different data representations

Churchill *et al.* [24] reviewed a wide range of collaborative settings and state that the following should be provided in order to support good group communication and problem solving:

- Shared context - the shared knowledge and context around the data
- Awareness of others - users being aware of others' actions

- Negotiation and communication - people being able to freely talk with each other
- Flexible and multiple viewpoints - showing different viewpoints depending on roles

As can be seen from the reviewed systems, there are a wide range of different ways to achieve these requirements. In addition, previous research has shown that groups need to be able to have access to externalization tools, such as notes or laptop computers that enable them to record their insights and organize the results of their analysis [80] [48]. It is also important to enable collaborators to have access to both individual and shared workspaces [43] [60], and to enable them to easily shift their focus from their own work to the work of their collaborators [32]. Marai *et al.* point out that people from different backgrounds want to see data represented in different ways, so there should be multiple representations available and a variety of tools for interacting with the data [82].

In this section we have categorized collaborative systems according to how they support collaboration through space and time. Another important element of these systems are the various roles that the users have, and how the technology can support these roles. In the next section we describe the different roles used in CIA systems.

8.4. Types of Participants in CIA

In collaborative systems participants may have different roles or types of engagements with the system. For example, during a data driven presentation there are typically one or more people presenting while other constituents are audience members that generally do not interact directly with the presentation material. The roles of the people in the collaborative setting define the level of engagement that they have. Isenberg *et al.* [58] discuss how there are three different levels of engagement with collaborative visualization systems:

- Viewing: people are consuming a data presentation without interacting with the data, such as in a lecture presentation.
- Interacting/exploring: people have the means to choose alternate views or explore the data.
- Sharing/creating: people are able to create and distribute new datasets and visualizations to be explored.

Zhu [142] discusses role-based collaboration and points out that for efficient collaboration there needs to be support for asymmetric expertise and authority. For example, in a meeting the collaborative system needs to allow a presenter to control the image presentation, while the images shown should be made visible to all of the viewers in the audience. Similar to theater acting, storytelling can be enhanced by adjusting your presentation to suite your audience and react to their response. Sole [116] points out that effective knowledge-sharing requires storytellers to streamline their narrative by removing (or temporarily hiding) preparatory parts of the analysis that may overwhelm or confuse the audience. Sole asserts that the other most essential part of a good narrative is to provide a surrogate experience for the recipient. Immersive Analytics uniquely offers a sensorial advantage for enveloping recipients in a story thereby increasing the effect of Suspension of Disbelief. For example, analysts within a CIA willingly interact with abstract visualizations of data that may not realistically represent the original source of that data.

Collaborative Immersive Analytics builds upon these archetypal roles, but also enables the ability to mix roles. Given that CIAs are necessarily more highly mediated and interactive than traditional visual analytics platforms, it may be quite natural for participants to switch back and forth between passive viewer and active explorer. In fact, Heer *et al.* [49] discuss how their sense.us platform was a social space for information visualization designed to facilitate data driven discussion and debate. CIA offers a unique opportunity for example in Command and Control scenarios where users may spend most of their time monitoring data feeds and then switch contexts into active analyst and explorer roles as problems arise. It is thus important that data representations and interfaces of CIAs can support fluid transitions between these roles. Another consideration when designing Collaborative Immersive Analytics is the number of creators and consumers. Here are some of the most common formats for collaborative analytics:

- One to self (e. g. data discovery that might be shared later)
- One to some (e. g. reporting findings to colleagues)
- One to many (e. g. presenting reports to stakeholders)
- Many to many (e. g. department heads presenting at employee town halls)
- Many to one (e. g. department heads presenting to CEO)
- Machine to one, some or many (e. g. AI returning results to analyst)

Up until about 10 years ago, the predominant method for analysis was through a guided analytics approach whereby data scientists created visualizations that were presented to and utilized by other users. In the Business Intelligence industry, this meant a very small group of individuals produced highly structured dashboards and reports which were consumed by specific departments within large organizations. Over the last 10 years though, there has been a massive shift to what is referred to as Self-Service Analytics in which users now have the ability to input, access, and analyze data directly by themselves. This transformation has enabled a new form of data discovery which allows for more people to ask more questions and solve more problems. This trend towards creating new collaborative analytics platforms is nicely articulated by the ManyEyes project [132] mentioned earlier. ManyEyes attempted to “democratize” visualization by not only serving as a discovery tool for anyone with data, but also as a platform to prompt discussions around data for large groups of users. This example best typifies the “many to many” form of collaboration.

Machine learning and artificial intelligence (AI) are being applied more and more towards analytics. There are many advanced analytics systems which employ

AI to automate various aspects of the analysis process including everything from data cleansing, preparation and modeling, to dynamically creating visualizations or data-driven narratives through natural language generation, to alerting users of "unusual activity" and predicting future trends. This new "analytics agent" can be considered as a third axis in a collaborative user matrix in Figure 12. Within a CIA, this collaboration with the AI could be represented through a friendly 3D avatar such as those we already interact with aurally through automated voice systems. However, ultimately AI systems will likely mature sufficiently so that they will replace some human knowledge workers through new forms of deep learning combined with expert systems.

This possible introduction of machine intelligence in the analysis process complicates further the design of CIA, as it adds a new level of complexity in the form of an additional actor or role (beyond the existing human ones), whose actions need to be made aware and interpreted by the human collaborators.

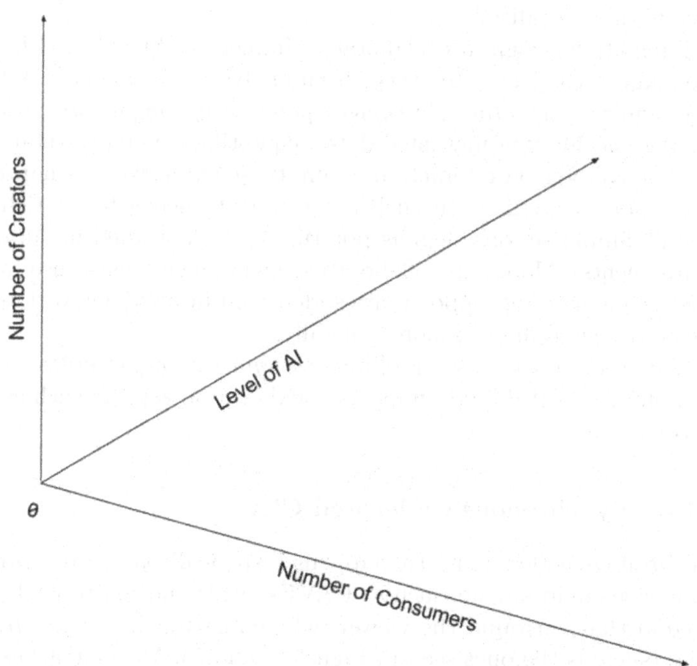

Fig. 12: Collaborative User Matrix.

Given that CIAs can offer more interactivity and potential for greater contribution by more participants, it can also encourage dialogue and debate around data analysis. If a chart is presented in 3D and one can easily move around it and interrogate it, will that simple shift in perspective also transform users into active listeners? Or can we go beyond simply allowing for the ability of multiple users with various roles within an Immersive Analytics environment to also enable them to have suitable means to effectively collaborate? In the next section we will explore how different types of interaction modalities enable participants within a CIA to engage in various analytic tasks.

8.5. Interaction in CIA Environments

Deciding on appropriate interactions to support any visual analysis task is important, as interactions facilitate the dialogue between analysts and their data [126]. When considering collaborative environments in particular, analysts are in dialogue not only with the data, but also with each other, and the choice of interaction technique can influence the nature of collaboration and the awareness of others [32,44]. For example, Prouzeau *et al.* [102] observed that when analyzing graphs on a wall display, pairs using techniques with a large visual footprint adopted tighter coordination strategies than pairs using techniques that were more visually localized.

Interaction design in Collaborative Immersive Analytics (CIA) environments faces similar challenges to other visual analysis environments [126]. For example they require *interactions to support potentially complex analytic tasks*, such as defining and filtering unwanted data, requesting new representations of the data, etc. The chapter on interaction covers these extensively (Chapter 4). Thus the interaction vocabulary in such environments needs to be rich enough to go beyond simple actions such as pointing (a task studied in detail in immersive environments). Moreover, collaborative environments must also take into account other challenges and opportunities identified in previous work on collaborative immersive environments more generally.

This section discusses preliminary *synchronous* interaction (co-located or distributed), as it directly impacts collaboration aspects such as awareness and coordination.

8.5.1. Synchronous Co-located CIA

Synchronous co-located CIA happens historically in shared **physically large** immersive environments such as CAVEs, walls and multi-display environments (MDEs) that surround the viewer, where analysts can *move freely around the space* (such as the ones seen in Figures 1 and 5). Movement has been linked to benefits such as avoiding occlusion by others in CAVEs [21], and correcting for possible visual distortion in walls [13].

Movement: While collaborative interaction from stationary positions with mice and keyboards is still possible [16,57], it does not leverage the full rendering capacities of these immersive environments. In CAVEs analysts can move inside the data itself and view it from different perspectives. With walls they can see data at different scales, coming close to the display to see details and further back to get an overview [7]. With tables, they can see data from different angles by moving

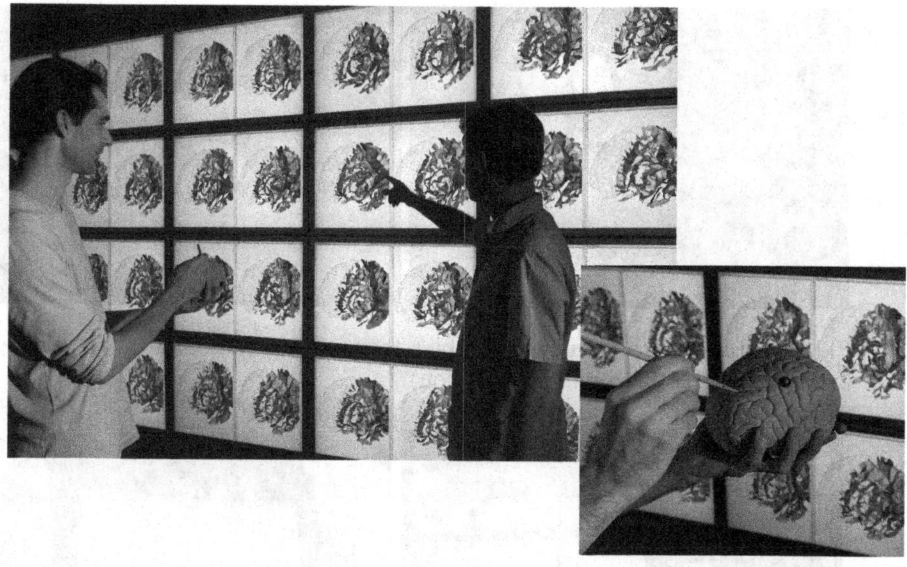

Fig. 13: Interaction using a tangible prop of a brain to rotate brain images, and a stick that defines the camera position (left), and close-up (right) from [39] (used with permission, ©CNRS-Phototheque - Cyril FRESILLON).

around the table. In all cases, movement can be seen as an implicit interaction for navigating in the data space. Movement has also been used as an explicit interaction, for example to trigger dynamic changes in content rendering [7], or to invoke actions such as dynamic filtering depending on the analyst's position and movement [63]. While such approaches can increase the interaction vocabulary, they need to be carefully considered in collaborative environments, where implicit actions as simple as moving may cause large scale visual changes that could disturb other analysts. This issue is particularly prominent in large-scale stereoscopic environments (such as CAVEs), where almost always only a single person controls perspective and interaction, even though multiple people can move in the space.

Pointing and Gestures: Existing work has looked at different interaction alternatives that support free movement. Research on CAVEs, walls and multi-display environments have considered extensively pointing techniques (using hands or dedicated devices) [4, 92, 93], that combined with on-screen menus and widgets, could cover the complex interaction needs in CIA environments. Pointing actions can be easily seen by colleagues, increasing the awareness of others. Nevertheless, the existence of persistent on-screen menus on the shared collaboration space takes up space that could be used for displaying data, while menus invoked on the fly can be disruptive to collaborators sharing the space.

As an alternative, hand or full-body gestures can activate commands (e. g., [117]) and provide a rich interaction vocabulary without taking up screen space. They provide awareness of the actions of others, given that these gestures are

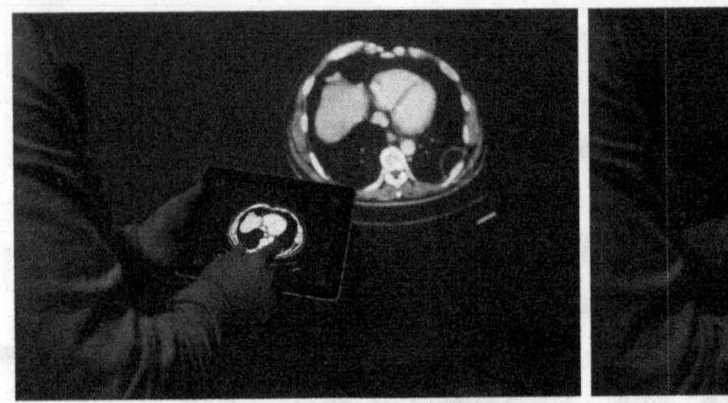
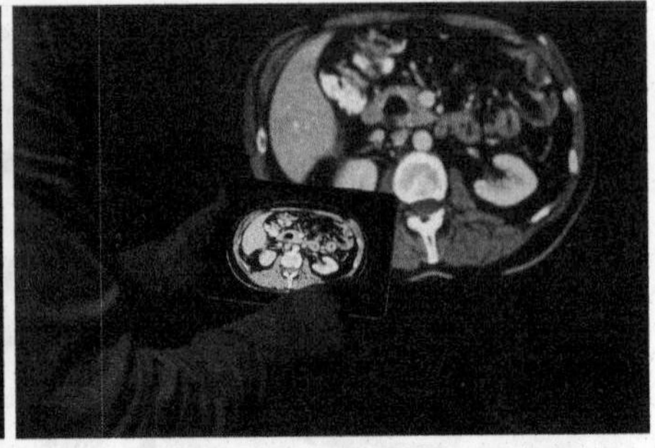

Fig. 14: Multi-touch input on a tablet to zoom and scroll through a stack of brain-scans [97] (used with permission).

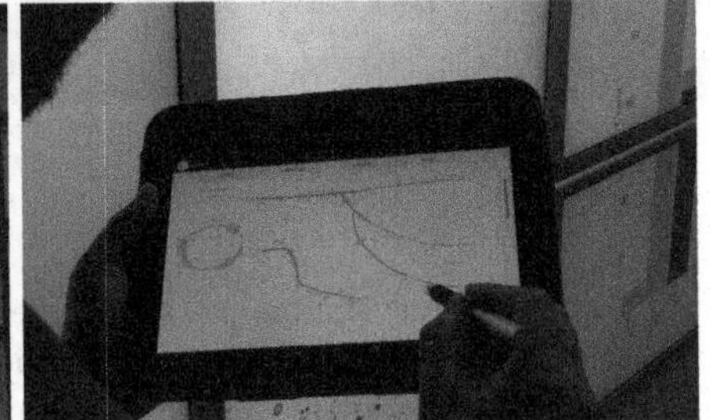

Fig. 15: A user sketching the sliders they need for their exploration [127] (used with permission).

easily seen by colleagues sharing the space. Nevertheless, full-body gestures can prove tiring during long periods of work [139] required by some analytics tasks [126], and gestural vocabularies can be large thus coming with a learning cost [69].

Dedicated Devices: Researchers have also examined the use of personal, dedicated, or generic, mobile devices. For example, in order to analyze brain scans on a wall display, Gjerlufsen *et al.* [39] suggested using a dedicated tangible prop of a brain to rotate and translate the scans (Figure 13), and physical tools to indicate camera viewing directions; Olwal *et al.* [97] suggested using dedicated software running on tablets to provide interaction tools and different views of the brain between colleagues in medical teams (Figure 14).

These examples illustrate the large possible range of such mobile devices in terms of both generalizability across analytic tasks, and awareness of others. Interaction with dedicated tangible props (such as a model of a brain), comes with a high degree of awareness since props used by colleagues are easy to identify, but their utility is limited to specific data domains and analysis tasks (exploring brain scans). On the other hand, more general purpose devices can be adapted across analysis tasks and data. For example, devices with multiple degrees of freedom (e. g., [11, 37]) allow for a rich input vocabulary while at the same time being general purpose. Existing mobile devices, such as smartphones and tablets, can also be appropriated, adapting their content to provide a personalized interface

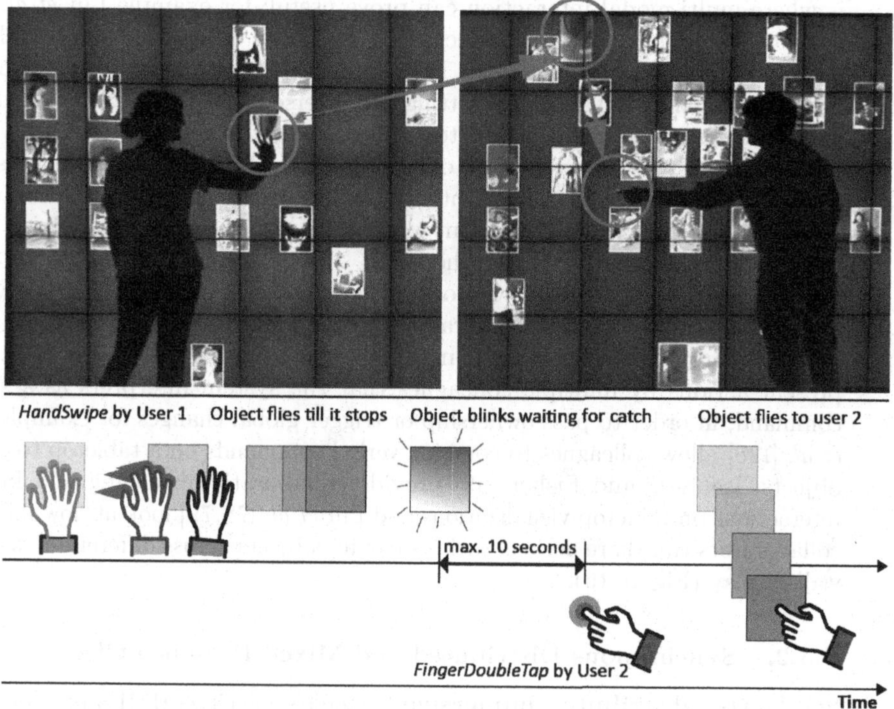

Fig. 16: A user throws an item and another performs a gesture to make it "fly" to their location in CoReach [79] (used with permission).

for analysis tasks or personal views of the data [97,134,140]. Mobile devices can also be combined with physical widgets [64] or be customized by analysts, for example allowing them to sketch their own interfaces based on their analysis needs [127] (Figure 15). Because these more general purpose personal devices can be adapted to help analysts perform many tasks, they usually provide limited awareness of the actions of others. In this case, additional awareness information needs to be given during collaboration, for example in the form of colored cursors, or other highlights to indicate the work of others [44]. Mobile devices, dedicated or general purpose, need to be carried around while analysts are moving, which could prove cumbersome in long duration analysis tasks.

Touch and other modalities: Physically large immersive environments often include displays that can act as touch surfaces. In the past researchers have considered direct touch interaction as input in collaborative analytics on very large surfaces such as walls [62,102] or tabletops [60,91]. Direct touch provides immediate awareness information about where others are working in the shared space, and allows for direct manipulation [112]. Nevertheless, touch technology may not be always available, and even if it is, it requires users to be close to the display, missing the benefits of movement discussed before. This is where multi-modal interaction can prove useful; for example Liu *et al.* [79] use a collection of collaboration techniques based on direct touch on a wall and distant interaction using mobiles. More generally, multimodal interaction can prove beneficial for collaborative settings for diverse reasons. For example, adding voice commands on a touch tabletop can enhance the gesture vocabulary and potentially increase awareness of others' actions [128]. Or providing personal devices coupled with the shared interactive surface, allows colleagues to fluidly move between individual and team work [110], and chose when to share their individual analysis results with others [85].

Collaborative actions: Co-located collaborative settings also allow the creation of new collaborative interaction techniques, where users combine their actions in order to create a single more powerful interactions. Morris *et al.* [90] present actions by multiple colleagues that the system interprets as a single command, in order to pass ownership or trigger global changes for example. Tse *et al.* [128] allow colleagues to combine verbal commands on a tabletop to group objects. Isenberg and Fisher [59] provide collaborative brushing and linking interactions on tabletop visualizations and Liu *et al.* [78,79] look at how multiple collaborators can share actions such as moving objects across different areas on a wall display (Figure 16).

8.5.2. Synchronous Distributed and Mixed Presence CIA

Synchronous **distributed immersive** technology, such as HMDs provides analysts with the ability to *chose whether to share exactly the same view or completely different ones.* As with individual analysis in these environments (see Chapter 4), a rich input vocabulary can be achieved using pointing and virtual menus [15], more elaborate gestures [6, 26, 74], or even mobile devices [36]. What is unique about this setting is that, contrary to physically large environments where awareness of others often comes from seeing the location and actions of others within a shared physical space, here analysts may be unaware of the focus and view of their colleagues. In order to maintain awareness of others, interaction needs to provide feedback not only to the user taking an action, but also to their colleagues. For example, researchers have proposed the use of avatars to represent their fellow analysts within the virtual world, starting from very abstract representation of others [10] to full 3D body models [101]. Analysts' actions need also be accompanied by feedback presented to their colleagues, for example in the form of highlights of their area of focus [38] that can be very fine grained (e. g., through eye-tracking [42]), and the ability to share views with others [96].

Given the introduction of **augmented reality** technology, it is possible to have scenarios where *analysts are physically co-located, but have personal views* of their data superimposed on the virtual environment. In these mixed reality environments, most interactions that are possible in physically large environments are possible here as well (with the exception possibly of touch interactions on shared surfaces). Nevertheless, in this context, awareness of actions can prove problematic. Even if the physical position of analysts and their physical actions (e. g., gestures) are visible, there is no guarantee that they are transparent to their colleagues since they are not sharing a common view. This problem is similar to the awareness challenges present in distributed environments. It may even be more pronounced in mixed reality settings: in distributed situations, representations of colleagues can be artificially placed close to their areas of focus; in a mixed reality setting, we have a strong visual presence of colleagues moving inside an analyst's field of vision (but not necessarily sharing a common view), that may be hard to override in order to represent their virtual focus.

Designing interaction for situations where some colleagues are co-located and some distributed, i.e., **mixed-presence** collaboration, presents possibly the biggest challenge. The analysis environment needs to provide awareness support for the actions of co-located colleagues, while at the same time providing representations of the distributed partners and/or their actions. All this, in an environment that is likely already occupied by large amount of visualized data.

8.5.3. Asynchronous CIA

So far, we have considered only synchronous interaction in collaborative environments. Nevertheless, analysis tasks can be long, requiring several work sessions [126], or analysts may work individually but share their analysis later on. These asynchronous analysis sessions can be done either distributed, or even co-located (working in shifts). In these case, some interaction challenges are similar to single user interaction. Nevertheless, there are new problems that arise when analysts **work asynchronously**, such as understanding where their colleagues left-off with their analysis, where they focused on, etc. More general, supporting hand-off in asynchronous analysis [141], both co-located and distributed, becomes crucial. Here, we require techniques that leave a trace of the analysis work and progress of colleagues. These can be explicit, for example annotations or summaries left behind for others [94,105]; implicit, such as summaries of all past interactions (as is done in [14]); or a combination of both, where the analysis system can help the analyst to tell a story [18,34,75,107] of their work to bring their colleagues up-to-speed (see Chapter 6).

8.6. Opportunities for Research

Collaborative Immersive Analytics is an emerging research field and it is still underexplored. As it is challenging to identify a pertinent path to explore in CIA, this section aims to provide a non-exclusive list of important research questions to guide research in this new domain. Previous work has identified important characteristics of Collaborative Visual Analytics. Heer [48] identified the following topics to explore:

- Division and allocation of work
- Common ground and awareness
- Reference and deixis [1]

[1] Deixis refers to words and phrases, such as "me" or "here", that cannot be fully understood without additional contextual information. Source: Wikipedia.

– Incentives and engagement
– Identity, trust, and reputation
– Group dynamics
– Consensus and decision making

Virtual/Augmented/Mixed reality, wall-size displays and tabletops can lead to more immersion and presence. The nature and affordances of such *immersive environments* may have an influence on how a group of users work together. This chapter presents a set of questions related to the space/time matrix and important topics previously identified in Collaborative Visual Analytics, with respect to immersive environments.

8.6.1. Virtual reality for Immersive Collaborative Analytics

CAVE-style setups and large display or multi-display environments are a natural space for collaboration. CAVE-style setups are rooms with screens surrounding the users. Collaborators view and talk to each other, and can, for example have face-to-face discussions. Collaboration in Virtual Reality can also be alternatively supported by networked head-mounted displays, or fishtanks. Cordeil *et al.* [28] found that performances were comparable between CAVE-style displays (Figure 17) and HMDs (Figure 18), but raised some usability issues for collaboration. However, there are other Virtual Reality displays that need to be compared for collaboration. Hence it is important to conduct research with different display form factors.

8.6.2. HMDs and face-to-face communication

While HMDs offer an alternative to wall displays and other CAVE-style environments, they obscure the face of collaborators. This can potentially be a major impairment as facial expressions are used as visual cues for different reasons, including establishing a common ground or assessing and discussing findings [48]. The study of Cordeil *et al.* [28] did not reveal a major issue with this impairment but they tested only low-level graph visualization tasks and did not test analytical reasoning. In this condition, using only conversation and gaze was probably sufficient to complete the tasks. An interesting opportunity for research is to measure the effect of not seeing the face expressions of collaborators:
– When they are sharing insights: how does it affect engagement?
– On the group dynamics: how does it affect leadership?

8.6.3. CIA and scale: number of users

Research has often studied collaborative tasks with head-mounted displays or shared large displays, involving only two collaborators. In real-life applications, collaboration potentially involves larger team sizes. There is a compelling case to study the impact of using both HMDs and shared displays, such as walls and tabletops, with large groups in terms of situation awareness. In order to design and develop future techniques, systems and platforms that support immersive and collaborative analytics, it is crucial to study how different group sizes collaborate with visualizations. A possible (non-restricted) list of research questions related to group size, could be:

– How do collaborators locate each other's positions in collaborative virtual environments?

– How do collaborators share insights with others (either in virtual or collocated environments)?

– How do collaborators share/find each other's cues?

8.6.4. Distant Collaborative Immersive Analytics

Little research has been focused on remote collaboration using immersive display technologies. Some studies have been carried out in the scientific visualization domain [31] and the robotics domain [73]. Those studies often investigate the ability of users to perform their tasks in such environments, and often use artificial or abstract tasks such as puzzle solving. However, collaborative analytics requires a higher level of engagement from collaborators when analyzing and understanding data. The study of engagement of team members in remote, immersive and collaborative data analytics remains widely unexplored. To this regard, the following research questions should be investigated:

– Does immersive and collaborative analytics bridge the distance gap in remote collaboration scenarios?

– What is the impact of immersion in collaborative analytics quality?

– What is the effect of immersion on remote collaboration: engagement, group dynamics?

8.6.5. The design space of Immersive and Collaborative Analytics

Immersive display technology is very heterogeneous. It includes head-mounted displays, CAVE-style environments, wall-sized displays, tabletops, and multi-display environments. Those displays also vary widely in size, resolution, and modality of interaction. Choosing which technology is more appropriate for the given tasks and needs of analysts, and designing for them, is a challenge. There is a great opportunity for research to define the design space of collaborative immersive analytics in order to guide the design of immersive collaborative platforms. Moreover, we can envision situations where a mix of these technologies can come in play, for example a group of analysts working in a CAVE and a colleague connecting remotely using a HMD. Understanding how collaborative analysis is affected by analysts using asymmetric technology (in terms of awareness, deixis, group dynamics), and how to design for it, is an important research direction.

8.6.6. Asynchronous collaboration

Collaboration can occur asynchronously for various reasons: collaborators work in shifts, in different time zones, they have different schedules, etc. In this situation, users view, analyze and understand data at different moments in time. We can identify two roles:

– A "hand over" role: users who have finished working with the visualizations

– A "take over" role: users who come after the previous group to keep working with the data visualization.

It is important to understand what the users' needs in those two roles are and how immersion can be used to better support hand-overs.

On one end, immersive technology can help preparing high fidelity handovers to communicate the results of data analysis. There are various ways to create a handover for the next users. For example, motion-tracking technology can be used to record precise hand gestures and interactions with the visualizations, and stereo cameras can record a user's body and face. Such recording can be used to facilitate telling a story (Chapter 6) about the work done with the visualizations. However, telling a story is only one form of asynchronous collaboration handover. A group of users may require the help and draw the attention of another user or a group of users to examine a specific issue. On the other end, a user who enters a collaborative space needs to be updated with the situation. The tasks of this user can be to consult the handover, resolve issues, answer questions, provide input for a specific problem, etc. In the context of Collaborative Immersive Analytics, it is unclear which techniques are better suited for specific scenarios. Hence, there is a research opportunity to study how to convey the state of progress of collaborative visualization in immersive and asynchronous collaborative analytics.

8.6.7. Channels for collaboration

Collaboration between members of a team is supported by various channels of communication. Those channels include (but are not limited to) oral communication, gaze direction, deixis (e. g. pointing) or feedback from other members' actions. Since CIA can simultaneously occur across different types of immersive technology, it seems important to evaluate, according to the users' tasks, which are the essential channels to support efficient group work.

8.6.8. Evaluation of CIA systems

The evaluation of CIA systems, as with all collaborative visual analysis systems is a challenging matter, as it needs to consider both task-related and teamwork related aspects [56]. Because collaborative environments incorporate a large number of variables to consider, they are often evaluated through field and laboratory observation studies [56]. The variables to consider increase in immersive environments, as colleagues may have asymmetric collaboration, be joining the work with different immersive technology, making evaluation even more challenging. Recent years, have also seen an increase in controlled experiment evaluations in collaborative immersive environments (e. g, [79], [102], [20], [78]), where researchers try to tease out effects of particular factors, including immersive technology. For example, Cordeil *et al.* [28] compared CAVE environments to Head-mounted displays in a graph analysis task (Fig. 18,17). Clearly, it is a mix of

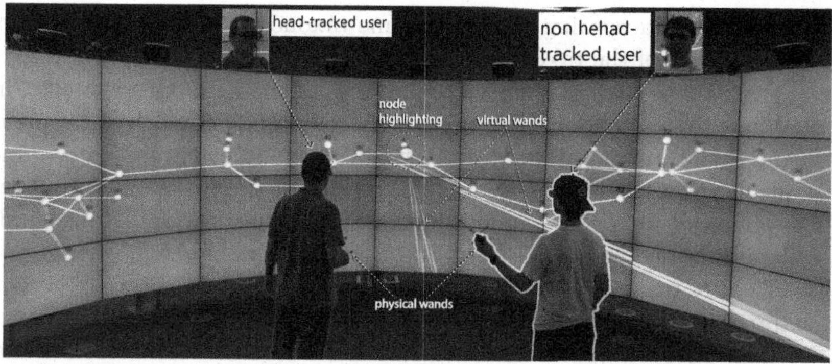

Fig. 17: Two users visualize a 3D network of abstract data in the CAVE2. The 3D immersive visualization can only be presented from the user wearing the head-tracker (left) [28] (used with permission).

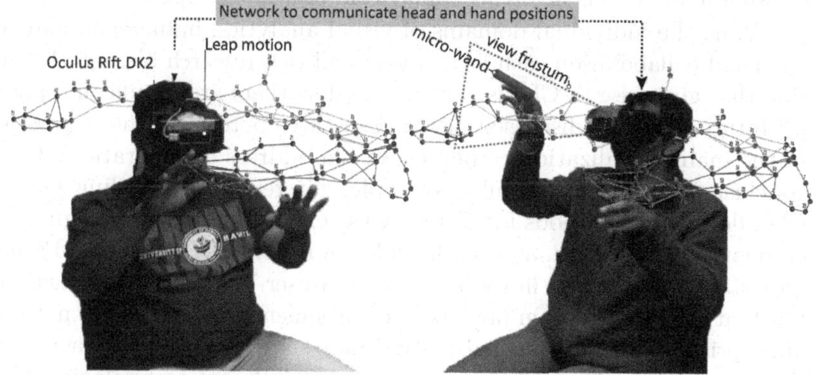

Fig. 18: Two users visualize a 3D network of abstract data in a network application with head-mounted displays. This platform allows independent head-tracking. Gaze cues and interactions are communicated on the network [28].

both open-ended and controlled evaluations that can provide practitioners with holistic insights. Hence, it is important to build evaluation frameworks for CIA, based on subjective, objective and collective measures to quantify the efficiency of collaboration. Such frameworks can certainly be built upon existing ones, for example ones coming from social presence [41].

8.7. Conclusion

This chapter introduced the concept of Collaborative Immersive Analytics (CIA), defined as the shared use of new immersive interaction and display technologies by more than one person, to support collaborative analytical reasoning and decision making. As shown in the introduction, CIA is at the intersection of the fields of Mixed Reality, Visual Analytics and CSCW and as such there are many technologies and approaches available for building CIA systems. These were classified according to a space-time taxonomy, and examples of systems in each quadrantof the taxonomy were provided.

From these examples we see some of the benefits of CIA systems, including enabling teams to work together, using emerging immersive technologies for intuitive data explorations, supporting multiple devices and tools, and seeing multiple representations of data. Perhaps most importantly CIA systems have the potential to enable teams to overcome the barriers of distance and time to collaborate together in the most effective way possible.

To fully realize this potential CIA systems must be carefully designed. The chapter covers the different roles collaborators have in such systems, such as viewing, interacting and sharing which should be accommodated in the system development. It also reviews the types of input modalities that could be used to design intuitive interaction. These include devices for capturing pointing and gestures, dedicated handheld devices, support for touch, and the use of collaborative actions involving input from multiple people.

While the individual domains of visual analytics, immersion, and computer mediated collaboration each have a long and rich research history, their combination that gives rise to CIA is very new and so there are significant opportunities for future work. As discussed, fewer than three percent of the papers published in the main visualization conferences even address collaboration. The chapter conclusion identifies a number of topics for research including using VR for CIA, developing methods for distant CIA, exploring the CIA design space, asynchronous collaboration, and methods for evaluating CIA systems. Perhaps most importantly is research in the area of multi-user interaction. Interaction modalities that may work well in immersive environments in general, are not necessarily appropriate for complex collaborative analysis work, that may last over several sessions, with participants connecting using different technologies. If and how technological asymmetry between colleagues can affect the quality of analysis work is still an open question.

Overall, Collaborative Immersive Analytics is an exciting new field with significant potential for improving how teams problem-solve, and presents many opportunities for ongoing research. CIA is at the same point that the field of visualization was at twenty years ago, and in the same way that visualization has become a key tool in the years since, we expect that CIA will dramatically change, and challenge, problem solving in the future.

References

1. Anslow, C.: Reflections on collaborative software visualization in co-located environments. In: IEEE International Conference on Software Maintenance and Evolution (ICSME). pp. 645–650. IEEE (2014)
2. Anwar, A., Klein, B., Berger, M., Arisona, S.M.: Value Lab Asia: A space for physical and virtual interdisciplinary research and collaboration. In: 19th International Conference on Information Visualisation (IV). pp. 348–353. IEEE (2015)
3. Arglasses(2016), http://arglassesguide.com/

4. Argelaguet Sanz, F., Andujar, C.: A survey of 3D object selection techniques for virtual environments. Computers and Graphics 37(3), 121–136(2013), https://hal.archives-ouvertes.fr/hal-00907787
5. Badam, S.K., Elmqvist, N.: Polychrome: A cross-device framework for collaborative web visualization. In: Proceedings of the Ninth ACM International Conference on Interactive Tabletops and Surfaces. pp. 109–118. ACM (2014)
6. Bai, H., Lee, G., Billinghurst, M.: Free-hand gesture interfaces for an augmented exhibition podium. In: Proceedings of the Annual Meeting of the Australian Special Interest Group for Computer Human Interaction. pp. 182–186. OzCHI '15, ACM, New York, NY, USA (2015)
7. Ballendat, T., Marquardt, N., Greenberg, S.: Proxemic interaction: Designing for a proximity and orientation-aware environment. In: ACM International Conference on Interactive Tabletops and Surfaces. pp. 121–130. ACM, New York, NY, USA (2010)
8. Belcher, D., Billinghurst, M., Hayes, S., Stiles, R.: Using augmented reality for visualizing complex graphs in three dimensions. In: Proceedings of the Second IEEE and ACM International Symposium on Mixed and Augmented Reality. pp. 84–93. IEEE (2003)
9. Benbunan-Fich, R., Hiltz, S.R., Turoff, M.: A comparative content analysis of face-to-face vs. asynchronous group decision making. Decision Support Systems 34(4), 457–469 (2003)
10. Benford, S., Fahlén, L.: A spatial model of interaction in large virtual environments. In: Proceedings of the Third Conference on European Conference on Computer-Supported Cooperative Work. pp. 109–124. ECSCW'93, Kluwer Academic Publishers, Norwell, MA, USA (1993)
11. Benko, H., Holz, C., Sinclair, M., Ofek, E.: NormalTouch and TextureTouch: High-fidelity 3D haptic shape rendering on handheld virtual reality controllers. In: Proceedings of the 29th Annual Symposium on User Interface Software and Technology. pp. 717–728. UIST '16, ACM, New York, NY, USA (2016)
12. Benko, H., Ishak, E.W., Feiner, S.: Collaborative mixed reality visualization of an archaeological excavation. In: Proceedings of the 3rd IEEE/ACM International Symposium on Mixed and Augmented Reality. pp. 132–140. IEEE Computer Society (2004)
13. Bezerianos, A., Isenberg, P.: Perception of visual variables on tiled wall-sized displays for information visualization applications. IEEE Transactions on Visualization and Computer Graphics 18(12), 2516–2525 (2012)
14. Bezerianos, A., Dragicevic, P., Balakrishnan, R.: Mnemonic rendering: An image-based approach for exposing hidden changes in dynamic displays. In: Proceedings of the 19th Annual ACM Symposium on User Interface Software and Technology. pp. 159–168. UIST '06, ACM, New York, NY, USA (2006)
15. Bowman, D.A., Wingrave, C.A.: Design and evaluation of menu systems for immersive virtual environments. In: Proceedings of the Virtual Reality 2001 Conference (VR'01). pp. 149–. VR '01, IEEE Computer Society (2001)
16. Bradel, L., Endert, A., Koch, K., Andrews, C., North, C.: Large high resolution displays for co-located collaborative sensemaking: Display usage and territoriality. International Journal of Human-Computer Studies 71(11), 1078–1088 (2013)
17. Card, S.K., Mackinlay, J.D., Shneiderman, B.: Readings in Information Visualization: Using Vision to Think. Morgan Kaufmann (1999)
18. Carpendale, S., Diakopoulos, N., Henry Riche, N., Hurter, C.: Data-Driven Storytelling. Dagstuhl Reports 6(2), 1–27(2016), https://hal-enac.archives-ouvertes.fr/hal-01348422

19. Carter, S., Mankoff, J., Goddi, P.: Building connections among loosely coupled groups: Hebb's rule at work. Computer Supported Cooperative Work (CSCW) 13(3-4), 305–327 (2004)
20. Chandler, T., Cordeil, M., Czauderna, T., Dwyer, T., Glowacki, J., Goncu, C., Klapperstueck, M., Klein, K., Marriott, K., Schreiber, F., et al.: Immersive analytics. In: Big Data Visual Analytics (BDVA), 2015. pp. 1–8. IEEE (2015)
21. Chen, W., Ladeveze, N., Clavel, C., Mestre, D., Bourdot, P.: User cohabitation in multi-stereoscopic immersive virtual environment for individual navigation tasks. In: 2015 IEEE Virtual Reality (VR). pp. 47–54 (2015)
22. Chen, Y., Alsakran, J., Barlowe, S., Yang, J., Zhao, Y.: Supporting effective common ground construction in asynchronous collaborative visual analytics. In: IEEE Conference on Visual Analytics Science and Technology (VAST). pp. 101–110. IEEE (2011)
23. Chung, H., North, C., Self, J.Z., Chu, S., Quek, F.: VisPorter: facilitating information sharing for collaborative sensemaking on multiple displays. Personal and Ubiquitous Computing 18(5), 1169–1186 (2014)
24. Churchill, E.F., Snowdon, D.N., Munro, A.J.: Collaborative virtual environments: digital places and spaces for interaction. Springer Science & Business Media (2012)
25. Clark, H.H., Brennan, S.E., et al.: Grounding in communication. Perspectives on Socially Shared Cognition 13(1991), 127–149 (1991)
26. Colaço, A., Kirmani, A., Yang, H.S., Gong, N.W., Schmandt, C., Goyal, V.K.: Mime: Compact, low power 3D gesture sensing for interaction with head mounted displays. In: Proceedings of the 26th Annual ACM Symposium on User Interface Software and Technology. pp. 227–236. UIST '13, ACM, New York, NY, USA (2013)
27. Cook, K.A., Thomas, J.J.: Illuminating the path: The research and development agenda for visual analytics. Tech. rep., Pacific Northwest National Laboratory (PNNL), Richland, WA (US) (2005)
28. Cordeil, M., Dwyer, T., Klein, K., Laha, B., Marriott, K., Thomas, B.H.: Immersive collaborative analysis of network connectivity: CAVE-style or head-mounted display? IEEE Transactions on Visualization and Computer Graphics 23(1), 441–450 (2017)
29. Craig, P., Huang, X., Chen, H., Wang, X., Zhang, S.: Pervasive information visualization: Toward an information visualization design methodology for multi-device co-located synchronous collaboration. In: IEEE International Conference on Computer and Information Technology; Ubiquitous Computing and Communications; Dependable, Autonomic and Secure Computing; Pervasive Intelligence and Computing (CIT/IUCC/DASC/PICOM). pp. 2232–2239. IEEE (2015)
30. Cruz-Neira, C., Sandin, D.J., DeFanti, T.A.: Surround-screen projection-based virtual reality: the design and implementation of the CAVE. In: Proceedings of the 20th Annual Conference on Computer Graphics and Interactive Techniques. pp. 135–142. ACM (1993)
31. Donalek, C., Djorgovski, S.G., Cioc, A., Wang, A., Zhang, J., Lawler, E., Yeh, S., Mahabal, A., Graham, M., Drake, A., et al.: Immersive and collaborative data visualization using virtual reality platforms. In: IEEE International Conference on Big Data (Big Data). pp. 609–614. IEEE (2014)
32. Dourish, P., Bellotti, V.: Awareness and coordination in shared workspaces. In: Proceedings of the 1992 ACM Conference on Computer-supported Cooperative Work. pp. 107–114. CSCW '92, ACM, New York, NY, USA(1992), http://doi.acm.org/10.1145/143457.143468

33. Edelson, D., Pea, R., Gomez, L., et al.: Constructivism in the collaboratory. Constructivist Learning Environments: Case Studies in Instructional Design 151 (1996)
34. Elias, M., Aufaure, M.A., Bezerianos, A.: Storytelling in visual analytics tools for business intelligence. In: IFIP Conference on Human-Computer Interaction. pp. 280–297. Springer (2013)
35. Ellis, S.E., Groth, D.P.: A collaborative annotation system for data visualization. In: Proceedings of the Working Conference on Advanced Visual Interfaces. pp. 411–414. ACM (2004)
36. Feiner, S., Macintyre, B., Höllerer, T.: A touring machine: Prototyping 3D mobile augmented reality systems for exploring the urban environment. In: Personal Technologies 1(4). pp. 74–81 (1997)
37. Flystick: http://www.ar-tracking.com/products/interaction/flystick2/ ([Online; accessed 05-Feb-2017])
38. Fraser, M., Benford, S., Hindmarsh, J., Heath, C.: Supporting awareness and interaction through collaborative virtual interfaces. In: Proceedings of the 12th Annual ACM Symposium on User Interface Software and Technology. pp. 27–36. UIST '99, ACM, New York, NY, USA (1999)
39. Gjerlufsen, T., Klokmose, C.N., Eagan, J., Pillias, C., Beaudouin-Lafon, M.: Shared substance: Developing flexible multi-surface applications. In: Proceedings of the SIGCHI Conference on Human Factors in Computing Systems. pp. 3383–3392. CHI '11, ACM, New York, NY, USA (2011)
40. Greenberg, S., Rounding, M.: The notification collage: posting information to public and personal displays. In: Proceedings of the SIGCHI Conference on Human Factors in Computing Systems. pp. 514–521. ACM (2001)
41. Gunawardena, C.N., Zittle, F.J.: Social presence as a predictor of satisfaction within a computer-mediated conferencing environment. American Journal of Distance Education 11(3), 8–26 (1997)
42. Gupta, K., Lee, G.A., Billinghurst, M.: Do you see what I see? the effect of gaze tracking on task space remote collaboration. IEEE Transactions on Visualization and Computer Graphics 22(11), 2413–2422 (2016)
43. Gutwin, C., Greenberg, S.: Design for individuals, design for groups: tradeoffs between power and workspace awareness. In: Proceedings of the 1998 ACM Conference on Computer Supported Cooperative Work. pp. 207–216. ACM (1998)
44. Gutwin, C., Greenberg, S.: A descriptive framework of workspace awareness for real-time groupware. Computer Supported Cooperative Work 11(3), 411–446 (2002)
45. Hackathorn, R., Margolis, T.: Immersive analytics: Building virtual data worlds for collaborative decision support. In: 2016 Workshop on Immersive Analytics (IA). pp. 44–47(March 2016) doi: 10.1109/IMMERSIVE.2016.7932382
46. Hauber, J., Regenbrecht, H., Billinghurst, M., Cockburn, A.: Spatiality in videoconferencing: trade-offs between efficiency and social presence. In: Proceedings of the 2006 20th Anniversary Conference on Computer Supported Cooperative Work. pp. 413–422. ACM (2006)
47. Heath, C., Luff, P.: Disembodied conduct: communication through video in a multi-media office environment. In: Proceedings of the SIGCHI Conference on Human Factors in Computing Systems. pp. 99–103. ACM (1991)
48. Heer, J., Agrawala, M.: Design considerations for collaborative visual analytics. Information Visualization 7(1), 49–62 (2008)
49. Heer, J., Viégas, F.B., Wattenberg, M.: Voyagers and voyeurs: supporting asynchronous collaborative information visualization. In: Proceedings of the SIGCHI Conference on Human Factors in Computing Systems. pp. 1029–1038. ACM (2007)

50. Hendrix, T.D., Cross II, J.H., Maghsoodloo, S., McKinney, M.L.: Do visualizations improve program comprehensibility? experiments with control structure diagrams for java. In: ACM SIGCSE Bulletin. vol. 32, pp. 382–386. ACM (2000)
51. Hill, G.W.: Group versus individual performance: Are N+ 1 heads better than one? Psychological Bulletin 91(3), 517 (1982)
52. Hiltz, S.R.: The virtual classroom: Learning without limits via computer networks. Intellect Books (1994)
53. Hutterer, P., Close, B.S., Thomas, B.H.: Supporting mixed presence groupware in tabletop applications. In: First IEEE International Workshop on Horizontal Interactive Human-Computer Systems (TableTop 2006). pp. 8–pp. IEEE (2006)
54. Imai, T., Johnson, A.E., Leigh, J., Pape, D.E., DeFanti, T.A.: The virtual mail system. In: Proceedings of IEEE Virtual Reality. p. 78. IEEE (1999)
55. Imai, T., Qiu, Z., Behara, S., Tachi, S., Aoyama, T., Johnson, A., Leigh, J.: Overcoming time-zone differences and time management problem with tele-immersion. In: The Proceedings of INET. pp. 18–21 (2000)
56. Isenberg, P., Bertini, E., Lam, H., Plaisant, C., Carpendale, S.: Empirical studies in information visualization: Seven scenarios. IEEE Transactions on Visualization & Computer Graphics 18, 1520–1536 (2012)
57. Isenberg, P., Bezerianos, A., Henry, N., Carpendale, S., Fekete, J.D.: CoCoNutTrix: Collaborative retrofitting for information visualization. IEEE Computer Graphics and Applications 29(5), 44–57(2009), https://hal.inria.fr/hal-00690020
58. Isenberg, P., Elmqvist, N., Scholtz, J., Cernea, D., Ma, K.L., Hagen, H.: Collaborative visualization: definition, challenges, and research agenda. Information Visualization 10(4), 310–326 (2011)
59. Isenberg, P., Fisher, D.: Collaborative brushing and linking for co-located visual analytics of document collections. In: Proceedings of the 11th Eurographics / IEEE - VGTC Conference on Visualization. pp. 1031–1038. EuroVis'09, The Eurographs Association & John Wiley & Sons, Ltd., Chichester, UK (2009)
60. Isenberg, P., Fisher, D., Ringel Morris, M., Inkpen, K., Czerwinski, M.: An exploratory study of co-located collaborative visual analytics around a tabletop display. In: Proceedings of Visual Analytics Science and Technology (VAST). pp. 179–186. IEEE, Salt Lake City, UT, United States(2010), https://hal.inria.fr/inria-00587236, received an honorable mention at VAST 2010
61. Ishii, H., Kobayashi, M., Arita, K.: Iterative design of seamless collaboration media. Communications of the ACM 37(8), 83–97 (1994)
62. Jakobsen, M.R., Hornbaek, K.: Up close and personal: Collaborative work on a high-resolution multitouch wall display. ACM Transactions on Computer-Human Interaction 21(2), 11:1–11:34 (2014)
63. Jakobsen, M.R., Sahlemariam Haile, Y., Knudsen, S., Hornbæk, K.: Information visualization and proxemics: Design opportunities and empirical findings. IEEE Transactions on Visualization and Computer Graphics 19(12), 2386–2395 (2013)
64. Jansen, Y., Dragicevic, P., Fekete, J.D.: Tangible remote controllers for wall-size displays. In: Proceedings of the SIGCHI Conference on Human Factors in Computing Systems. pp. 2865–2874. CHI '12, ACM, New York, NY, USA (2012)
65. Johansen, R.: Groupware: Computer support for business teams. The Free Press (1988)
66. Johnson, A., Leigh, J.: Tele-immersive collaboration in the CAVE research network. In: Collaborative Virtual Environments. pp. 225–243. Springer (2001)
67. Johnson, A., Roussos, M., Leigh, J., Vasilakis, C., Barnes, C., Moher, T.: The nice project: Learning together in a virtual world. In: Proceedings of the IEEE Virtual Reality Annual International Symposium. pp. 176–183. IEEE (1998)

68. Johnson, C.: Top scientific visualization research problems. IEEE Computer Graphics and Applications 24(4), 13–17 (2004)
69. Keates, S., Robinson, P.: The use of gestures in multimodal input. In: Proceedings of the Third International ACM Conference on Assistive Technologies. pp. 35–42. Assets '98, ACM, New York, NY, USA (1998)
70. Kim, K., Javed, W., Williams, C., Elmqvist, N., Irani, P.: Hugin: A framework for awareness and coordination in mixed-presence collaborative information visualization. In: ACM International Conference on Interactive Tabletops and Surfaces. pp. 231–240. ACM (2010)
71. Kinnect(2016), https://developer.microsoft.com/en-us/windows/kinect
72. Klapperstueck, M., Czauderna, T., Goncu, C., Glowacki, J., Dwyer, T., Schreiber, F., Marriott, K.: ContextuWall: Multi-site collaboration using display walls. Journal of Visual Languages and Computing 46, 35 – 42(2018) doi: 10.1016/j.jvlc.2017.10.002
73. Kratz, S., Ferriera, F.R.: Immersed remotely: Evaluating the use of head mounted devices for remote collaboration in robotic telepresence. In: 2016 25th IEEE International Symposium on Robot and Human Interactive Communication (RO-MAN). IEEE (aug 2016)
74. Leapmotion(2016), https://www.leapmotion.com/
75. Lee, B., Henry Riche, N., Isenberg, P., Carpendale, S.: More than telling a story: A closer look at the process of transforming data into visually shared stories. IEEE Computer Graphics and Applications 35(5), 84–90 (2015)
76. Leigh, J., Brown, M.D.: Cyber-commons: merging real and virtual worlds. Communications of the ACM 51(1), 82–85 (2008)
77. Leigh, J., Johnson, A.E., Brown, M., Sandin, D.J., DeFanti, T.A.: Visualization in teleimmersive environments. Computer 32(12), 66–73 (1999)
78. Liu, C., Chapuis, O., Beaudouin-Lafon, M., Lecolinet, E.: Shared interaction on a wall-sized display in a data manipulation task. In: Proceedings of the 34th International Conference on Human Factors in Computing Systems. pp. 2075–2086. CHI '16, ACM (2016)
79. Liu, C., Chapuis, O., Beaudouin-Lafon, M., Lecolinet, E.: CoReach: Cooperative gestures for data manipulation on wall-sized displays. In: ACM (ed.) Proceedings of the 35th International Conference on Human Factors in Computing Systems. CHI '17, Denver, United States(2017), https://hal.archives-ouvertes.fr/hal-01437091
80. Mahyar, N., Sarvghad, A., Tory, M.: Note-taking in co-located collaborative visual analytics: Analysis of an observational study. Information Visualization 11(3), 190–204 (2012)
81. Mahyar, N., Tory, M.: Supporting communication and coordination in collaborative sensemaking. IEEE Transactions on Visualization and Computer Graphics 20(12), 1633–1642 (2014)
82. Marai, G.E., Forbes, A.G., Johnson, A.: Interdisciplinary immersive analytics at the electronic visualization laboratory: Lessons learned and upcoming challenges (2018)
83. Mark, G., Carpenter, K., Kobsa, A.: Are there benefits in seeing double? A study of collaborative information visualization. In: CHI'03 Extended Abstracts on Human Factors in Computing Systems. pp. 840–841. ACM (2003)
84. McCarthy, J.F., Costa, T.J., Liongosari, E.S.: Unicast, outcast & groupcast: Three steps toward ubiquitous, peripheral displays. In: International Conference on Ubiquitous Computing. pp. 332–345. Springer (2001)

85. McGrath, W., Bowman, B., McCallum, D., Hincapié-Ramos, J.D., Elmqvist, N., Irani, P.: Branch-explore-merge: Facilitating real-time revision control in collaborative visual exploration. In: Proceedings of the 2012 ACM International Conference on Interactive Tabletops and Surfaces. pp. 235–244. ITS '12, ACM, New York, NY, USA (2012)
86. Milgram, P., Kishino, F.: A taxonomy of mixed reality visual displays. IEICE Transactions on Information and Systems 77(12), 1321–1329 (1994)
87. Millán, J.d.R.: Brain-computer interfaces. Tech. rep., The MIT Press (2002)
88. Moraes, A.C., Eler, D.M., Brega, J.R.: Collaborative information visualization using a multi-projection system and mobile devices. In: 18th International Conference on Information Visualisation (IV). pp. 71–77. IEEE (2014)
89. Morozov, M., Gerasimov, A., Fominykh, M.: vAcademia–educational virtual world with 3D recording. In: 2012 International Conference on Cyberworlds (CW). pp. 199–206. IEEE (2012)
90. Morris, M.R., Huang, A., Paepcke, A., Winograd, T.: Cooperative gestures: Multi-user gestural interactions for co-located groupware. In: Proceedings of the SIGCHI Conference on Human Factors in Computing Systems. pp. 1201–1210. CHI '06, ACM, New York, NY, USA (2006)
91. Morris, M.R., Lombardo, J., Wigdor, D.: Wesearch: Supporting collaborative search and sensemaking on a tabletop display. In: Proceedings of the 2010 ACM Conference on Computer Supported Cooperative Work. pp. 401–410. CSCW '10, ACM, New York, NY, USA (2010)
92. Nacenta, M.A., Sallam, S., Champoux, B., Subramanian, S., Gutwin, C.: Perspective Cursor: Perspective-based interaction for multi-display environments. In: Proceedings of the SIGCHI Conference on Human Factors in Computing Systems. pp. 289–298. CHI '06, ACM, New York, NY, USA (2006)
93. Nancel, M., Pietriga, E., Chapuis, O., Beaudouin-Lafon, M.: Mid-air pointing on ultra-walls. ACM Transactions on Computer-Human Interaction 22(5), 62 pages (2015)
94. Nassani, A., Bai, H., Lee, G., Billinghurst, M.: Tag It!: AR annotation using wearable sensors. In: SIGGRAPH Asia 2015 Mobile Graphics and Interactive Applications. pp. 12:1–12:4. SA '15, ACM, New York, NY, USA (2015)
95. Nature specials "big data" (2008)
96. Nguyen, T.T.H., Duval, T., Fleury, C.: Guiding Techniques for Collaborative Exploration in Multi-Scale Shared Virtual Environments. In: GRAPP International Conference on Computer Graphics Theory and Applications. pp. 327–336. Barcelona, Spain(2013), https://hal.archives-ouvertes.fr/hal-00755313
97. Olwal, A., Frykholm, O., Groth, K., Moll, J.: Design and evaluation of interaction technology for medical team meetings. In: Human-Computer Interaction – INTERACT 2011. pp. 505–522. Springer Berlin Heidelberg (2011)
98. Pauchet, A., Coldefy, F., Lefebvre, L., Picard, S., Bouguet, A., Perron, L., Guerin, J., Corvaisier, D., Collobert, M.: Mutual awareness in collocated and distant collaborative tasks using shared interfaces. Human-Computer Interaction–Interact 2007 pp. 59–73 (2007)
99. Poole, A., Ball, L.J.: Eye tracking in hci and usability research. Encyclopedia of Human Computer Interaction 1, 211–219 (2006)
100. Pousman, Z., Stasko, J.: A taxonomy of ambient information systems: four patterns of design. In: Proceedings of the Working Conference on Advanced Visual Interfaces. pp. 67–74. ACM (2006)

101. Prince, S., Cheok, A.D., Farbiz, F., Williamson, T., Johnson, N., Billinghurst, M., Kato, H.: 3DD Live: Real time interaction for mixed reality. In: Proceedings of the 2002 ACM Conference on Computer Supported Cooperative Work. pp. 364–371. CSCW '02, ACM, New York, NY, USA (2002)
102. Prouzeau, A., Bezerianos, A., Chapuis, O.: Evaluating multi-user selection for exploring graph topology on wall-displays. IEEE Transactions on Visualization and Computer Graphics p. 14 pages(2016), https://hal.archives-ouvertes.fr/hal-01348578
103. Regenbrecht, H., Haller, M., Hauber, J., Billinghurst, M.: Carpeno: interfacing remote collaborative virtual environments with table-top interaction. Virtual Reality 10(2), 95–107 (2006)
104. Rice, R.E.: Computer-mediated communication and organizational innovation. Journal of Communication 37(4), 65–94 (1987)
105. Robinson, A.C.: Collaborative synthesis of visual analytic results. In: 2008 IEEE Symposium on Visual Analytics Science and Technology. pp. 67–74 (2008)
106. Robinson, P., Tuddenham, P.: Distributed tabletops: Supporting remote and mixed-presence tabletop collaboration. In: Second Annual IEEE International Workshop on Horizontal Interactive Human-Computer Systems (TABLETOP'07). pp. 19–26. IEEE (2007)
107. Satyanarayan, A., Heer, J.: Authoring narrative visualizations with ellipsis. Computer Graphics Forum 33(3), 361–370 (2014)
108. Sawyer, S., Farber, J., Spillers, R.: Supporting the social processes of software development. Information Technology & People 10(1), 46–62 (1997)
109. Schmalstieg, D., Fuhrmann, A., Hesina, G., Szalavári, Z., Encarnaçao, L.M., Gervautz, M., Purgathofer, W.: The studierstube augmented reality project. Presence: Teleoperators and Virtual Environments 11(1), 33–54 (2002)
110. Seifert, J., Simeone, A., Schmidt, D., Holleis, P., Reinartz, C., Wagner, M., Gellersen, H., Rukzio, E.: Mobisurf: Improving co-located collaboration through integrating mobile devices and interactive surfaces. In: Proceedings of the 2012 ACM International Conference on Interactive Tabletops and Surfaces. pp. 51–60. ITS '12, ACM, New York, NY, USA (2012)
111. Shaffer, E., Reed, D.A., Whitmore, S., Schaeffer, B.: Virtue: Performance visualization of parallel and distributed applications. Computer 32(12), 44–51 (1999)
112. Shneiderman, B.: Direct manipulation: A step beyond programming languages. Computer 16(8), 57–69 (1983)
113. Skog, T., Ljungblad, S., Holmquist, L.E.: Between aesthetics and utility: designing ambient information visualizations. In: IEEE Symposium on Information Visualization (INFOVIS 2003). pp. 233–240. IEEE (2003)
114. Snowdon, D., Grasso, A.: Diffusing information in organizational settings: learning from experience. In: Proceedings of the SIGCHI Conference on Human Factors in Computing Systems. pp. 331–338. ACM (2002)
115. Soares, A.G.M., dos Santos, C.G.R., Mendonça, S.D.P., Carneiro, N.J.S., Miranda, B.P., de Araújo, T.D.O., de Freitas, A.A., de Morais, J.M., Meiguins, B.S.: A review of ways and strategies on how to collaborate in information visualization applications. In: 20th International Conference on Information Visualisation (IV). pp. 81–87. IEEE (2016)
116. Sole, D., Wilson, D.: Storytelling in organizations: The power and traps of using stories to share knowledge in organizations. LILA (2002)
117. g speak: http://www.oblong.com/g-speak ([Online; accessed 05-Feb-2017])

118. Stasko, J., Catrambone, R., Guzdial, M., McDonald, K.: An evaluation of space-filling information visualizations for depicting hierarchical structures. International Journal of Human-Computer Studies 53(5), 663–694 (2000)
119. Sun, G.D., Wu, Y.C., Liang, R.H., Liu, S.X.: A survey of visual analytics techniques and applications: State-of-the-art research and future challenges. Journal of Computer Science and Technology 28(5), 852–867 (2013)
120. Tang, A., Boyle, M., Greenberg, S.: Understanding and mitigating display and presence disparity in mixed presence groupware. Journal of Research and Practice in Information Technology 37(2), 193–210 (2005)
121. Tang, A., Neustaedter, C., Greenberg, S.: Videoarms: embodiments for mixed presence groupware. In: People and Computers XX—Engage, pp. 85–102. Springer (2007)
122. Tang, J.C., Minneman, S.: VideoWhiteboard: video shadows to support remote collaboration. In: Proceedings of the SIGCHI Conference on Human Factors in Computing Systems. pp. 315–322. ACM (1991)
123. Teasley, S., Covi, L., Krishnan, M.S., Olson, J.S.: How does radical collocation help a team succeed? In: Proceedings of the 2000 ACM Conference on Computer Supported Cooperative Work. pp. 339–346. ACM (2000)
124. Terrenghi, L., Quigley, A., Dix, A.: A taxonomy for and analysis of multi-person-display ecosystems. Personal and Ubiquitous Computing 13(8), 583 (2009)
125. Thomas, J.J.: Illuminating the path: the research and development agenda for visual analytics (2005)
126. Thomas, J.J., Cook, K.A.: A visual analytics agenda. IEEE Computer Graphics and Applications 26(1), 10–13 (2006)
127. Tsandilas, T., Bezerianos, A., Jacob, T.: SketchSliders: Sketching widgets for visual exploration on wall displays. In: Proceedings of the 33rd Annual ACM Conference on Human Factors in Computing Systems. pp. 3255–3264. CHI '15, ACM, New York, NY, USA (2015)
128. Tse, E., Greenberg, S., Shen, C., Forlines, C., Kodama, R.: Exploring true multi-user multimodal interaction over a digital table. In: Proceedings of the 7th ACM Conference on Designing Interactive Systems. pp. 109–118. DIS '08, ACM, New York, NY, USA (2008)
129. Turoff, M., Hiltz, S.R., Bahgat, A.N., Rana, A.R.: Distributed group support systems. MIS quarterly pp. 399–417 (1993)
130. Veerasamy, A., Belkin, N.J.: Evaluation of a tool for visualization of information retrieval results. In: Proceedings of the 19th Annual International ACM SIGIR conference on Research and Development in Information Retrieval. pp. 85–92. ACM (1996)
131. Viegas, F.B., Wattenberg, M.: Communication-minded visualization: A call to action. IBM Systems Journal 45(4), 801 (2006)
132. Viegas, F.B., Wattenberg, M., Van Ham, F., Kriss, J., McKeon, M.: Manyeyes: a site for visualization at internet scale. IEEE Transactions on Visualization and Computer Graphics 13(6) (2007)
133. Vogel, D., Balakrishnan, R.: Interactive public ambient displays: transitioning from implicit to explicit, public to personal, interaction with multiple users. In: Proceedings of the 17th Annual ACM Symposium on User Interface Software and Technology. pp. 137–146. ACM (2004)
134. Voida, S., Tobiasz, M., Stromer, J., Isenberg, P., Carpendale, S.: Getting practical with interactive tabletop displays: Designing for dense data, "fat fingers," diverse

interactions, and face-to-face collaboration. In: Proceedings of the ACM International Conference on Interactive Tabletops and Surfaces. pp. 109–116. ITS '09, ACM, New York, NY, USA (2009)

135. Ware, C., Franck, G.: Evaluating stereo and motion cues for visualizing information nets in three dimensions. ACM Transactions on Graphics (TOG) 15(2), 121–140 (1996)
136. Willett, W., Heer, J., Hellerstein, J., Agrawala, M.: CommentSpace: structured support for collaborative visual analysis. In: Proceedings of the SIGCHI conference on Human Factors in Computing Systems. pp. 3131–3140. ACM (2011)
137. Woolley, A.W., Chabris, C.F., Pentland, A., Hashmi, N., Malone, T.W.: Evidence for a collective intelligence factor in the performance of human groups. Science 330(6004), 686–688 (2010)
138. Yasojima, E.K.K., Meiguins, B.S., Meiguins, A.S.G.: Collaborative augmented reality application for information visualization support. In: 16th International Conference on Information Visualisation (IV). pp. 164–169. IEEE (2012)
139. Yoo, B., Han, J.J., Choi, C., Yi, K., Suh, S., Park, D., Kim, C.: 3D user interface combining gaze and hand gestures for large-scale display. In: CHI '10 Extended Abstracts on Human Factors in Computing Systems. pp. 3709–3714. CHI EA '10, ACM, New York, NY, USA (2010)
140. von Zadow, U., Büschel, W., Langner, R., Dachselt, R.: SleeD: Using a sleeve display to interact with touch-sensitive display walls. In: Proceedings of the Ninth ACM International Conference on Interactive Tabletops and Surfaces. pp. 129–138. ITS '14, ACM, New York, NY, USA (2014)
141. Zhao, J., Glueck, M., Isenberg, P., Chevalier, F., Khan, A.: Supporting Handoff in Asynchronous Collaborative Sensemaking Using Knowledge-Transfer Graphs. IEEE Transactions on Visualization and Computer Graphics 24(1), 340–350(2018), https://hal.inria.fr/hal-01565560
142. Zhu, H.: From WYSIWIS to WISINWIS: role-based collaboration. In: 2004 IEEE International Conference on Systems, Man and Cybernetics. vol. 6, pp. 5441–5446. IEEE (2004)
143. Zimmer, B., Kerren, A.: Ongrax: A web-based system for the collaborative visual analysis of graphs. Journal of Graph Algorithms and Applications 21(1), 5–27 (2017)

9. Just 5 Questions: Toward a Design Framework for Immersive Analytics

Kim Marriott[1], Jian Chen[2], Marcel Hlawatsch[3], Takayuki Itoh[4], Miguel A. Nacenta[5], Guido Reina[6], and Wolfgang Stuerzlinger[7]

[1] Monash University, Australia
Kim.Marriott@monash.edu
[2] Computer Science and Engineering, The Ohio State University, USA
chen.8028@osu.edu
[3] Visualization Research Center, University of Stuttgart (VISUS), Germany
Marcel.Hlawatsch@visus.uni-stuttgart.de
[4] Dept. of Information Sciences, Ochanomizu University, Japan
itot@is.ocha.ac.jp
[5] University of St Andrews, Scotland
mans@st-andrews.ac.uk
[6] Visualization Research Center, University of Stuttgart (VISUS), Germany
guido.reina@visus.uni-stuttgart.de
[7] School of Interactive Arts + Technology (SIAT), Simon Fraser University, Canada
w.s@sfu.ca

Abstract. We present an initial design framework for immersive analytics based on Brehmer and Munzner's "*W*hat-Why-How" data visualisation framework. We extend their framework to take into account *Who* are the people or teams of people who are going to use the system, and *Where* is the system to be used and what are the available devices and technology. In addition, the *How* component is extended to cater for collaboration, multisensory presentation, interaction with an underlying computational model, degree of fidelity and organisation of the workspace around the user. By doing so we provide a framework for understanding immersive analytics research and applications as well as clarifying how immersive analytics differs from traditional data visualisation and visual analytics.

Keywords: immersive analytics, visual analytics, data visualisation, information visualisation, design framework

9.1. Introduction

This chapter is a first step toward a design framework for Immersive Analytics (IA). Such a design framework is intended to serve two important purposes. The first is to provide methodological support for the development and evaluation of IA applications. The second is to provide a way of organising, understanding, and analysing IA research. In addition, such a framework should clarify how IA

K. Marriott et al. (Eds.): Immersive Analytics, LNCS 11190, pp. 259–288, 2018.
https://doi.org/10.1007/978-3-030-01388-2_9

differs from traditional data visualisation and visual analytics applications and research.

Our design framework brings together the various aspects of IA research explored in the previous chapters: use of spatial immersion, multisensory analytics, natural interaction, responsive human-in-the-loop analytics, situated analytics and collaboration. It is based upon Brehmer and Munzner's [4] well-known "*What-Why-How*" data visualisation framework. But we have extended this in three main ways.

First, to provide necessary contextual information about the intended IA applications we extend the framework with two additional questions:

- *Where* is the system to be used including on what kind of platform, and
- *Who* are the people or teams of people who are going to use the system?

Where allows us to take into account different interaction and display capabilities such as the degree of spatial immersion or world knowledge, i.e. knowledge of the physical environment, as well as the characteristics of the physical environment in which the application will be run. For instance, is the system to be used in a controlled environment like an office or in the field?

Who allows us to take into account different types of collaboration as well as user characteristics and needs. For instance, is the application to be used by a single analyst or a group of analysts, or is it designed to communicate data findings to the local community?

The second major modification is to the *How* component. We extend this by considering all sensory channels (not only vision), adding support for collaboration, including a representation of oneself and others (i. e.avatars), explicitly considering how to position views in the 3D environment around the user as well as the degree of representation fidelity.

The third modification is to broaden the *What-Why-How* framework to explicitly include the use of computer models so as to better capture all aspects of human-in-the-loop analytics. This includes machine-learning based data modelling and optimisation-based decision support in which interactive visualisation is used to understand and refine the computational model as well as to understand the original data. This adds other aspects to *What* and *How*: the kind of analytics provided, and the idioms used to build, use and understand the analytical model.

The resulting five question framework, *Where-What-Who-Why-How*, provides a rich multidimensional categorization for designing IA applications and understanding IA research. However, given the current immaturity of the field, the proposed framework should be viewed as a work in progress and will undoubtedly require refinement in light of future research.

In Section 9.2., we review previous design frameworks for data visualisation, scientific visualisation and visual analytics as well as the What-Why-How framework. We then sketch in Section 9.3. a high-level view of the major components and processes in an IA application. In Section 9.4., we present the five question design framework for IA. In Section 9.5. we show how the framework applies to six existing applications. Finally, in Section 9.6. we discuss some research questions and issues suggested by the framework including evaluation and conclude the Chapter in Section 9.7.

9.2. Design Frameworks for Data Visualisation & Visual Analytics

Data visualisation frameworks and taxonomies fall into a number of different categories. The first category focuses on the structure of the *visual representations* and how the underlying data is *mapped* to a visual representation. Starting with Bertin [3] these frameworks detail how low-level graphical primitives, with geometric and non-geometric visual attributes (such as colour), can be combined to create sophisticated data visualisations [31, 50]. Others detail useful mappings between different kinds of data and visual representation [6, 52].

The second kind of framework focuses on the user *tasks* and the purposes for which the visualisation is being used. The sense-making loop [39] captures the high-level process by which analysts make sense of data while the knowledge generation model [42] considers the processes used for human-in-the-loop knowledge discovery. Both are widely used in visual analytics. A related model, called the problem-solving loop, has been suggested for human-in-the-loop optimisation [30].

There has also been considerable attention focussed on developing lower-level task taxonomies for data visualisation and visual analytics [1,2,17,23,44,53] or for specific kinds of data [28]. Many of these also suggest appropriate visualisation and/or interaction idioms for the tasks. A framework emphasising cognitive aspects of data visualisation has also been proposed [36].

Another category of frameworks, called *pipelines*, emphasise computer and user processes [46]. Card *et al.*'s [7] well-known data visualisation pipeline has three main steps: structuring and filtering the raw data, mapping data onto visualisation primitives, and rendering of the visualisation. The knowledge discovery pipeline [47] captures the processes for human-in-the-loop generation of a computational model for the data. It consists of data integration, cleaning, warehousing and selection, data mining, pattern (model) evaluation and rendering of the visualisation.

More recently, Brehmer and Munzner [4] introduced the *What-Why-How* design framework for data visualisation. Refined and elaborated by Munzner [34], this is widely used in the data visualisation community. It combines the task-oriented and data-oriented frameworks, capturing that the choice of visual and interaction idioms depend upon both data and task. As its name suggests, it is built around three fundamental questions:

- *What* is the kind of data to be visualised?
- *Why* is the data being visualised–what task does the user wish to perform?
- *How* is the data visually represented and how should interaction with that representation work? That is, what data visualisation and interaction idioms should be employed?

A number of researchers have explored some of the issues arising in data visualisation applications that move beyond the traditional desktop, e.g. interaction [27], placement of 2D views [15] and data physicalisation [20, 51]. However, to the best of our knowledge there has been no previous attempt to develop a general design framework for analytic applications in immersive environments.

9.3. Architecture of IA Applications

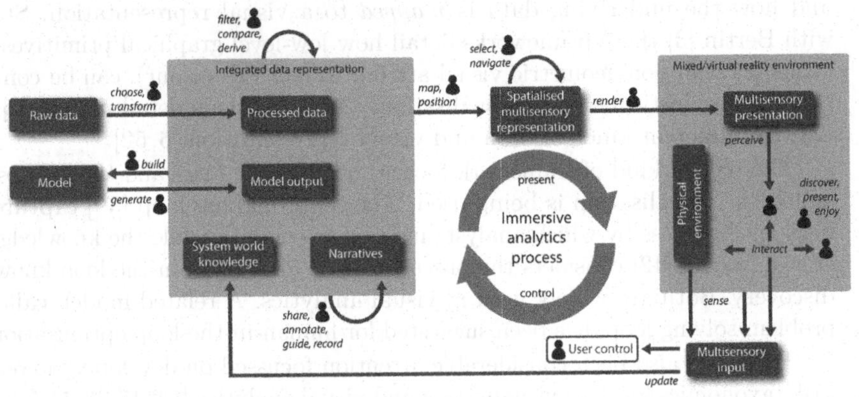

Fig. 1: Abstract architecture of an immersive analytics application that supports collaboration in a mixed-reality environment. Boxes represent data, while arrows indicate processing steps or interaction.

As a first step in developing a design framework for IA we sketch the abstract architecture of a generic IA application.[8] This is shown in Figure 1. Not all components would be needed in all IA applications.

At the highest level the immersive analytics process consists of a tightly coupled *presentation* and *control* loop that allows users to *discover* the answer to their question, *present* findings or simply *enjoy* exploring the data [4]. At the architecture's core is the data visualisation pipeline after Card *et al.* [7], generalised to *map* data to a multisensory representation whose elements are *positioned* in the mixed-reality environment. *Rendering* is generalised from simple visual rendering to include other modalities such as auralization, haptic presentation or data physicalisation. The user can *choose* and *transform* the raw data to create the processed data. They can *filter*, *compare* and *derive* new data from existing data, *navigate* through the multisensory presentation or *select* elements [17] as part of the analytics process [22]. The pipeline is further extended in five ways:

[8] The architecture is idealised and does not show how data and processes might be shared in a distributed setting.

1. In order to cater for mixed-reality presentations and data physicalisation, the physical environment is considered to be part of the presentation. Information about the physical environment—and the location and pose of users—is gathered through sensors and is part of the integrated data representation. It is termed *system world knowledge* [33].
2. Furthermore, interaction is now blended [14]. Users can interact with the IA application through conventional controllers like touchscreens or with voice commands. Alternatively, gestures, physical navigation in the environment or manipulation of objects in the environment can be sensed using appropriate devices and employed for user control in addition to updating the system world knowledge.
3. To more fully capture the importance of analytics, the pipeline now explicitly includes models. In the case of knowledge discovery this might be a new classification model learnt from the data or an existing model fitted to the data. In decision support this might be an instance of an optimisation model instantiated with the current data. Or in scientific modelling it might be the use of simulation to predict behaviour. The model is *built* from the data and used to *generate* trends, solutions, simulations, clusters or to test hypotheses [42].
4. Collaboration is a fundamental component of many immersive analytics applications. Users may be co-located in the same physical environment or work together remotely in a mixed-reality environment. Collaboration may be synchronous or asynchronous. Regardless, users experience a fused multisensory presentation and can interact with the immersive analytics application and with each other either directly or through the application.
5. Collaboration and provenance are supported by *narratives*. These are composed of *annotated* scenes or interactions, sequences of annotated views, text, etc., that are used to *record* a history of user actions. Users can communicate with collaborators and external stakeholders by *sharing* and *guiding* other users through these narratives [17, 40].

9.4. The 5 Question Design Framework for IA

We now describe how Brehmer and Munzner's *What-Why-How* framework can be extended to provide a design framework for immersive analytics applications. Table 1 summarises the extensions. In short we need to provide more contextual information about *who* the intended users of the application are and *where* and on what platform they intend to use it, as well as by extending the kinds of idioms considered in *how* to include spatial immersion, collaboration and multisensory presentation. We now look at these in more detail.

9.4.1. Where

In traditional data visualisation and visual analytics the default, often implicit, assumption is that data visualisation is taking place on the desktop and so details

What-Why-How Framework	**5 Question Framework**
	Where
	Presentation
	Interaction
	World Knowledge
	Environment
What	*What*
Dataset Types	Dataset Types
Tables, Networks, Fields, Geometry	Tables, Networks, Fields, Geometry, **Function**
Dataset Availability	**Dataset Generation**
	Who
	User
	Collaboration
Why	*Why*
High-level Tasks	High-level Tasks
Consume	Discover, Present, Enjoy
Discover, Present, Enjoy	
Produce	
Annotate, Record, Derive	
Medium-level Tasks	Medium-level Tasks
Search: Lookup, Locate, Browse, Explore	Search: Lookup, Locate, Browse, Explore
Query: Identify, Compare, Summarize/Overview	Query: Identify, Compare, Summarize/Overview
	Annotate, Record, **Share, Guide**
	Derive, **Build, Use**
How	*How*
Encode	Encode
Manipulate	Manipulate
Facet	Facet & **Position**
Reduce	Reduce
	Collaborate
	Render
	Model

Table 1: The *What-Why-How* data visualisation design framework and the proposed IA design framework. Extensions and modifications are shown in **bold**.

of the output and interaction devices can be ignored. In IA applications, however, platform capabilities significantly affect the design of the most appropriate analytics tool.

Presentation: Different output devices such as desktop, HMD-based VR, AR, smartphone, smartwatch, tablet, large-wall or tangible display have quite different resolutions, viewport sizes and capabilities. This large range of sizes and capabilities mean that there is no single best visual idiom and the choice will depend upon the output device. Furthermore, new output devices introduce new challenges that go well beyond traditional GUI design. Consider, for example, that a user standing close to the left side of a wall-sized touch display will not be able to directly see and/or interact with content that is shown on the other end of the wall [21, 35].

Moreover, as discussed in Chapter 2, these output devices differ in how well the display of 3D content is supported. For instance, the use of depth on a traditional desktop display may not be effective because of the limited depth cues but quite effective when using a desktop fish tank VR display or a modern head-mounted VR display because motion perspective and binocular disparity support better depth perception.

Finally, presentation is not limited to vision. Other modalities such as sound or touch may be provided in an immersive environment. Which modalities are provided and the capabilities of the presentation devices is also part of *Where* (see Chapter 3).

Interaction: Another component of *Where* are the interaction modalities provided by the system (e.g., natural language, touch, gesture and tangible controllers). It is important that the interaction modalities are suited to the environment and the user behavior. For example, in an AR setting in which the user can freely move around, mouse or keyboard input can be cumbersome and touch, gesture, or a laser pointer [37] may be more suitable (see Chapter 4, Section 4.5.).

World knowledge: Another important characteristic of an immersive platform is the extent of world knowledge the system has access to (see Milgram *et al.* [33]). System world knowledge requires the platform to have sensors that allow it to sense its physical environment—objects and their position, lighting, and the position of the user—as well as an internal model of the environment which abstracts and makes sense of the raw sensor data. The range of system world knowledge in IA systems goes from traditional data visualisation on a desktop computer in which the platform is oblivious to its physical environment, to AR platforms like the Microsoft HoloLens which provide a sophisticated model of the objects in the environment.

Environment: The final component of *Where* are the characteristics of the environment in which the application is to run. These include physical aspects like the level of ambient noise or light, as well as social aspects such as whether users expect to be frequently interrupted.

However, it is important to recognise that the ability to use other sensory modalities, interaction modalities or world knowledge does not necessarily mean that they should be used. The choice of whether to use these is part of the *How* aspect of the design framework.

9.4.2. What

The *What* component of Brehmer and Munzner's framework covers the type of the original data and pre-processing before visualisation. For an in-depth description of the data types, we refer the reader to Munzner [34] since this aspect is largely independent of whether the application is immersive or not.

We have added one new generic dataset type to the framework: *function*. In Munzner [34] only *explicit* data representations are considered. These provide a set of data samples to describe an object and use interpolation between the data samples to model continuous objects. For example, in a mesh, the object is specified using a set of vertices as well as a topology describing the interconnection of these vertices. Depending on the topology, samples at the vertices can then be interpolated appropriately across the resulting surface. However, in scientific computing applications, *implicit representations* that use an analytic description of the object, e.g., equations defining a surface, are also common. Implicit representations can be computed from terse parametric descriptions, a very simple example being spheres generated from just a radius and a position. These analytic descriptions have to be evaluated, i.e. sampled, at an adequate frequency to compute an appropriate (visual) appearance of the object. The *function* datatype captures the use of such implicit data representations.

The *What-Why-How* framework also considers *dataset availability*, i.e. whether a dataset is static or dynamic. We generalise this to consider interactive *generation* of data. As well as considering whether raw data is static or dynamic, *dataset generation* details data preprocessing and any underpinning analytics model, as well as the level of interaction supported.

Efficiency of data processing is a major concern for IA because of latency: delay in rerendering of the scene due to user interaction. Slow data processing can disrupt the user experience (and thus immersion) (also see Chapter 5). Efficiency depends upon how directly the data is mapped to its presentation, i.e., how much processing of the data is performed before it is mapped to the presentation channels. For example, multi-dimensional scaling or topological analysis methods like vector field topology require extensive processing of the data. Directness is a continuum, different methods require a different amount of data processing.

9.4.3. Who

In traditional data visualisation the diverse perceptual, cognitive and physical capabilities of the user population are rarely taken into account. A notable exception is colour blindness for which there exist colour blindness simulators and design guidelines. The default scenario also assumes a single user rather than a collaborative setting. These two aspects are considered explicitly in our framework.

User: In IA the use of non-visual presentation modalities and alternative input modes (e.g., gesture, touch and speech) results in a much wider range of user capabilities and preferences that need to be taken into account. While this means that it is now more likely that a particular user will be unable or prefer not to use some of these modalities, there is also the opportunity to improve access by providing alternative modalities. We also need to take into account cultural conventions, age, educational level and familiarity with immersive technology when developing personal analytic applications and narrative visualisations.

Collaboration: If the IA application is to be used collaboratively the tool must support this. Thus an important part of the design context is to answer the following questions. Is the tool to be used collaboratively? If so, how many people will be involved in the collaboration (a few or many hundreds)? Do they have different roles, and what does this entail? Are users collaborating locally or remotely? Are they collaborating synchronously or asynchronously? (see Chapter 8).

9.4.4. Why

Brehmer and Munzner [4] identified three high-level *consume* tasks of *discover*, *present* and *enjoy.* These respectively captured the use of data visualisation to discover new information, communicate findings and the casual use of data visualisation application for entertainment. We feel these also capture the high-level use of IA applications. In addition, Munzner [34] identified three high-level *produce* tasks–*annotate*, *record* and *derive.* These were distinguished from the *consume* tasks because they add information to the data store. We think this distinction between *consume* tasks and *produce* tasks is unhelpful since, in our opinion, the three *produce* tasks are instead medium-level tasks that are often subcomponents of the higher-level *consume* tasks.

We organised the medium-level tasks around three activities:

- **Traditional data visualisation:** Based on Brehmer and Munzner [4], we identify three kinds of tasks: *search* which captures looking-up an item, locating an item, browsing and exploring the dataset; *query* which identifies/details a single item, compares or summarises multiple items and *derive* which produces new data items from old data items by, for instance, changing type or by using arithmetic or statistical operations. *Search* and *query* encompass the slightly lower level tasks of filter, sort, select and navigate identified by Heer and Schniderman [17].
- **Model use:** Based on Sacha *et al.* [42], models have two associated activities [42]: *Build* the model by, for instance, learning it from the data or instantiating a predefined model with the data, and *use* the model to produce new data such as trend lines, clusters or solutions to an optimisation problem.[9]

[9] In the *What-Why-How* framework model use would be regarded as an example of *generating* new data. However, we feel that it is useful to distinguish between simple

- **Narratives:** Based on Heer and Schniderman [17] and Ragan *et al.* [40], we have four tasks associated with narratives: *annotate* visualisations to document/communicate findings, *record* narratives and history for provenance, review and sharing, *share* views, narratives and annotations for collaboration and communication, and *guide* users through analysis tasks or narratives.

9.4.5. How

A major modification to Brehmer and Munzner's framework is the need to generalise the *How* component. Munzner [34] divides *How* into four aspects. As shown in Table 1 we extend this classification by introducing *render*, *model* and *collaboration* aspects and adding view placement in the virtual world to *facet.*

- **Encode:** How data is mapped to visual and spatial variables as well as to other sensory channels in each view;
- **Facet and Position:** How different views are arranged and combined, and where they are placed in the immersive environment;
- **Render:** Degree of fidelity and choice of graphics rendering model;
- **Manipulate:** The choice of user interaction idioms for controlling data manipulation and presentation;
- **Reduce:** The different ways for aggregating and filtering data;
- **Collaborate:** Idioms for collaboration including construction of narratives and providence;
- **Model:** Idioms for building and using analytical models.

While we still feel this classification is useful, in immersive analytics the different aspects are not as clearly separated as they are in a desktop environment. For instance, with data physicalisation or blended situated analytics interfaces encoding and manipulation are closely linked because the same artefact is used for both data display and input.

Encode: Generating a view of the data requires the designer to map data dimensions to different *visual variables* (also called *visual channels*) in order to construct a visual idiom or metaphor. For example, one data dimension can be mapped to the height of a rectangle, another to its position in one dimension and a third to its colour, which results in a bar chart. The visual variables can be classified as spatial properties (position, size, orientation, aggregated shape—line, glyph, etc.), visual surface properties (hue, saturation, luminance, texture), and motion and blinking (motion pattern, velocity and timing, and direction) [48].

Traditional information visualisation eschews the use of the third dimension, depth. However, as discussed in Chapter 2 there are tasks (*Why*) for which the use of a third dimension in a view may in fact be beneficial, especially if the display platform provides head-tracked binocular presentation (*Where*). If depth

data transformations or computations such as subtracting two attributes to give a new attribute, and task involving true computational analytics.

is used as a visual variable then a key design decision is to choose which depth cues to use. When doing so it is important to take account of dependencies between depth cues [48].

Occlusion, the need for supporting viewer movement and/or navigation as well as challenges in precisely determining position and distances between points are potential disadvantages of using depth. Shadows, navigation grids, drop lines, transparency, use of orthogonal projection rather than linear perspective are techniques that may mitigate these disadvantages. Furthermore, the use of linked 3D and 2D representations allows both overview and fine-grained comparison and control [38]. Choosing which, if any, of these techniques to use is another design decision.

While vision will remain the most important and commonly used sensory channel for encoding data because of its high-bandwidth and low-level parallel processing, immersive environments offer the possibility to use non-visual variables to present data. There a number of good reasons for doing so. A number of studies suggest that multisensory feedback increases the feeling of spatial immersion [11, 18, 19, 41, 43] and both haptic and sound can be used to attract attention, with the advantage that sound can be used to direct attention to items which are out of view. There are also environments and users for which visual presentations are not suited. The choice of which other sensory channels to use and the choice of mapping is also part of the *encoding*–see Chapter 3.

Facet and Position: One of the most interesting research questions raised by immersive analytics is how to arrange multiple views and viewing canvases with respect to each other, with respect to the viewer, and with respect to objects in the physical environment (see Chapter 2). Only the first of these is considered in Brehmer and Munzner's framework since viewing canvases are implicitly assumed to be arranged on desktop display. Because of these other questions we prefer to call this aspect *Facet and Position* rather than simply *Facet*.

Arrangement of different viewing canvases is relatively simple in a full-screen representation on 2D output devices such as a standard monitor. If a window system is in use, visualisations can be stacked and occlude each other. Large, wall-sized displays expand the workspace of the user substantially. In an immersive VR environment the user can potentially place views anywhere in a virtual 3D room. As for visual analytics, view management algorithms such as grouping views and showing exploratory workflows might benefit IA interface design [29].

The widest range of options arises with the use of AR: a canvas can be embedded into the real world, it can be projected onto a real-world surface, it can be mixed into the real world without explicit delineation or it might be printed (in 2D or 3D) to become an object in the real world. In all cases, placement (position, orientation, scaling) can be arbitrarily controlled but should relate to the task at hand (not too small, not too far away from the user etc.). Placement is constrained by the environment: you may not wish to obscure some objects and there may be a semantic meaning if a canvas is close to a particular object in the environment. As discussed in Chapter 2, currently there is no standard metaphor for arranging views in mixed reality presentations: suggestions include 2D views [15,16], embodied 3D views [5,10] or blended views in which physical objects provide the view frame [14].

Another important question is the *viewer's relationship* to the view or viewing canvases. This includes the initial placement of the user. Is the user placed inside one of the views to give an egocentric view of the data or do they have an exocentric view of the data? Is the viewpoint chosen so as to minimise occlusion? Another question is the relative size of the user and the view. In a traditional desktop setting, when scaling a bar chart only the space on the screen is considered. In mixed reality, the size of the bar chart is likely to have more impact on the viewer's understanding of its importance. A bar chart as large as the viewer might provide a different impression to one the size of a book. More generally, arrangement of viewing canvases needs to take account the physical and cognitive costs of moving and/or navigating between the different canvases, see Chapter 4.

A further consideration is the degree to which the user's *situational awareness* is manipulated. Perception of the physical environment can be altered by the mixed-reality application. It might choose to hide or simplify/abstract certain aspects of the environment in order to reduce distraction to the user or to focus attention to task-relevant objects in the environment (e.g. a server rack with only the relevant machine visible or just the relevant network port etc.).

A final consideration is how to *link* elements in these different canvases. This might by brushing or using lines to connect them, e.g. [9].

Render: There are two fundamentally different *display methods* for rendering graphics. The object-space approach "draws" objects, usually geometry, onto the image plane using an explicit projection. The projected shape is computed and filled with the respective color values. Virtually all desktop information visualisation platforms use this approach. In immersive environments, however, it also common to use an image-space approach in which colour values of the image are obtained by computing the contribution of the objects to the corresponding image element. A common method is ray casting/tracing, where a ray is traced through virtual space and every time an object is hit, the respective contribution to the image is computed. While object-space methods are commonly used for explicitly represented objects/metaphors, image space approaches can easily be used with explicit and implicit representations (indirect ray-casting can be done per glyph [32]).

An overarching aspect to *How* in immersive analytics is the degree of *reproduction fidelity.* Even if some visual properties are not used as visual variables, they may be used to create more realistic visualisations and so increase spatial immersiveness. For example, a variety of textures might be provided even if they are not explicitly used to encode properties of the data. Different rendering methods provide differing degrees of realism, from more abstract display methods like wireframe rendering to photo-realistic output with global illumination effects like ray tracing and path tracing. More realistic rendering methods usually require more computation power and therefore their use is often limited because of this.

Reproduction fidelity is also linked to the use of other sensory channels and affordances for embodied interaction. The behaviour of virtual objects can be made consistent with the physical world in various degrees, usually via a simulation running in the background. Starting from complete disregard of natural laws, realism can be increased from rigid/soft collision to simulation of physico-chemical processes like combustion, though this obviously depends on the availability of computational power and suitable models. In principle, object properties like inertia, density, momentum or charge revealed through their behavior during interaction might be used as non-visual encodings of data attributes (see Chapter 3). However, care is needed as spatial immersion will probably be negatively affected if visual and non-visual variables are not in accord. For example, it would feel incongruous if a smaller object that appeared similar to a larger object had greater inertia than the larger object.

Manipulate: User control and interaction is at the heart of immersive analytics. Two interrelated aspects distinguish many IA applications from traditional visual analytics: interaction in 3D virtual environments rather than 2D, and the use of so-called natural interaction modalities such as gesture, speech or touch rather than mouse and keyboard. Importantly, interaction methods and modalities in IA need to take into account proximity to the display and the characteristics of human attention [27].

The traditional WIMP-based desktop environment has standard idioms for low-level data manipulation tasks. However, in IA manipulation tasks related to navigate, select, arrange, change, filter, aggregate, and control are still very much the focus for research, partially because of the ever growing variety of interaction devices (see Chapter 4). LaViola *et al.* [26] report an astonishing variety of 3D UI manipulation techniques. A basic goal has been the development of interaction techniques that are natural yet allow high-levels of user efficiency, effectiveness, and comfort while diminishing the impact from inherent human and hardware limitations. Interaction attributes, such as distance to the target, target scale, precision required, domain specificity, and number of targets, affect manipulation accuracy. There is also a close relationship between the input device and manipulation metaphors, e.g., the degrees of freedom in the manipulation, e.g., whether or not two-handed input is allowed. In general, techniques using smaller and faster muscle groups (e.g., fingers) support more precise manipulation than larger muscle groups (arm and torso).

The development of more effective low-level manipulation techniques and input devices will remain a focus of research in the VR community. This will fuel research in IA into the design and evaluation of higher-level interaction idioms that take advantage of these new techniques and devices as well as advances in other input modalities such as speech.

Another important focus of IA research will be the development of interfaces that provide physically embodied interactions and affordances [12] and support responsive, fluid interactions [13] that allow users to remained immersed in their task (see Chapter 4 for more detail).

Collaborate: Support for collaboration is an important component of many IA applications. As discussed more fully in Chapter 8 there are many facets to consider: types and roles of participants, management of private and shared views in synchronous collaboration, representation of self and remote participants, maintenance of group awareness and channels of communication in distributed synchronous collaboration, as well as communication channels and hand-over in asynchronous collaboration.

Collaboration may be with other analysts or with stakeholders. Regardless there is a need to communicate findings. Thus the choice of idioms for storytelling, i.e. the construction of narrative visualisations, and for analysis providence fall into this component of *How.* This includes mechanisms for annotation, recording and sharing as well as choice of narrative structure, rhetoric, transitions, etc.

Reduce: This aspect is unchanged from Munzner [34]. It covers idioms for reducing items and attributes by filtering or aggregation.

Model: Neither Brehmer and Munzner [4] or Munzner [34] explicitly consider idioms for building or generating results from any underlying analytics model. However, the choice of idioms for these tasks is an important component of many IA applications and is likely to significantly impact user engagement.

Creation and evaluation of a model necessitates finding information and supporting evidence, finding relations in the information, extracting meaning, schematizing that information and re-evaluation. IA systems can support such modelling by displaying relevant data/information, model output, the models themselves (if this makes sense) and the workflows used to construct them. New challenges arise around the creation, (potentially automatic) arrangement, representation, and the manipulation of models in an IA system. Such manipulation may require new interaction and visualisation idioms that allow users to refine a model by changing parameters or the model itself, to understand the appropriateness and fitness of a model, as well as to compare multiple alternative models.

Responsive algorithms with timely, clear, and easily understandable feedback are a necessity to support any modeling activity. Moreover, predictability and stability in response to user interaction is also important, as with any good user interface (see Chapter 5).

9.5. Using the Design Space Framework

In this section we look at six representative data analytics applications from the literature and analyse them in terms of the design framework we have discussed. These have been chosen to cover various aspects of IA including immersion in virtual-reality and mixed-reality, embodied interaction, responsive analytics, situated analytics and collaboration.

The first example, shown in Figure 2, is an example of a visualisation that is not designed to be immersive and one that is barely interactive: the only user

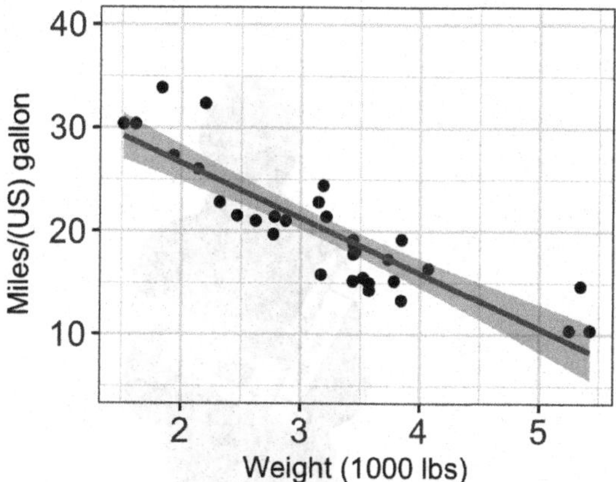

Fig. 2: Simple scatter plot and linear regression model with standard error created with R.

interaction is zooming and panning. It is intended to provide a benchmark for comparison with the following more immersive examples. It is a scatterplot, one of the most widely used visualisations for understanding multidimensional data, that has been created with R using ggplot2 [49] for display in a standard desktop environment. Linear regression has been used to fit a linear model to the data with an associated confidence interval.

The second example, shown in Figure 3, is also based on the scatterplot. However, it is designed to be much more immersive. It is a VR application for the HTC Vive HMD that allows the analyst to use the Vive controllers to interactively create, manipulate and position one-dimensional data axes and two- and three-dimensional scatter plots and scatter plot matrices (SPLOMs) in the space around the viewer [10]. Views are naturally built from the data axes in the virtual environment using embodied direct manipulation to move the axes into the requisite position to form the view. When two visualisations are close to one another data elements in the two views are linked by lines, allowing the user to dynamically create parallel coordinate plots and similar kinds of linked multivariate data visualisations. There is no underlying analytics but users can filter data and rescale the axes. Tables 2 and 3 show a detailed comparison between the first two examples in terms of our design framework.

Our third example is another VR application, this time for network data visualisation–see Figure 4 and Table 4. It is taken from Kwon *et al.* [24, 25]. This application introduces a spherical network layout designed to immersively display network data in a VR setting. The basic graph visualisation is a node link diagram. Clustering analysis is performed before layout and position and colour is used to show the clusters. Clustering is not interactive. Edge bundling is used to aggregate edges. The main novelty in this example is in the egocentric placement of the node-link diagram. It is arranged on a spherical layout around

Fig. 3: Creating a 2D scatter plot using the ImAxes VR visualisation application [10]. Image courtesy M. Cordeil.

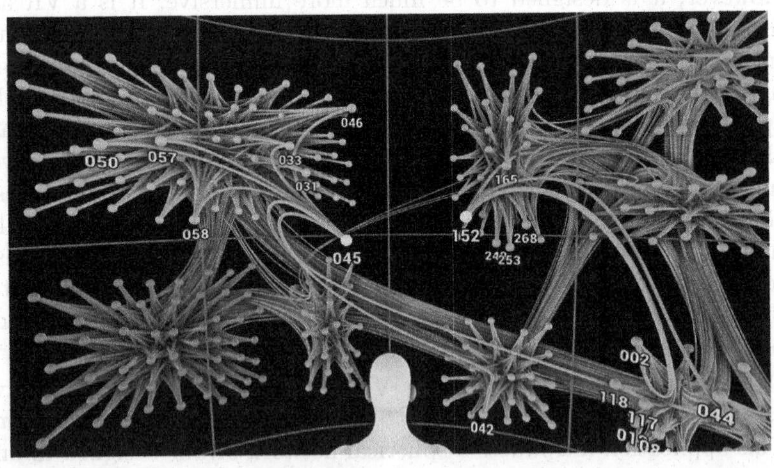

Fig. 4: Egocentric network data visualisation in VR from [24]. © 2016 IEEE. Reprinted, with permission, from [24].

Where	
Presentation	Standard monitor
Interaction	Mouse and keyboard
World knowledge	None
Environment	Controlled indoor
What	
Dataset types	Two-dimensional tabular data
Dataset generation	Static data; pre-computed linear regression + standard error; non-interactive analytics
Who	
User	Analyst; sighted
Collaboration	Single user
Why	
High-level tasks	Discover outliers, clusters, and trends
Medium-level tasks	Compare, summarize, lookup, browse
How	
Encode	Scatter plot (attributes mapped to position of points on a 2D plane), line showing regression model and polygon showing confidence interval; no use of 3D or depth cues; no use of non-visual variables
Manipulate	Standard mouse-based zooming and panning
Collaborate	Collaboration and narrative creation not supported
Facet & position	Standard 2D windowing; no situational awareness; exocentric view; monitor in front
Render	Explicit object-space; low reproduction fidelity
Reduce	No
Model	No interactive analytics

Table 2: Design analysis 1–Simple scatter plot with linear regression

the user, i.e., the user is surrounded by the graph. Since the visualisation shows abstract data, the visual representation is not aimed at realism and standard geometry rendering with some basic lighting is used. The paper provides no indication about collaborative scenarios. Interestingly, a user study [24] indicates that the user can perform certain tasks better with the spherical layout compared to a traditional 2D layout in the virtual environment suggesting that, at least for some tasks in VR, egocentric layouts may be preferable to more standard exocentric data visualisations.

Our next example is an interactive optimisation application for treatment planning in low-dosage rate prostrate brachytherapy [30]–see Figure 5 and Table 5. This is an example of an immersive analytics application that relies on sophisticated human-in-the-loop analytics. Optimisation is used to plan where

Where	
Presentation	HMD VR (HTC VIVE)
Interaction	VIVE controllers
World knowledge	Head and controller tracking
Environment	Controlled indoor
What	
Dataset types	Multi-dimensional tabular data
Dataset generation	Static data; no preprocessing or underlying analytics
Who	
User	Analyst; sighted, ambulatory and ability to use HMD and controllers
Collaboration	Single user
Why	
High-level tasks	Discover outliers, clusters, and trends
Medium-level tasks	Compare, summarize, lookup, browse
How	
Encode	2- or 3-D scatter plot or SPLOM (two or three attributes mapped to position of points on a 2D plane or 3D cube); standard head-tracked VR depth cues; no use of non-visual variables
Manipulate	Embodied direct manipulation for creation and placement of 2- or 3-D scatter plots and SPLOMs using controller buttons and controller tracking
Collaborate	Collaboration and narrative creation not supported
Facet & position	User-controlled placement in 3D space; no situational awareness; exocentric view of visualisations and egocentric arrangement of visualisations around user; elements in views are linked by lines when user moves two views close to one another
Render	Explicit object-space; medium reproduction fidelity
Reduce	Filtering
Model	No interactive analytics

Table 3: Design analysis 2–Multidimensional VR analytics tool (ImAxes).

to place radioactive seeds in the prostrate so as to irradiate the region where the tumour is likely to be but not overdose sensitive tissue such as the urethra or rectum. The tool allows the user to create a gallery of treatment plans using interactive optimisation and then choose the preferred treatment. It has three viewing modes. In presentation mode the user can see a treatment plan on a 3D view of the prostrate with linked 2D axial, sagittal and coronal slices. Volume

Where	
Presentation	HMD VR (Oculus Rift DK2)
Interaction	Mouse, head tracking
World knowledge	Head and controller tracking
Environment	Controlled indoor
What	
Dataset types	Network data
Dataset availability	Static data, precomputation of clusters
Who	
User	Analyst. Ability to use HMD, stereo and normal color perception required
Collaboration	Collaboration and narrative creation not supported
Why	
High-level tasks	Discover network connectivity and structure
Medium-level tasks	Browse, explore
How	
Encode	Node-link diagram representation laid out on the surface of a sphere, colour differentiates clusters; standard VR depth cues
Manipulate	Node hovering, node highlighting (propagating to edges), node selection
Collaborate	Collaboration and narrative creation not supported
Facet & position	Egocentric placement of sphere around seated viewer; no situational awareness; single view
Render	Explicit object-space; medium reproduction fidelity–lighting
Reduce	Edge bundling
Model	No interactive analytics

Table 4: Design analysis 3–Egocentric network data visualisation.

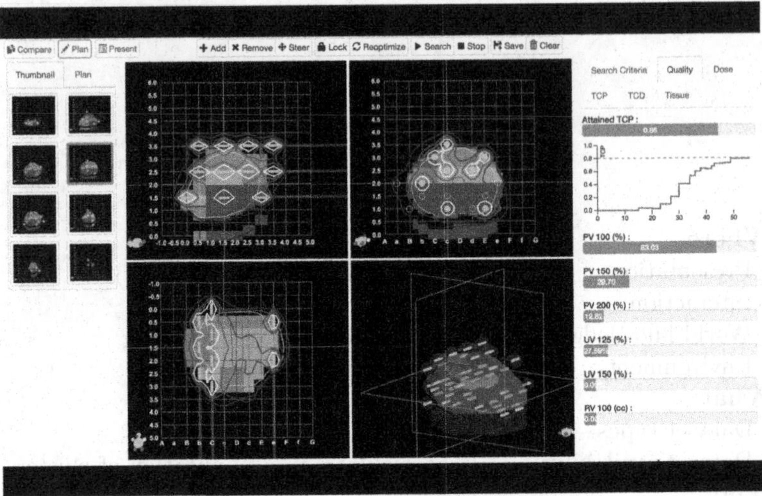

Fig. 5: Prostrate brachytherapy treatment planning with interactive optimisation [30].

rendering and contours, respectively, show the dosage, tumour cell density (TCD) or tumour control probability (TCP) in these 3D and 2D views. In addition summary statistics are shown in a bar chart. This example is interesting because of the idioms supporting responsive interactive optimisation. In planning mode the use can automatically generate a new treatment plan and then manually adjust the position of seeds, or re-optimise part of the plan, while in comparison mode the user can compare two treatment plans. The application runs on a standard desktop computer.

Our fifth example is an immersive visual analysis of spintronics (spin electronics) in quantum mechanics using a three-wall CAVE environment. It illustrates immersive co-located collaborative data analysis. Interactions of atoms in quantum mechanics are extremely complex. Their analysis relies on computer simulations recording electron spin, a vector with magnitude (charge density) and orientation at each sampling site. Quantum physicists are interested in how the electrons interact with magnetic fields or other electrons with spin. Figure 6 shows the display of a quantum simulation dataset of 255,772 spins in a CAVE immersive environment. Large spin magnitude variations can be queried on demand using either information-rich virtual environments [8] or SplitVectors glyphs [54, 55]. In analyzing quantum physics simulation results, physicists can extract scientific insights about their data by: a) using visualisation to understanding the large scale (global overview using the results of the entire simulation); b) interactively querying the data to identify clusters or topological structures satisfying criteria such as an equation for symmetry in order to build a qualitative understanding of pattern distributions (e.g., magnitude and orientation distribution and changes, symmetry structures, magnitude and orientation); c) visually comparing the

Where	
Presentation	Standard monitor
Interaction	Mouse and keyboard
World knowledge	None
Environment	Controlled indoor
What	
Dataset types	3D spatial and field
Dataset generation	Input data are tumour cell density (TCD), prostrate and other organ volumes; optimisation computes seed placement, dosage and tumour control probability (TCP); optimisation is interactive
Who	
User	Brachytherapy treatment planner; sighted.
Collaboration	No (though plans may be reviewed and revised collaboratively)
Why	
High-level tasks	Discover treatment plan
Medium-level tasks	Use optimisation model to create plans, compare plans
How	
Encode	3D volume rendering, 2D projections with derived contours; 2D bar and line charts; no use of non-visual variables; standard desktop monitor depth cues
Manipulate	Mouse-controlled cutting plane manipulation and rotation of 3D view
Collaborate	Collaboration and narrative creation not supported
Facet & position	Standard 2D windowing; no situational awareness; exocentric view; linked 3D/2D views
Render	Explicit object-space; low reproduction fidelity
Reduce	Thumbnail view of treatment plans in gallery
Model	User computes gallery of treatment plans; can modify optimisation goal function; manipulate solution; re-optimise part of solution

Table 5: Design analysis 4–Prostrate brachytherapy treatment planning

differences between or within datasets to understand extremes, ratios, and value distributions in selected regions. The CAVE environment allows small groups of physicists to stand together to view and discuss the visualisations on the walls of the CAVE. A disadvantage is that only one user is head-tracked so the other participants' binocular presentation is distorted if they are not standing close together. Quantum physicists have commented that using a CAVE environment

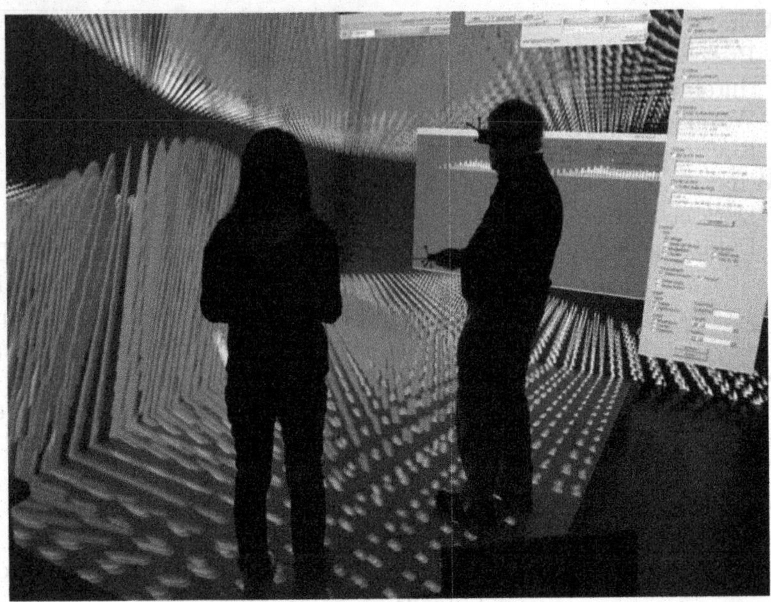

Fig. 6: Immersive visual analysis of quantum physics simulation in the CAVE at NIST using the encoding methods in Zhao *et al.* [54] and Zhao and Chen [55].

lets them detect spatial pattern changes more effectively than is possible in a desktop environment.

Our final example is an AR tool for environmental monitoring [45]–see Figure 7 and Table 7. This is an example of immersive *in situ* analytics, i.e. situated analytics. The AR tool is part of a larger application that allows environmental engineers and scientists, engineers and builders working for regional authorities and private companies as well as specialists such as hydrographers to develop a shared understanding of particular environments, and to develop and discuss potential solutions to environmental issues. The complete application runs on a combination of mainframes, laptops and mobile tablet PCs.

Here we focus on the mobile tablet tool for visualising sensor data in the field. The tool allows data to be overlaid on top of the environment viewed through the tablet. The environment can be shown at different levels of abstraction, while the sensor data can be compared with simulations that have been precomputed on the mainframe. Since a small mobile device is used, only a small part of the environment is augmented. Different types of visual representations are used: visual markers for sensor positions, text boxes for sensor information, line and color plots for sensor data. Some of them are just blended into the video view, others are mapped onto the surface of the environment, e.g., a temperature visualisation based on colour mapping. The visualisations are not aimed at realism; a rather abstract representation of the data is used.

Where	
Presentation	CAVE (three-wall); stereoscopic projected display
Interaction	Wand for hand-tracking, head-tracking, keyboard input
World knowledge	Head and hand tracking
Environment	Controlled indoor low-light
What	
Dataset types	Raw spintronics vector data
Dataset generation	Pre-computation of data using computer simulation; interactive computation of topology (contours), symmetry, groups, and clusters
Who	
User	Physicists (domain experts); sighted, ambulatory and ability to use wand and keyboard
Collaboration	Co-located collaboration by small groups
Why	
High-level tasks	Discover unknown/disjoint spatial structures
Medium-level tasks	Derive, query, search
How	
Encode	3D vectors (raw, derived contours); 2D projections; standard head-tracked VR depth cues;
Manipulate	Standard navigation–details-on-demand, drill down, cutting planes
Collaborate	Shared view in same physical workspace; direct communication through speech and gesture
Facet & position	Egocentric and exocentric view; egocentric placement of view around viewers; multiple views arranged using standard windowing system
Render	Explicit world-space; medium reproduction fidelity–lighting
Reduce	Regions of interest selection; feature selection; filtering
Model	Interactive clustering, group and feature identification.

Table 6: Design analysis 5–Immersive visual analysis of quantum physics simulation in a CAVE

The AR tool is designed to support distributed collaboration. This is between users on-site as well as between on-site and off-site users. A shared view service and voice communication supports synchronous collaboration while geo-referenced annotations support construction of narratives for asynchronous collaboration.

This last example highlights the importance of considering the working environment and platform when developing immersive analytics applications

Fig. 7: Environmental monitoring in the field with AR [45]. Reprinted by permission from Springer Nature: Personal and Ubiquitous Computing [45], COPYRIGHT 2012.

as mobile hardware like tablets typically have limited computational power and relatively small display size. Furthermore, because of the remote location and possibly hostile weather conditions, network connectivity and equipment robustness as well as the ability to use the equipment while wearing gloves were important design considerations.

9.6. Research Questions and Issues

This chapter suggests a number of research directions. The most obvious is to refine the design framework as we learn from future successful (and unsuccessful) IA applications. As part of this we need to develop evidence-based design rules and a portfolio of idioms to help designers answer the various aspects of *How*. We particularly need guidelines and successful idioms for interaction, workspace arrangement and collaboration in mixed-reality environments, design of multi-modal presentations, and integration of different kinds of analytics into responsive interactive analysis tools.

A second fundamental research question is how do we *evaluate* and *validate* the design of an IA application. Immersive analytics brings together the virtual reality, data visualisation and visual analytics communities. Each field has developed its own evaluation methods, all of which are relevant to immersive analytics. All fields heavily rely on controlled user studies to evaluate task performance (speed, errors and accuracy) as well as user preferences. Virtual reality researchers have developed methods to evaluate spatial and social presence (the degree of spatial and social immersion) (see Chapter 1) and investigate how immersive technologies affect this. Data visualisation and visual analytics consider scalability and expressiveness of visual representations and scalability and responsiveness of algorithms. Both make use of ethnographic methods such as contextual inquiry to better understand the application domain. Visual analytics, in particular, employs in-the-wild studies, smaller focussed studies using domain experts and participative use-driven evaluation. For immersive analytics to succeed, we believe that researchers will need to demonstrate through such in-the-wild studies that the adoption of immersive analytics solutions can increase productivity, improve team collaboration and reduce costs in real-world applications. What is missing are ways to measure user engagement, emotional response and psychological immersion. Furthermore, while some data visualisation researchers have investigated memorability and learnability (accessibility, naturalness, discoverability and affordances) this is uncommon. Development of standard measures and techniques for measuring all of these different aspects is an important research direction.

Where	
Presentation	Mobile tablet
Interaction	Touch screen
World knowledge	Positions and object types from GPS, user tracking, geo-referenced data
Environment	Uncontrolled outdoors
What	
Dataset types	Spatially embedded sensor data; plans, maps & 3D data
Dataset generation	Sensor data is dynamic; statistical analysis, simulation data pre-computed
Who	
User	On-site environmental scientist, engineers etc; Ambulatory, sighted.
Collaboration	Synchronous and asynchronous distributed collaboration
Why	
High-level tasks	Discover patterns in environmental data; discover and evaluate solutions to environmental issues
Medium-level tasks	Search, compare, annotate, share, guide
How	
Encode	Digital overlays of 1/2/3D data visualisations on the environment
Manipulate	Typical navigation idioms
Collaborate	Voice communication, position and view sharing, graphics, text and voice annotation
Facet & position	Geo-referenced overlays as well as standard window manager
Render	Explicit object-space
Reduce	Filtering, aggregation
Model	Not applicable in AR tool as simulations may take many hours and are run off-line

Table 7: Design Analysis 6: AR Environmental Monitoring Tool

A third class of research questions relate to broader ergonomic, health and societal concerns. We know that virtual reality environments can lead to motion-sickness and fatigue. What are the possible health risks of long term use of mixed mode and virtual reality environments? Do we need to develop guidelines for ethical design of user studies so as to mitigate these risks? What are appropriate ergonomic standards for the workplace? How do people outside a virtual world communicate or interrupt someone who is in a virtual world? E.g., imagine you are wearing your HMD performing some data exploration in a virtual world and your colleague wants to notify you that you have a guest. What are the societal benefits and disadvantages of immersive telepresence and remote working/home office scenarios? We have already seen concerns about mixed-reality HMDs being used to record events without permission. What level of real-time analysis of the objects and people in your environment with results displayed in your head-mounted mixed reality display is permissible?

9.7. Conclusion

We have presented an design framework for immersive analytics based around five questions, *Where-What-Who-Why-How*, that extends Brehmer and Munzner's well known *What-Why-How* design framework for data visualisation. It extends the framework by considering the context in which the analysis is taking part: *Where* takes into account the capabilities of the immersive analytics platform and the type of physical environment, while *Who* takes into account the number of users and their characteristics and needs. The *How* component is also more complex in immersive analytics because it may include the use of non-visual representations, collaboration, 3D arrangement of views in the user's environment and the use of analytics for data modelling and decision support.

We believe the design framework provides a good basis for designing IA applications as well as suggesting directions for further research. However, given the current immaturity of the field, the proposed framework should be viewed as a work in progress and further development of the design framework is also, we believe, an important topic for future immersive analytics research.

Acknowledgements

Marriott acknowledges support by the Australian Research Council Discovery Scheme, project DP180100755.

References

1. Amar, R., Eagan, J., Stasko, J.: Low-level components of analytic activity in information visualization. In: Information Visualization, 2005. INFOVIS 2005. IEEE Symposium on. pp. 111–117. IEEE (2005)
2. Andrienko, N., Andrienko, G.: Exploratory analysis of spatial and temporal data: a systematic approach. Springer Science & Business Media (2006)

3. Bertin, J.: Semiology of graphics: diagrams, networks, maps. University of Wisconsin Press (1983)
4. Brehmer, M., Munzner, T.: A multi-level typology of abstract visualization tasks. IEEE Transactions on Visualization and Computer Graphics 19(12), 2376–2385 (2013)
5. Butscher, S., Hubenschmid, S., Müller, J., Fuchs, J., Reiterer, H.: Clusters, trends, and outliers: How immersive technologies can facilitate the collaborative analysis of multidimensional data. In: Proceedings SIGCHI Conference on Human Factors in Computing Systems. pp. 90:1–90:12 (2018)
6. Card, S.K., Mackinlay, J.: The structure of the information visualization design space. In: Proceedings of the IEEE Symposium on Information Visualization. pp. 92–99. IEEE (1997)
7. Card, S.K., Mackinlay, J.D., Shneiderman, B.: Readings in information visualization: using vision to think. Morgan Kaufmann (1999)
8. Chen, J., Pyla, P.S., Bowman, D.A.: Testbed evaluation of navigation and text display techniques in an information-rich virtual environment. In: Proceeedings of IEEE Virtual Reality. pp. 181–289. IEEE(2004) doi: 10.1109/VR.2004.1310072
9. Collins, C., Carpendale, S.: VisLink: Revealing relationships amongst visualizations. IEEE Transactions on Visualization and Computer Graphics 13(6), 1192–1199 (2007)
10. Cordeil, M., Cunningham, A., Dwyer, T., Thomas, B.H., Marriott, K.: ImAxes: Immersive axes as embodied affordances for interactive multivariate data visualisation. In: Proceedings of the 30th Annual ACM Symposium on User Interface Software and Technology. pp. 71–83. ACM (2017)
11. Dinh, H.Q., Walker, N., Hodges, L.F., Song, C., Kobayashi, A.: Evaluating the importance of multi-sensory input on memory and the sense of presence in virtual environments. In: Proceedings IEEE Virtual Reality. pp. 222–228 (1999)
12. Dourish, P.: Where the Action Is: The Foundations of Embodied Interaction. MIT Press (2001)
13. Elmqvist, N., Vande Moere, A., Jetter, H.C., Cernea, D., Reiterer, H., Jankun-Kelly, T.J.: Fluid interaction for information visualization. Information Visualization 10(4), 327–340(Oct 2011) doi: 10.1177/1473871611413180
14. ElSayed, N.A., Smith, R.T., Marriott, K., Thomas, B.H.: Context-aware design pattern for situated analytics: Blended model view controller. Journal of Visual Languages & Computing 44 (2018)
15. Ens, B., Hincapié-Ramos, J.D., Irani, P.: Ethereal planes: a design framework for 2D information space in 3D mixed reality environments. In: Proceedings of the 2nd ACM Symposium on Spatial User Interaction. pp. 2–12. ACM (2014)
16. Feiner, S., MacIntyre, B., Haupt, M., Solomon, E.: Windows on the world: 2D windows for 3D augmented reality. In: Proceedings of the 6th Annual ACM Symposium on User Interface Software and Technology. pp. 145–155. ACM (1993)
17. Heer, J., Shneiderman, B.: Interactive dynamics for visual analysis. Queue 10(2), 30 (2012)
18. Hoffman, H.G.: Physically touching virtual objects using tactile augmentation enhances the realism of virtual environments. In: Proceedings. IEEE 1998 Virtual Reality Annual International Symposium. pp. 59–63 (1998)
19. Hoffman, H.G., Hollander, A., Schroder, K., Rousseau, S., Furness, T.: Physically touching and tasting virtual objects enhances the realism of virtual experiences. Virtual Reality 3(4), 226–234 (1998)

20. Jansen, Y., Dragicevic, P.: An interaction model for visualizations beyond the desktop. IEEE Transactions on Visualization and Computer Graphics 19(12), 2396–2405 (2013)
21. Jota, R., Nacenta, M.A., Jorge, J.A., Carpendale, S., Greenberg, S.: A comparison of ray pointing techniques for very large displays. In: Proceedings of Graphics Interface 2010. pp. 269–276. Canadian Information Processing Society (2010)
22. Keim, D., Kohlhammer, J., Ellis, G. (eds.): Mastering the Information Age: Solving Problems with Visual Analytics. Eurographics Association (2010)
23. Keller, P.R., Keller, M.M.: Visual Cues: Practical Data Visualization. IEEE Press (1993)
24. Kwon, O.H., Muelder, C., Lee, K., Ma, K.L.: A study of layout, rendering, and interaction methods for immersive graph visualization. IEEE Transactions on Visualization and Computer Graphics 22(7), 1802–1815(July 2016) doi: 10.1109/TVCG.2016.2520921
25. Kwon, O.H., Muelder, C., Lee, K., Ma, K.L.: Spherical layout and rendering methods for immersive graph visualization. In: 2015 IEEE Pacific Visualization Symposium (PacificVis). pp. 63–67(April 2015) doi: 10.1109PACIFICVIS.2015.7156357
26. LaViola Jr, J.J., Kruijff, E., McMahan, R.P., Bowman, D., Poupyrev, I.P.: 3D User Interfaces: Theory and Practice. Addison-Wesley Professional (2017)
27. Lee, B., Isenberg, P., Riche, N.H., Carpendale, S.: Beyond mouse and keyboard: Expanding design considerations for information visualization interactions. IEEE Transactions on Visualization and Computer Graphics 18(12), 2689–2698 (2012)
28. Lee, B., Plaisant, C., Parr, C.S., Fekete, J.D., Henry, N.: Task taxonomy for graph visualization. In: Proceedings of the 2006 AVI Workshop on Beyond Time and Errors: Novel Evaluation Methods for Information Visualization. pp. 1–5. ACM (2006)
29. Li, G., Bragdon, A.C., Pan, Z., Zhang, M., Swartz, S.M., Laidlaw, D.H., Zhang, C., Liu, H., Chen, J.: VisBubbles: a workflow-driven framework for scientific data analysis of time-varying biological datasets. In: SIGGRAPH Asia 2011 Posters. p. 27. ACM (2011)
30. Liu, J., Dwyer, T., Marriott, K., Millar, J., Haworth, A.: Understanding the relationship between interactive optimisation and visual analytics in the context of prostate brachytherapy. IEEE Transactions on Visualization and Computer Graphics 24(1), 319–329 (2018)
31. Mackinlay, J.: Automating the design of graphical presentations of relational information. ACM Transactions On Graphics (ToG) 5(2), 110–141 (1986)
32. McDonnel, B., Elmqvist, N.: Towards utilizing GPUs in information visualization: A model and implementation of image-space operations. IEEE Transactions on Visualization and Computer Graphics 15(6), 1105–1112(2009) doi: 10.1109/TVCG.2009.191
33. Milgram, P., Takemura, H., Utsumi, A., Kishino, F.: Augmented reality: a class of displays on the reality-virtuality continuum. Proc. SPIE 2351, 282–292 (1995)
34. Munzner, T.: Visualization Analysis and Design. CRC Press (2014)
35. Nacenta, M.A., Sakurai, S., Yamaguchi, T., Miki, Y., Itoh, Y., Kitamura, Y., Subramanian, S., Gutwin, C.: E-conic: a perspective-aware interface for multi-display environments. In: Proceedings of the 20th Annual ACM Symposium on User Interface Software and Technology. pp. 279–288. ACM (2007)
36. Patterson, R.E., Blaha, L.M., Grinstein, G.G., Liggett, K.K., Kaveney, D.E., Sheldon, K.C., Havig, P.R., Moore, J.A.: A human cognition framework for information visualization. Computers & Graphics 42, 42–58 (2014)

37. Petford, J., Nacenta, M.A., Gutwin, C.: Pointing all around you: selection performance of mouse and ray-cast pointing in full-coverage displays. In: Proceedings of the 2018 CHI Conference on Human Factors in Computing Systems. p. 533. ACM (2018)
38. Piringer, H., Kosara, R., Hauser, H.: Interactive focus+ context visualization with linked 2D/3D scatterplots. In: Proceedings of the Second International Conference on Coordinated and Multiple Views in Exploratory Visualization. pp. 49–60. IEEE (2004)
39. Pirolli, P., Card, S.: The sensemaking process and leverage points for analyst technology as identified through cognitive task analysis. In: Proceedings of International Conference on Intelligence Analysis (2005)
40. Ragan, E.D., Endert, A., Sanyal, J., Chen, J.: Characterizing provenance in visualization and data analysis: An organizational framework of provenance types and purposes. IEEE Transactions on Visualization and Computer Graphics 22(1), 31–40(Jan 2016), https://doi.org/10.1109/TVCG.2015.2467551 doi: 10.1109/TVCG.2015.2467551
41. Ranasinghe, N., Jain, P., Thi Ngoc Tram, N., Koh, K.C.R., Tolley, D., Karwita, S., Lien-Ya, L., Liangkun, Y., Shamaiah, K., Eason Wai Tung, C., Yen, C.C., Do, E.Y.L.: Season traveller: Multisensory narration for enhancing the virtual reality experience. In: Proceedings of the 2018 CHI Conference on Human Factors in Computing Systems (CHI). pp. 577:1–577:13. ACM, New York, NY, USA (2018)
42. Sacha, D., Stoffel, A., Stoffel, F., Kwon, B.C., Ellis, G., Keim, D.A.: Knowledge generation model for visual analytics. IEEE Transactions on Visualization and Computer Graphics 20(12), 1604–1613 (2014)
43. Sanchez-Vives, M.V., Slater, M.: From presence to consciousness through virtual reality. Nature Reviews Neuroscience 6(4), 332–339 (2005)
44. Shneiderman, B.: The eyes have it: A task by data type taxonomy for information visualizations. In: Proc. IEEE Symposium on Visual Languages. pp. 336–343. IEEE Press (1996)
45. Veas, E., Grasset, R., Ferencik, I., Grünewald, T., Schmalstieg, D.: Mobile augmented reality for environmental monitoring. Personal and Ubiquitous Computing 17(7), 1515–1531(2013), http://dx.doi.org/10.1007/s00779-012-0597-z doi: 10.1007/s00779-012-0597-z
46. Wang, X.M., Zhang, T.Y., Ma, Y.X., Xia, J., Chen, W.: A survey of visual analytic pipelines. Journal of Computer Science and Technology 31(4), 787–804 (2016)
47. Ward, M.O., Grinstein, G., Keim, D.: Interactive data visualization: foundations, techniques, and applications. CRC Press, 2nd edn. (2015)
48. Ware, C.: Information Visualization: Perception for Design (3rd Ed.). Elsevier (2013)
49. Wickham, H.: A layered grammar of graphics. Journal of Computational and Graphical Statistics 19(1), 3–28(2010) doi: 10.1198/jcgs.2009.07098
50. Wilkinson, L.: The grammar of graphics. Springer Science & Business Media (2006)
51. Willett, W., Jansen, Y., Dragicevic, P.: Embedded data representations. IEEE Transactions on Visualization and Computer Graphics 23(1), 461–470 (2017)
52. Wright, H.: Introduction to Scientific Visualization. Springer Science & Business Media (2007)
53. Yi, J.S., ah Kang, Y., Stasko, J.: Toward a deeper understanding of the role of interaction in information visualization. IEEE Transactions on Visualization and Computer Graphics 13(6), 1224–1231 (2007)

54. Zhao, H., Bryant, G.W., Griffin, W., Terrill, J.E., Chen, J.: Validation of SplitVectors encoding for quantitative visualization of large-magnitude-range vector fields. IEEE Transactions on Visualization and Computer Graphics 23(6), 1691–1705 (2017)
55. Zhao, H., Chen, J.: Bivariate separable-dimension glyphs can improve visual analysis of holistic features. IEEE Transactions on Visualization and Computer Graphics (Under revision) (2018), https://arxiv.org/abs/1712.02333

10. Immersive Analytics Applications in Life and Health Sciences

Tobias Czauderna[1], Jason Haga[2], Jinman Kim[3], Matthias Klapperstück[1], Karsten Klein[1,3,4], Torsten Kuhlen[5], Steffen Oeltze-Jafra[6], Björn Sommer[1,4], and Falk Schreiber[1,4]

[1] Monash University, Australia
{tobias.czauderna,matthias.klapperstueck}@monash.edu
[2] National Institute of Advanced Industrial Science and Technology, Japan
jh.haga@aist.go.jp
[3] University of Sydney, Australia
jinman.kim@sydney.edu.au
[4] University of Konstanz, Germany
{karsten.klein,bjoern.sommer,falk.schreiber}@uni-konstanz.de
[5] RWTH Aachen University, Germany
kuhlen@vr.rwth-aachen.de
[6] Innovation Center Computer Assisted Surgery, University of Leipzig, Germany
steffen.oeltze-jafra@medizin.uni-leipzig.de

Abstract. Life and health sciences are key application areas for immersive analytics. This spans a broad range including medicine (e. g., investigations in tumour boards), pharmacology (e. g., research of adverse drug reactions), biology (e. g., immersive virtual cells) and ecology (e. g., analytics of animal behaviour). We present a brief overview of general applications of immersive analytics in the life and health sciences, and present a number of applications in detail, such as immersive analytics in structural biology, in medical image analytics, in neurosciences, in epidemiology, in biological network analysis and for virtual cells.

Keywords: immersive analytics, applications, life sciences, health sciences

10.1. Background

10.1.1. Motivation

Life and health sciences cover a broad range of scientific fields that study living organisms, such as biochemistry, biology, physiology, neurosciences and areas which are concerned with the science and delivery of healthcare. Life and health sciences are important application areas for immersive analytics (IA). In addition, they are a model field of application for IA, as on the one hand they are creating and collecting large amounts of data for analysis, and on the other hand have always been an early adaptor of new approaches and technologies for both data acquisition and analytics, see the next section for some examples.

K. Marriott et al. (Eds.): Immersive Analytics, LNCS 11190, pp. 289–330, 2018.
https://doi.org/10.1007/978-3-030-01388-2_10

With the great progress that has been made in unravelling the mysteries of life, the questions to be answered and the data under investigation are becoming more and more complex, and hence more and more sophisticated methods for analysis are required. Due to the wide range of modalities and methods for data acquisition that are used in the life and health sciences, including imaging techniques, high-throughput (omics) technologies, personal health monitoring, etc., there is the further challenge to integrate quite diverse data sets and data types into a visual analytics approach to allow the user to gain an accurate insight into the processes in a living organism [115]. In addition, the dynamics of these processes need to be covered in order to understand the underlying mechanisms. The fact that the data spans multiple orders of magnitude in time and space constitutes a further challenge.

10.1.2. Initial Immersive Analytics Approaches

Immersive analytics can help by combining data analytics methods, multi-sensory input and output, and technologies along the reality-virtuality continuum into immersive environments that allow the user to cope with more complex data while keeping focused on a particular research question. For some of the challenges in the life and health sciences, first steps have been taken towards supporting an immersive analytics workflow, for example, for:

- brain activity analysis [28,100]
- improving peoples' long-term health behaviour [83,93]
- training and simulation in medicine [17,112,113]
- planing in radiotherapy [19]
- investigating climate change effects on the great barrier reef [97,98]
- analytics of animal movements [99]
- docking of molecules [3,95] and
- the integrative exploration and analysis of data in complex cellular environments [125,127].

In particular, virtual reality (VR) and augmented reality (AR) medicine is a strong area of application and immersive technologies are already used, e. g., in surgical practice.

10.1.3. Application Examples

In the following we present several diverse application examples in detail. These application examples have been picked to show both the breadth and depth of the emerging field of immersive analytics [14], and it should be noted that these examples are not an exhaustive list of current approaches. For each example we discuss traditional methods as well as novel immersive methods, provide a critical analysis and look to the future of immersive analytics developments.

10.2. Case Study 1: Molecular Scientific Visualisation in Structural Biology

The field of structural biology encompasses the study of protein or nucleic acid structures and their relationship to the function of the molecule. It is now a mature field that uses a variety of experimental techniques from molecular biology, biochemistry, and biophysics to resolve and map molecular structures at the atomic scale [12, 87]. The challenge is to better understand the details of molecular interactions that will lead to further discoveries in macromolecular function. The inherently three-dimensional nature of molecules makes them a natural and logical target domain for 3D visualisation applications. This is especially important in drug design where visualisation helps the user to validate virtual screening results as well as to discover structural trends in binding or unknown interactions between molecules. The earliest effort in this area was by Levinthal *et al.* [82], who built one of the first interactive computer systems for the visualisation of protein structures, where a user could control the rate of rotation of the molecule. Subsequently, many different molecular visualisation applications have been developed, these now support the field of 3D molecular scientific visualisation.

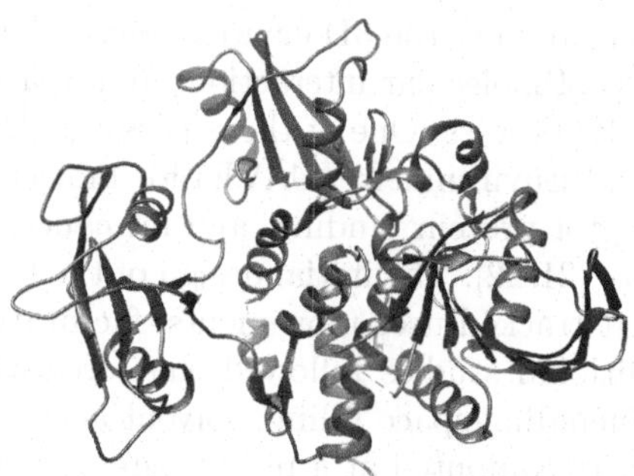

Fig. 1: Visualisation of the wild-type Src homology 2 (SH2)-domain containing protein tyrosine phosphatase-2 (SHP2, PDBID: 4DGP). Orange-red denotes alpha-helices, purple denotes beta-strands, and grey denotes other coil structures. The visualisation has depth cues to indicate portions of the molecule that are behind others.

10.2.1. Traditional Methods

The ability to visualise computational models of biological structures in a meaningful way is a mature field with many different tools that exist to help researchers visualise their results (see Fig. 1 for an example). The details of each of these tools are beyond the scope of this chapter, however, a large list of these tools is available at the RSCB PDB website [109]. Of these tools, one of the most popular is Chimera [16], which is an extensible molecular modelling package for desktop computers. Other similar desktop tools include Jmol [57], PyMOL [105], RasMol [108] and VMD [142]. Some web-based tools such as GLmol [44] are being created that are platform independent to offer greater flexibility in their use. Many of these desktop tools are being ported for use on high-resolution tiled display walls that present a single logical display area with pixel counts in the hundreds of millions range [96]. This allows this technology to be used in a variety of applications and can support displaying multiple types of content simultaneously. One example is a modified version of a tool called ViewDock designed to run on large tiled display walls [80] and, more recently, a JavaScript version of this tool designed for greater platform portability [122]. All of these software development efforts are creating a stable set of tools for molecular visualisation, with high accuracy and resolution on 2D displays.

10.2.2. Immersive Methods

Concurrently, as the development of desktop tools progressed, several research groups began to design high-end virtual reality (VR) based immersive environments for molecular visualisation, in an effort to cater for the inherently 3D nature of molecular structures. These immersive environments allow the user to visualise and navigate in a true 3D environment and are very advantageous for investigating details of molecular interactions and dynamics, as molecular function is an inherently 3D process. One of the earliest implementations used the CAVE Automatic Virtual Environment (CAVE) for molecular dynamics of membrane protein and receptor protein binding, and for cancer, specifically simulations of the p21 active site [21, 22]. The initial design of the CAVE was a projection-based environment that tracked user movements, facilitating navigation through the 3D model. Additional studies followed that created algorithms for molecular representation including space filling, solvent accessible, and molecular surface models, which were computed at a remote site and transferred to the CAVE for visualisation [1].

A series of papers also explored the user-interface for virtual environments, specifically for molecular visualisation. Up to 4 molecules could be compared in real-time before frame-rates decreased [88] and a case-study confirmed the feasibility of the virtual reality environment for molecular visualisation [89]. However, the interactive manipulation and navigation required six-degrees-of-freedom to achieve precise, intuitive control. A customised wand with head and hand tracking was used for interactive manipulation of the molecules, but it was also found that cordless gamepads were a suitable and usable input device [90]. Some desktop tools have been extended to work with VR including RasMol [108] and PyMol [141, 143]. There also is a tool designed for interactive protein manipulation in a CAVE, with the purpose of providing a framework for a human-in-the-loop optimisation process for protein folding [20].

In addition to the CAVE, different configurations of the projection-based system were created including a desktop version and a single wall configuration, both of which allowed multiple people to share the VR experience [26]. There is a commercial desktop environment called zSpace [157] that provides a virtual reality setup. It is smaller in scale and cost but allows the same collaborative interactivity that a CAVE provides and can be used for molecular visualisation with PyMol and Avogadro [6,158]. There are also some fledgeling efforts in using augmented reality (AR) with molecular models. The rise in 3D printing has enabled structural biologists to print their own physical models of peptide backbones and attach fiducial markers for AR to overlay 3D virtual representations of electrostatic fields or space-filling models [40,41]. This merging of tangible objects with virtual data has potential in research to elucidate new information and the potential to be a powerful teaching tool as well [5].

Most recently, there is research in using head-mounted displays (HMD) for the immersive visualisation of molecular structures. Stone *et al.* have improved ray tracing algorithms for the VMD tool and improved the overall performance of video streaming of molecular visualisations in HMD [134].

10.2.3. Critical Analysis

From a technological perspective, these efforts successfully provide immersive visualisation of proteins. Both collaborative analysis and interaction modalities with molecular models are ongoing areas of research; however, these technologies do not provide a suitable environment for analysis of large numbers of molecular interactions, which can be important in drug discovery efforts. Tiled display walls can depict molecular dynamics, but there are no truly high-throughput methods to compare hundreds of interactions. Some tools facilitate the high-throughput analysis of virtual screening data to help address this issue on tiled display walls [122]. Both VR and AR modalities are very limited in the number of structural comparisons that can be done. Thus, there is a need to scale these modalities to take advantage of big data. Moreover, with the recent exponential increase in biological datasets, including genomic, proteomic, and network data, none of these methods provides a data-rich, immersive environment for structural biology. There is currently no solution that presents multiple types of data in an integrated fashion. One example would be incorporating both genomic information and relevant patent information when analysing structural interactions during the drug discovery process. Patent data that can be accessed from within a single user interface can inform researchers how their discoveries relate to current commercial efforts. There are some efforts to integrate sequence-structure analysis [86] and genomic networks [91] with protein visualisation in the traditional desktop tools, but an immersive analytic approach has yet to be developed. Importantly, there appears to be slow adoption of these immersive environments by structural biologists. This is partially due to the fact that immersive environments until recently have been several orders of magnitude more expensive than desktop computers and require specialised hardware, facilities, and extensive support staff. At this time, however, we are at a turning point with the technologies. HMDs are now becoming commodity level hardware [92] and it is opening the possibility to have an immersive analytics environment that a user can dive into and perform molecular analytics and/or drug discovery.

10.2.4. Future in Immersive Analytics

Although the technologies themselves are well established, there is a lack of comprehensive usability studies with these technologies investigating how beneficial they are for structural biologists. Future efforts must go beyond the visualisation of molecules. As explored through three case-studies in a recent paper from Marai *et al.* [85] at the Electronic Visualization Laboratory, some data representations fit naturally into a 3D paradigm, and others are best left in 2D. This is highly dependent on the users and the interaction between them during collaborations, so multiple data representations can be better and more effective than a single shared representation (see Chap. 2). Thus, integration of other heterogeneous data sets will be a key driver of the adoption and usability of these immersive analytic environments for structural biologists and will provide exciting opportunities for immersive analytics as a whole.

10.3. Case Study 2: Explorative Analysis of *In-Silico* Experiments in Neuroscience

10.3.1. Traditional Methods

While for the last two decades, computer science mostly concentrated on classical scientific visualisation as a tool in neuroscience for the analysis of medical imaging and microscopy data, recently the discipline of visual analytics has attracted more and more attention in the field of computational neuroscience. In particular, so-called *in-silico* experiments are a rather new approach in neuroscience, which attempts to understand the mechanisms of the (human) brain by simulating huge, biologically realistic neuronal networks at the scale of single neuro-cortical columns, brain areas and even complete brains. The two most prominent simulation tools in the field are NEURON [13] and NEST [39]. To gain insight into the simulation data, the exploration methods developed and used by neuroscientists range from simple raster plots, where neural activity is plotted over time, to diagrams of derived parameters, up to complex statistical analyses. Important analysis goals are to detect meaningful spiking patterns of clusters of neurons at different temporal as well as spatial scales and to, finally, establish relationships between brain structures, functions and connectivity.

10.3.2. Immersive Methods

It can be argued that a more advanced visual analysis, combining a more interactive, explorative workflow with immersive visualisation techniques, has the potential to further support neuroscientists to answer their research questions. A visualisation tool for neuroscientific analysis of *in-silico* experiments called VisNEST that is inherently based on the concept of immersive analytics is currently being developed [74,75,100].

Since the identification of correlations between a brain's structure, function, and connectivity at the different temporal as well as spatial scales is essential for the assessment of large-scale neuronal network simulations, VisNEST builds on a multi-view paradigm. This paradigm has already proven its potential in many other domains and is nowadays a mainstream method in visual analytics. In a nutshell, the idea of multi-view visualisation is to combine a number of specialised information displays and semantically link their content in order to interactively explore possible relationships in the data. In this context, linking means that changes in either view are automatically transferred to all other views. In the concrete example of VisNEST, structural and dynamic information is combined via geometrical and more abstract views in order to effectively and efficiently support neuroscientists in the exploration phase of a neuronal network model analysis. Here, linking may relate to both spatial as well as temporal aspects of the data.

The central view in the VisNEST framework consists of a geometrical representation of brain areas, thus addressing the macroscopic scale. In this view, the aggregated neural activity per brain region is colour-coded. If in an analysis session a specific area is selected, the corresponding raster plot shows up and allows for an exploration of the spiking activities at the resolution of individual neuron populations. They are synchronised in time with the brain area view, thus allowing the user to assess the interaction between microscopic and macroscopic scales. Beyond these two basic views, VisNEST offers dynamic bar plots of mean spike rates for each area and for the multiple layers within the areas, providing an overview of the network's activity and a means to identify oscillating spiking patterns. Additional views resulting from advanced statistical analyses can be easily added to the framework and semantically linked to other views. Beyond these geometrical and abstract, diagram-style views, graph-style views are currently under development, these show the communications between brain areas, area layers and clusters of neurons and thus make the temporal dynamics of a network's activity assessable in an intuitive way.

10.3.3. Critical Analysis

The question of whether or not neuroscientific tools like VisNEST can profit from immersive analytics techniques is currently being investigated (see Fig. 2). While web-based approaches are required by neuroscientists, allowing them to conveniently access simulation results from their desk, it can be argued that by means of web interfaces it is difficult, if not impossible, to provide a powerful, explorative multi-view analysis for complex, large-scale neuronal network simulations, both in terms of performance and display infrastructure.

In the VisNEST framework specific geometrical views of brain structures and densely-connected, weighted 3D graphs reveal highly complex structures. As such, an egocentric, stereoscopic projection of these views might help to assess complex

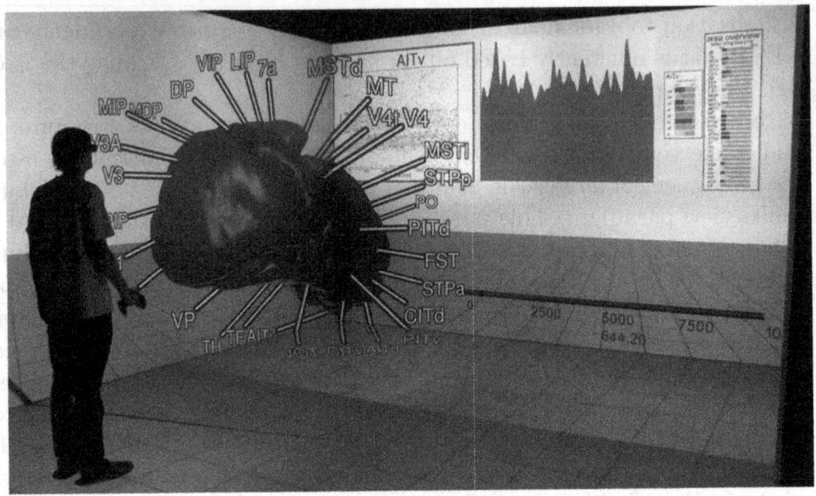

Fig. 2: Aiming at an integrative analysis of simulated, biologically realistic neuronal networks at multiple scales, VisNEST links geometrical 3D views with abstract 2D views in an immersive environment.

spatial relationships in the data. Furthermore, the sheer screen real-estate and high resolution of modern immersive or semi-immersive displays, consisting of multiple LCD panels or (edge-blended) projectors arranged in a matrix layout, are crucial features for carrying multiple views, maintaining essential qualities like the readability of individual plots or their legends, and allowing users to switch between views at the blink of an eye.

10.3.4. Future in Immersive Analytics

Initial expert reviews with neuroscientists have been carried out based on a model simulating 32 areas of the visual cortex of a macaque brain which has been simulated using the NEST code. These studies indicate that the multi-view design significantly supports the domain experts in the exploration of parameter impact on large-scale activity, the assessment of detailed spiking patterns, and the comparison of structural and functional relationships [100]. Immersive visualisation of geometrical views and direct interaction with the data in 3D space have been rated as meaningful features. Yet, aside from anecdotal evidence, there is no formal evaluation for this statement. After several months of experience with the early VisNEST prototype, it turns out that neuroscientists prefer to run them on semi-immersive VR systems, like small-scale PowerWalls, allowing for stereoscopic, head-tracked rendering and direct interaction in 3D space, while fitting into the scientists' office environment. Only occasionally do neuroscientists use fully-immersive systems like the RWTH Aachen University's aixCAVE. They primarily call upon this system to demonstrate research results to stakeholders and the broader public [75]. Since head-mounted displays are by design not particularly suitable for this purpose, it remains questionable if they will become accepted for this application. In terms of tool functionality, neuroscientists pointed out that in the longer term, a practical immersive analytics framework should go beyond the range of functions provided by our initial prototype. In particular, it should allow for comparative analyses across multiple simulation runs with varying network parameters or even different simulation algorithms, and a comparison of simulation and experimental data.

10.4. Case Study 3: Exploration of Virtual Cells in Cytology

Cell visualisation and modelling is a classical field where immersive analytics methods can be applied. Although the term immersive analytics was coined a relatively short time ago [14], cell visualisation has to cope since a long time with aspects like representation and exploration in virtual environments. Naturally, for many information visualisation-related purposes it is not necessary to pay particular attention to the spatial structure of the cell. For example, if just the localisation of a specific protein has to be visualised disconnected from its spatial context, such as a protein-protein interaction network, it is not necessary to visualise 3D structures. Simple approaches visualising compartments in two dimensions are here sufficient [10,156]. And although only two dimensions have to be taken into account for network drawings, it is already a quite demanding task to map nodes to specific areas by using, e. g., human-readable constrained-based layout [30, 67, 120]. However, especially in fields like scientific visualisation, the illustration of spatial structures plays a very important role.

10.4.1. Traditional Methods

In computational biology the simulation of 3D cells has a long tradition. Approaches like VCell (The Virtual Cell) were developed one and a half decades ago and are still used by many cell biologists and bioengineers [84]. From the beginning, VCell supported the simulation based on compartmental and/or spatial models which can be based on experimentally derived geometries. Using cell simulation, users try to predict changes inside a living cell in terms of, e. g., concentration changes over time. Recently, virtual cell approaches unite different integrative bioinformatics approaches, combining spatial with mathematical modelling by using the methodology of data integration [15]. Other approaches focus on the integration and visualisation of multimodal biological data including 3D data [115]. Often, this data is modelled in form of networks with additional annotations, which are visualised for exploration and analysis. Due to the size and complexity of these networks, the result is often the (in)famous hairball, which might look quite attractive to some people at the first glance, but fails to provide a reasonable tool to scientist to explore complex data in 3D [78].

One reason is that even today in the scientific community most 3D visualisations are provided by a two-dimensional medium: the print-out of a publication on a piece of paper, a scientific poster or a PDF. This is the case although there are many alternative ways to present 3D structures, e. g., models created by 3D printers, 3D stereoscopic anaglyph print-outs for posters (see also Fig. 4), and Adobe PDF which provides the option to embed 3D models.

An important sub-field of scientific visualisation is the illustration of cytological structures and their processes. One famous animation is the "Inner Life of a Cell" produced by Harvard University, screened first in 2006 at SIGGRAPH. Well-recognised artists like Drew Berry, David S. Goodsell, and Gaël McGill/Digizyme created high-quality visualisations and animations which helped to illustrate these processes to a broader public. As an important aspect of their work they mimicked the reality of the cell as accurate as possible by incorporating state-of-the-art research results. For example, Drew Berry created a number of videos for the digital biology textbook "E.O. Wilson's Life on Earth", demonstrating the impact of this technology on education [149].

The 3D modelling of cells is traditionally based on the interpretation of microscopic images, using tools like Blender, Autodesk 3DS Max or Maya. Approaches like cellPACK try to simplify the cell modelling process by duplication of molecular structures based on PDB models, see also Sec. 10.2. and [59, 60]. Today, there are a large number of different approaches providing biologists and bioinformaticians access to the 3D modelling of cytological complexes [54,128,130]. Visualisation and modelling of cells are also important in education. Here, edutainment-based approaches such as Meta!Blast are being developed which provide an alternative method to teach school students the structure of the cell [151]: the user has to navigate a small space-craft-like device through a cell environment, in order to complete various tasks. As cell models tend to contain large structures with high granularity, effective visualisation approaches are being developed which make use of GPU acceleration for smooth interactive exploration [34].

Whereas these approaches focus on the visualisation of structural data such as cellular compartments, there are efforts to combine structure with abstract data such as biological networks. First approaches that associated metabolic pathways with simple geometric structures were developed many years ago: MetNet3D/VR and the Interactorium [147, 152]. Already at this time, a CAVE was used to explore the data presented in MetNet3D/VR by using a wand-like device and a small tablet PC which could be used to navigate in the virtual environment [152]. Complex metabolic networks were simplified to show direct connections between interacting cell components, represented by cubes. These cubes could be expanded to show their internal networks. The Interactorium was not optimised to be used in CAVEs, but it provided a simplified environment to navigate through protein-protein interaction networks of a yeast cell. The cell components were presented as simple shapes: spheres; moreover, it was possible to visualise protein structures of single molecules in this 3D environment. More recent solutions combine networks with geometric representation of cell models [130]. Sommer *et al.* developed a visual analytics method to predict localisations based on different database entries using sub-cellular localisation charts [126].

Where 3D data is explored, 3D-stereoscopic visualisation (S3D) technologies play a pivotal role. Already in the 1990s structural biologists, in particular crystallographers, were making use of the 3D-stereoscopic screens of special CRT monitors in combination with active shutter glasses. In cell visualisation, where many complex structures have to be analysed, stereoscopic visualisation can help to improve the spatial perception of cells. This is also helpful for educational approaches where the aim is to improve the spatial understanding for high school or undergraduate students [129]. For example, the previously mentioned game Meta!Blast supports S3D visualisation by using NVIDIA 3D Vision. Other more artistic approaches such as CytoViz take cell visualisation as an example to map data streams–such as network transfer information–to cellular organisms, manipulating their behaviour and structure [123]. In addition, commercial software such as Amira has provided S3D for more than a decade.

10.4.2. Immersive Methods

How is it possible to apply today's technology to create fully or semi-immersive data interactions providing analytical capabilities? For abstract 3D structures, such as the previously mentioned biological networks, S3D visualisation could be a tool to improve visual perception. In the network visualisation community, classical 3D network layouts are often criticised. But visual experiments of Greffard *et al.* [46] showed important differences between stereoscopy, the classical 3D perspective and 2D perspective. They concluded that using S3D is advantageous in the context of the detection of numerous clusters of variable density and with many overlaps. Whereas for a small number of clusters the 2D visualisation outperforms S3D in terms of error rate, for more complex structures S3D provided better results than 2D and classical 3D visualisation [46] (also see Chap. 2).

On the other hand, the stereoscopic visualisation comes also with drawbacks, as two perspectives have to be rendered. For example, a critical aspect is the avoidance of crosstalk which is defined by Woods [150] as "the incomplete isolation of the left and right image channels so that one image leaks into the other"; the perception of crosstalk is also better known as ghosting. Therefore, methods have to be implemented to optimise the stereoscopic vision based on the current perspective and the location of the viewer. For cell visualisation, e. g., the interactive projection plane method was developed [129] and implemented in CELLmicrocosmos (Cm) CellExplorer [130]. Stereoscopic visualisation alone is not sufficient to create an appropriate virtual image of the cell that is able to illustrate spatial relationships. Therefore, exploration techniques are required to allow the user to navigate in the virtual environment. While a lot of effort has been put into the optimisation of navigation methods for 2D computer screens, 3D navigation is still an open field for development (see Chap. 4).

The Cm CellExplorer software provides 3D cell visualisation which can be combined with biological networks based on gene/protein localisation, and an optimised 3D navigation supporting six degrees of freedom (6DOF). This navigation is based on navigation known from first-person computer games. For

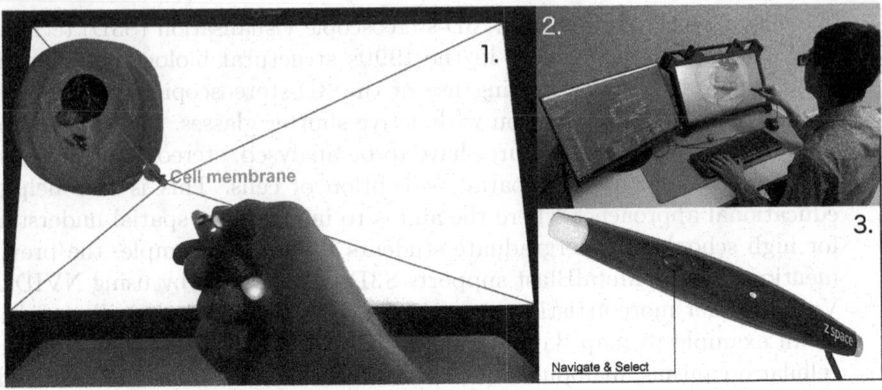

Fig. 3: The *CELLmicrocosmos CellExplorer* using a *zSpace* providing hybrid-dimensional visualisation and navigation: 1.) Navigation is performed with a 3D arrow providing 3D navigation, 2.) The zSpace on the right side provides stereoscopic 3D visualisation and navigation, the standard monitor on the left side can be used for visualisation of networks in 2D, 3.) All basic navigation capabilities can be performed with the stylus pen and a single button.

the following three navigation modes only a mouse operating in two dimensions and a keyboard are required: Floating (mouse selection and movement using the keyboard), Flight mode (movement using the mouse), and Object-bound mode (movement around a selected object).

Nowadays, new devices such as the zSpace [157] are available. This device provides head tracking, stereoscopic visualisation and a stylus pen which can be used for navigation in 3D space. In contrast to head-mounted displays (HMD), this is a semi-immersive technology. Therefore, the user is not fully immersed in the virtual environment and is still able to perceive and interact with the real environment. The big advantage of similar technologies is the fact that they can be used over longer time periods, as issues like simulator sickness do not occur.

The term "Hybrid-dimensional visualisation" describes 2D and 3D visualisation which can be used side-by-side. One example is Aquaria, a web-based tool which combines molecular 3D representations of proteins with 2D representations of the corresponding protein sequence. The user can select specific areas of the sequence and directly highlight the corresponding 3D location in the protein [101]. Moreover, this approach was also combined with a quite popular and affordable 3D interaction technology, the Leap Motion [117]. By using hand gestures, the user can move the protein, whereas mouse and keyboard can be used to explore the 2D information on the screen. The previously mentioned CellExplorer can also be used for hybrid-dimensional visualisation. Biological networks can be visualised side-by-side in 2D and in 3D by using PathwayIntegration [130]. Fig. 3.2 shows on the right side the zSpace which is used to explore a cell model associated with a metabolic pathway in 3D, as well as a standard 2D monitor on the left side. Here, the original metabolic pathway is shown, using a 2D layout [131]. The stylus pen shown in Fig. 3.3 is used in conjunction with a 3D arrow to navigate and select the different cell components (see Fig. 3.1). Well-established standards, such as SBML, KGML and SBGN [52, 64, 81], can be supported by combining PathwayIntegration and corresponding pathway analysis tools, such as VANTED and SBGN-ED [24, 25, 72, 116, 127].

The first version of CellExplorer was developed for single-user mode, but an extended version for educational purposes supports small groups of up to three people. For the purpose of larger group presentations, the tool was adapted to the CAVE2 environment at Monash University. The CAVE2 is a large 330° virtual environment providing space for up to 30 people which is used for educational tours, presentations, but also scientific discussions during which specific questions are elaborated [36]. Because it also provides stereoscopic visualisation, it is often used to explore new biological structures, such as proteins, cells, tissues, up to the whole human body. Due to the advent of affordable HMDs - which might replace CAVEs for many single-user analysis tasks in the near future–group presentations will become the major use case for these large visualisation facilities [18, 23] (and as discussed in Sec. 10.3.).

10.4.3. Critical Analysis

Scientific artists generating highly relevant videos for outreach and educational purposes do usually not make use of S3D visualisation as it demands additional resources which are usually not covered by the production costs. On the other hand, we showed that especially cell visualisation profits from S3D [129]. So a first step towards immersive analytics in this area would be to support S3D visualisations. Then it would be possible to combine these animations with immersive analytics-based approaches, e. g., by linking videos to special locations in virtual cell models and creating in this way an immersive interactive learning experience.

Another basic problem is that previous approaches–such as MetNetVR [153] for hierarchical visualisation of metabolic networks using VR–were optimised for the CAVE. So there are only a few facilities in the world which provide compatible technology. This will change now by transferring similar approaches to affordable HMD technology. An important aspect of future developments will be to provide software for researchers which can be easily installed and used on local machines. For this purpose, new human-computer interaction approaches will have to be developed and optimised. Of course, there are still application areas for CAVEs, but their usage has to be focused more on group presentations [125]. Here, another problem is that usually expert users are required who are able to work with this kind of environments.

To tackle this problem in an exemplary solution, the aforementioned combination of CellExplorer and zSpace was used in the context of a CAVE (CAVE2) for an improved navigation experience in the use case of a presenter and an audience. This approach, called Space Map, is a World In Miniature-related technique [133] where both presenter and audience have different views onto the 3D world. The overall target is here to simplify 3D navigation in a way that in

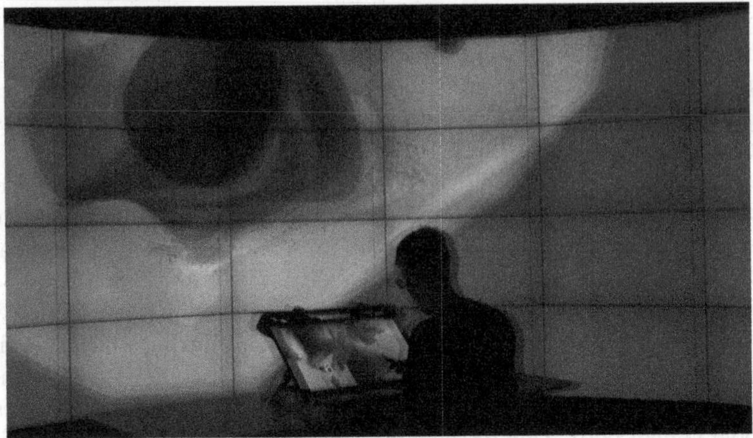

Fig. 4: The image shows a live image of the Space Map approach. The zSpace is used as a World In Miniature device which shows an overview map of the virtual environment. By using the stylus pen the user can select specific positions in the 3D environment and navigate to these locations. This is an anaglyph red-cyan stereoscopic image.

the future also biologists can handle the navigation inside a CAVE without the need of an additional person doing the navigation.

Usually, the 3D-stereoscopic perspective of the environment is optimised for the presenter, using head-tracked glasses plus a wand-like device for navigation. In contrast, the Space Map approach optimises the stereoscopic experience for the audience [125,133], see Fig. 4. The presenter uses the zSpace to obtain a 3D-stereoscopic view of the virtual world and uses the stylus pen to point in 3D where the view of the CAVE2 should be navigated to, see Fig. 4 (background). This helps the presenter to maintain the overview in the 3D environment, to smoothly navigate between different positions in 3D space, as well as to optimise the stereoscopic effect for specific locations. First user studies showed that there is some training required for new users, especially as the regular user is not familiar with navigating in a virtual 3D space. However, many users learned after a short introduction within a few minutes how to use this technology. Especially expert CAVE users familiar with the wand navigation learned quite fast how to use the stylus pen. Still, it is not easy to convince an expert user to abandon the wand [125]. Here, additional studies are required to compare different user attitudes and the perception of the audience in a wand-navigated environment versus a Space Map-navigated environment.

10.4.4. Future in Immersive Analytics

Existing approaches for virtual cells already provide functionalities such as

– import of 3D structures of segmented cells,

- mapping of network and other data onto the 3D cell model,
- usage of localisation information from data warehouses, and
- interactive exploration in 3D environments.

Therefore, changes can be directly perceived in the virtual model representing a biological entity. In the future, it will be possible to interactively change the parameters of a simulation and directly visualise the resulting changes in the 3D environment. In the context of a simulated virtual cell model, it would be possible to observe spatial changes if the location of a specific gene or protein is altered. And whereas today usually only local areas are interactively simulated, such as the interaction of proteins with small molecules, this could be done on a larger scale in the future [29]. In this way it would be possible to simulate and visualise an environment at the mesoscopic as well as molecular scale, i. e., enabling users to observe how small changes in the molecular structure impact the large structure of the whole cell.

A promising example is the Allen Cell Explorer which uses web technologies to present cellular structures directly derived from microscopy. With generative modelling approaches the recognition of cell components is automatised [61]. In this way, a large database of different cell models will be generated, which will be a highly relevant resource to explore and analyse cytological structures. With recent VR-ready web technologies, such as WebGL, it would be possible to visualise these structures directly in, e. g., an HMD such as the HTC Vive, and to compare and experience the differences between different cell structures.

10.5. Case Study 4: Image Analytics in Medicine

Medical imaging plays a critical and indispensable role in modern healthcare. Multi-dimensional medical imaging modalities such as positron emission tomography (PET), computed tomography (CT), and magnetic resonance imaging (MRI) enables the depiction of the interior of a human body, in a non-invasive manner, for routine clinical analysis and medical intervention such as for diagnosis and pre-operative planning. These modalities are acquired in multi-dimensional space (e. g., 4D functional MRI which comprises of 3D MRI volumes acquired repeatedly over time within a single scanning session), multi-modal (e. g., PET-CT and PET-MR where two modalities are acquired sequentially in a single scan so that the images are registered), and temporal sequences (e. g., scans of the same patient after treatment). Such volumetric imaging data (i. e., the shape, size, and location of the structures are natively specified in 3D space) consist of a stack of 2D slices that collectively represent the 3D information. An example of a PET-CT image is given in Fig. 5. It shows the conventional visualisation reliant on 2D cross-sectional views in (a) to (c), together with 3D direct volume rendering (DVR) for an abdominal CT in (d). The computer-generated 3D DVR helps users accurately interpret, for example, the shape of vascular structures and its spatial relationship with the neighbouring spine.

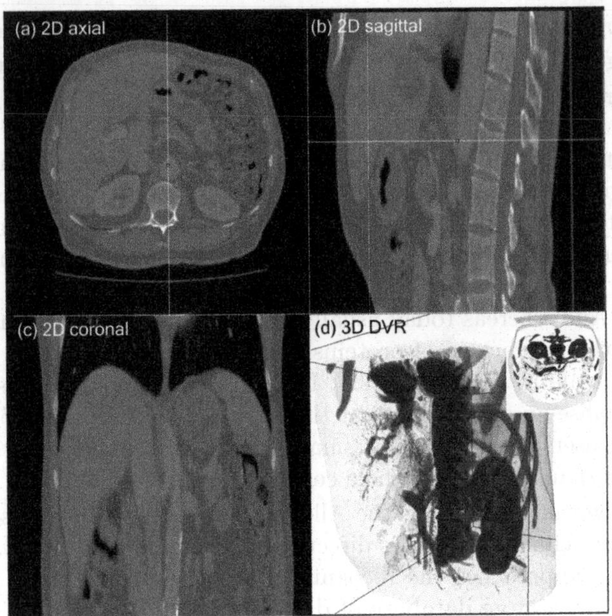

Fig. 5: 2D vs 3D where 3D allows users to better assimilate 3D information, e. g., the shape of vessels and the spatial relationship with the neighbouring spine.

10.5.1. Traditional Methods

There are now vast amounts of medical imaging data available and there are increasing demands on users to interpret and use this data. To aid the users, there have been tremendous research efforts geared towards developing medical image analysis algorithms for use in clinical decision support (CDS) systems. These algorithms are designed to automatically derive image semantics, such as the recognition of anatomical structures and detection of tumour structures as regions of interest (ROIs). Large-scale projects with the objective to understand the human brain are producing a multitude of image analysis algorithms [53], e. g., to characterise schizophrenia patients according to their active brain regions [42]. In another example, the Visual Concept Extraction Challenge in Radiology (VISCERAL) project [79] is aimed at creating an evaluation infrastructure and software to allow the anatomy and pathology identification benchmarks to be carried out efficiently and effectively. The state of the art in CDS in modern clinical research and patient care are evidence-based processes where it is widely accepted that the information from patient populations (big medical data) can improve diagnosis and patient management. The use of population data has largely been embraced in medical image analysis, e. g., in image classification where population data is used to learn from prior examples [76], anatomical shape modelling constructed by averaging large number of patient data [118], and in medical image structure classification where visual image features are transfer-learned from a model that is pre-trained on a massive imaging data repository (millions of images) [8].

However, these automated algorithms that depend on big data for prior knowledge are becoming highly complex, and it is difficult for the users to understand the reasoning which leads to the results. Further, fine-tuning of the algorithm parameters are often required, and this process is time-consuming and difficult. Another challenge is the dependency of the algorithms on the training data, as rare or unique disease patient cases which are not included in the training data may not be detected. In current CDS systems, the information may become noise and thus may be detrimental, rather than supporting the decision making.

There has been growth in the field of iterative and adaptive CDS systems with examples such as user interaction, via relevance feedback and iterative refinement [155]. However, these approaches rely upon the user to sift through potentially hundreds of related results from varying parameters. They must then filter out the useful from irrelevant data (noise) which can lead to information overload. The difference between the automated decision support and the user's intent, i. e. the semantic gap, also allows for the possibility that relevant data with outlier features may be ignored.

10.5.2. Immersive Methods

As an alternative to relevance feedback and user interactions, a new suite of approaches has emerged in the form of visual analytics (VA). VA relies on the integration of computer processing together with an intuitive visual user interface based on cognitive science and it aims to provide meaningful information that is immediate, relevant and understandable to individual users or communities [50]. Most of the research that attempted to incorporate VA with biomedical imaging has focused on providing interactivity to image analysis algorithms such as ROI segmentation and region classification. In one earlier work, interactive approaches to low-level medical image processing were introduced by Glaßer *et al.* [43] where they presented their work on the exploration and analysis of breast tumours from DCE-MRI data. Raidou *et al.* [106] proposed a tool for the visual exploration of imaging-derived heterogeneous tumour tissue characteristics. Geurts *et al.* [38] presented their work on the application of VA concepts in which visual comparison was provided in order to evaluate the quality of the automated image segmentation based on statistical shape models. Two types of visual evaluations were proposed: (i) a global quality view, where a scatterplot matrix was used for pairwise comparisons between the algorithm; and (ii) a regional quality view, which presented the result from a clustering algorithm that identified regions of common quality across the segmented data set for each algorithm. Klemm *et al.* [71] presented their work on an interactive visual analysis approach to shape variance visualisations of segmented structures. These were augmented with information visualisation techniques so that non-image data could be used to identify subject groups with unusual organ shapes and pathologies.

In another VA example, 2D and 3D visualisations were combined to present the time activity and network connectivity data from functional magnetic resonance imaging (fMRI) data to users in a way that illuminates meaning and discovery. Statistical analysis of fMRI, such as independent components analysis, is providing new scientific and clinical insights into data with capabilities such as characterising traits of schizophrenia. However, with existing approaches to fMRI analysis, there are a number of challenges that prevent it from being fully utilised, including understanding exactly what a significant activity pattern is, which structures are consistent and different between individuals and across the population, and how to deal with imaging artefacts such as noise. VA has been presented as a step towards solving these challenges by visualising the data to users in an interactive and exploratory fashion. This includes using circular layouts that represent network connectivity and volume renderings with *in situ* network diagrams. A fMRI visualisation system called Cerebrum VA (CereVA) [28] was presented as an approach to providing a VA solution to the identified challenges [27]. Fig. 6 depicts the user interface.

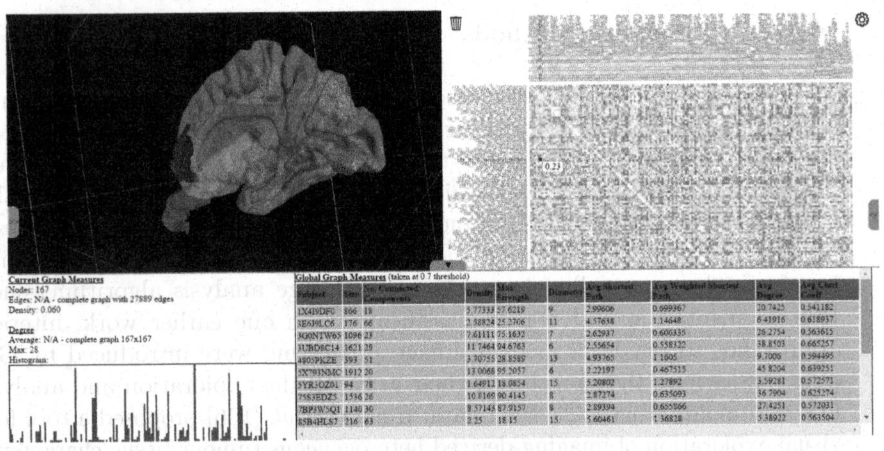

Fig. 6: Overview of the CereVA interface comparing two fMRI correlation networks: 3D rendering and volume display on the left; network abstraction (Heat map) on the right; statistical network analysis at the bottom.

Whilst there has been increasing use of VA for medical image analysis, the application of immersive analytics (IA) is only starting to be explored to visualise medical image volumes. As an example, the CereVA project was expanded to explore the potential in immersive analytics through a VR setting as shown in Fig. 7.

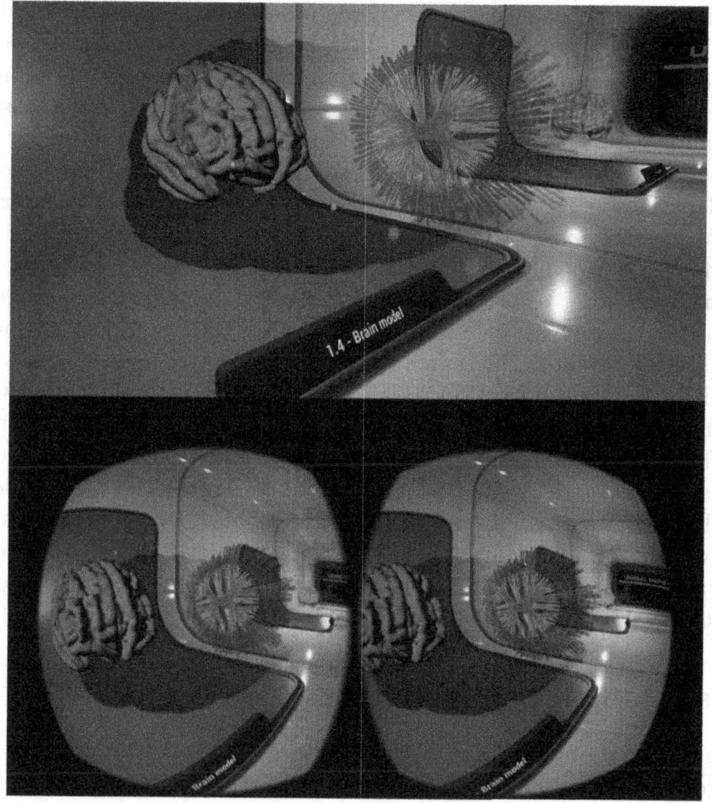

Fig. 7: An illustration of adjacency in volume rendering and visual analytics in a VR environment: in the first row, the brain on the left has an ROI highlighted in red. The radial graph on the right is from CereVA, showing the correlation between brain regions. The brain in the background represents the time-point in a temporal set of scans or another subject that can be compared. Moving around in the scene highlights similarities and differences on the radial graph in the middle. The bottom row shows the stereoscopic view when rendered in VR (with an Oculus Rift).

10.5.3. Critical Analysis

Apart from medical image analysis algorithms, such as image segmentation and classification, there is a great opportunity to use VA and IA approaches more broadly with CDS systems. Currently, VA has been demonstrated for use in image retrieval and in visual semantic representations. Content-based image retrieval (CBIR) is a search technique based on the similarity of visual features that has demonstrated potential benefits for medical diagnosis, education and research [94]. However, clinical adoption of CBIR is partially hindered by the difference between the computed image similarity and the user's search intent, the semantic gap, with the end result that relevant images with outlier features may not be retrieved. Furthermore, most CBIR algorithms do not provide intuitive explanations as to why the retrieved images were considered similar to the query (e. g., which subset of features were similar), hence it is difficult for users to verify if relevant images, with a small subset of outlier features, were missed. Users, therefore, resort to examining irrelevant images and there are limited opportunities to discover these missed images. One solution is to enable a guided visual exploration of the search space through a tool named Visual Analytics for Medical Image Retrieval (VAMIR) [77]. An overview of the VAMIR interface is shown in Fig. 8 where the VA approach is applied to facilitate interactive exploration of the entire dataset using the query image as a point-of-reference. A user study and several case studies demonstrated the capabilities of VAMIR in the retrieval of CT images and multi-modality PET-CT images. The system allowed users, who may not be experts in retrieval algorithms, to explore the feature space with assistance from the retrieval process to discover the images that they consider similar, thereby reducing the semantic gap.

10.5.4. Future in Immersive Analytics

The potential of immersive methods in medical image analysis is only starting to be realised. With the rapid advancements in medical image acquisition technology and computational processing capabilities, greater amounts of imaging volume and derived information from them to be visualised and analysed by the users. To fully utilise the imaging data, appropriate visualisation that is coupled with image analysis algorithms to support efficient navigation and interrogation of the data needs to be developed. The research to date has identified the limitations of current, traditional methods for visualisation, and is becoming increasingly reliant on visual analytics approaches to medical image analysis, and is now starting to explore visualisation with immersive analytics.

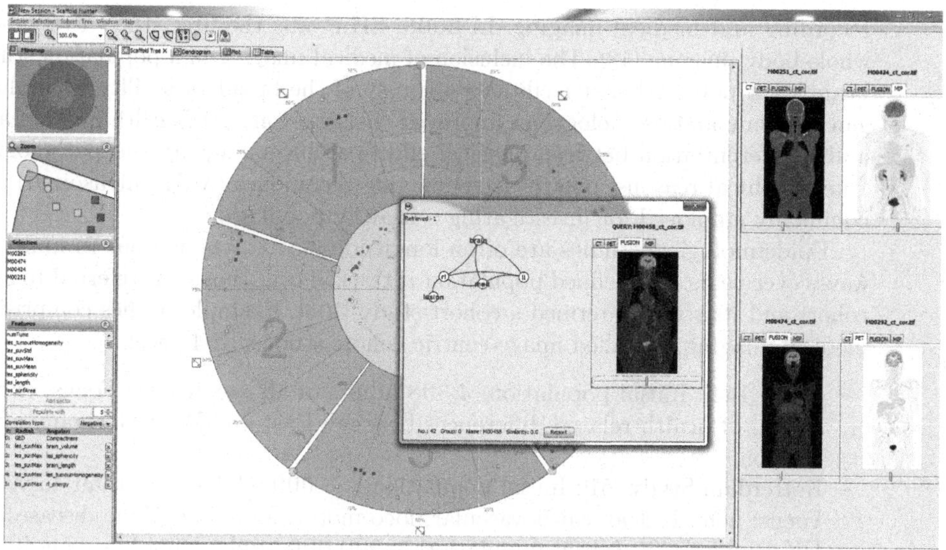

Fig. 8: The VAMIR interface. The major visualisation and interaction components are presented; volumes displayed are coronal and sagittal PET-CT, fused PET-CT, and projection images from a PET-CT scan.

10.6. Case Study 5: Population Study Analytics in Epidemiology

Epidemiology is a branch of medicine. In contrast to clinical medicine, it does not focus on the diagnosis and treatment of a specific disease in a single patient. Instead, epidemiology investigates the occurrence and distribution of health-related events in defined populations [103]. The term defined population refers to individuals sharing a common characteristic such as gender, ethnicity, health condition or residential area (close to a nuclear plant or the seashore etc.). Important goals of epidemiological investigations are: (i) determination of prevalence and incidence of diseases, i. e., number of diseased people at a certain point in time and number of people falling ill within a specified time period and (ii) identification and characterisation of risk factors that are casually related to changes in relevant health conditions.

Epidemiology has huge consequences, also for clinical medicine. Mildred Vera Peters demonstrated that in treating early-stage breast cancer, breast-conserving surgery followed by radiation therapy is as effective as radical mastectomy while at the same time having a much lower emotional impact [102]. A wide range of public campaigns, screening recommendations, and treatment suggestions as for instance, passive smoking protection, safer sex education, vaccination plans, breast and prostate cancer screening, and suggestions for diabetes treatment, are all based on epidemiological research.

Population studies are the main vehicle of epidemiological research. They collect hundreds of socio-demographic, lifestyle-related and health-related variables for thousands of individuals in a defined population by means of interviews, questionnaires and various medical examinations. Studies in modern epidemiological research, such as the Study of Health in Pomerania (SHiP) [144], comprise laboratory tests of blood, urine and DNA, sleep monitoring, electrocardiogram (ECG) recording and medical imaging. In 2008, SHiP was the first study to include whole-body imaging [49]. The inclusion of medical imaging in a population study bears great potential as it facilitates a survey of the broad variability in vital organ anatomy and physiology, an improved characterisation of health and disease, and a differentiation between physical effects of normal ageing and pathologies. Due to ethical reasons, non-invasive imaging techniques (MRI, ultrasound) are commonly employed for investigating a healthy population.

Epidemiological studies are often longitudinal, i. e., carried out in multiple waves over years. If a defined population is tracked over time, it is referred to as a cohort and its study is termed a cohort study [103]. Example studies comprising medical imaging, so-called image-centric cohort studies [104], are:

- SHiP [144]: Initial population: 4,308 adults of all age groups; Focus: explanation of health-related differences between East and West Germany after reunion.
- Rotterdam Study [51]: Initial population: ≈8,000 adults older than 45 years; Focus: neurological, cardiovascular, loco motor, and ophthalmic diseases.
- UK Biobank [2]: Initial population: ≈500,000 adults aged between 40-69 years; Focus: diseases with high prevalence in ageing society such as cancer, heart diseases, stroke, diabetes, and dementia.
- Norwegian Cognitive Ageing Study [154]: Initial population: 170 adults (120 female) aged between 46-77 years; Focus: understanding of relationship between brain anatomy, cognitive function, and genetics.
- German National Cohort [37]: Initial population: ≈200,000 adults aged between 20-69 years; Focus: understanding the causes of widespread diseases such as cancer, dementia, diabetes and cardiovascular diseases.

The quality of population study data is in general very high due to highly standardised and formalised data acquisition and subsequent data preparation, and rigorous quality control by experts. Datasets are comprehensively described by a data dictionary precisely defining all variables and their value ranges. However, some specifics of the data need to be considered using visual analytics approaches.

The complexity and heterogeneity of population study data are very high. Image data and derived data such as segmentation masks further increase the complexity. The collected variables relate to physical measures, aspects of lifestyle, socio-demographic factors and to visual, hearing and cognitive function. Some variables have been collected only at later stages due to technological advances or have been removed after a re-evaluation of their reliability. Other variables are only available for a subpopulation, e. g., childbirth status, or are based on follow-up questions, e. g., the number of cigarettes smoked per day is only recorded for individuals who smoke. The variables differ with respect to their data type: nominal, ordinal, or quantitative, e. g., are occupation, income level, and body height. Dichotomous variables assume only binary values (yes or no). The data type of a variable determines the set of appropriate visualisation techniques.

The analysis of epidemiological studies is hampered by unreliable and missing data. A classical example of the former are self-reports of drinking behaviour and sexual practices, which tend to be biased towards socially accepted answers. Study data may be incomplete due to individuals who drop out of the study since they pass away or move. Further reasons may be a refusal to answer particular interview questions or ineligibility for a certain imaging procedure.

10.6.1. Traditional Methods

The standard data analysis workflow in epidemiology focuses on non-image data and is driven by an a priori hypothesis, which often evolved from observations of physicians in their clinical routine (Fig. 9 (a)). For instance, the onset of a particular disease may be seen more frequently in people with a specific lifestyle. In the course of verifying the hypothesis, either a new population study is initiated or a large-scale study is analysed retrospectively given that the prevalence of the disease is high enough in the studied population. A list of variables potentially related to the hypothesis is then extracted from the study data. Next up, subgroups of individuals are defined by categorising variables, e. g., age is divided into 20 years bins in order to determine a per-group risk of falling ill with the disease.

From the list of variables, confounders must be identified and later considered when interpreting the results. For instance, the effects of alcohol consumption on a certain health condition may be overestimated when the potentially confounding variables of smoking and diet are neglected. Without the control of confounders, wrong causal relationships may be derived from the associations of variables.

Finally, associations between the variables and the investigated disease are determined using statistical methods such as regression analysis. The associations indicate whether variables/factors influence the disease thereby confirming or disproving the given hypothesis. The statistical significance of this influence (p-value) and the relative risk of falling ill with the disease relative to a factor represent important outcomes of epidemiological research. Visualisation plays a minor role in the standard epidemiological workflow and is restricted to statistical plots such as histograms, Kaplan-Meier curves and odds ratio plots.

Incorporating the analysis of image data of a population into the workflow poses challenges [136]. The images itself are too complex to be fed directly into the analysis pipeline which is tailored to variables aggregated in a data table. Moreover, epidemiologists are not interested in the images themselves but in descriptors, which characterise the phenomena of interest. For instance, in an investigation of lumbar back pain by Klemm *et al.* [70], the lumbar spine was detected in the image data of a population by means of a hierarchical finite element model [107]. Once fitted to the spine in the images of an individual, the model captured the position and orientation of the vertebrae as well as the bending of the spinal canal. Based on the segmentation results, average models of subpopulations were computed and analysed [71]. Furthermore, numerical measures characterising the bending of the spinal canal were derived, integrated into the data table and jointly investigated with the non-image data [69]. This approach can be generalised to other phenomena of interest.

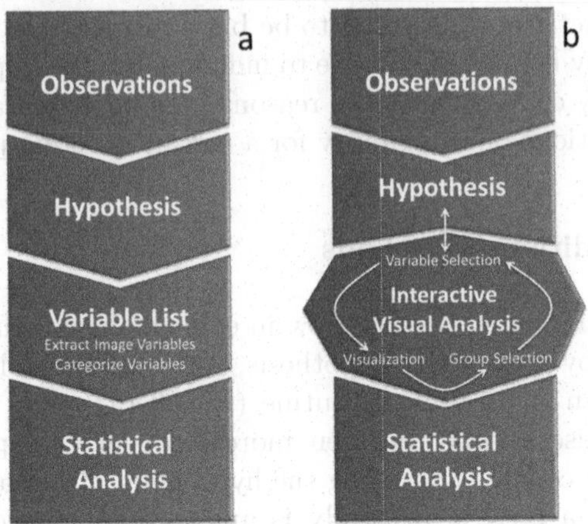

Fig. 9: (a) Standard data analysis workflow in epidemiology. Variables are manually extracted from the data table and categorised to form subgroups. (b) The standard workflow is complemented by an interactive visual analysis step. It installs a feedback loop and allows for a more flexible variable selection and categorisation. Image adapted from [71].

10.6.2. Immersive Methods

While immersive environments are not yet used in evaluating population study data, visual analytics approaches designed to tightly engage an epidemiologist have been proposed. The standard data analysis workflow in epidemiology is sequential and based on an a priori hypothesis and a rather static definition of subgroups. Visual analytics approaches incorporate the epidemiologist in an interactive and iterative analysis process and thereby, support hypothesis generation and a flexible subgroup definition as part of an extended workflow yielding a more immersive experience. Turkay *et al.* [138] investigated data from the Norwegian Cognitive Ageing Study employing their dual analysis coordinated multiple views (CMV) framework. They demonstrated the generation of new hypotheses in pair analysis sessions with domain experts. Klemm *et al.* [71] proposed the integration of an interactive visual analysis step into the standard epidemiological workflow (Fig. 9 (b)). In their CMV framework, variables can be added or removed from the analysis via drag and drop and the definition of subpopulations (group selection) can be adjusted interactively, both triggering an update of the statistical analysis (Fig. 10). Angelelli *et al.* [4] proposed a dedicated data model for visual analytics of population study data that accounts for data heterogeneity. They further presented an implementation of the model in a CMV framework, which was utilised for hypothesis generation in an investigation of the Norwegian Cognitive Ageing Study. Bernard *et al.* [7] presented a visual-interactive system for the analysis of prostate cancer cohorts and demonstrated its integration in an epidemiological workflow for hypothesis testing and generation.

Krause *et al.* [73] presented an approach to subpopulation definition based on temporal patterns of interest and pattern matching.

The data mining component of the analytics process facilitates a data-driven definition of subpopulations revealing more complex, hidden patterns. For instance, individuals may be clustered according to variables derived from image data or socio-demographic and lifestyle-related variables. The resulting clusters can then be interrelated with other variables. Klemm *et al.* [71] clustered a SHiP subpopulation regarding their spinal canal bending and related each cluster, e. g., to self-reported back pain and the level of physically demanding work. They augmented the bar chart and mosaic plot of their coordinated multiple views system by interactive small multiples of average lumbar spine shape. For instance in a bar chart of back pain clusters, the mean shape per bar/cluster is displayed and coloured according to its deviation from the mean of the entire population (Fig. 10 (b)). In a follow-up work, Klemm *et al.* [69] trained decision tree classifiers to predict lumbar back pain indicators based on image-derived variables and compared the predictive power of different types of decision trees by means of generalised pairs plots [32].

10.6.3. Critical Analysis

Visual analytics and interactive visual analysis are relatively new concepts to epidemiologists. Most of the described approaches have been implemented in CMV frameworks which are highly interactive and very flexible. While being an advantage on one hand, a lack of guidance on which views to use when and for what type of variables can also represent a hurdle for epidemiologists. Moreover, the frameworks incorporate data mining techniques whose parameters need to be fine-tuned. For instance, adjusting the parameters of a clustering algorithm is often necessary in order to define reasonable subgroups. However, fine-tuning these parameters represents another hurdle since epidemiologists are in general no data mining experts. As a consequence, most CMV frameworks were used in pair analytics sessions of a domain expert and a computer scientist. The computer scientist knows the specifics of data analysis and visualisation and can tweak the corresponding parameters. The domain expert knows how to fine-tune application-specific analytical components, can interpret intermediate analysis results and poses the relevant questions to proceed. While this separation yields hypotheses in a shorter time, it hampers the immersion of the epidemiologist into the data and their analysis.

10.6.4. Future in Immersive Analytics

In order to increase immersion, approaches are required that facilitate a more engaging and autonomous use of the CMV framework by the epidemiologist. This includes the suggestion of optimal views based on the variable type and the number of variables to be investigated. Klemm *et al.* [71] proposed to update the appropriate plot type whenever the user is dragging a new variable to the analysis canvas (Fig. 10 (d)). For instance, one continuous variable is represented by a

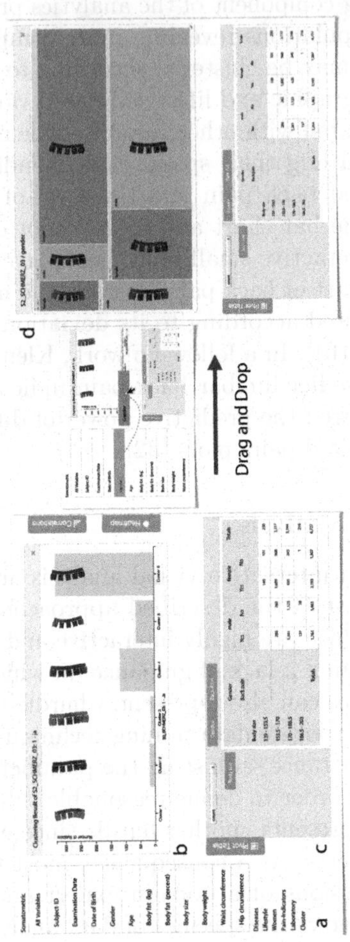

Fig. 10: Coordinated multiple views framework for the analysis of population study data demonstrated by lower back pain investigation [71]. *(a)* Sidebar containing all variables of the study. *(b)* Analysis canvas where variables can be dragged and visualisations are created. A bar chart of back pain clusters is shown. *(c)* Pivot table for opposing the categories of interesting variables. *(d)* The categorical variable gender is dragged from the sidebar and dropped over the bar chart thereby causing the replacement of the chart by a mosaic plot relating pain clusters and gender. Bar chart and mosaic plot are augmented by a mean shape of the lumbar spine displayed for each subgroup. *Image courtesy of Paul Klemm.*

histogram. Adding a second continuous variable changes the plot to a scatter plot and adding a third to a parallel coordinates plot [55]. For incrementally adding solely categorical variables, a mosaic plot [47] is employed while generalised pairs plot [32] are applied for a combination of continuous and categorical variables. Another step toward an increased immersion is to make data mining more accessible to non-experts and help them in finding optimal solutions without knowing details of the underlying algorithm. Related work in image processing provides visual guidance through an abstraction of the parameter space of segmentation and clustering techniques [121,137].

Storytelling with data gives the epidemiologist an opportunity to communicate the analysis process, e. g., to a colleague who may be more immersed by a sequence of orchestrated visualisations than by a pure display of the analysis results. Storytelling requires a way of monitoring and protocolling the analysis workflow. A suitable approach based on a film-strip metaphor has been proposed in the context of CMV systems by van den Elzen *et al.* [140]. It supports capturing all intermediate steps of an analysis process which can then be revisited and adapted using a rewind and fast-forward navigation mechanism.

The concurrent investigation of population image and non-image data may benefit from being carried out in an immersive environment as discussed for the investigation of brain's structure, function, and connectivity (Sec. 10.3., Fig. 2). For instance, shape models of the spine of subpopulations can be related to lifestyle and socio-demographic factors. Population study data are often acquired with a spatial reference, e. g. the street address. Relating attributes to geographical location can be crucial when the latter is suspected of having an impact on the investigated phenomenon, e. g. distance to the sea and hence, access to fresh fish on the incidence of thyroid disorders. The comprehension of such relations may be supported by linked geographical maps and abstract 2D attribute views presented in an immersive environment.

10.7. Case Study 6: Collaborative Immersive Analytics in Life and Health Sciences

Collaboration is a major part of immersive analytics and plays an important role in applications from the life and health sciences domain (see Chap. 8). In this application example, the focus is on collaboration as a way for remote or co-located groups of people to investigate a given problem or dataset using visual analytics to gain an understanding of the problem or dataset [48,56].

10.7.1. Traditional Methods

Local and remote visual collaboration is being used already in different domains, e. g., scientists share data and images with remote collaborating labs for discussion and experiment planning, doctors share X-ray images with colleagues to discuss further patient treatment and manufacturers share schematics, photos etc. with clients to discuss details of fabrication. Interaction is an important aspect of collaboration in immersive and visual analytics [65], and in all of these examples users share and annotate static content, such as images, for collaborative exploration and understanding using interactive methods with the ultimate goal to support knowledge generation and decision making.

In the last few years a variety of software and/or hardware products have been released supporting local and remote collaboration in various application areas:

- online text document sharing, e. g., Evernote, Google Drive;
- online image sharing + image annotation, e. g., A.nnotate, Marqueed, RealtimeBoard;
- screen sharing using video conferencing software, e. g., Google Hangouts, Skype, TeamViewer, Zoom;
- source code sharing, e. g., Git repositories, Subversion repositories;
- interactive whiteboards, e. g., Hitachi Interactive Whiteboard, Smoothboard Air;
- meeting room collaborative environments, e. g., Cisco Spark Board, DisplayNote, Google Jamboard, Intel Unite, Microsoft Surface Hub;
- large display environments for collaboration, e. g., SAGE2 [111], Jupiter Canvas, Mersive Solstice; and
- video conference systems, e. g., Polycom, Cisco Immersive TelePresence.

Text document, image or source code sharing solutions are often cloud-based [63] and lack privacy. Even with paid services, data is not necessarily private since it is most often stored on non-private servers which might be an issue in collaborations when data cannot be disclosed. Screen sharing solutions have the disadvantage that only one person at a time can manipulate the content and the resolution depends on the device sharing its screen. Interactive whiteboards require specialised hardware and not all support remote collaboration. Most proprietary solutions such as Intel Unite, Jupiter Canvas, and Mersive Solstice offer limited extensibility or integration of customised applications.

Furthermore, since the 1980s several research projects have been run on local collaboration using large displays and corresponding interaction methods. Examples are CAV [31], Colab [132], i–LAND [135], Augmented Surfaces [110], iRoom [58], MultiSpace [33], Table-Centric Interactive Spaces [148], and IMPROMPTU [9]. An overview of recent projects can be found in Brown *et al.* [11].

10.7.2. Immersive Methods

Immersive analytics employs novel display and interaction hardware such as large display walls, zSpace [157], recent head-mounted displays (HMD) [146], touch devices and similar low-cost equipment to bring immersive collaboration into offices and labs (see Chap. 1). Such a democratising access to new technology is possible thanks to affordable consumer grade hardware which is available nowadays.

This section focuses on ContextuWall [68], an open source collaboration tool supporting a wide variety of available hardware and enabling users to share and annotate images. The ContextuWall system is designed as a client-server-display framework with: the client being the interface for the user to share content, the server synchronising its content with multiple remote sites, and the display rendering shared content and associated annotations (see Fig. 11).

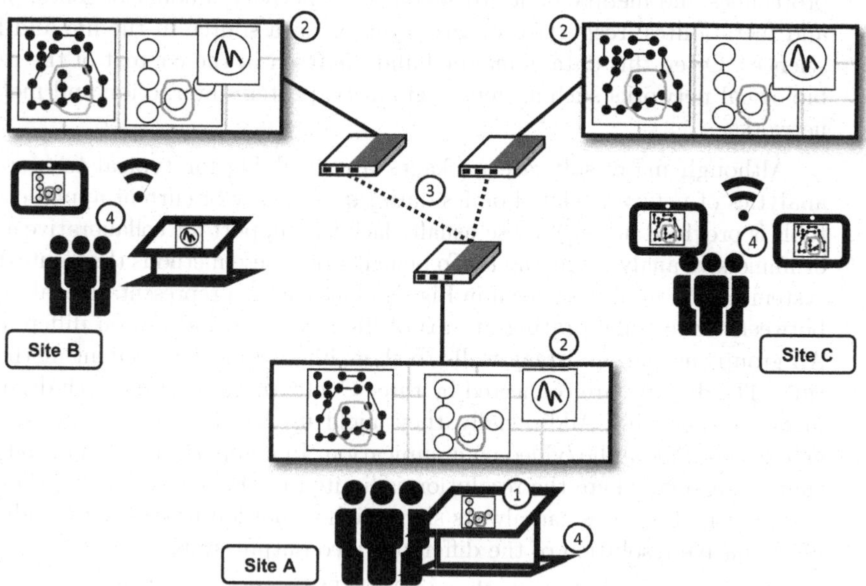

Fig. 11: Application of the ContextuWall system where site A started to share high-resolution images with site B and site C using the ContextuWall client (1). All sites use display wall systems (2) with different sizes (aspect ratios) to show the images which are synchronised over the server network (3). The participating sites collaborate by arranging the content on the display as well as annotating content using their portable or touch table devices which run the ContextuWall client (4), enabling each site to focus the discussion on particular details.

ContextuWall can connect multiple remote sites, runs under full control in an organisation's network, and makes use of various display technologies from consumer grade to professional and highly-priced hardware (e. g. Cave Automatic Virtual Environment–*CAVE* [36]). It creates a virtual shared large desktop supporting different display configurations and provides synchronised interactive exploration as well as simultaneous manipulation of displayed content from multiple connected sites. The client for sharing and annotating content can be any smartphone, tablet, notebook or touch table computer running at least Microsoft Windows 8 or Android 5.0. Possible display configurations to show shared and annotated content can range from single screen displays to clustered multi-screen displays [114] utilising different software frameworks, such as the omegalib framework [35], SAGE2 [111], or the Unity Game Engine [139].

The following use-case is a typical application for collaborative analysis using the ContextuWall system with a multi-site setup (as seen in Fig. 11). It shows how scientists can work, analyse and exchange information about a large-scale omics data set in a distributed lab environment. Omics data, such as transcriptomics, proteomics and metabolomics (describing the activity/amount of genes, proteins and metabolites, respectively), are a major data source in the life and health sciences. Often this data is mapped and analysed in the context of the relevant biological networks such as gene-regulatory, protein-interaction and metabolic networks.

Although many software packages are available for typical tasks of data analytics of network-related omics data (an overview of current approaches and tools is provided in [66]), these usually lack the support for collaborative analysis or immersive analytics methods. To benefit from these methods the ContextuWall system can be set up as shown in Fig. 11. This shows a representative lab meeting between three collaborating groups of life scientists, located on different sites. All groups use large display walls to show high-resolution content at the same time. The displays are connected by three ContextuWall servers, each driving one display respectively. Additionally, they might use a video conferencing system to enable separate audio/video communication. In comparison to a normal screen sharing session, where the resolution is limited to the device sharing the screen, the participating sites can always share high-resolution images taking advantage of the native resolution of the different video output systems.

One group, located at site A, uses VANTED [62,116], a JAVA-based software for visualising experimental data on biological networks, which is extendible by add-ons. A specific add-on has been developed to enable VANTED to share images of entire networks or selected network regions of interest with data and/or analysis results mapped onto the network on large display walls using the ContextuWall system (see Fig. 12). In this example, a biologist located on site A starts the discussion by displaying a metabolic network (in this case derived from the MetaCrop/MetaAll database [119,145]) with experimental data obtained in their own labs mapped onto the network. This enriched network is shared as a high-resolution image which can be zoomed, panned and annotated using the ContextuWall client to get an overview of both the network and its mapped data. During the discussion scientists on site B and site C are then interested in particular regions of this network which they would like to investigate in more detail. They can engage with their colleagues and interactively annotate regions of interest using their own clients, these annotations can be directly seen by the colleagues on all sites. As a next step, for example, the group at site A can provide additional data for the annotated regions in VANTED and these new selections are then shared as additional high-resolution images between the groups. The entire network, as well as selected parts, can be viewed simultaneously on all sites and arranged next to each other creating a factual context. After some discussion within or between the participating groups, colleagues on site B would like to see more details about a particular element in the network. Site A can now create another detailed image of this element. All images can be investigated on the displays on all sites at the same time giving the scientists a method to move from an overview to a detailed view without losing the context. At any point in time, users can download the full-sized images including the annotations added throughout the discussions.

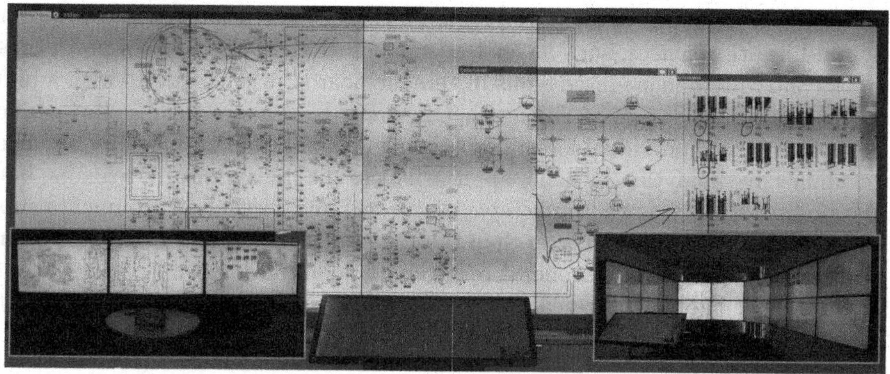

Fig. 12: A scenario showing a power wall in the background, a three 4k screen setup in the lower left and a system with 18 4k screens in the lower right of the figure. All systems run their own ContextuWall server. Each site can use their clients (tablet or touch table devices) respectively to annotate the content. The images shown are compiled from the MetaCrop database [45, 119].

10.7.3. Critical Analysis

The ContextuWall system is a first step towards collaboration in immersive analytics. With its three-tier client-server-display infrastructure, it enables users to combine a variety of technologies including affordable consumer hardware to set up an environment for local and remote collaboration. Using touch-enabled devices and large displays to share and annotate images users on multiple sites can connect and work together on a jointly used virtual desktop. Currently, ContextuWall is limited to sharing and annotation of static 2D content only. To be more generally useful for immersive analytics applications in the life and health sciences an extension will be necessary that allows sharing and annotation of static as well as dynamic 3D content using standard and stereoscopic display technologies to incorporate mixed 2D and projected/stereoscopic 3D content [124]. The annotation of 3D content could be made available in two different ways: 1) placement of a 2D annotation canvas as a texture in 3D space, and 2) brushing annotations on the 3D content using 3D tracked wand hardware.

Immersive analytics is still lacking solid foundations for several aspects including the definition of immersion in analytics processes, metrics for its quantification, and the quantification of its effects on analysis performance. All these aspects also affect collaboration, and there are only very few studies so far which evaluate performance for collaborative tasks in immersive environments, such as the study of Cordeil *et al.* [18].

10.7.4. Future in Immersive Analytics

Collaborative data analysis is a requirement for many challenging tasks in the life and health sciences, such as for the collaborative development of new drugs and for interdisciplinary discussions in tumour boards, where experts with a different background need to work together in order to solve problems that cannot be solved by an individual alone. Supporting collaboration is thus a requirement for immersive analytics for many applications in the life and health sciences, but also an opportunity as the immersive real world and virtual environments support, e. g., co-location much better than the classical keyboard and mouse environments. While there is a lot of general research on collaboration and co-presence, there is however not much research yet on collaboration in virtual environments for complex data analytics (see Chap. 8).

10.8. Challenges and Outlook

In summary, this chapter has promised a variety of application examples of Immersive Analytics (IA) in the Health and Life Sciences. Each particular example summarised traditional visualisation methods followed by a discussion of novel Immersive Analytics methods, a critical analysis and some outlook towards the future of IA in this specific field. There are many open challenges as well as research opportunities including better support of collaboration for teams in immersive environments, novel scalability solutions to deal with the huge amount of data and improved complexity handling addressing the complexity of the data (i. e., data integration) as well as the complexity of analysis tasks.

Each application example in this chapter details particular challenges and opportunities. There is yet a lack of formal evaluation and comprehensive usability studies applying immersive technologies in the health and life sciences to provide evidence how beneficial those technologies are for the domain. Either not much research has been conducted yet, e. g., on collaboration in immersive environments for complex data analytics, or research has only just been started to explore the capabilities of immersive analytics for health and life sciences. However, the exploration and analysis of integrated heterogeneous data sets from the domain, e. g., 2D image data or 3D volume data and additional non-image data, will likely benefit from being carried out in immersive analytics environments.

We hope that this overview will provide a starting point for investigations and will inspire others to do their own projects for immersive analytics in the Health and Life Sciences. There are many open research questions and challenges as well as interesting applications for IA approaches.

References

1. Akkiraju, N., Edelsbrunner, H., Fu, P., Qian, J.: Viewing geometric protein structures from inside a CAVE. IEEE Computer Graphics and Applications 16(4), 58–61 (1996)
2. Allen, N., Sudlow, C., Downey, P., Peakman, T., Danesh, J., Elliott, P., Gallacher, J., Green, J., Matthews, P., Pell, J., Sprosen, T., Collins, R.: UK Biobank: Current status and what it means for epidemiology. Health Policy and Technology 1(3), 123–126 (2012)
3. Anderson, A., Weng, Z.: VRDD: applying virtual reality visualization to protein docking and design. Journal of Molecular Graphics and Modelling 17, 180–186 (1999)
4. Angelelli, P., Oeltze, S., Turkay, C., Haász, J., Hodneland, E., Lundervold, A., Lundervold, A.J., Preim, B., Hauser, H.: Interactive visual analysis of heterogeneous cohort study data. IEEE Computer Graphics and Applications 34(5), 70–82 (2014)
5. Asai, K., Takase, N.: Learning molecular structures in a tangible augmented reality environment. International Journal of Virtual and Personal Learning Environments 2(1), 1–18 (2011)
6. Avogadro. http://avogadro.cc/, [last accessed 20/04/17]
7. Bernard, J., Sessler, D., May, T., Schlomm, T., Pehrke, D., Kohlhammer, J.: A visual-interactive system for prostate cancer cohort analysis. IEEE Computer Graphics and Applications 35(3), 44–55 (2015)
8. Bi, L., Kim, J., Kumar, A., Wen, L., Feng, D., Fulham, M.: Automatic detection and classification of regions of fdg uptake in whole-body pet-ct lymphoma studies. Computerized Medical Imaging and Graphics 60, 3–10 (2017)
9. Biehl, J.T., Baker, W.T., Bailey, B.P., Tan, D.S., Inkpen, K.M., Czerwinski, M.: IMPROMPTU: A new interaction framework for supporting collaboration in multiple display environments and its field evaluation for co-located software development. In: Proceedings of the SIGCHI Conference on Human Factors in Computing Systems. pp. 939–948. CHI '08, ACM, New York, NY, USA (2008)
10. Binder, J.X., Pletscher-Frankild, S., Tsafou, K., Stolte, C., O'Donoghue, S.I., Schneider, R., Jensen, L.J.: COMPARTMENTS: unification and visualization of protein subcellular localization evidence. Database 2014(1), bau012 (2014)
11. Brown, J., Wilson, J., Gossage, S., Hack, C., Biddle, R.: Surface computing and collaborative analysis work. Synthesis Lectures on Human-Centered Informatics, Morgan & Claypool Publishers (2013)
12. Campbell, I.D.: The march of structural biology. Nature Reviews Molecular Cell Biology 3(5), 377–381 (2002)
13. Carnevale, N.T., Hines, M.L.: The NEURON Book. Cambridge University Press, New York, NY, USA (2006)
14. Chandler, T., Cordeil, M., Czauderna, T., Dwyer, T., Glowacki, J., Goncu, C., Klapperstueck, M., Klein, K., Marriott, K., Schreiber, F., Wilson, E.: Immersive analytics. In: IEEE Big Data Visual Analytics (BDVA) 2015. pp. 73–80. IEEE eXpress Conference Publishing (2015)
15. Chen, M., Hofestädt, R.: Approaches in integrative bioinformatics: towards the virtual cell. Springer Publishing Company, Incorporated (2014)
16. Chimera. http://www.cgl.ucsf.edu/chimera/, [last accessed 20/04/17]
17. Coles, T.R., John, N.W., Gould, D., Caldwell, D.G.: Integrating haptics with augmented reality in a femoral palpation and needle insertion training simulation. IEEE Transactions on Haptics 4(3), 199–209 (2011)

18. Cordeil, M., Dwyer, T., Klein, K., Laha, B., Marriot, K., Thomas, B.H.: Immersive collaborative analysis of network connectivity: CAVE-style or head-mounted display? IEEE Transactions on Visualization and Computer Graphics 23, 441–450 (2017)
19. Cosentino, F., John, N.W., Vaarkamp, J.: An overview of augmented and virtual reality applications in radiotherapy and future developments enabled by modern tablet devices. Journal of Radiotherapy in Practice 13(3), 350–364 (2014)
20. Crivelli, S., Kreylos, O., Hamann, B., Max, N., Bethel, W.: ProteinShop: a tool for interactive protein manipulation and steering. Journal of Computer-Aided Molecular Design 18(4), 271–285 (2004)
21. Cruz-Neira, C., Leigh, J., Papka, M.E., Barnes, C., Cohen, S.M., Das, S., Engelmann, R., Hudson, R., Roy, T., Siegel, L., Vasilakis, C., DeFanti, T.A., Sandin, D.J.: Scientists in wonderland: A report on visualization applications in the CAVE virtual reality environment. In: Proceedings of 1993 IEEE Research Properties in Virtual Reality Symposium. pp. 59–66 (1993)
22. Cruz-Neira, C., Sandin, D.J., DeFanti, T.A.: Surround-screen projection-based virtual reality: the design and implementation of the CAVE. In: Proceedings of the 20th Annual Conference on Computer Graphics and Interactive Techniques (SIGGRAPH '93). pp. 135–142. ACM (1993)
23. Cruz-Neira, C., Sandin, D.J., DeFanti, T.A., Kenyon, R.V., Hart, J.C.: The CAVE: audio visual experience automatic virtual environment. Communications of the ACM 35(6), 64–72 (1992)
24. Czauderna, T., Klukas, C., Schreiber, F.: Editing, validating and translating of SBGN maps. Bioinformatics 26(18), 2340–2341 (2010)
25. Czauderna, T., Wybrow, M., Marriott, K., Schreiber, F.: Conversion of KEGG metabolic pathways to SBGN maps including automatic layout. BMC Bioinformatics 14, 250 (2013)
26. Czernuszenko, M., Pape, D., Sandin, D., DeFanti, T., Dawe, G.L., Brown, M.D.: The ImmersaDesk and infinity wall projection-based virtual reality displays. ACM SIGGRAPH Computer Graphics 31(2), 46–49 (1997)
27. de Ridder, M., Jung, Y., Huang, R., Kim, J., Feng, D.D.: Exploration of virtual and augmented reality for visual analytics and 3D volume rendering of functional magnetic resonance imaging (fMRI) data. In: IEEE Big Data Visual Analytics (BDVA) 2015. pp. 49–56. IEEE eXpress Conference Publishing (2015)
28. de Ridder, M., Klein, K., Kim, J.: CereVA - visual analysis of functional brain connectivity. In: Proceedings of the 6th International Conference on Information Visualization Theory and Applications (IVAPP2015). pp. 131–138. SciTePress (2015)
29. Dreher, M., Piuzzi, M., Turki, A., Chavent, M., Baaden, M., Férey, N., Limet, S., Raffin, B., Robert, S.: Interactive molecular dynamics: scaling up to large systems. Procedia Computer Science 18, 20–29 (2013)
30. Dwyer, T., Marriott, K., Schreiber, F., Stuckey, P.J., Woodward, M., Wybrow, M.: Exploration of networks using overview+detail with constraint-based cooperative layout. IEEE Transaction on Visualization and Computer Graphics 14(6), 1293–1300 (2008)
31. Ellis, S.E., Groth, D.P.: A collaborative annotation system for data visualization. In: Proceedings of the Working Conference on Advanced Visual Interfaces. pp. 411–414. AVI '04, ACM, New York, NY, USA (2004)
32. Emerson, J.W., Green, W.A., Schloerke, B., Crowley, J., Cook, D., Hofmann, H., Wickham, H.: The generalized pairs plot. Journal of Computational and Graphical Statistics 22(1), 79–91 (2013)

33. Everitt, K., Shen, C., Ryall, K., Forlines, C.: MultiSpace: Enabling electronic document micro-mobility in table-centric, multi-device environments. In: Proceedings of the First IEEE International Workshop on Horizontal Interactive Human-Computer Systems. pp. 27–34. TABLETOP '06, IEEE Computer Society, Washington, DC, USA (2006)
34. Falk, M., Krone, M., Ertl, T.: Atomistic visualization of mesoscopic whole-cell simulations using ray-casted instancing. In: Computer Graphics Forum. vol. 32, pp. 195–206. Wiley Online Library (2013)
35. Febretti, A., Nishimoto, A., Mateevitsi, V., Renambot, L., Johnson, A., Leigh, J.: Omegalib: A multi-view application framework for hybrid reality display environments. IEEE Virtual Reality pp. 9–14 (2014)
36. Febretti, A., Nishimoto, A., Thigpen, T., Talandis, J., Long, L., Pirtle, J.D., Peterka, T., Verlo, A., Brown, M., Plepys, D.: CAVE2: a hybrid reality environment for immersive simulation and information analysis. In: IS&T/SPIE Electronic Imaging. pp. 864903.1–12. International Society for Optics and Photonics (2013)
37. German National Cohort Consortium: The German National Cohort: Aims, study design and organization. European Journal of Epidemiology 29(5), 371–382 (2014)
38. Geurts, A., Sakas, G., Kuijper, A., Becker, M., von Landesberger, T.: Visual comparison of 3D medical image segmentation algorithms based on statistical shape models. In: Duffy, V.G. (ed.) Proceedings of the Sixth International Conference on Digital Human Modeling – Applications in Health, Safety, Ergonomics and Risk Management. Part II: Ergonomics and Health, Lecture Notes in Computer Science, vol. 9185, pp. 336–344. Springer International Publishing (2015)
39. Gewaltig, M.O., Diesmann, M.: NEST (neural simulation tool). Scholarpedia 2(4), 1430 (2007)
40. Gillet, A., Sanner, M., Stoffler, D., Goodsell, D., Olson, A.: Augmented reality with tangible auto-fabricated models for molecular biology applications. In: Proceedings of the Conference on Visualization '04 (VIS '04). pp. 235–242. IEEE Computer Society (2004)
41. Gillet, A., Sanner, M., Stoffler, D., Olson, A.: Tangible interfaces for structural molecular biology. Structure 13(3), 483–491 (2005)
42. Giraldo-Chica, M., Woodward, N.D.: Review of thalamocortical resting-state fMRI studies in schizophrenia. Schizophrenia Research 180, 58–63 (2017)
43. Glaßer, S., Preim, U., Tönnies, K., Preim, B.: A visual analytics approach to diagnosis of breast DCE-MRI data. Computers & Graphics 34(5), 602–611 (2010)
44. GLmol. http://webglmol.osdn.jp/index-en.html, [last accessed 20/04/17]
45. Grafahrend-Belau, E., Weise, S., Koschützki, D., Scholz, U., Junker, B.H., Schreiber, F.: MetaCrop - a detailed database of crop plant metabolism. Nucleic Acids Research 36, D954–D958 (2008)
46. Greffard, N., Picarougne, F., Kuntz, P.: Visual community detection: An evaluation of 2D, 3D perspective and 3D stereoscopic displays. In: International Symposium on Graph Drawing. pp. 215–225. Springer (2011)
47. Hartigan, J.A., Kleiner, B.: Mosaics for contingency tables. In: Computer Science and Statistics: Proceedings of the Symposium on the Interface. pp. 268–273 (1981)
48. Heer, J., Agrawala, M.: Design considerations for collaborative visual analytics. Information Visualization 7(1), 49–62 (2008)
49. Hegenscheid, K., Kühn, J., Völzke, H., Biffar, R., Hosten, N., Puls, R.: Whole-body magnetic resonance imaging of healthy volunteers: Pilot study results from the population-based SHIP study. RoFo: Fortschritte auf dem Gebiete der Röntgenstrahlen und der Nuklearmedizin 181(8), 748–759 (2009)

50. Hermann, M., Klein, R.: A visual analytics perspective on shape analysis: State of the art and future prospects. Computers & Graphics 53, Part A, 63–71 (2015)
51. Hofman, A., Brusselle, G.G., Murad, S.D., van Duijn, C.M., Franco, O.H., Goedegebure, A., Ikram, M.A., Klaver, C.C., Nijsten, T.E., Peeters, R.P., Stricker, B.H.C., Tiemeier, H.W., Uitterlinden, A.G., Vernooij, M.W.: The Rotterdam study: 2016 objectives and design update. European Journal of Epidemiology 30(8), 661–708 (2015)
52. Hucka, M., Finney, A., Sauro, H.M., Bolouri, H., Doyle, J.C., Kitano, H., Arkin, A.P., et al.: The systems biology markup language (SBML): a medium for representation and exchange of biochemical network models. Bioinformatics 19, 524–531 (2003)
53. The human brain project. https://www.humanbrainproject.eu/, [last accessed 20/04/17]
54. Im, W., Liang, J., Olson, A., Zhou, H.X., Vajda, S., Vakser, I.A.: Challenges in structural approaches to cell modeling. Journal of Molecular Biology 428(15), 2943–2964(2016)
55. Inselberg, A., Dimsdale, B.: Parallel coordinates: a tool for visualizing multi-dimensional geometry. In: Proceedings of IEEE Visualization. pp. 361–378 (1990)
56. Isenberg, P., Elmqvist, N., Scholtz, J., Cernea, D., Ma, K.L., Hagen, H.: Collaborative visualization: definition, challenges, and research agenda. Information Visualization 10(4), 310–326 (2011)
57. Jmol. http://jmol.sourceforge.net/, [last accessed 20/04/17]
58. Johanson, B., Fox, A., Winograd, T.: The interactive workspaces project: Experiences with ubiquitous computing rooms. IEEE Pervasive Computing 1(2), 67–74 (2002)
59. Johnson, G.T., Autin, L., Goodsell, D.S., Sanner, M.F., Olson, A.J.: ePMV embeds molecular modeling into professional animation software environments. Structure 19(3), 293–303 (2011)
60. Johnson, G.T., Autin, L., Al-Alusi, M., Goodsell, D.S., Sanner, M.F., Olson, A.J.: cellPACK: a virtual mesoscope to model and visualize structural systems biology. Nature Methods 12(1), 85–91 (2015)
61. Johnson, G.R., Donovan-Maiye, R.M., Maleckar, M.M.: Generative modeling with conditional autoencoders: Building an integrated cell. arXiv preprint arXiv:1705.00092 (2017)
62. Junker, B.H., Klukas, C., Schreiber, F.: VANTED: A system for advanced data analysis and visualization in the context of biological networks. BMC Bioinformatics 7(1), 109.1–13 (2006)
63. Kahin, B., Keller, J.H.: The self-governing internet: coordination by design. In: Kahin, B., Keller, J.H. (eds.) Coordinating the Internet, pp. 3–38. MIT Press (1997)
64. Kanehisa, M., Goto, S., Sato, Y., Furumichi, M., Tanabe, M.: KEGG for integration and interpretation of large-scale molecular data sets. Nucleic Acids Research 40(1), D109–D114 (2012)
65. Kerren, A., Schreiber, F.: Toward the role of interaction in visual analytics. In: Proceedings of the Winter Simulation Conference. vol. 420, pp. 1–13 (2012)
66. Kerren, A., Schreiber, F.: Network visualization for integrative bioinformatics. In: Chen, M., Hofestädt, R. (eds.) Approaches in Integrative Bioinformatics: Towards the Virtual Cell, pp. 173–202. Springer (2013)
67. Kieffer, S., Dwyer, T., Marriott, K., Wybrow, M.: Hola: Human-like orthogonal network layout. IEEE Transactions on Visualization and Computer Graphics 22(1), 349–358 (2016)

68. Klapperstück, M., Czauderna, T., Goncu, C., Glowacki, J., Dwyer, T., Schreiber, F., Marriott, K.: ContextuWall: peer collaboration using (large) displays. In: IEEE Big Data Visual Analytics (BDVA) 2016. pp. 7–14 (2016)
69. Klemm, P., Glaßer, S., Lawonn, K., Rak, M., Völzke, H., Hegenscheid, K., Preim, B.: Interactive visual analysis of lumbar back pain. In: International Conference on Information Visualization Theory and Applications (IVAPP). pp. 85–92 (2015)
70. Klemm, P., Lawonn, K., Rak, M., Preim, B., Tönnies, K.D., Hegenscheid, K., Völzke, H., Oeltze, S.: Visualization and analysis of lumbar spine canal variability in cohort study data. In: Bronstein, M., Favre, J., Hormann, K. (eds.) International Workshop on Vision, Modeling and Visualization (VMV). pp. 121–128 (2013)
71. Klemm, P., Oeltze-Jafra, S., Lawonn, K., Hegenscheid, K., Völzke, H., Preim, B.: Interactive visual analysis of image-centric cohort study data. IEEE Transactions on Visualization and Computer Graphics 20(12), 1673–1682 (2014)
72. Klukas, C., Schreiber, F.: Dynamic exploration and editing of KEGG pathway diagrams. Bioinformatics 23(3), 344–350 (2007)
73. Krause, J., Perer, A., Stavropoulos, H.: Supporting iterative cohort construction with visual temporal queries. IEEE Transactions on Visualization and Computer Graphics 22(1), 91–100 (2016)
74. Kuhlen, T.W., Hentschel, B.: Towards an explorative visual analysis of cortical neuronal network simulations. In: Grandinetti, L., Lippert, T., Petkov, N. (eds.) Brain-Inspired Computing: First International Workshop, BrainComp 2013, Revised Selected Papers, pp. 171–183. Springer International Publishing (2014)
75. Kuhlen, T.W., Hentschel, B.: Towards the ultimate display for neuroscientific data analysis. In: Amunts, K., Grandinetti, L., Lippert, T., Petkov, N. (eds.) Brain-Inspired Computing: Second International Workshop, BrainComp 2015, Revised Selected Papers, pp. 157–168. Springer International Publishing (2016)
76. Kumar, A., Kim, J., Lyndon, D., Fulham, M., Feng, D.: An ensemble of fine-tuned convolutional neural networks for medical image classification. IEEE Journal of Biomedical and Health Informatics 21(1), 31–40 (2017)
77. Kumar, A., Nette, F., Klein, K., Fulham, M., Kim, J.: A visual analytics approach using the exploration of multidimensional feature spaces for content-based medical image retrieval. IEEE Journal of Biomedical and Health Informatics 19(5), 1734–1746 (2015)
78. Lander, A.D.: The edges of understanding. BMC Biology 8(1), 40.1–4 (2010)
79. Langs, G., Hanbury, A., Menze, B., Müller, H.: VISCERAL: Towards large data in medical imaging – challenges and directions. In: Greenspan, H., Müller, H., Syeda-Mahmood, T. (eds.) Medical Content-Based Retrieval for Clinical Decision Support: Third MICCAI International Workshop, MCBR-CDS 2012, pp. 92–98. Springer Berlin Heidelberg, Berlin, Heidelberg (2013)
80. Lau, C.D., Levesque, M.J., Chien, S., Date, S., Haga, J.H.: ViewDock TDW: high-throughput visualization of virtual screening results. Bioinformatics 26(15), 1915–1917 (2010)
81. Le Novère, N., Hucka, M., Mi, H., Moodie, S., Schreiber, F., Sorokin, A., Demir, E., Wegner, K., Ghazal, P., et al.: The systems biology graphical notation. Nature Biotechnology 27, 735–741 (2009)
82. Levinthal, C., Barry, C.D., Ward, S.A., Zwick, M.: Computer graphics in macromolecular chemistry. In: Emerging Concepts In Computer Graphics, pp. 231–253. W. A. Benjamin (1968)
83. Liao, Z., Kong, L., Wang, X., Zhao, Y., Zhou, F., Liao, Z., Fan, X.: A visual analytics approach for detecting and understanding anomalous resident behaviors in smart healthcare. Applied Sciences 7(3), 254.1–13 (2017)

84. Loew, L.M., Schaff, J.C.: The Virtual Cell: a software environment for computational cell biology. Trends in Biotechnology 19(10), 401–406 (2001)
85. Marai, G.E., Forbes, A.G., Johnson, A.: Interdisciplinary immersive analytics at the Electronic Visualization Laboratory: lessons learned and upcoming challenges. In: IEEE VR 2016 Workshop on Immersive Analytics. pp. 1–6 (2016)
86. Meng, E.C., Pettersen, E.F., Couch, G.S., Huang, C.C., Ferrin, T.E.: Tools for integrated sequence-structure analysis with UCSF Chimera. BMC Bioinformatics 7(1), 339–348 (2006)
87. Moore, P.B.: Structural biology: Past, present, and future. New Biotechnology (2016), in press
88. Moritz, E., Meyer, J.: Virtual exploration of proteins. In: Proceedings of the Second IASTED International Conference on Visualization, Imaging, and Image Processing (VIIP 2002). pp. 757–762 (2002)
89. Moritz, E., Meyer, J.: Interactive 3D protein structure visualization using virtual reality. In: Proceedings of the Fourth IEEE Symposium on Bioinformatics and Bioengineering (IEEE BIBE 2004). pp. 503–507 (2004)
90. Moritz, E., Wischgoll, T., Meyer, J.: Comparison of input devices and displays for protein visualization. ACM Crossroads 12(2), 19–26 (2005)
91. Morris, J.H., Huang, C.C., Babbitt, P.C., Ferrin, T.E.: structureViz: linking Cytoscape and UCSF Chimera. Bioinformatics 23(17), 2345–2347 (2007)
92. Morrison, J.: Will chemists tilt their heads for virtual reality? Chemical & Engineering News 94(14) (2016)
93. Mueller, J., Butscher, S., Reiterer, H.: Immersive analysis of health-related data with mixed reality interfaces: potentials and open questions. In: Workshop Immersive Analytics 2016 (in conjunction with ISS 2016) (2016)
94. Müller, H., Kalpathy-Cramer, J., Caputo, B., Syeda-Mahmood, T., Wang, F.: Overview of the first workshop on medical content–based retrieval for clinical decision support at MICCAI 2009. In: Medical Content-Based Retrieval for Clinical Decision Support. Lecture Notes in Computer Science, vol. 5853, pp. 1–17. Springer Berlin Heidelberg (2010)
95. Nadan, T., Haffegee, A., Watson, K.: Collaborative and parallelized immersive molecular docking. In: Allen, G., Nabrzyski, J., Seidel, E., van Albada, G.D., Dongarra, J., Sloot, P.M.A. (eds.) Computational Science – ICCS 2009: 9th International Conference Proceedings, Part II, pp. 737–745. Springer Berlin Heidelberg (2009)
96. Ni, T., Schmidt, G.S., Staadt, O.G., Livingston, M.A., Ball, R., May, R.: A survey of large high-resolution display technologies, techniques, and applications. In: Proceedings of the IEEE Conference on Virtual Reality (VR 2006). pp. 223–236. IEEE Computer Society (2006)
97. Nim, H., Done, T., Schreiber, F., Boyd, S.: Interactive geolocational and coral compositional visualisation of great barrier reef heat stress data. In: IEEE Big Data Visual Analytics (BDVA) 2015. pp. 1–7 (2015)
98. Nim, H.T., Wang, M., Zhu, Y., Sommer, B., Schreiber, F., Boyd, S.E., Wang, S.J.: Communicating the effect of human behaviour on the Great Barrier Reef via mixed reality visualisation. In: IEEE Big Data Visual Analytics (BDVA) 2016. pp. 1–6 (2016)
99. Nim, H.T., Sommer, B., Klein, K., Flack, A., Safi, K., Nagy, M., Fiedler, W., Wikelski, M., Schreiber, F.: Design considerations for immersive analytics of bird movements obtained by miniaturised GPS sensors. In: Bruckner, S., Hennemuth, A., Kainz, B., Hotz, I., Merhof, D., Rieder, C. (eds.) Eurographics Workshop on Visual Computing for Biology and Medicine. The Eurographics Association (2017)

100. Nowke, C., Schmidt, M., Albada, S.J.V., Eppler, J.M., Bakker, R., Diesmann, M., Hentschel, B., Kuhlen, T.W.: VisNEST – interactive analysis of neural activity data. In: IEEE Symposium on Biological Data Visualization (BioVis). pp. 65–72 (2013)
101. O'Donoghue, S.I., Sabir, K.S., Kalemanov, M., Stolte, C., Wellmann, B., Ho, V., Roos, M., Perdigão, N., Buske, F.A., Heinrich, J.: Aquaria: simplifying discovery and insight from protein structures. Nature Methods 12(2), 98–99 (2015)
102. Peters, M.V.: Cutting the "gordian knot" in early breast cancer. Annals of the Royal College of Physicians and Surgeons of Canada 8, 186–192 (1975)
103. Porta, M.S., Greenland, S., Hernán, M., dos Santos Silva, I., Last, J.M. (eds.): A Dictionary of Epidemiology. Oxford University Press, 6th edn. (2014)
104. Preim, B., Klemm, P., Hauser, H., Hegenscheid, K., Oeltze, S., Tönnies, K., Völzke, H.: Visual analytics of image-centric cohort studies in epidemiology. In: Linsen, L., Hamann, B., Hege, H.C. (eds.) Visualization in Medicine and Life Sciences III: Towards Making an Impact, pp. 221–248. Springer International Publishing (2016)
105. PyMOL. https://www.pymol.org/, [last accessed 20/04/17]
106. Raidou, R.G., van der Heide, U.A., Dinh, C.V., Ghobadi, G., Kallehauge, J.F., Breeuwer, M., Vilanova, A.: Visual analytics for the exploration of tumor tissue characterization. Computer Graphics Forum 34(3), 11–20 (2015)
107. Rak, M., Engel, K., Tönnies, K.D.: Closed-form hierarchical finite element models for part-based object detection. In: International Workshop on Vision, Modeling and Visualization (VMV). pp. 137–144 (2013)
108. RasMol. http://www.openrasmol.org/, [last accessed 20/04/17]
109. RCSB PDB: Molecular graphics software links. http://www.rcsb.org/pdb/static.do?p=software/software_links/molecular_graphics.html, [last accessed 20/04/17]
110. Rekimoto, J., Saitoh, M.: Augmented surfaces: A spatially continuous work space for hybrid computing environments. In: Proceedings of the SIGCHI Conference on Human Factors in Computing Systems. pp. 378–385. CHI '99, ACM, New York, NY, USA (1999)
111. Renambot, L., Marrinan, T., Aurisano, J., Nishimoto, A., Mateevitsi, V., Bharadwaj, K., Long, L., Johnson, A., Brown, M., Leigh, J.: SAGE2: A collaboration portal for scalable resolution displays. Future Generation Computer Systems 54, 296–305 (2016)
112. Ribeiro, M.L., Lederman, H.M., Elias, S., Nunes, F.L.S.: Techniques and devices used in palpation simulation with haptic feedback. ACM Computing Surveys 49(3), 48.1–28 (2016)
113. Ritsos, P.D., John, N.W., Roberts, J.C.: Standards in augmented reality – towards prototyping haptic medical AR. In: 8th International AR Standards Meeting. Perey Research & Consulting (March 2013)
114. Roberts, J.C., Ritsos, P.D., Badam, S.K., Brodbeck, D., Kennedy, J., Elmqvist, N.: Visualization beyond the desktop – the next big thing. IEEE Computer Graphics and Applications 34(6), 26–34 (2014)
115. Rohn, H., Klukas, C., Schreiber, F.: Creating views on integrated multidomain data. Bioinformatics 27(13), 1839–1845 (2011)
116. Rohn, H., Junker, A., Hartmann, A., Grafahrend-Belau, E., Treutler, H., Klapperstück, M., Czauderna, T., Klukas, C., Schreiber, F.: VANTED v2: a framework for systems biology applications. BMC Systems Biology 6(1), 139.1–13 (2012)
117. Sabir, K., Stolte, C., Tabor, B., O'Donoghue, S.: The molecular control toolkit: Controlling 3D molecular graphics via gesture and voice. In: 2013 IEEE Symposium on Biological Data Visualization (BioVis). pp. 49–56. IEEE (2013)

118. Schmid, J., Kim, J., Magnenat-Thalmann, N.: Robust statistical shape models for MRI bone segmentation in presence of small field of view. Medical Image Analysis 15(1), 155–168 (2011)
119. Schreiber, F., Colmsee, C., Czauderna, T., Grafahrend-Belau, E., Hartmann, A., Junker, A., Junker, B.H., Klapperstück, M., Scholz, U., Weise, S.: MetaCrop 2.0: managing and exploring information about crop plant metabolism. Nucleic Acids Research 40, D1173–D1177 (2012)
120. Schreiber, F., Dwyer, T., Marriott, K., Wybrow, M.: A generic algorithm for layout of biological networks. BMC Bioinformatics 10, 375 (2009)
121. Schultz, T., Kindlmann, G.L.: Open-box spectral clustering: Applications to medical image analysis. IEEE Transactions on Visualization and Computer Graphics 19(12), 2100–2108 (2013)
122. Sera, C., Matlock, S., Watashiba, Y., Ichikawa, K., Haga, J.H.: Hydra: a high-throughput virtual screening data visualization and analysis tool. Procedia Computer Science 80, 2312–2316 (2016)
123. Silva, B.A.L., Renambot, L.: CytoViz: an artistic mapping of network measurements as living organisms in a VR application. In: Proc. SPIE 6490, Stereoscopic Displays and Virtual Reality Systems XIV. vol. 6490, pp. 64901U.1–11. International Society for Optics and Photonics (2007)
124. Sommer, B., Barnes, D., Boyd, S., Chandler, T., Cordeil, M., Klein, K., Nguyen, T.D., Nim, H., Stephens, K., Vohl, D., Wang, S., Wilson, E., McCormack, J., Marriott, K., Schreiber, F.: 3D-Stereoscopic immersive analytics projects at Monash University and University of Konstanz. In: Proceedings IS&T Electronic Imaging - Stereoscopic Displays and Applications XXVIII. pp. 5.179–187 (2017)
125. Sommer, B., Hamacher, A., Kalutza, O., Czauderna, T., Klapperstück, M., Biere, N., Civico, M., Thomas, B., Barnes, D.G., Schreiber, F.: Stereoscopic space map - semi-immersive configuration of 3D-stereoscopic tours in multi-display environments. In: Proc. IS&T Electronic Imaging - Stereoscopic Displays and Appl. XXVII. pp. 5.1–9 (2016)
126. Sommer, B., Kormeier, B., Demenkov, P.S., Arrigo, P., Hippe, K., Ates, Ö., Kochetov, A.V., Ivanisenko, V.A., Kolchanov, N.A., Hofestädt, R.: Subcellular localization charts: A new visual methodology for the semi-automatic localization of protein-related data sets. Journal of Bioinformatics and Computational Biology 11(1), 1340005.1–18 (2013)
127. Sommer, B., Schreiber, F.: Integration and virtual reality exploration of biomedical data with CmPI and VANTED. Information Technology 59(4), 181–190 (2017)
128. Sommer, B.: Membrane packing problems: A short review on computational membrane modeling methods and tools. Computational and Structural Biotechnology Journal 5(6), e201302014.1–13 (2013)
129. Sommer, B., Bender, C., Hoppe, T., Gamroth, C., Jelonek, L.: Stereoscopic cell visualization: from mesoscopic to molecular scale. Journal of Electronic Imaging 23(1), 011007.1–11 (2014)
130. Sommer, B., Künsemöller, J., Sand, N., Husemann, A., Rumming, M., Kormeier, B.: CELLmicrocosmos 4.1: an interactive approach to integrating spatially localized metabolic networks into a virtual 3D cell environment. In: Fred, A., Filipe, J., Gamboa, H. (eds.) Proc. Intl. Conf. Bioinformatic (BIOINFORMATICS 2010). pp. 90–95 (2010)
131. Sommer, B., Wang, S.J., Xu, L., Chen, M., Schreiber, F.: Hybrid-dimensional visualization and interaction - integrating 2D and 3D visualization with semi-immersive navigation techniques. In: IEEE Big Data Visual Analytics (BDVA) 2015. pp. 65–72. IEEE eXpress Conference Publishing (2015)

132. Stefik, M., Foster, G., Bobrow, D.G., Kahn, K., Lanning, S., Suchman, L.: Beyond the chalkboard: Computer support for collaboration and problem solving in meetings. Communications of the ACM 30(1), 32–47 (1987)
133. Stoakley, R., Conway, M.J., Pausch, R.: Virtual reality on a WIM: interactive worlds in miniature. In: Proceedings of the SIGCHI Conference on Human Factors in Computing Systems. pp. 265–272. ACM Press/Addison-Wesley Publishing Co. (1995)
134. Stone, J.E., Sherman, W.R., Schulten, K.: Immersive molecular visualization with omnidirectional stereoscopic ray tracing and remote rendering. In: 2016 IEEE International Parallel and Distributed Processing Symposium Workshops (IPDPSW). pp. 1048–1057 (2016)
135. Streitz, N.A., Geissler, J., Holmer, T., Konomi, S., Mueller-Tomfelde, C., Reischl, W., Rexroth, P., Seitz, P., Steinmetz, R.: i-LAND: An interactive landscape for creativity and innovation. In: Proceedings of the SIGCHI Conference on Human Factors in Computing Systems. pp. 120–127. CHI '99, ACM, New York, NY, USA (1999)
136. Tönnies, K.D., Gloger, O., Rak, M., Winkler, C., Klemm, P., Preim, B., Völzke, H.: Image analysis in epidemiological applications. it - Information Technology 57(1), 22–29 (2015)
137. Torsney-Weir, T., Saad, A., Möller, T., Hege, H.C., Weber, B., Verbavatz, J.M., Bergner, S.: Tuner: Principled parameter finding for image segmentation algorithms using visual response surface exploration. IEEE Transactions on Visualization and Computer Graphics 17(12), 1892–1901 (2011)
138. Turkay, C., Lundervold, A., Lundervold, A.J., Hauser, H.: Hypothesis generation by interactive visual exploration of heterogeneous medical data. In: Human-Computer Interaction and Knowledge Discovery in Complex, Unstructured, Big Data, pp. 1–12. Springer (2013)
139. Unity Game Engine. https://unity3d.com/, [last accessed 20/04/17]
140. van den Elzen, S., van Wijk, J.J.: Small multiples, large singles: A new approach for visual data exploration. Computer Graphics Forum 32(3pt2), 191–200 (2013)
141. Virtalis. https://www.virtalis.com/vr-for-pymol/, [last accessed 20/04/17]
142. VMD. http://www.ks.uiuc.edu/Research/vmd/, [last accessed 20/04/17]
143. VMD required libraries and related programs. http://www.ks.uiuc.edu/Research/vmd/allversions/related_programs.html, [last accessed 20/04/17]
144. Völzke, H., Alte, D., Schmidt, C.O., Radke, D., Lorbeer, R., Friedrich, N., Aumann, N., Lau, K., Piontek, M., Born, G., et al.: Cohort profile: the study of health in Pomerania. International Journal of Epidemiology 40(2), 294–307 (2011)
145. Weise, S., Grosse, I., Klukas, C., Koschützki, D., Scholz, U., Schreiber, F., Junker, B.H.: Meta-All: a system for managing metabolic pathway information. BMC Bioinformatics 7, 465 (2006)
146. Wheeler, A.: Understanding virtual reality headsets. http://www.engineering.com/Hardware/ArticleID/12699/, [last accessed 20/04/17]
147. Widjaja, Y.Y., Pang, C.N.I., Li, S.S., Wilkins, M.R., Lambert, T.D.: The interactorium: Visualising proteins, complexes and interaction networks in a virtual 3D cell. Proteomics 9(23), 5309–5315 (2009)
148. Wigdor, D., Shen, C., Forlines, C., Balakrishnan, R.: Table-centric interactive spaces for real-time collaboration. In: Proceedings of the Working Conference on Advanced Visual Interfaces. pp. 103–107. AVI '06, ACM, New York, NY, USA (2006)

149. Wilson, E.O., Ryan, M., McGill, G., Berry, D.: E.O. Wilson's Life on Earth. Wilson Digital (2012)
150. Woods, A.J.: How are crosstalk and ghosting defined in the stereoscopic literature? In: Proc. SPIE 7863, Stereoscopic Displays and Applications XXII. vol. 7863, pp. 78630Z.1–12. International Society for Optics and Photonics (2011)
151. Wurtele, E.S., Bassham, D.C., Dickerson, J., Kabala, D.J., Schneller, W., Stenerson, M., Vasanth, A.: Meta!Blast: a serious game to explore the complexities of structural and metabolic cell biology. In: Proceedings of the ASME 2010 World Conference on Innovative Virtual Reality. pp. 237–240 (2010)
152. Wurtele, E.S., Li, J., Diao, L., Zhang, H., Foster, C.M., Fatland, B., Dickerson, J., Brown, A., Cox, Z., Cook, D.: MetNet: Software to build and model the biogenetic lattice of Arabidopsis. Comparative and Functional Genomics 4(2), 239–245 (2003)
153. Yang, Y., Wurtele, E.S., Cruz-Neira, C., Dickerson, J.A.: Hierarchical visualization of metabolic networks using virtual reality. In: Proceedings of the 2006 ACM International Conference on Virtual Reality Continuum and Its Applications. pp. 377–381. ACM (2006)
154. Ystad, M.A., Lundervold, A.J., Wehling, E., Espeseth, T., Rootwelt, H., Westlye, L.T., Andersson, M., Adolfsdottir, S., Geitung, J.T., Fjell, A.M., Reinvang, I., Lundervold, A.: Hippocampal volumes are important predictors for memory function in elderly women. BMC Medical Imaging 9(1), 17.1–15 (2009)
155. Zhao, F., Xie, X.: An overview of interactive medical image segmentation. Annals of the BMVA 2013(7), 1–22 (2013)
156. Zhu, L., Malatras, A., Thorley, M., Aghoghogbe, I., Mer, A., Duguez, S., Butler-Browne, G., Voit, T., Duddy, W.: CellWhere: Graphical display of interaction networks organized on subcellular localizations. Nucleic Acids Research 43, W571–W575 (2015)
157. zSpace. http://zspace.com, [last accessed 20/04/17]
158. zSpace Showcase 3D Platform. http://zspace.com/about/press-releases/zspace-inc.-showcases-3d-platform-for-biotechnology-and-molecular-modeling, [last accessed 20/04/17]

11. Exploring Immersive Analytics for Built Environments

Tom Chandler[1], Thomas Morgan[1], and Torsten Wolfgang Kuhlen[3]

[1] Monash University
tom.chandler@monash.edu
tom.morgan@monash.edu
[2] RWTH Aachen University
kuhlen@vr.rwth-aachen.de

Abstract. This chapter overviews the application of immersive analytics to simulations of built environments through three distinct case studies. The first case study examines an immersive analytics approach based upon the concept of "Virtual Production Intelligence" for virtual prototyping tools throughout the planning phase of complete production sites. The second study addresses the 3D simulation of an extensive urban area (191 square kilometres) and the attendant immersive analytic considerations in an interactive model of a sustainable city. The third study reviews how immersive analytic overlays have been applied for virtual heritage in the reconstruction and crowd simulation of the medieval Cambodian temple complex of Angkor Wat.

Keywords: immersive analytics, crowd simulation, interactive simulations, immersive 3D visualisation, augmented reality, tangible interfaces, CAVE

11.1. Introduction and Overview

In simulations of the built environment, the 3D format is much more than a graphical gimmick. It is crucial to discern essential information such as line-of-sight issues, material flows and intersections of objects, all which are best remedied by a full 3D, dynamic reconstruction. Such spaces, whether mediated through a laptop screen or in a specially constructed CAVE environment, are spatially immersive because they depict environments–a factory, a cityscape, a reconstructed cultural landscape–in a realistic way. When navigating through these environments, the user has the benefit of familiar and proportionate visual cues such as walls, streets and computer-generated characters that provide the virtual space with perspective and relative position. While analytic features can overlay and augment these ready-made immersive environments, the organization of 3D models into sets or layers can also function as visual analytic features in their own right. For example, 3D model sets of architectural typologies, vegetation assemblies or walking figures can be interchanged in real time, revealing contrasts, patterns and interdependencies in the data that weren't previously apparent.

K. Marriott et al. (Eds.): Immersive Analytics, LNCS 11190, pp. 331–357, 2018.
https://doi.org/10.1007/978-3-030-01388-2_11

The utility of 3D models have been familiar to architects, engineers and urban planners for some time, but new Immersive Analytic interfaces, augmentations and overlays promise to significantly extend the interpretation and exploration of virtual environments. This chapter explores the application of Immersive Analytic features in simulations of built environments in three case studies that are situated variously in the present, the future and the past. The first case study examines an immersive analytics approach based upon the concept of 'Virtual Production Intelligence' for virtual prototyping tools throughout the planning phase of complete production sites. The second study models the addresses the 3D simulation of an extensive urban area (191 square kilometres) and the attendant immersive analytic considerations in an interactive model of a sustainable city of the near future. Notably, both of these case studies propose models of present built environments as a foundation for the prototyping of future scenarios. The third study takes a landscape of the present day–the world heritage listed Cambodian temple complex of Angkor Wat–almost a millennium back into the past, and reviews how immersive analytic overlays have been applied for the reconstruction of the complex and the simulation of crowds over a 24-hour cycle in medieval times.

11.2. Case Study 1: Planning and Visualisation in Production Engineering

In high-wage countries, the complexity of production processes has increased dramatically. It has been state-of-the-art for quite some years now to make use of virtual prototyping tools throughout the planning phase of complete production sites. In such virtual production systems, a tremendous number of process parameters have to be determined with the goal of making high-quality products. While these process parameters are highly interdependent, the knowledge about how to optimize production processes is dispersed among various experts from different fields working on diverse aspects of designing and optimizing procedures, which makes production planning a highly collaborative and interdisciplinary task. Last but not least, the data generated in virtual production environments is highly heterogeneous.

To meet the challenges above, a first attempt has been made just recently to follow an immersive analytics approach that is based on the concept of "Virtual Production Intelligence" (VPI), which in turn builds on the concept of business intelligence in terms of data aggregation, data condensation, and data exploitation. The VPI strives at an integrative, collaborative decision support for complex production planning processes in different design domains. Factory and Machine are two design domains, where virtual reality (VR), scientific visualization (SciVis) and information visualization (InfoVis) are used in combination to support planners in evaluating and reviewing layouts before implementing them in real factories and machines.

The work presented here is a Research Area in the Cluster of Excellence "Integrative Production Technology for High-Wage Countries". The Cluster is a major long-term project started in 2006, in which over 25 research departments of RWTH Aachen University, Germany, are collaborating with industrial companies across disciplines on new technologies in multiple fields of production, like virtualization, individualized production, hybrid production systems, and self-optimizing production. Within the VPI Research Area, the following RWTH institutes work closely together: The Institute of Information Management in Mechanical Engineering, the Visual Computing Institute, the Department of Factory Planning from the Laboratory for Machine Tools and Production Engineering, and the Nonlinear Dynamics of Laser Manufacturing Processes Instruction and Research Department.

The following paragraphs do not present original research by themselves, but instead are mostly an excerpt from various, previously published outcomes of the project [19], focussing particularly on the immersive analytics aspects of the VPI.

In the field of production engineering, immersive analytics should reduce and accelerate planning efforts and increase planning efficiency by providing an integrative analysis in immersive virtual environments. VPI mainly follows this approach and integrates the planning and optimization of the two design domains Factory and Machine. The heart of the VPI platform is an analytics engine providing, among other things, domain-specific data exploration, advanced data mining techniques, modules for correlation and sensitivity analyses, and a consolidation of planning data in the involved design domains based on domain ontologies [5,19]. The VPI analytics engine is operated via a Web-based platform but can, on top of that, be coupled to an immersive virtual environment, making the VPI an immersive analytics tool. The VPI offers a seamless explorative space by linking and integrating geometric, scientific as well as information visualization.

Design domain factory In the context of factory layout planning, VR-based support tools have already been realized by others, demonstrating that a visualization and interaction in immersive environments provides a significant added-value as compared to non-immersive, monitor-based systems (see e. g. [6,9]). One of the strengths of walkthroughs in immersive VR is that planners can experience a factory in its original scale. This can, e. g., be used to manually check workplace visibility in a rather natural fashion and thereby ensure important lines of sight between related workplaces. While the existing tools allow for virtual walkthroughs of factory models and the modification of the factory layout from within the virtual environment by placing or rearranging shop-floor equipment, the VPI tool goes beyond this by leveraging visual analytics and providing a much higher level of integration of heterogeneous planning data into the model. With the VPI, geometrical data of the factory layout is combined with visualizations that offer access to additional relevant planning data, with the goal to further increase the usefulness of VR-based factory design. By this, the VPI wants to make a fundamental contribution to the realization of the vision of the digital factory. The overall VPI solution hypothesis is that a combination of semantical enrichment of planning data by a comprehensive information model on the one hand, and smart human-machine interaction via 3D, immersive user interfaces on the other hand, is advantageous for factory planning and the optimization process. Solutions of simulations of factory or production processes are linked together in such a way that interdependencies in the planning tasks can be identified and analyzed flexibly.

Within the VPI project, we developed a prototype of an immersive analytics factory planning platform called the *Factory Layout Planning Assistant (flapAssist).* A key goal of flapAssist is to not only create an appealing rendering of factory layouts but to elaborate methods and tools that support the factory planners in their daily work. flapAssist offers traditional functionality, e. g., virtual walkthroughs (see Figure 1) and positioning of machines, but combines them with visualization concepts that have been newly developed to better support the planning and optimization process. Above all, material flows provided by the VPI analytics engine are a crucial type of planning data. In flapAssist, material flows are presented as a 3D overlay embedded into the immersive representation of factory models. As shown in Figure 2, inter-machine material flows are visualized via color-coded arcs. Alternatively, a card-style visualization can be used to visualize the accumulated material flow in which specific machines participate. Since material flow matrices can become rather complex, leading to a cluttered, confusing visualization, planners have the possibility to interactively filter out the flow information of those machines that are not in the focus of interest for the current task. Beyond the visualization of material flow data, flapAssist offers a support tool to aid the planner to optimize the position of individual machines with respect to the material flow matrix. Since material flow costs are not the only criterion affecting the factory layout, a fully automated approach is not effective here. Instead, the tool simply suggests where to move a user selected machine, taking into account the entire material flow for that machine. Via online communication with the VPI analytics engine, planners get immediate feedback on their changes and can thus quickly iterate between different optimization scenarios (see Figure 3).

Design domain machine To optimize configurations of complex machines, an analysis of high-dimensional parameter spaces is often necessary. As an example, in laser cutting machine tools typical parameters are laser power, laser pulse duration, beam radius, beam thickness level, Rayleigh length, and beam focal position. To identify optimal machine configurations for a specific production task, it is not feasible to simulate a machine for all possible parameter combinations in a straight-forward way. Instead, the process running on such a machine is simulated for selected combinations of parameters only, while other configurations are interpolated from these selected combinations via metamodels. For the design domain Machine, therefore, we identified metamodeling techniques as being crucial for the VPI approach. For an optimization of machine parameters based on metamodels, it is important to analyse correlations between parameters. Thus, the concept of linked multiple views seems appropriate to explore the data. We, therefore, developed a new visual analytics application called *Metamodel Slicer (memoSlice)*, which mainly builds on an interactive exploration of metamodels via linked multiple views. While a detailed introduction to metamodels in production

Fig. 1: Immersive virtual reality support for factory layout planning.

engineering would go far beyond the scope of this section (for details see e. g., [1]), the visualization concept of memoSlice shall be briefly described here (see figure 4 and [16]).

As required by domain experts, an adequate workflow should allow for an integrated overview as well as in-depth analysis of metamodels. Following this workflow requisite, memoSlice offers three main views of the data. Via the scatterplot matrix view, planners can gain a fast outline of the data. It contains one scatterplot for every possible pair of parameter-criterion combination and thus gives an overview of the distribution of values.

For a detailed examination, the hyperslice view [36] shows a matrix of 2D plots which display all possible axis-aligned slices through one focal point of the data space. In the matrix, the graphs shown on the diagonal represent axis-aligned 1D slices through the common point, allowing for a quick navigation through the parameter space.

In contrast to the HyperSlice view, the 3D view visualizes a single three-dimensional slice instead of several two-dimensional ones. The 3D view contains three crossed 2D-slices whose intersection point matches the projection of the focal point. Additionally, a direct volume rendering of a 3D-slice is superimposed. Thus, the 3D view does not give an overview over all dimensions but instead shows all information along three visible parameters, thereby providing more context than 2D slices.

Integrative analysis of the design domains Factory and Machine While a planning tool for the design domain Factory, like flapAssist, quite obviously can profit from an immersive analytics approach, since a lot of geometrical data is involved, an application like memoSlice for planning and optimization of the design domain Machine follows a more "conventional" visual analytics approach, where the

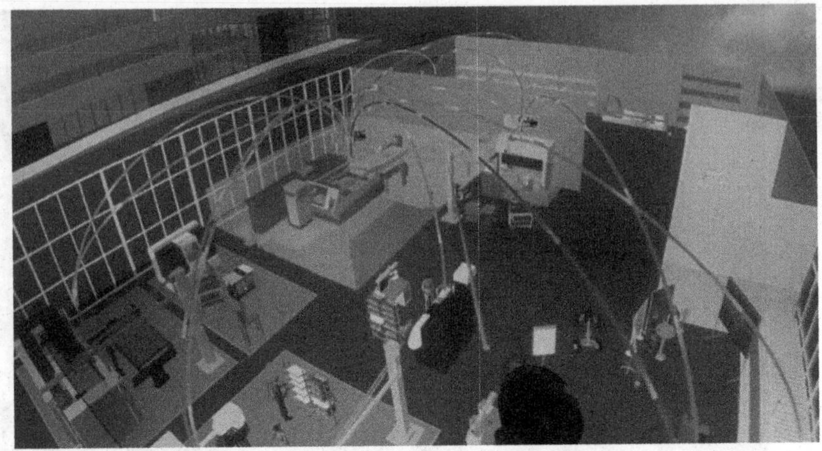

Fig. 2: Visualization of material flow.

aspect of immersion, if at all, plays a minor role. In fact, in the concrete example of memoSlice, the only 3D aspect that might profit from a stereoscopic, egocentric perspective, is related to the direct volume rendering in the 3D view, whereas the other views are considered as classical InfoVis visualizations, where a desktop environment might be more appropriate.

Having the ultimate goal in mind, i. e., to provide an integrative and explorative analysis of both design domains, flapAssist and memoSlice should no longer be stand-alone applications though. In a fully integrative planning and optimization process it should, for instance, be possible to instantaneously experience how machine configuration variations affect factory-related parameters, like material flows. Therefore, we have integrated memoSlice into flapAssist, where it serves as a widget for machine configuration (see Figures 5 and 6).

To enable interactive exploration of such a highly integrative scenario, a high degree of responsiveness is an absolute prerequisite (also see Chapter 5). Thus, the Virtual Production Intelligence relies on task-based parallelization techniques with a specific user-centred prioritization scheme and streaming updates to guarantee fast response times, without impairing the user's workflow. Even as stand-alone applications, the computational loads in flapAssist and memoSlice are rather high and require high-end computing hardware and parallelism. In memoSlice, for instance, the update of hyperslice views during user interaction requires the computation of radial basis functions for every pixel. Therefore, hierarchical parallelization schemes are applied here that are specialised for this use case.

Data annotation in immersive analytics tools An important issue of existing VR-based factory planning tools and, most probably, any VR-based analysis tool in science and technology, is the lack of efficient workflows for creation and access to annotations. Therefore, we developed an annotation framework, which can be

Fig. 3: Interactive optimization of a digital factory's shop-floor layout.

used with flapAssist and memoSlice but, in principle, with any other immersive analytics application, too [28].

As previously described in [19], a variety of annotations can be created via our framework, like labels or viewpoint annotations, and linked to different types of data, like text, voice comments, images, or sketches. To capture all these different data types, the annotation system provides a selection of interaction metaphors. Since standard keyboards typically do not work for entering text from within an immersive virtual environment, in our annotation framework text entries can be accomplished via smartphone input or, alternatively, via a speech-based system called *Swifter*, that we specifically designed for simplicity while maintaining good performance (see Figure 7) [28].

An annotation server based on Web services stores the annotation data in a standardized way so that it should be easy to integrate it not only into the VPI platform, but also into any other infrastructure. By this, annotations become accessible to all involved parties, thereby supporting truly collaborative factory planning.

Conclusions and lessons learned from this use case With the Virtual Production Intelligence platform, a first prototypical immersive analytics demonstrator for a use case in production engineering is under development, focusing on an integrative approach for planning and optimization tasks in the design domains Factory and Machine. A formal evaluation in terms of comprehensive user studies is still to be performed to evaluate whether an immersive analytics approach is, in fact, superior to a non-immersive Visual analytics approach for this use case. Expert studies for the evaluation of single system components have been already conducted with promising results. By means of the VPI approach, combining

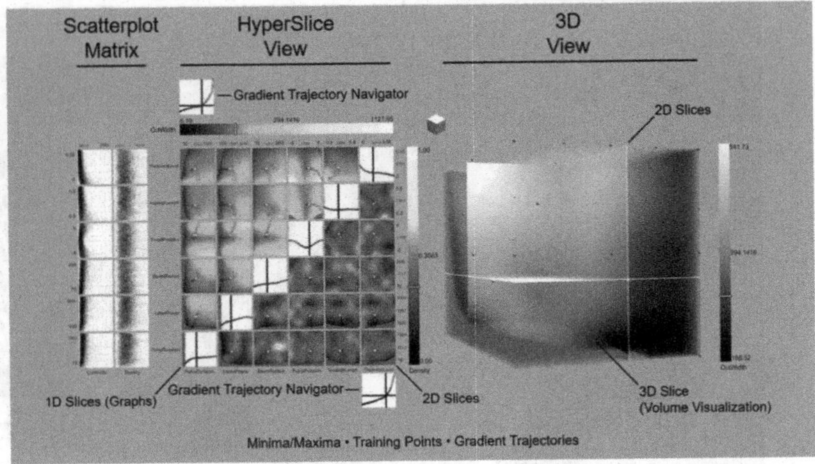

Fig. 4: The linked multiple view concept of memoSlice.

life-sized virtual walkthroughs of entire factories with further meta information of factory layouts and single machines, it becomes possible to compare design alternatives in an intuitive, cost-effective and timely fashion.

While real-time, low latency visualization and interaction are an issue in any immersive VR application in general, our case study clearly demonstrates that performance is an even bigger challenge in immersive analytics scenarios. Due to a high integration level of heterogeneous, partially large, data and computationally expensive analysis algorithms, efficient data management, as well as advanced, hierarchical parallelization strategies with user-centric priority schemes, need to be applied to make the analysis an explorative, human-in-the-loop experience. Furthermore, we consider a powerful annotation framework as crucial for any immersive analytics tool, making it possible to extract information and insight from immersive analysis sessions. Annotation data should be stored in a standardized way, so that it can be used in a variety of setups and further processed by collaborators in subsequent immersive or non-immersive analysis sessions.

11.3. Case Study 2: Immersive Analytics in the Interactive Visualisation of Sustainable Cities

Achieving liveable, sustainable and resilient cities of the future requires an in-depth understanding of the complexities, uncertainties and priorities that characterise urban communities, environments and infrastructures. In this context, infrastructure planners, designers and managers are seeking innovative processes that communicate across communities and lead to robust planning outcomes.

This chapter outlines immersive analytics considerations in the interactive exploration of virtual city environments under different future scenarios. The project's case study is the Elster catchment, an extensive area in the south-eastern

Fig. 5: Factory and machine planning in an immersive environment, integrating geometric and abstract information in a unified analytics tool.

suburbs of Melbourne, Australia. An immersive 3D model of the suburb, alongside support for interactive climate scenarios, was assembled at Monash University to engage various stakeholders and communities as the region moves into a more climate-uncertain future. Such stakeholders include the local government authorities that intersect with the Elster Catchment, the relevant water boards and government bodies, and local residents. As such the model presents an ideal case study for the communication of complex data to a broad range of users of varying technical and disciplinary expertise. It as an example of immersive story-telling (see Chapter 6)

This case study aims to address a set of core concerns that cut to the heart of the idea of the 'model' in the emerging field of immersive analytics. The first core concern is the idea of the model as simulation. The case study embeds practices and approaches that anticipate *immersive analytics* presence in the design, communication, and encountering of urban space.

A 'fluid' model and an engine for cities The project commenced with a comprehensive water and rain-loading model for the entire catchment of the Elster Creek in south-eastern metropolitan Melbourne. The watershed rises in the former sandy heathlands of the south-east, falling down toward Port Phillip Bay. Its lower reaches, which drain what was once the Elwood swamp, are extensively channelized and subject to regular flooding. The creek wraps up a microcosm of issues facing Australian urban ecologies; both vulnerable and dangerous; a

Fig. 6: Integration of factory and machine planning, bird's eye view into the RWTH Aachen aixCAVE.

contested space between the natural and the man-made whose exigencies are only exacerbated by climate change.

The rain-loading model considered the watershed as a cohesive system in which planning upstream could deliver substantial benefits downstream. The model offered a way of recording the impact of a series of small and medium scale interventions, such as water run-off retention, streetscaping, and domestic rainwater tanks, during a set of forecast rain and tidal surge events.

The model, while comprehensive, suffered from many of the issues that affect complex data visualisation in that it requires existing spatial/analytical skills and a passing understanding of the methodology of the study. Other ideas engaged through the model–like changes in the morphology of the urban space, shifts in density and housing approaches–are also less evident in the static outputs of the model-as-maps. The core issue, however, was an absent sense of tangibility and immediacy. That is, the scope and scale of the flooding impacts were not immediately legible, and the ways in which differing scenarios might impact the same space of the city was not readily apparent. Finally, the model embedded issues with what Ian Bogost terms simulation fever–the issue around completeness and accuracy in the simulation of events.

Bogost places emphasis on the narrative capacity of simulations, suggesting that; "A simulation is a representative of a source system via a less complex

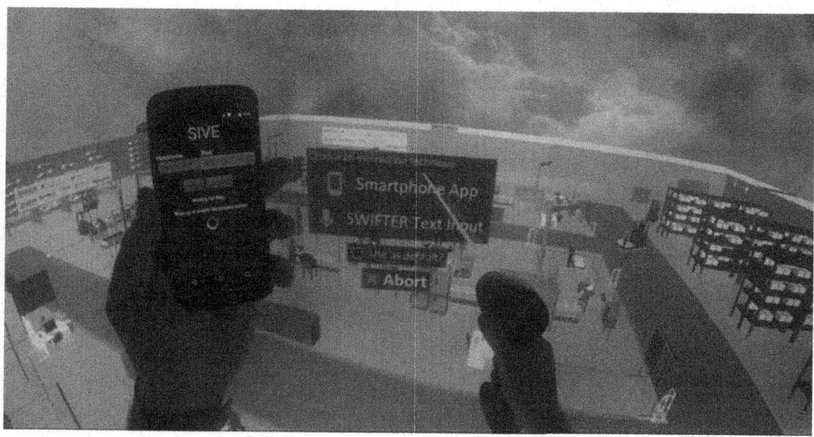

Fig. 7: Creating annotations for smartphone-based communication with the VPI analytics engine.

system that informs the user's understanding of the source system in a subjective way." [3, p. 98] More importantly, these simulations provide 'fungible' insights, narrative structures into reality, rather than a one to one mapping between the model and reality. Bogost goes on to suggest that; "What simulation games create are biased, nonobjective modes of expression that cannot escape the grasp of subjectivity and ideology." [3, p. 99] While Bogost uses this in the sense of interactive simulations as games, we want to argue that this holds true for all interactive and immersive spaces.

As the model was to be used to buttress and support a series of community outreach workshops that were aimed at clarifying and communicating the outcomes, the cooperative research centre for water (CRC for Water) commissioned an interactive virtual model of the suburb of Elwood that could illustrate a set of outcomes from the earlier water modelling.

The last two decades have seen a number of key texts on the idea of computable and simulatable cities. At one level this is an offshoot of the concepts and ideas bandied around by the cybernetic model of the city as a digital/human organism in the 1960s. We might find this in the ambivalent attitude of figures such as DeLanda [10, pp. 95-96], and the strange reductive processes of actor-network-theory (ANT) in the context of the city. A second thread (no less reductive) is the drive to image and model large cities, sites that appear to resist imagining *in toto*. Work by Pascal Müller *et al.* [23, 26], at the ETH, then Procedural, and finally at ESRI, sets the stage for the comprehensive modelling and imaging of cities.

So there is a question around the nature of this material. Approaches to 3D city models tend to proceed from the structure of the transportation network–either generated or inherited from spatial data. These are used to create developable blocks which can be further subdivided to serve as the starting point for generating

Fig. 8: The suburb of Elwood sits 8 kilometres south of Melbourne's CBD (left). The site forms the creek-mouth of the Elster catchment (right) and is subject to regular pluvial and fluvial flooding.

geometry based on land-use, lot size and orientation. It is, however, possible to neatly sidestep this process; the best asset for the initial generation, in this scenario, is the existing footprint of the dwelling–which embeds a kind of latent history of the site and the tectonics. 'Swamped,' an architectural design studio that ran parallel to the CRC investigation, furnished a set of building footprints as shapefiles with associated metadata. This was material that would have proven useful to the architectural students in the studio and indexed the apparent age of the property, the number of stories and the presence of at-grade car-parking.

These simple data points, combined with the footprint, provide seeds for the construction of dwelling geometry across the Elster catchment. The particular grammars act as analytical placeholders, distilling (visual) meaning out of otherwise undifferentiated footprints and data-tables. Combined with a road network, Cityengine is able to provide an index of street 'frontages' and the grammars are able to adjust to reflect this. The grammars are often able to identify the presence of extensions or renovations as the building footprint has additional vertices or extends beyond the expected scale of the historical type.

As a general procedure, the model involved a high-level separation between formal styles–historical styles associated with the age of the building. Elwood is a heterogeneous mix of styles–ranging from late-Victorian terrace houses, through federation and bungalow styles in the regions reclaimed from the swamp, to post-war brown-brick apartments, and contemporary developments along commercial arteries and the foreshore.

The 3D spatial model allowed for the superimposition of analytical material across the site–and allowed us to use it as a design seed–embedding further narrative intelligence into the model.

Areas subject to inundation or heat-stress varied depending on the parameters of the underlying simulation. The analytical component was represented as a set

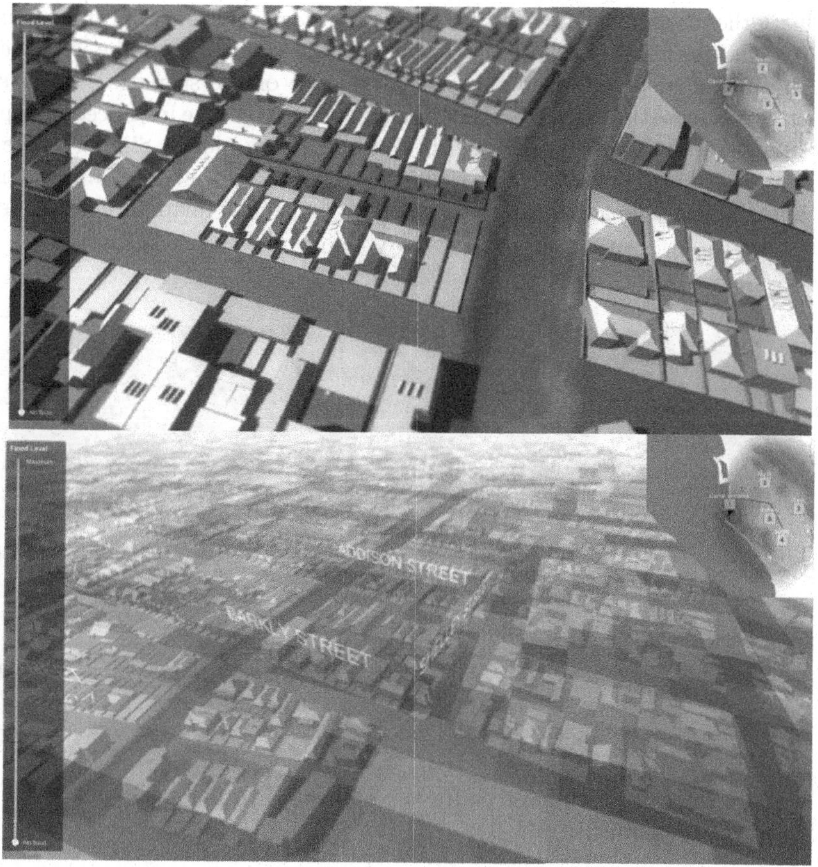

Fig. 9: Heat Island modelling was used to seed 'stressed' environments in the model–this affected the type, extent, and condition of vegetation. The nature of this information shifted from explicit (temperature) to implicit (vegetation type) as the user navigated down to street level.

of colour shifts or modifications to underlying models; areas subject to repeat flooding were paler, or the generative grammars of buildings were adapted to puncture and reveal underlying structure as if they had fallen into disuse and disrepair. Areas subject to increased heat-stress had a corresponding die-back in projected vegetation, and a 'browning out' in their resulting colouration. The simulation tracked changes in ground-cover that could influence future micro-climates. At the large scale, these were represented using the grid-cells of the simulation–giving a comprehensive overview of temperatures and stresses. But at the finer building scale, these were represented directly–imaging stressed and thriving gardens, and showing the extent of future green-space for each building lot.

Other dynamic details were used to code elements of the overarching narrative–incremental features such as water-tanks or solar panels could be instanced across the model, depending on the ethical valence of the scenario. Water sensitive streetscape features–such as swales and planting–could be instanced in appropriate sites based on stresses identified in the underlying model. Similarly, the stresses placed on building stock by rising waters and heat-stress can be directly, if hyperbolically, imaged using the narrative register of dilapidation and decay (see Figure 10).

Fig. 10: Impacts of climatic shifts were conveyed through the 'image' of the built fabric of the suburb.

Critical and narrative elements are also communicated through procedural means–the surrounding city is dynamic, and hints at larger economic and socio-political conditions that might be attached to the underlying data model–the condition and coherence of the city skyline changing in response to the valences and registers of the scenario–shifting from ruin to shining, coruscating object as the overall story shifts from climate disaster to anti-fragile responses.

Finally, the model is able to communicate using other channels–i. e., spatial awareness, things that are coded as stories and performances. This scaffolds off a capacity for coherent immersive environments to function as narrative or story spaces, and in doing so communicate complex insights. While the immersive analytics field is young, similar affective powers are evidenced in the landscapes of games and simulations. In this mode, the purpose of the model or simulation is more than just a site for representation or computation. As critic Steve Fuller outlines, a possibility is that; "The point of *virtual reality* is to realise the latent potential of the actual world, typically by getting us to see or do things that we probably would not under normal circumstances but could under the right circumstances." [15, p. 105]

Fig. 11: The model offers the capacity to image extreme scenarios, and scaffold them off recognisable visual miscellanea to further entrench the enormity of future changes.

For a site in the built environment, which engages with multiple stakeholders and necessitates creative re-imaginings of the world, this is the direct benefit of an immersive analytical model. Where immersive analytics differs from virtual reality in that it not only allows for the consideration of other possibilities but also offers concrete and direct information and data that allow stakeholders to act on these possibilities.

Conclusions and lessons learnt from the use case Immersive Analytic models of the built environment have the capacity to act as 'transformative narratives' – tools to prompt speculation and corresponding act on such speculation. Renata Tyszczuk frames transformative narratives as:

"... those stories that have an open-endedness that makes space for the unforeseen–a future we cannot ever really understand. Such stories have agency: they can provoke us to think about how we might live with the prospect of uncertain futures, how we can prepare for situations we cannot anticipate, to think through our responsibilities to others and help develop our adaptive capacities." [33, p. 133]

The Elwood visualisation was commissioned to serve a straightforward purpose–the communication of sea-level and storm surge scenarios in an uncertain future. However, the combination of the robust underlying data model and recognisable built spaces allowed for powerful synergies. The immersive analytical model allowed the discrete time-steps of a severe weather event to be experienced as an *event*–as a space and a territory that unfolded around the viewer/participant, with storm clouds rolling in across the bay and floodwaters engulfing the old Edwardian houses along Barkly Street.

From an architectural and urban design perspective, the immersive analytic model differs from normative design models. It is not a design outcome but a continuum of potential responses–a set of Tyszcuck's 'transformative narratives.' Critically, they allow what are often disparate disciplines (design, engineering, planning) to communicate in a common site and model and to share this with a broader community. The model ties together various data sets that would not commonly be intersected or superimposed–and in their correlation creates new adjacencies and awarenesses. The completed asset immerses the wide array of actors and stakeholder in a rich and contingent set of futures, and ultimately, compel us all to engage and to *act with new knowledge.*

Citizen actors/agents engaged with the model with a sense of desperation or alarm. The mixture of contingent scenarios (in which some houses were rendered uninhabitable) reasserted the contingent nature of all actions in this space. The discussion turned toward the myriad of choices available to planners and designers in this space–to ways of bypassing path determinism. As we move forward, a manner and method to capture this insight would be desirable–increasingly integrating this into the immersive, analytical environment–closing the cycle of the decision and discussion loop.

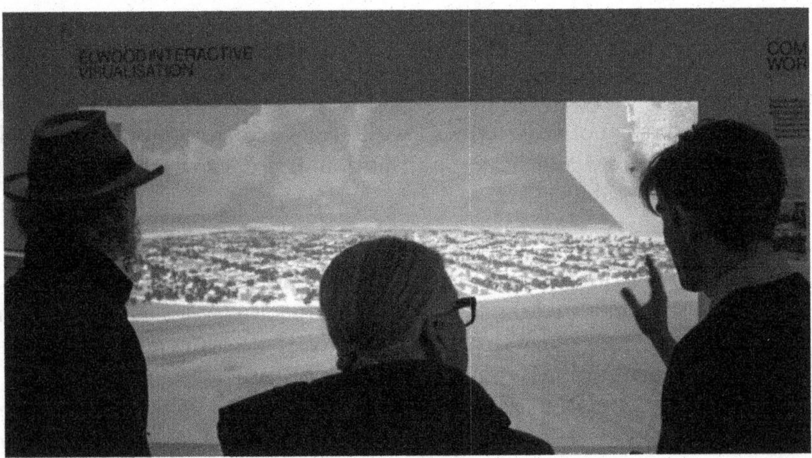

Fig. 12: The interactive visualisation forms the crux of further discussions with community, stakeholders, and designers.

11.4. Case Study 3: Crowd Simulations in a Virtual Model of Medieval Angkor

The third case study in this chapter overviews a research project at the Faculty of IT at Monash University that attempts to visualize how the Angkor Wat complex might have operated almost a millennium ago. Broadly, the aims of this project are twofold. The first aim is to leverage from data obtained in recent archaeological surveys to craft a comprehensive virtual reconstruction of Angkor Wat as the centrepiece in the medieval Cambodian metropolis of Angkor in the 12th century; this is the 'built environment' component of this study. The second aim is the simulation and tracking of thousands of animated 'agents' as they enter, exit and circulate around the complex–the immersive analytic component of this study. As an academic exploration that uses simulation to test how assumptions can be made more precise, the primary users of this system are archaeologists and historians. That said, provided it can be mediated in an educational context, an interactive simulation of daily life medieval Angkor Wat would make an ideal exercise in the Australian high school history curriculum, where the civilization of Angkor was recently nominated as a key depth study.

Constructed in the 12th century by the Khmer king Suryavarman II, the temple of Angkor Wat in Cambodia is a world famous heritage site and the largest religious monument on earth. The temple's well-preserved stone architecture and decorative reliefs have been the subject of extensive scholarship [20,24,29,30], but until recently, the wooden settlement that once lay within the temple's enclosure walls remained unknown. In 2013, LIDAR archaeological surveys confirmed a grid pattern of roads and household ponds, suggesting a regular layout of dispersed but substantial wooden dwellings [13].

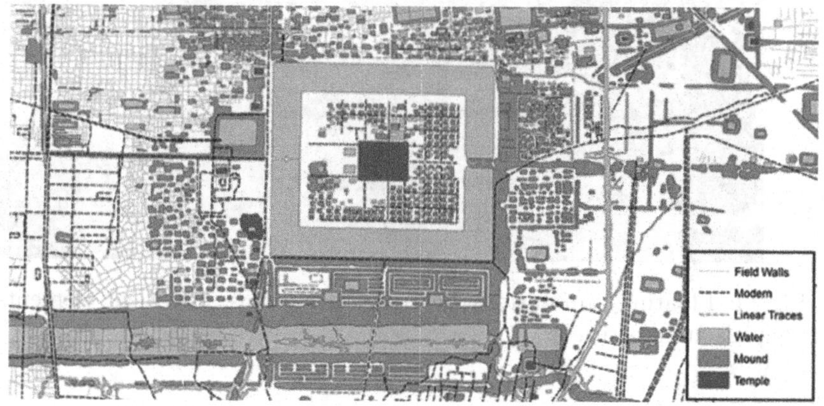

Fig. 13: A preliminary archaeological map of Angkor Wat (at centre, surrounded by a square moat) and its environs based on an analysis of Lidar imagery. *Image courtesy of Damian Evans / Khmer Archaeology Lidar Consortium*

Our simulation of the Angkor Wat enclosure in historical times is guided by two primary constraints in space and time. The temporal constraint was a single day set at some indeterminate date in the 12th century. In contrast to broad scale 'virtual archaeology' studies that plot change over centuries, such as the Rome Reborn Project [14], this simulation focuses specifically on just 24 hours: a day in the medieval life of Angkor Wat. The spatial constraints are delineated in the 1500 by 1300 metre space of the Angkor Wat enclosure bounded by its 200-metre wide moat. However, these spatial limits are only meaningful in describing the Angkor Wat complex as a two dimensional map and not as a simulated built environment. If we were only concerned with simulating the hypothetical flow of crowds around Angkor Wat, a map-based traffic simulation could have sufficed. A flat map (as in Figure 13) with multiple layers of cartographical data would allow us to plot the movement of human figures as points moving along the 2D vector lines around polygon boundaries. However, while a purely two-dimensional simulation would undoubtedly have analytic qualities, it would hardly be immersive

In a similar manner to the accompanying case studies in this chapter, the data that facilitates spatial immersion in the reconstruction of Angkor Wat in medieval times is not only intrinsically 3D in format, but comes with its own particular complexities.

Fig. 14: Floating annotations describe various art historical elements in the temple's architecture.

To begin with, there is the 3D modelling of the ornate and architectural complexity of the stone edifice of the temple, its gates and walls. Though worn and at risk of collapsing in places today, the stone architecture of Angkor Wat is very much still in place. As such, its virtual reconstruction doesn't require the careful weighing of varying degrees of uncertainties as those deduced from faint imprints, such as the gladiatorial school or auxiliary fortress of Carnuntum [25, 34]. The reconstruction of the urban settlement surrounding the temple revealed by Lidar mapping, however, did need to account for a number of uncertainties. Angkor was essentially a green and wooden city, thick with trees shading the timber and thatch dwellings of its inhabitants (see Figure 15). Our simulation had to account for the likely species of trees and plants for Angkor in the 12th century drawn from epigraphic [18], archaeological [27] and historical botanic studies [2]. The patterning of vegetation was randomised and clustered in open spaces between the approximately 283 mounds and 250–300 ponds within the Angkor Wat enclosure [31, p. 1444]. Moreover, because the excavation data supported a scenario where "temple personnel of modest material wealth occupied relatively insubstantial, perishable structures located on mounds in the immediate vicinity of the temple" [31, p. 1452], our models of thatched, roofed houses were drawn from studies in traditional Khmer architecture [11, 32]. Given these uncertainties, one of the primary advantages of a 24-hour cycle was the opportunity to alter, adjust and re-order architectural and vegetation assemblies at initialization, each time the simulation started up.

Fig. 15: The cultural landscape surrounding the temples, showing wooden dwellings on raised stilts, vegetation assemblies derived from archaeological pollen cores, and smoke from cooking fires.

The 3D animated models of human figures presented their own complexities, for they had to be planned as mobile collections of artefacts, insignia and motifs. The adornment of the Angkorian populace, so well attested in the bas reliefs [22, 30], opens up the visualisation of the fabrics that cloth them [17] of the jewellery that adorns them, and even–speculatively for medieval Angkor–the magical talisman tattoos on their skin. And then there are the things that they carry–the balanced baskets and shouldered loads–and, if we are to visually model social hierarchies and distinctions, the colours and sumptuary motifs on the parasol that retainers hold aloft behind over their masters (see Figure 16).

This virtual space, rich in the hues of greenery, patterned cloth and gilded spires, constituted the immersive foundation for augmented textural, temporal and cartographic information. Floating descriptive 'signifiers' in white text would appear above walking figures and architectural elements when the viewer moved close to them (see Figures 14 and 16). A plan map of the temple enclosures in the top right of the screen specified the position of the viewer's camera as a yellow circle (see Figures 14, 15 and 16) and the time of day was recorded in a slider at the base of the screen. Each agent in the visualisation was also tracked by summary statistics; a coloured circle indicated their category (explained below) and floating lines of text listed their destination and the time each agent had been active within the visualisation space. Though these overlaid features were arguably interactive and dynamic in the immersive space of the visualisation, the purpose they served was more descriptive than analytical.

If immersive analytics can be broadly defined as the exploration of how new interaction and display technologies can be used to support analytical reasoning and decision making [7] then in this simulation of Angkor Wat the key analytic concern was the visualization of the cumulative movement of agent groups. Early attempts in envisaging agent motion trails and patterns of aggregate activity in the visualization of the Angkor Wat enclosure consistently ran up against limits in processing power and memory, not to mention the limits of the Unity engine in tracking vast numbers of animated meshes. Consequently, we resolved to split the simulation and visualisation into two separate but linked applications; the visualisation would render the details of the animated scene, and the simulation would deal with the tracking the agent paths under differing scenarios. And there were quite a lot of agent paths to deal with.

Current archaeological estimates suggest that at its peak, the Angkor Wat complex may have housed up to 4,500 residents within its walls. If preliminary inferences can be made from the Ta Prohm inscriptions, the temple was serviced by a workforce of 25,000 and a support population of 125,000 people [12, p. 1410]. Pending further excavations and historical research, not a great deal is certain about the daily activities of the historical 'agents' we are attempting to simulate. Admittedly some speculation is involved in this venture and we must extrapolate the numbers, categories and activities of our agents from the Ta Prohm and Preah Khan temple inscriptions [8, 21]. Our intention was to construct a hypothetical space that presents not one but several possibilities, and can accommodate for varying shades in between. Figure 16 shows our initial attempts at visualising these estimates as crowds of walking figures or 'agents' moving in, out and around the Angkor Wat complex over a 24-hour period. Luckily, only a fraction of the estimated workforce of 25,000 needed to be present at any one time in the simulation. Working on the assumption that the populace attached to the temple worked on an alternating fortnightly roster, we could reduce the workforce the total numbers of agents on any given day by 50%. Given that many of the agents essentially disappeared when they entered the temple or exited from the edges of the simulation, a further reduction could be made by only tracking agents who were both moving around and in view. What the agents were doing at any given time depended upon how we categorized them.

We divided these crowds of animated 12th century Cambodians into four broad categories: *visitors, residents, commuting workers* and *suppliers*. All agents were guided by broadly similar rules, though each agent category was given a

Fig. 16: Each agent is tracked by summary statistics. A coloured circle indicates their category (blue for commuting workers, red for residents, green for suppliers, yellow for visiting elites) and a floating 'signifier'- revealed when the camera approaches close by–shows their destination and the time they have been spent within the confines of the visualisation space.

different agenda for navigating the space of the enclosure. The *resident* category of agents circulated between the residential blocks and the temple but did not venture beyond the temple walls. The *commuting worker* category, by far the most numerous, entered the complex from any gate and make their way to a random point in the enclosure, where they would remain for a number of hours before leaving the complex by the same way they came. The *supplier* category of agents behaved much like the commuting workers except that they did not venture inside the complex but instead approached the gates, stopped briefly, and then returned the way they came. The *visitor* category–comprised of high-status individuals and their retainers–entered the temple through the central western gates, make their way along the interior stone causeway, after a random number of hours, returned the way they arrived.

Our simulated 24 hours is provisionally set in the dry season and we designed two 'pulses' of activity during daylight hours; the first was from dawn until 11am and the second from around 2pm to dusk. During the hottest time of the day, between 11am and 2pm, activity would be more subdued. During these times, the agents were programmed to avoid travelling and to seek shade, preferably near the wooden dwellings, where they would sit in groups to pass the time in company. Between 2pm and 6pm (dusk) commuting workers would again start to arrive or leave the complex.

When testing scenarios about how the workforce of Angkor Wat would have entered, exited and moved around the temple, a dynamic overlay that superimposed each agent's motion trail over time and space as moved around

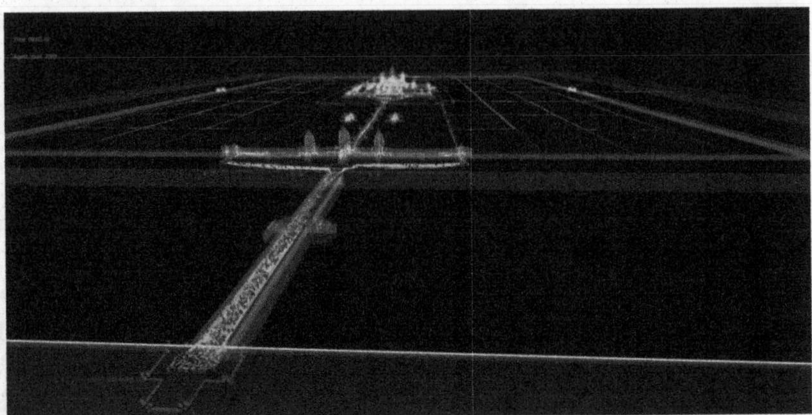

Fig. 17: A test visualisation of the tracking of agent paths during the early hours of the day. The mass of green and blue on the western causeway the red colours indicating residents and the green indicating suppliers. The trails mark the passage of the agent over time. *Image created by Kingsley Stephens*

the complex (see Figures 17 and 18) was a valuable device to visualise the consequences of agent decisions en masse. By turning off the textures and lighting and adopting an 'x-ray view' in the model, the residual colour coded trails the agents left behind as they ventured toward their destination meant that key thoroughfares and efficient routes became overlaid and thickened with colours the more that agents opted for them. Each agent was programmed to follow the shortest path (using an A* algorithm) to travel from point A to B, but with the proviso that certain paths were likely off-limits to certain agent categories and so too were certain gateways. Because the agent paths were coloured according to their category, the emergent effect was a 'heatmap' that visualised the overall distribution, destination and circulation of thousands of agents over the course of the day. Because slight changes to the rules governing the agent categories could result in vivid colour and phase changes in the map, the effect of the parts–thousands of individual characters making simple decisions–could be analysed as a whole.

As well as tinkering with agents numbers in general hypothetical tests, such as shifting the drop-offs in morning and afternoon activities and adding or subtracting numbers of agents in each category, we could also move toward testing our model against more particular scenarios. For example, restricting the central western gates to the elites (the visitor category) would see the animated populace branch out from a multi-coloured stream into a trident divided by social hierarchy, where the commuting worker and supplier categories separated from the visitor category and made their way into the complex through alternate gates. Another test concerned hypothetical structures. The recent discovery of multiple breaches in the north and south walls of the complex suggested that these too were once used as thoroughfares in medieval times [4]. While there is no evidence of bridges across the moat on either of these sides of the complex today, the existence of bamboo bridges of light construction in medieval times is a plausible hypothesis to test. The ability to toggle a hypothetical bridge across the north and south sides of the moat 'on and off' meant that agents would cross the bridges to achieve their destination if the bridges were present, with the result that the agent paths weave in and out to link the interior of the complex to the outer sides of the moat like the struts of a spiders web. If the bridges were absent, agents would have to take an alternate path to their destination by a considerably longer route.

Conclusions and lessons learnt from the use case Given the inherent challenges of visualising the past with incomplete data, our simulation was bound to be more explorative than predictive. Does a simulation proposing new access points into Angkor Wat support the hypothesis that wooden bridges existed there in medieval times? In lieu of hard evidence such as the remains or imprints of bridge posts under the mud of the moat, the answer remains equivocal. However, anything that can force assumptions to be more precise remains valuable in the investigation of the civilisation of Angkor.

Certainly, more could have been made of interactive aspects of the simulation especially in enabling the user to alter the weightings of agent numbers and goals in real time. As it was the simulation's variables and the layout of the 3D structures could only be altered offline. It followed that aspects of interactivity and immersion while spatially 'deep' were restricted in function. In navigating the simulation, the user's interaction was limited to a free roving camera, however, whether the user moved through the sky or along the roads, the texturing and animation of the thousands of 3D models populating the space ensured a visual consistency that meant the user was immersed in a cohesive virtual world. The addition of sound, belatedly mentioned here, underscored the spatial immersion with a sonic dimension. Samples drawn from field recordings were assigned specific locations within the enclosure and coded so that they faded in and out of earshot as the user moved between their source points. Thus, the sound of a conch shell horn emanating from the inner sanctums of the temple is loud when the user is near it, but muted when they are further away. And if the viewer floated the camera close to groupings of animated people they would discern fragments of conversations in Khmer, but if they moved the camera up above the tree line these sounds gradually diminish, and instead they would hear the wind ruffling the leaves of the sugar palm trees.

Though superimposed diagrams, floating 'signifiers' and motion trails that faded over time augmented the simulation with some analytic features, the key analytic feature of the immersive space was the library of 3D models themselves. It follows that in an immersive, contextual historical space where every evidence-based reconstruction relates to those around it, there is something to be said for the immersive analysis of the historical 'likelihood' of the 3D reconstructions themselves. For example, when the simulation was presented on a 3840 x 1080 multi-projector interleaved display at Monash SensiLab, visiting historians and archaeologists, while spatially and sonically immersed, were able to analyse whether particular 3D reconstructions in the Angkor Wat enclosure were plausible or implausible for medieval Angkor given the other models–including walking figures–around them.

Finally, there were the unexpected, serendipitous visualisations that emerged from the application of immersive analytics at Angkor Wat, one such example being the overnight visualisation in Figure 18.

Fig. 18: A test visualisation of the tracking of agent paths through the enclosure overnight. *Image created by Mike Yeates*

We have no firm evidence for activities at Angkor Wat through the night. At any rate, when night fell upon our virtual model our agents had almost all departed or retired indoors. However, our simulation accommodated for a small number of residential agents walking back and forth from the temple throughout the evening. The overlaying of agent paths in Figure 18 showed the trails of these wanderings along dark roads not unlike the slow exposure photography of cars through an urban centre at night. Though we have not yet modelled and animated the small ceramic oil lamps these nocturnal agents would have carried, the visualisation was nevertheless a surprising one. Here was a world famous monument that had been digitally reconstructed countless times, but always in the hard ambient occlusion of a simulated sun. This overnight visualisation suggested an intriguing view of the paths taken over night at a preindustrial centre lit only by the moon.

11.5. Conclusion

While the word model conjures up different meanings according to the discipline using it, a broad description is that a model is a mental representation of an external phenomenon [35]. A model might be simple, complex, metaphorical or physical. It can be conveyed through prose, diagrams or cultural practice. Perhaps the most easily recognised definition of a model is a scaled representation of a real object, as in a 'model' aeroplane, or a scale architectural model constructed carefully from cut segments of wood and plastic. While the built environments depicted in the illustrated figures of the above case studies are all digital, they share an easy visual interpretability because they seek to mimic visual and spatial reality directly. The added third dimension that all these case studies share means that they have transformed factory floor plans, city street atlases and archaeological survey maps beyond cartography into cohesive and self-contained virtual worlds. The fact that the virtual environments in the case studies discussed above can accommodate realistic 3D human figures further underscores the fact that they depict a *model* of reality that is recognisable, and recognisably 'immersive' in a way that a 'business model' or 'theoretical model' isn't.

This familiarity offers certain advantages as well as challenges. Because the environments incorporate familiar spatial cues navigation is intuitive whether the viewer walks through the environment in first person mode or floats above the scene. However, the fact that we are mostly navigating within an immersive environment presents a challenge to embed annotations and other documentation and to allow these to be viewed consistently within the environment without losing immersion, occlusion issues, and unnecessarily complicating the user experience. The issues of motion sickness and latency are more critical in simulations of the built environment than in other subject fields where graphics are usually centred and not presented as scale models of real spaces.

Despite these caveats, the advantages discussed in the above case studies are manifold. By enabling life-sized walkthroughs in immersive VR planners can not only experience a factory in its original scale but also compare, with the aid of analytic meta information, design alternatives in an efficient and intuitive manner. For the visualisation of sustainable cities, the combination of the underlying data model and recognisable built spaces allowed for powerful synergies; namely the discrete time-steps of a severe weather event to be experienced as an *event*–as a space and a territory that unfolds around the viewer. And, finally, there are the unexpected insights that emerged from the application of the immersive analytic tracking of animated characters–agents–following simple rules as they navigate reconstructed paths and avenues in a re-built environment of long ago.

References

1. Al Khawli, T., Eppelt, U., Schulz, W.: Sensitivity analysis of laser cutting based on metamodeling approach. In: Handbook of research on computational simulation and modeling in engineering, pp. 618–639. IGI Global (2016)
2. Blench, R.: A history of fruits on the southeast asian mainland. Occasional Paper 4, 115–37 (2008)
3. Bogost, I.: Unit operations: An approach to videogame criticism. MIT Press (2008)
4. Brotherson, D.: The fortification of Angkor Wat. Antiquity 89(348), 1456–1472 (2015)

5. Büscher, C., Meisen, T., Schilberg, D., Jeschke, S.: VPI-FP: an integrative information system for factory planning. International Journal of Production Research (2015) doi: doi:10.1080/00207543.2015.1057298
6. Caputo, F., Di Gironimo, G., Marzano, A.: A structured approach to simulate manufacturing systems in virtual environments. In: Congreso International de Ingegneria Grafica. pp. 73–80 (2006)
7. Chandler, T., Cordeil, M., Czauderna, T., Dwyer, T., Glowacki, J., Goncu, C., Klapperstueck, M., Klein, K., Marriott, K., Schreiber, F., Wilson, E.: Immersive Analytics. In: Big Data Visual Analytics (BDVA) 2015. pp. 73–80. IEEE eXpress Conference Publishing(2015) doi: 10.1109/BDVA.2015.7314296
8. Cœdès, G., Cordier, P.: La stèle de ta-prohm. Bulletin de l'École française d'Extrême-Orient 6(1/2), 44–85 (1906)
9. Corves, B., Loftus, M.: Designing an immersive virtual reality interface for layout planning. Journal of Material Processing Technology 107(1–3), 425–430 (2000)
10. DeLanda, M.: A new philosophy of society: Assemblage theory and social complexity. A&C Black (2006)
11. Dumarçay, J., Royère, P.: Cambodian architecture: Eighth to thirteenth centuries, vol. 12. Brill (2001)
12. Evans, D., Fletcher, R.: The landscape of Angkor Wat redefined. Antiquity 89(348), 1402–1419 (2015)
13. Evans, D.H., Fletcher, R.J., Pottier, C., Chevance, J.B., Soutif, D., Tan, B.S., Im, S., Ea, D., Tin, T., Kim, S.: Uncovering archaeological landscapes at Angkor using lidar. Proceedings of the National Academy of Sciences 110(31), 12595–12600 (2013)
14. Frischer, B.: The Rome reborn project. How technology is helping us to study history. OpEd. University of Virginia (November 10, 2008) (2008)
15. Fuller, S.: Humanity 2.0: What it means to be human past, present and future. Springer (2011)
16. Gebhardt, S., Hentschel, B., Kuhlen, T.W., Al Khawli, T., Schulz, W.: Hyperslice visualization of metamodels for manufacturing processes. In: IEEE Vistualization Poster Proceedings (2013)
17. Green, G.: Traditional textiles of Cambodia : cultural threads and material heritage. Published and distributed in Thailand by River Books, Bangkok, Thailand (2003)
18. Jacob, J.: The ecology of Angkor. Evidence from the Khmer inscriptions. In: Stott, P.A. (ed.) Nature and Man in South East Asia, pp. 109–127. School of Oriental and African Studies, London (1978)
19. Jeschke, S., Kampker, A., Kuhlen, T.W., Schuh, G., Schulz, W., Al Khawli, T., Büscher, C., Eppelt, U., Gebhardt, S., Kreisköther, K., Pick, S., Reinhard, R., Tercan, H., Utsch, J., Voet, H.: Virtual production intelligence (VPI). In: Integrative Production Technology, pp. 177–251. Springer International Publishing (2017)
20. Mannikka, E.: Angkor Wat: Time, space, and kingship. University of Hawaii Press, Honolulu (1996)
21. Maxwell, S.: The stele inscription of preah khan, angkor: text with translation and commentary. UDAYA, Journal of Khmer Studies 8, 1–114 (2008)
22. Maxwell, T.S.: Of gods, kings, and men: the reliefs of Angkor Wat. Silkworm Books (2006)
23. Müller, P., Wonka, P., Haegler, S., Ulmer, A., Van Gool, L.: Procedural modeling of buildings. ACM Transactions On Graphics (ToG) 25(3), 614–623 (2006)
24. Nafilyan, G.: Angkor Vat, description graphique du temple. Ècole française d'Extrême-Orient, A. Maisonneuve, Paris, (1969)

25. Neubauer, W., Seren, S., Hinterleitner, A., Doneus, M., Löcker, K., Trinks, I., Nau, E., Pregesbauer, M., Kucera, M., Verhoeven, G.: The discovery of a gladiatorial school at Carnuntum. In: 10th International Conference on Archaeological Prospection. pp. 423–426. Austrian Academy of Sciences (2013)
26. Parish, Y.I., Müller, P.: Procedural modeling of cities. In: Proceedings of the 28th Annual Conference on Computer Graphics and Interactive Techniques. pp. 301–308. ACM (2001)
27. Penny, D., Pottier, C., Fletcher, R., Barbetti, M., Fink, D., Hua, Q.: Vegetation and land-use at Angkor, Cambodia: A dated pollen sequence from the Bakong temple moat. Antiquity 80(309), 599–614 (2006)
28. Pick, S., Kuhlen, T.W.: A framework for developing flexible virtual-reality-centered annotation systems. In: Proceedings of the IEEE Conference on Virtual Reality, SEARIS workshop (2015)
29. Roveda, V.: Khmer mythology secrets of Angkor Wat. Weatherhill Inc., Trumbull, Connecticut (1997)
30. Roveda, V., Poncar, J.: Sacred Angkor: The carved reliefs of Angkor Wat. Published and distributed by River Books, Bangkok (2002)
31. Stark, M.T., Evans, D., Rachna, C., Piphal, H., Carter, A.: Residential patterning at Angkor Wat. Antiquity 89(348), 1439–1455 (2015)
32. Tainturier, F.: Wooden architecture of Cambodia: A disappearing heritage. Center for Khmer Studies, Publishing Dept, Phnom Penh, Cambodia (2006)
33. Tyszczuk, R., Smith, J., Clark, N., Butcher, M.: ATLAS: Geography, architecture and change in an interdependent world. Black Dog Publishing (2012)
34. Valdelomar, J.T., Brandtner, J., Kucera, M., Wallner, M., Sandici, V., Neubauer, W.: 4D investigation of digital heritage an interactive application for the auxiliary fortress of Carnuntum. In: Digital Heritage, 2015. vol. 2, pp. 81–84. IEEE (2015)
35. Webb, M.E.: Computer-based modelling in school history. In: Martin, A.S.L., D, Y. (eds.) Information Technology and the Teaching of History International Perspectives, pp. pp 211–218. Harwood, Amsterdam (1997)
36. van Wijk, J., van Liere, R.: Hyperslice: visualization of scalar functions of many variables. In: Proceedings of the 4th Conference on Visualization. pp. 119–125 (1993)